DATA JOURNALISM
Inside the global future

Cover illustration

We wanted to find out whether the authors of this book form the nucleus of an advocacy network, and how connected that network might be. We harvested the Twitter data for each author and all their friends and created a force-directed network chart in D3. It shows both the network nucleus (coloured nodes and links) and the network reach (white nodes and links). You can explore the interactive version at flyingbinary.com/dj-global-future

Datajournalist: Jacqui Taylor (jacqui.taylor@flyingbinary.com)

Visualisation: Ian Taylor (ian.taylor@flyingbinary.com)

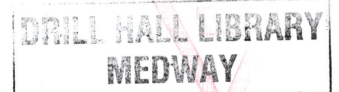

Data: twitter.com

DATA JOURNALISM
Inside the global future

EDITED BY

TOM FELLE, JOHN MAIR
and
DAMIAN RADCLIFFE

Published 2015 by Abramis academic publishing

www.abramis.co.uk

ISBN 978 1 84549 663 0

Printed and bound in the United Kingdom

Typeset in Garamond 11pt

Abramis is an imprint of arima publishing.

arima publishing
ASK House, Northgate Avenue
Bury St Edmunds, Suffolk IP32 6BB
t: (+44) 01284 700321

www.arimapublishing.com

Contents

Tables and figures

Tables

Figures

Acknowledgements

Data journalism is the new punk? So argues the doyen of DJers, Simon Rogers, late of *the Guardian* and now Google's Data Editor in San Francisco. Certainly it is the *topic du jour* for journalism academics, and it is a key skillset and in high demand in newsrooms in London, New York, and other media capitals worldwide.

This volume – the fourteenth in the series of 'hackademic' texts for Abramis and the second book on data journalism – attempts give voice to new ideas, challenges sacred cows, and (hopefully) educates, enlightens and, dare we suggest, entertains occasionally as well. It adds to the growing volume of such texts that are trying both to understand the many changes occurring in digital journalism, plot them, and in some cases map the way forward into what is not quite virgin territory for reporters, but certainly a frontier that has only just begun to be charted.

Books such as these live and die by the quality of contributions and as ever we are indebted to our many writers for the calibre of their various chapters. You have been unstinting in your dedication and without your efforts, patience, and kindness despite our many barking requests and a torrent of gruff emails, valuable projects such as this would never get to print. Contributions are ordered into sections by subject area, so the ordering of chapters should not be seen as any reflection on quality. In that vein, the editors have listed their names alphabetically and each has laboured and toiled equally in the minor miracle required to produce this text.

We thank Richard and Pete Franklin of Abramis, who support and publish this and other volumes in the series in double-quick time with great aplomb and little fuss. Likewise our gratitude is due to The Media Society and City University London's Department of Journalism for their support, and to Jacqui Taylor of Flying Binary for the cover illustration.

Finally we thank our families, who have to put up us while we carefully crafted what you now hold in your hands with late night edits and general grumpiness, all the while supplying us with endless cups of tea and chocolate biscuits; and whom suffered our ill-temper with great grace and patience.

Tom Felle, London
John Mair, Oxford
Damian Radcliffe, Oregon
November 2015

The editors

Tom Felle lectures at the Department of Journalism, City University London, and was previously a lecturer and Head of Journalism at the University of Limerick, Ireland. He worked for almost a decade as a journalist, including as a correspondent with the *Independent News and Media* group (Dublin, Ireland); as deputy editor of the *Irish Echo* (Sydney, Australia); as Bureau Chief of the *Lebanon News Agency* (Beirut, Lebanon); and had postings in Brussels and London. He has published on topics including local journalism; newspapers in the digital era; journalism's role in democracy; press freedom, ethics and regulation; freedom of information, accountability and sunshine laws; and data journalism. He is co-editor of *FOI at 10: freedom fighting or lazy journalism?* (Abramis, with John Mair) and *Ireland and the Freedom of Information Act* (MUP, with Maura Adshead). Email tom.felle.1@city.ac.uk / Twitter @tomfelle

John Mair has taught journalism at the Universities of Coventry, Kent, Northampton, Brunel, Edinburgh Napier, Guyana and the Communication University of China. He has now edited 14 'hackademic' volumes over the last five years on subjects ranging from trust in TV, the health of investigative journalism, reporting the 'Arab Spring' to three volumes on the Leveson Inquiry. He and Richard Lance Keeble invented the sub-genre. John also invented the Coventry Conversations which attracted 350 media movers and shakers to Coventry University while the podcasts of those have been downloaded five million times worldwide. Since then, he has launched the Northampton Chronicles, MediaMondays at Napier and most recently the Harrow Conversations at Westminster. In a previous life, he was an award-winning producer/director for the BBC, ITV and Channel Four and a secondary school teacher. Email johnmair100@hotmail.com

Damian Radcliffe is the Carolyn S Chambers Professor in Journalism at the University of Oregon, an Honorary Research Fellow at Cardiff University's School of Journalism, Media and Culture Studies, and a Fellow of the Royal Society for the encouragement of Arts, Manufactures and Commerce (RSA). A former content creator with 20 years' experience in senior and mid-level editorial, research and policy positions, Damian writes regularly about digital trends in social media, technology, and innovations in journalism, for major media outlets such as CBS Interactive, *The Huffington Post* and the BBC College of Journalism. He has held posts at the BBC, the UK Communications Regulator Ofcom, Qatar's Ministry of Information and Communications Technology (ictQATAR), and as an independent analyst and consultant. In 2013 he was part of the Internet Society's Next Generation Leaders programme and between 2005 and 2008 he led a multi-award winning partnership between the NGO Volunteering Matters and the BBC. Twitter @damianradcliffe / web www.damianradcliffe.com

Contributors

Helena Bengtsson is Editor, Data Projects at *the Guardian* in London, UK. She previously worked as the Database editor at Sveriges Television, Sweden's national television broadcaster. In 2006 and 2007, she was Database editor at the Center for Public Integrity in Washington, DC. In 2010, she was awarded the *Stora Journalistpriset* (Great Journalism Award) for Valpejl.se, a website profiling every candidate in that season's Swedish elections. She tweets at @HelenaBengtsson

Kathryn Corrick is an independent consultant and former Head of Content and Learning at the Open Data Institute. Kathryn was UK chair of the Online News Association until 2013. She has been a Journalist in Residence for Kingston University from 2011 to 2013 and a visiting lecturer at the University of East Anglia, Bournemouth University and Ravensbourne. From 2001 until 2006 she worked as online production editor and then online manager of the *New Statesman* magazine. Email kathryncorrick.co.uk or tweet @kcorrick

Eva Constantaras is the Internews Data Journalism Advisor and a freelance data journalist and data journalism trainer. She studied the evolution of data journalism in developing countries through a Fulbright Fellowship in Colombia and as a Google Scholar in Spain. She has launched data journalism initiatives in Kenya, Sudan, Palestine, Afghanistan, China, Sri Lanka, Myanmar, Colombia, El Salvador, Guatemala and Mexico on topics ranging from ranging from organized crime and election transparency to extractive industries and health system corruption. Email evaconstantaras@gmail.com

Andy Dickinson is a senior lecturer in online and digital journalism and researcher at the University of Central Lancashire. Based in the Media Innovation Studio, he is interested in the places that data, technology, journalism and the community meet. He blogs as andydickinson.net

Steve Doig holds the Knight Chair in Journalism at the Walter Cronkite School of Journalism and Mass Communication of Arizona State University. Before joining ASU in 1996, he was Associate Editor/Research of the *Miami Herald*, where he worked for 20 years. Data journalism projects on which he worked at *The Herald* and at ASU have won the Pulitzer Prize for Public Service, the Investigative Reporters and Editors Award, the Goldsmith Prize for Investigative Reporting, the George Polk Award for Medical Reporting, and other recognition. His email address is steve.doig@asu.edu, and his Twitter handle is @sdoig

Gavin Freeguard (@GavinFreeguard) is a senior researcher at the Institute for Government, where he leads the *Whitehall Monitor* project. He was previously political adviser on culture, media and sport to Harriet Harman MP, senior editor at the Media Standards Trust and deputy director of the Orwell Prize. He holds an undergraduate degree in history and politics from Merton College, Oxford and a master's in the history of political thought from UCL and QMUL. He also runs a daily data journalism newsletter, Warning: Graphic Content (@WarningGraphicC).

Adam Frost (@adamfrostuk) and **Tobias Sturt** (@skelington) are, respectively, the Content Director and Creative Director of Graphic, an agency specialising in data visualisation and information design with work that encompasses everything from infographics, animation and interactive data visualisation to the fathomless horrors of PowerPoint. They also teach *Guardian* Masterclasses and corporate seminars in infographics and communication with and about data. Adam Frost's award-winning infographic work (with various designers) has been published in many places including *the Guardian*, *The New Statesman*, Buzzfeed, Mashable and Taschen Books' 'Understanding the World – The Atlas of Infographics'.

Jan Goodey is a lecturer in the Department of Journalism and Publishing at Kingston University, London. He runs a module entitled 'Digital detectives: data journalism'. He freelances on environmental issues and has been a regular contributor to *Red Pepper* magazine, *The Ecologist*, *The Independent* and *the Guardian.* He helps run the asset-tracker.org website. Email jangoodey@phonecoop.coop

Alexander B Howard is a writer and editor based in Washington, DC. From August 2013 to May 2014, he was a fellow at the Tow Center for Digital Journalism at Columbia University. He is a columnist at TechRepublic; the founder of 'E Pluribus Unum,' a blog focused on open government and technology; and a contributor to TechPresident, among other publications. In 2013 he was a fellow at the Networked Transparency Policy Project in the Ash Center for Democratic Governance and Innovation at the Kennedy School of Government at Harvard University. Previously, he was the Washington correspondent for *Radar* at O'Reilly Media, where he chronicled the emergence of open data and open government movements around the world.

Kathryn Hayes lectures in journalism at the University of Limerick and runs a news agency in Ireland's mid-west region supplying daily news to a number of national Irish newspapers and broadcast media outlets. Kathryn has been contributing to The *Irish Times* newspaper from the Limerick region since 2003 and is a regular Limerick stringer for Ireland's national broadcaster RTE. She is currently involved in journalism research as a PhD candidate at the University of Limerick. Email kathryn.hayes@ul.ie or tweet @hayes_cait

Jonathan Hewett is Director of Interactive and Newspaper Journalism at City University London. His research interests include social media, data journalism, and the teaching and learning of journalism. Jonathan has led and taught on journalism programmes since 1997. He welcomes suggestions, corrections and other constructive feedback, plus offers of help, funding, coffee and chocolate to J.C.Hewett@city.ac.uk or @jonhew.

Bella Hurrell and **John Walton** work for the BBC's Visual Journalism team. Set up in 2012 the team produces graphics, maps and interactive projects for BBC News. Recent awards won by the team include the 2015 Global Editors Network data app of the year and the Royal Statistical Society's best data visualisation for 2015.

Liz Hannaford is a lecturer in Multimedia Journalism at Manchester Metropolitan University. This chapter is based on a journal article she wrote for *Journalism Education* (2015) Vol. 4 No. 1. She is founder and co-organiser of Hacks/Hackers Manchester. Previously, she was a broadcast journalist at BBC World Service and has worked extensively in Russia, Ukraine and Uzbekistan making radio documentaries, reporting, working with local media and training local journalists. She blogs about her efforts to become more 'technical' at www.LizHannaford.com.

Gabriel Keeble-Gagnère is Senior Informatics Analyst for the Australia-China Centre for Wheat Improvement at Murdoch University, Perth, Australia. He has a BSc in Mathematics and Computer Science from Imperial College, London, and a Maîtrise Master's in Pure Mathematics from Pierre and Marie Curie University, Paris, France. While he works in bioinformatics, he has a strong interest in cryptography and topics related to internet security.

Megan Lucero is the Data Journalism Editor at *The Times* and *The Sunday Times* in London. She was part of their first data journalism team and led its development from a small supporting unit to a key component of *Times* investigations. Her team's data mining and analysis brought many issues into the public discourse, including widespread use of blood doping in athletics and high profile figure's participation in tax avoidance schemes. She spearheaded a political data unit for analysis in the lead up to and during the UK's last General Election. She tweets at @Megan_Lucero

Isabelle Marchand is data journalist at PRISM, part of the WPP group. She produces visualisations, infographics and interactive infographics for the Ford Motor Company. She completed a Masters in International Journalism at Brunel University, as well as a Masters in Written Press at the French Ecole Superieur de Journalisme de Paris. Her email is isabelle.mvs@gmail.com, and she tweets at @isabellemvs

Dr Martin Moore is director of the Centre for the Study of Media, Communication and Power at the Policy Institute at King's and a Senior Research Fellow at King's College London. **Dr Gordon Ramsay** is deputy director of the Centre and a Research Fellow at King's College London.

Matteo Moretti grew up and worked for years in the web and motion design industry, researching data visualisation and generative design. Presently he works as a researcher at the Faculty of Design and Arts at the Free University of Bozen-Bolzano, where he teaches web and interactive graphics, research methodologies, and visual journalism practice. He also co-founded the research platform on visual journalism teaching, visualjournalism.unibz.it. People's Republic of Bolzano, his last research project, won the Data Journalism Award 2015 in Barcelona during the GEN Summit 2015. His email is hello@matteomoretti.com and he tweets at @teo_moretti

Sanjit Oberai works as data editor of Quintillion, an online news web portal that tracks news across India. Prior to this, he was deputy editor and product head of IndiaSpend, India's first data journalism initiative. He is the ambassador for Infogr and also the co-founder of the Data Meet chapter in Mumbai, India. He completed an MBA in finance from Bombay University in 2007. Twitter: @sanjit_oberai. Syed Nazakat is an award-winning journalist and editor-in-chief of the Centre for Investigative Journalism, a non-profit organisation he founded to promote the cause of watchdog journalism in India. In 2015 he also set-up a data journalism initiative focussed on Indian healthcare, called Health Analytics India. Twitter: @SyedNazakat. **Rakesh Dubbudu** is an engineer by education and an activist by passion. He is the founder of Factly. He has been working on issues related to Right to Information (RTI) for a decade. He has authored many reports on the status of the RTI legislation and has been a Government of India Fellow on RTI. He is also associated with various organisations working in the area of transparency and accountability in governance and has ground level experience of issues. Twitter: @rakeshdubbudu. **Govindraj Ethiraj** is founder of IndiaSpend and was previously the founding editor-in chief of Bloomberg TV India, a 24-hours business news service launched out of Mumbai in 2008 and a partnership between Bloomberg LLP and the UTV Group in India. Prior to setting up Bloomberg TV India, he worked with *Business Standard* as editor (new media). He also worked with CNBC-TV18 and *The Economic Times*. Twitter: @govindethiraj. **Nisha Thompson** is co-founder of Data Meet India. She has a background in online community organising and has worked for the Sunlight Foundation in Washington DC, with online communities to use US government data to hold elected officials accountable. She moved to Bangalore in October 2010 where contributed to a research report on open government data in India for the Centre for Internet and Society. Twitter: @fakenisha. **John Samuel Raja** is co-founder of How India Lives, a data search engine for public data. Prior to this, he worked as financial journalist for 11 years for *The Economic Times*, *Mint*,

Business Standard and *Outlook Business*. In 2012, John was selected as Tow Knight Fellow in the City University of New York's entrepreneurial journalism program. He holds a Masters in Econometrics. Twitter: @johnraja

Nick Phipps is an editor at Sky News with experience across network, 24-hour and digital news. Before assuming his role as election editor, he spent 18 months in Abu Dhabi as executive editor for the launch for Sky News Arabia. Between 2008 and 2011, Nick was head of business at Sky News, leading the unit through the financial crisis. Nick began his career at ITN in 1994 as a news trainee. His roles there included science and medical producer, Europe producer and programme editor at ITV News.

Ændrew Rininsland is a newsroom developer at *The Times* and *The Sunday Times*, alongside being the creator of AxisJS (axisjs.org) and a maintainer of C3.js (c3js.org). He is also a contributor to *The Times* Digital Development Blog (medium.com/digital-times). Ændrew can be found on Twitter via @aendrew.

Zara Rahman is a researcher and writer based in Berlin, Germany. She has been working in data activism and information accessibility among civil society for over five years, and most recently worked with Open Knowledge and the School of Data where she led their fellowship programme and carried out numerous data journalism workshops, supporting their data literacy efforts among journalists and civil society. She is a fellow at the Centre for Internet and Human Rights and now works with the engine room, carrying out research on technology and data in advocacy. You can find Zara on Twitter @zararah, or at mail@zararah.net.

Simon Rogers is Data Editor at Google. He was previously Data Editor at Twitter, and spent 15 years at *the Guardian* – where he created its Datablog. He is author of *Facts are Sacred* (Faber and Faber, 2013).

Emily Shackleton is a journalist who specialises in digital reporting, social media and current affairs. A recent MA Interactive Journalism graduate from City University London, she has had pieces of data journalism published by the *Press Gazette, The Media Briefing, The Independent* and the *i100*. She began learning her craft while studying for her BA in English at the University of Nottingham, editing the features section of her student publication Impact Magazine that won Best Website of the Year at the Guardian Student Media Awards at the end of her tenure. Her interests include current affairs, transport and the media.

Jonathan Spencer manages the BBC News Visual Journalism computer graphics team. His development team is responsible the delivery of all of BBC News real time computer graphics content from the creation of newsroom templates through to the virtual reality graphics used in BBC election coverage. Jonathan is an experienced television graphic designer, experimental video and sound maker. After studying Fine Art painting in the 1980s Jonathan moved into computer animation, he has won a number of international design awards.

Nicole Smith Dahmen is an Assistant Professor at the School of Journalism and Communication at the University of Oregon. Her research focuses on ethical and technological issues in visual communication, with emphasis on photojournalism in the Digital Age. Dahmen's research is published in such leading journals as *American Behavioral Scientist*, *Visual Communication Quarterly*, and *Journalism Studies*. In regard to technology, her work examines the visual presentation of mass-mediated information and associated technologies, both from a content and effects perspective. She blogs about Visual Communication in the Digital Age at http://nicoledahmen.wordpress.com

After a 20-year career in the BBC, including spells in charge of the Croatian and Macedonian language services, and of the training department of the BBC World Service, **Jonathan Stoneman** became a freelance trainer and consultant in 2010. He soon developed a passion for data, and devotes his professional activities to training journalists how to use data – particularly open data, and is an associate trainer with the Open Data Institute in London. Email jonathan.stoneman@gmail.com

Jacqui Taylor has 25 years of implementing technology across the world. She co-founded FlyingBinary after implementing a European banking regulatory change using web science principles. An appointment to the Open Data User Group in the Cabinet Office recognised her as a web scientist of influence in the era of 'big data'. Her role at the British Standards Institute defining the ISO data standards for Smart Cities on behalf of the UK moves her data journalism work into the Internet of Things arena, a global IT driven change which will transform all our daily lives. Jacqui trains advanced analysts on the science of data visualisation and is a regular speaker on cloud adoption, big data, smarter analytics and profiting from the 'Internet of Things'.

Section 1:
Data journalism for beginners

John Mair

Data journalism is where it is at in modern journalism. Wannabe hacks planning to enter the 'profession' are well advised to be numerate as well as literate. Apart from all else they can expect an uplift of 25 per cent on their starting salary and being firmly in demand for the future and at the cutting edge now. Simon Rogers is a rock star figure in the data journalism world. He founded *the Guardian*'s Datablog and has gone upwards and onward from that to Twitter and now to Google in Silicon Valley. But, in his opening chapter, first published in *the Guardian*, he likens data journalism not to rock but to punk with its tradition of 'anyone can do it' philosophy:

> '*...data journalism incorporates such a wide range now of styles from visualisation to long-form articles. The key thing they have in common is that they are based on numbers and statistics – and that they should aim to get a 'story' from that data'.*

But like the punk movement of three decades ago, DJ is a great leveller:

> *'There's a great democratisation of data going on. Rather than the numbers belonging to the experts, they belong to all of us – and data journalism is part of that reclaiming of the facts'.*

Emily Shackleton is a newbie, a wannabe on the way to making it. She's just graduated from the *Ecole des Sciences Po* of data journalism – City University London – and offers some practical advice on mistakes and how to avoid them. Some of those stem from wrongly separating the journalism from the data...

'Data journalism is just like any other journalism - the fundamentals of being able to sniff out a good story are still the same. But instead of contacts and press releases, your core piece of information is a dataset.'

And like all good journalism, it's all about the reporting, stupid! (to misquote Bill Clinton).

'The number one mistake that data journalism students make is forgetting the good old fashioned reporting. Despite coming from a long tradition of on-the-ground reporting, data journalists appear to sometimes forget to talk to people.'

And remember it's not just about charts and pretty infographics. In 'Data journalism: A-Z from pitch to delivery' Jan Goodey, who is a journalism teacher rather than learner, guides some of his class towards producing a practical campaigning result through simple digging and asking the right questions of the right people – another not to be forgotten tool of journalism. They analysed Local Government Pension Fund investment data and brought to light some ethical dilemmas, with local councils seeking to make returns while at the same being arbiters on planning proposals in the nascent fracking industry in the UK.

Data journalism is the 'Johnnie Come Lately' of journalism, especially in the journalism academe and most especially in the UK, argues Jonathan Hewett of City University London. He provides a potted history of its development in the USA, Europe and the UK. It is a *tour de force* of intellectual history. It has taken two decades for 'CAR' reporting to gain respectability as 'data journalism' and to gain and retain footholds away from the investigative margins in the mainstream of broadsheet journalism, in papers such as the *Financial Times*, *the Guardian* and *The Times*. As he puts it in his contribution:

'Data journalism draws on wider foundations and aspirations than CAR, and it now appears to be flourishing. Certainly it is in everyday use in some parts of journalism, although it takes many different forms and its practitioners vary from solo operators to large teams. Its spread, successes and diversity surely qualify data journalism to be a worthy successor.'

Hewett is in many senses the Galileo of DJ in the British academe; his pedagogy lives on in many newsrooms. Long may he flourish.

Storytelling is a vexed subject in data visualisation but Adam Frost and Tobias Sturt, formerly of the Eton of DJ – *the Guardian* – argue not only is it inevitable but necessary for communicating with an audience, which means we have to understand storytelling as well as we understand our data. First they debunk some over-use of the moniker in popular commercial culture:

'Storytelling' is a fashionable term, widely touted as a magic bullet for a diverse range of professions, from estate agents ('Show more than just boring pictures. Sell the story!' (Studeo, 2015) to architects ('Story telling is at the heart of great place-making.' The Architecture Foundation, 2015). Stefan Sagmeister recently ranted: 'I read an interview with somebody who designs roller coasters and he referred to himself as a storyteller. No,

*f**khead, you are not a storyteller, you're a roller coaster designer. And that's fantastic!' (Sagermeister, 2015)'*

Their recipe for good data storytelling is simple:

'When you're working with data, the concept of storytelling is doubly problematic. Data suggests objectivity, evidence, facts. Storytelling suggests subjectivity, bias, lies.'

But treated with care and clarity that circle can be squared:

'In the balance between beauty, accuracy and clarity, the greatest of these is clarity.... And it is only through the clarity of our communication that our audience will appreciate the accuracy of our data representation, because it only then that they will understand it well enough to use'.

Ultimately, though, the author/reporter is as important in this as in other media products:

'As with any kind of authorship, it is the combination of a great tale and a great teller that creates the most enduring work'.

Back to filthy lucre. Data journalism is fast growing with increasing employment opportunities. If legacy media often look for experienced applicants, marketing offers good salary prospects to young graduates. Data journalist Isabelle Marchand (to declare an interest one of my students at Brunel University who developed a DJ interest on reading the first edition of this book!) compiles some tricks and tips to help beginners creating advertising visualisations. She is realistic about what she is doing for the Ford Motor Company:

'Journalism is often synonymous with long hours, low pay and little recognition. The good news is that data journalism, especially related to communications, is a well-paid area, and it is in the interest of your employer to publicise your productions.'

Finally in this section, is the future of data journalism really the past? Can today's data journalists learn lessons from history? The BBC's Bella Hurrell and John Walton look to visualisations by Florence Nightingale and Charles Booth from two centuries ago to find out. For them, platforms will determine data visualisation:

'Many of the big data stories of the future will be designed to be consumed primarily on mobile phones (and have to be designed for that small mobile area).

And, as with all media, the audience expects more and better not static product:

'As all journalists, not just data journalists, become more sophisticated at using data so will our readers. They will routinely expect personally relevant data in addition to a national picture or general overview.'

So, these are the beginnings of a journey into the worlds of data journalists. Worlds apart but worlds that are increasingly the mainstream in journalism today.

Why data journalism is the new punk

Simon Rogers argues that data journalism draws on the great tradition of punk to celebrate the 'anyone can do it' philosophy

This is a chord … this is another … this is a third. NOW FORM A BAND. So went the first issue of British punk fanzine, *Sideburns*, in 1977 in the 'first and last part in a series'. It might be 35-years-old, but this will do nicely as a theory of data journalism in 2015. Why? Arguably punk was most important in its influence, encouraging kids in the suburbs to take up instruments, with little or no musical training. It represented a DIY ethos and a shake-up of the old established order. It was a change. Crucial to it was the idea: anyone can do it.

Is the same true of data journalism? Do you need to be part of a major news operation, working for a big media company to be a data journalist? Now is the time to examine this. In May 2010, we published a piece on how journalists would be flooded with a 'tsunami of data'. Five years on and data journalism is part of the fabric of what we, and many other news organisations do.

Data journalism has its roots – or many of them – in CAR, going back to the 1960s in the USA. But even if they had heard of this computer-assisted reporting stuff, how many UK journalists were using spreadsheets for data analysis by (say) 2008 – at least, outside of financial and business journalism? How many people were actually teaching it here?

What is it? I would say data journalism incorporates such a wide range now of styles – from visualisation to long-form articles. The key thing they have in common is that they are based on numbers and statistics – and that they should aim to get a 'story' from that data. The ultimate display of that story, be it words or graphics, is irrelevant, I think – it's more about the process. There are even different streams now – short-form, quick-and-dirty data visualisations of the kind many news organisations do daily, right through to complex investigations and visualisations such as our riots data analysis or the kind of projects that make the shortlist of the Data Journalism Awards, from around the world. So, can we still say that anyone can do data journalism; in the first and last part in a series. Would this work?

1) This is a dataset.
2) Here's another.
3) Here are some free tools.
4) NOW BE A DATA JOURNALIST

OK, it lacks a certain 1976 grittiness, but the theory is there. You don't have to be a developer or a coder to be a data journalist. We asked our Twitter followers what they thought. A couple stand out to me: 'Maybe everyone can do it, but not everyone can do it well'; and 'like so many other things, done well is a mix of art and science.' Mutual disregard for shared constructs of authority? Shared overarching aim of revealing reality away from the facade? But is that enough? The thing about data journalism is that there are so very many 'chords' – just the free ones could fill several training manuals: Google fusion tables, Tableau, Gephi, OutWit Hub, Google Refine … Can anyone really do it?

Dan Sinker knows about both data and punk: he heads up the Knight-Mozilla News Technology Partnership and is a former editor of *Punk Planet.* He says there are some parallels – with a crucial difference.

> *'While I agree with the premise – it's never been easier to do this stuff than it is right now – I think there are a few steps beyond just learning three chords when doing data journalism. For one, Legs [McNeil, who coined the word 'punk'] didn't really say a band needed to be *good* but I'd like to think we'd require that for data journalism. The theory goes that the punk bands we remember best are the ones that were good – but there needed to be a whole lot of kids experimenting and sounding awful before they got there. For what it's worth, I like the fact that there are many just trying stuff out, even if it is forgettable – because some of it will be amazing.'*

Data journalism – the great leveller

In fact, data journalism is a great leveller. Many media groups are starting with as much prior knowledge and expertise as someone hacking away from their bedroom. Many have, until very recently, no idea where to start and great groups of journalists are still nervous of the spreadsheets they are increasingly confronted with. It's rare for the news site reader to find themselves as powerful as the news site editor, but that's where we are right now – and that power is only increasing as journalists come to rely more and more on their communities for engagement and stories. Says Sinker:

> *'Where I think there are more parallels are in the fact that this is a young community (in years if not always age), and one that's actively teaching itself new tricks every day. That same vitality and excitement that motivated punk, it's motivating news hackers right now.'*

Meanwhile, more and more news teams are discovering that data equals stories and are bulking up their teams. Some would say it's just an extension of work they've always done, but that's to ignore the huge shift in power the web has created. 'Some people think that this stuff is instant,' says Sinker. 'Even though there are incredible tools now, there is still a learning curve.' Out there in the world, there are lots of people who have just formed a band and got on with it – despite the obstacles.

Take the data team at *La Nacion*, recently shortlisted for the Data Journalism Awards for their work on transport subsidies. When the team started, it was sparse, to say the least, says Florencia Coelho.

> *We had no web programmer or CAR [computer assisted reporting] people in our newsroom. We gathered an interactive designer and we self-taught Tableau with their free training videos in what we called our Tableau days, in a Starbucks at a shopping mall in Buenos Aires.*

The team is still not exactly huge – but it is easily the best data journalism site in South America and one of the most innovative around. It's not all about investigative reporting. First, all reporting probably counts as investigative journalism, but if you want to play semantics, then I will see your 'investigative' and raise you 'analytical'. Not all data journalism has to bring down the government – it's often enough for it to shine a light in corners that are less understood, to help us see the world a little clearer. And if that's not investigative, what is?

Democratisation of data

There's a great democratisation of data going on. Rather than the numbers belonging to the experts, they belong to all of us – and data journalism is part of that reclaiming of the facts. Even at the OECD, users' voices are part of the process, making up the core analysis that lies at the heart of the Better Life Index on well-being. And, just to be clear – data journalism doesn't have to mean data visualisation. It is not about producing charts or intricate graphics – the results of data journalism just happen to lend themselves to that. Sometimes a story is best told in images and infographics, other times it works as words and stories. It's the ultimate in flexible formats.

But, when it comes to visualisations, what really comes across from this analysis of Visual.lys most viral infographics is how sometimes the simplest things can flood the web. Single charts are likely successful because they are easy to consume; the viewer only needs to learn how to read one 'chunk' of visualisation to get the whole story. Simplicity lends itself to quick understanding and sharing, whereas complexity can prevent a viewer from reaching those points. Curiously, mixed charts, which is what we commonly think of as the typical form of an infographic, is the least successful here, perhaps because they take more mental work to consume completely, again pointing to simplicity and brevity as strengths in visual communication.

As the post points out, however, sometimes things done messily can still be hits – it's the information that's vital. People are willing to forgive a lack of perfection; they are much less forgiving for those who get the facts wrong. Data visualisation experts will always say: allow the data to choose the visualisation, that it's crucial for the visualisation to fit the numbers – and not the other way around. That question equally applies itself to whether something needs a visualisation in the first place.

Of course, for some people, this will never be journalism. But then, who cares? While they are worrying about the definitions, the rest of us can just get on with it. Punk eventually turned into new wave, new wave into everyday pop and bands that just aren't as exciting. But what it did do is change the climate and the daily weather. Data journalism is doing that too. In the words of Joe Strummer: 'people can do anything'.

Common mistakes data journalism learners make - and how to avoid them

Recent graduate and journalist Emily Shackleton offers some practical advice for novices on how to avoid the pitfalls when working with and visualising data

Introduction

Data journalism is in vogue - or experiencing a 'moment' as so many of its commentators state. In fact, it is what students including myself have paid £9,000 to learn while undertaking City University London's prestigious and still relatively new Interactive Journalism Masters programme that has an entire module dedicated to it. It has never been so prevalent in British media, and so easy for journalists to produce. Tools such as Datawrapper exist where writers can simply insert a selection of data from a spreadsheet into a website, and a visualisation appears instantaneously. Andrew Hill, the creator of mapping service CartoDB that allows you to make a beautiful interactive map within minutes, explained last year in an interview for City Interactive students' website *Interhacktives* that the reason the tool was created was to allow everyone to make complicated-looking maps. 'We think everyone has the ability to create interesting visualisations and tell important stories with data,' he said. 'We created CartoDB to make it easier, faster, and less expensive' (Scott, 2014).

If there is one piece of advice that I could impart after a year of grappling with data while studying for my MA though, it is that there is more to it than being able to chuck in a few visualisations. There are a range of skills and knowledge that you need to deploy, some which as a data learner can take a while to truly understand and have the confidence to exercise effectively. In some ways, as you enter industry as a professional journalist armed with a plethora of data skills, you never stop learning - and in a rapidly changing industry that is no bad thing.

To save yourself some time, here, with a mixture of personal experience from doing my MA at City and advice from data journalism experts themselves, I will go through the most common mistakes learners seem to make when embarking on mastering this increasingly popular craft.

Misinterpreting numbers

Data journalism is just like any other journalism - the fundamentals of being able to sniff out a good story are still the same. But instead of contacts and press releases, your core piece of information is a dataset. Dealing with numbers means a good understanding of statistics and ways of analysing raw data can obviously be incredibly helpful. However, if you are anything like me then that may not be easy at first. In a lot of ways I was the average journalism student: graduated with a good undergraduate degree in an arts subject (English, in my case), and previously some kind of editor or contributor of my institution's student publication with the trials and tribulations of maths in the GCSE long behind me. I did not have the benefit of a natural inclination towards maths and statistics.

I, and people like me, can take a small, brief comfort in the fact that journalists and numbers have famously never got on. In his call for more scientific rigour in data journalism, Alberto Cairo even proclaims that journalists have a well-known allergy to maths and scientific method. 'Some even proudly boast about it,' he writes. 'Many in our profession still stick to flawed practices, such as asking the same questions to two or more sources and then just reporting their answers, without weighing the evidence and then pointing out which opinion is better grounded.' (Cairo, 2014)

So how can someone without a background in maths or statistics get to grips with data and apply more scientific rigour to their analysis? There are so many ways to analyse data that they almost merit a separate book of their own. Yet, there are a couple of major lessons that I have learned over the last year that strike me as key things to remember if you are just starting out. At City, we had the privilege and pleasure of being taught by some of the most prestigious data journalists. One of whom was James Ball, the former special projects editor at *the Guardian.* In a particularly useful data theory lecture, he introduced us to one of the most important rules to remember about data analysis: correlation does not equal causation.

This rule becomes particularly significant in line charts where, as the next section will show, variables over a period of time can be compared in order to find a relationship or correlation. However, as Tyler Vigen's *Spurious Correlations* website and book humorously illustrate by correlating random variables, there is a folly in putting together two that seem to correlate and forming a causation conclusion about their relationship.

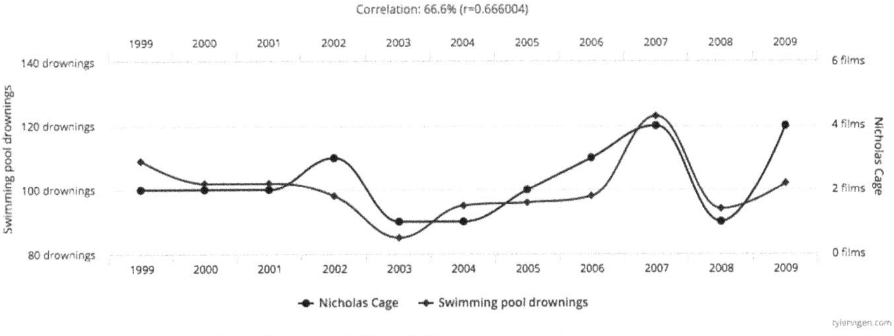

Figure 1: The dangers of correlation: Just because films that Nicolas Cage has been in and people drowning in swimming pools follow a similar trend, it does not mean one caused the other (Vigen 2015).

Vigen (2015) says that the project was just a 'fun way to look at correlations and to think about data [...] The charts on this site aren't meant to imply causation nor are they meant to create a distrust for research or even correlative data'. However, it illustrates a significant point about the danger of interpreting a correlation or relationship between two variables, whether they be related or not. It could, as the graph of Nicolas Cage films and swimming pool deaths shows, be a complete coincidence.

Portraying data in proportion has been something else important that I have learned as a data journalism learner. There are many factors that could be influencing the results of your data, which if not dealt with can throw your story and its angle completely out. Population, for example, when not taken into account can create an inaccurate picture of what is going on, especially when it comes to mapping. If you were trying to show the spread of a dangerous infection across the UK then you might find that you are simply illustrating areas with a high population density if you just put the raw data into a mapping tool. Instead you will need to work out proportional numbers per a certain amount of the population - so perhaps per thousand or million population.

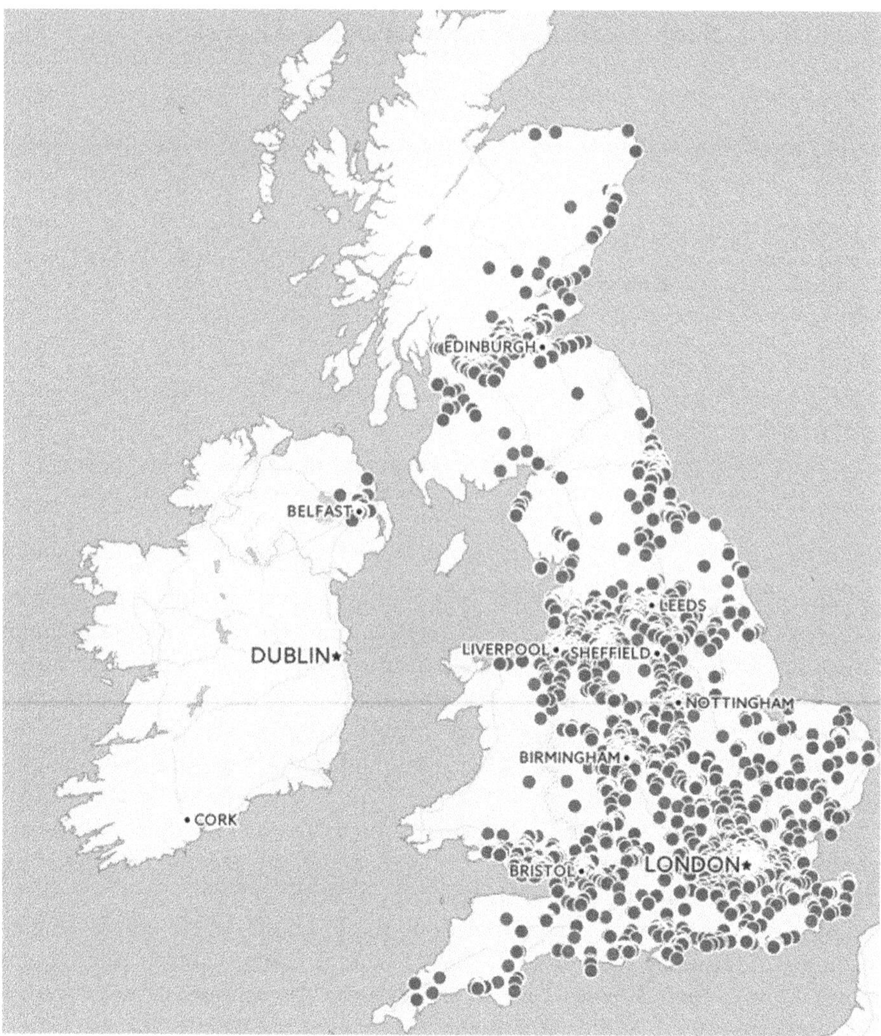

Figure 2: Mapping the UK's swear words on Twitter for The Independent using CartoDB: Without taking population into account, the points on the map naturally cluster around cities with large populations (Shackleton, 2015).

The entire focus of your story may become vastly different as a result. The image below shows the change in news line in an article that I wrote for the *Press Gazette* that exposed a gap in the capital's local newspaper coverage. It occurred once I took each region's population into account.

Local newspapers and hyperlocals update

File Edit View Insert Format Data Tools Add-ons Help All changes saved in

	A	B	C	D	E
1	**Region**	**No. of newspapers**	**Population**	**Newspapers per million population**	
2	East Midlands	69	4,537,400	15	
3	East of England	105	5,862,400	18	
4	London	93	8,204,400	11	
5	North East	28	2,596,400	11	
6	North West	110	7,056,000	16	
7	Northern Ireland	59	1,806,900	33	
8	Scotland	142	5,254,800	27	
9	South East	157	8,652,800	18	
10	South West	124	5,300,800	23	
11	Wales	60	3,063,800	20	
12	West Midlands	77	5,608,700	14	
13	Yorkshire and Th	62	5,288,200	12	
14					
15					

Figure 3: The difference proportional numbers can make: Without taking into account population as a variable that can distort results, London's local newspaper scene does not look too bad (Shackleton, 2015; Office of National Statistics, 2013; Jicreg, 2014; British Newspapers Online, 2014; ABC, 2014).

Before I calculated the number of newspapers per million population, the North East seemed to have the least. Once the variable of population density was controlled, the reality of London's local newspaper coverage became apparent.

Using the wrong tool

A pie chart for comparing two different things, a bar chart to show composition, or a line chart when it is not a time series - you name the error, and it is out there in everyday data journalism. Using the wrong tool can have a huge impact on how a reader absorbs the story. A line chart, for example, that is usually employed to show changes over a certain period – decreases and increases – could imply a confusing, non-existent trend when applied to illustrate other variables.

Channel 4's Fact Check made this mistake recently in a piece about George Osborne's 2015 Budget and what it was not telling you. One line chart aims to show the difference in ages between Tory and Labour voters, where the value of the x axis is age instead of time.

It suggests a continuous trend between age and party preference, where the older a voter becomes the more likely they are to be a Tory voter, instead of treating the voters of different ages as separate values. While the data is continuous, it actually shows the preferences of a sample of voters at a specific point of time that makes the use of a line chart inaccurate.

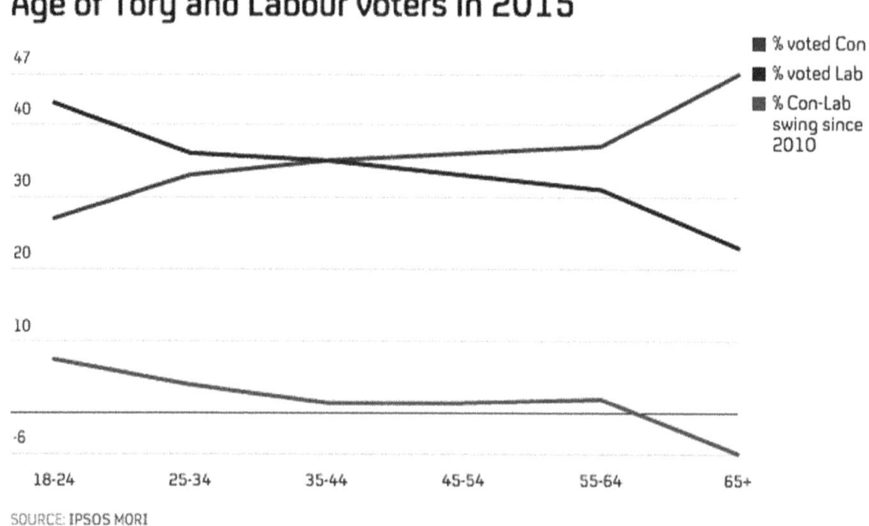

Figure 4: From Channel 4's Fact Check: A line chart used incorrectly.

So which chart or visualisation should be used for what? Below are the five of the most common charts and graphs that you might be using when starting out with data journalism, and when they should be used.

Chart/graph	Use
Line chart	To show a relationship or correlation over time.
Bar chart	To compare the number, frequency or mean of discrete variables. There are different types of bar charts including grouped, stacked or horizontal.
Pie chart	To show how much of a whole different components make up, e.g the distribution of people visiting attractions in London. They should contain no more than six categories.
Histogram	To show data in a bar chart that is continuous instead of discrete. This might include the height and weight of children of certain ages at a specific point in time.
Maps	To show a relationship between a variable and geographical location.

Table 1: Types of visualisations and their uses. *Source: University of Leicester*

Not putting the audience at the heart of the article

If analysing data was not tricky enough for data journalism beginners, it turns out visualisation can be complicated too. A lot more complicated. Once you start truly looking into the possibilities out there, a whole world of D3, javascript and other programming languages reveals itself. However, a narrow focus on tools and complex coding can lead journalists down a path that Paul Bradshaw describes as 'tool-led' as opposed to 'story-led'. Bradshaw, writer of the Online Journalism Blog and lecturer at Birmingham City University, shows concern for a teaching of data where it becomes 'something without journalism' instead. 'Will we end up with 'tool-centric' journalists in the same way as we had shovelware journalists?' he asks on his blog (Bradshaw, 2015).

Bradshaw identifies a reliance on tools as a key mistake data beginners make in a bid to show off what they have learned. 'People choose to show off their technical skills rather than just tell a story. It is the visual equivalent of the aspiring novelist who uses a 12 letter word to show off their vocabulary, despite the fact that 50 per cent of their audience won't know what you mean, and the other 50 per cent just thinks you're an egotistical prat.' (Bradshaw, 2015)

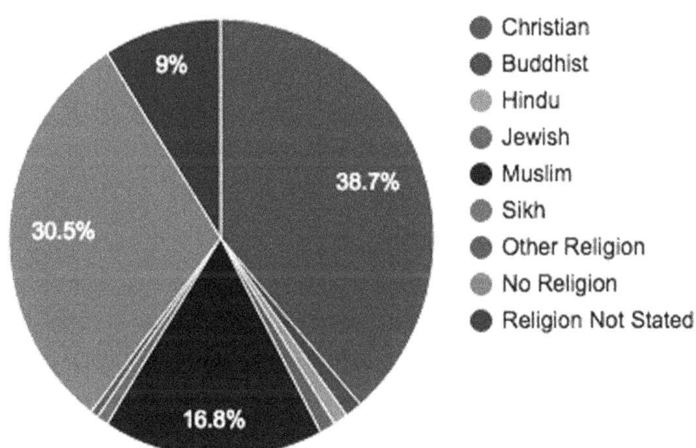

Figure 5: An early pie chart of mine gone wrong: Even basic tools such as Google Sheets charts can lead to unnecessary complexity.

It is the mistake of forgetting the purpose of your data investigation - you have to tell a story to those less in the know than you, the informer. In a time of snapshot news consumption moreover, where readers, as Tony Haile (2014) from Chartbeat has revealed, will spend an average time of 15 seconds on an article, you only have a limited amount of time to catch the readers' attention or convey the information. However complex your issue or topic might be, the reader needs to understand or at least be intrigued by what is going on with a visualisation at a glance.

Putting data out of context

Too much simplicity, however, is also an error many data journalists, let alone trainee journalists, are prone to make. A trend that is very common now is the 'this one graph shows you everything' headline, favoured by *Quartz*, *Vox* and many other publishers throwing their efforts into data journalism. Most issues, however, are often too complex to put into a single graph with a single dataset, and need context to fill in knowledge gaps.

Clara Guibourg, online writer for *City AM*, suggests breaking down seemingly enormous figures, such as that in public spending, and see if it still seems unreasonable.

'"Taxpayers paying more than $1 billion for illegal immigrant children," headlines yell out. "Benefits spending up £6.4 billion." The figures sound outrageous, astronomical even. It's tempting to want to splash on them. But public spending figures have a tendency to be, well, astronomical,' she writes on her blog (Guibourg, 2015). 'Put it into context: Break it down per person and you may find that in fact they're totally reasonable' (ibid).

Documentary context might also be necessary - can you identify why a trend has happened? What is the history behind that particular issue? *The Guardian*'s Datablog, set up in 2009 by Simon Rogers, is a much referenced example of data journalism done right in this way. A recent article, for example, about the shift in Vladimir Putin's approval rating includes an explanation of what has changed under Putin's government to give the data more background and context, offering Russia's state dominance of the media as a potential explanation.

The 'I can't talk to people' mistake

The number one mistake that data journalism students make is forgetting to do the good old fashioned reporting. Despite coming from a long tradition of on-the-ground reporting, data journalists appear to sometimes forget to talk to people. As Bradshaw observes:

> *'This is easily the most common. It's enjoyable to dig into data and find interesting things - but many people stop there. Some want to paint themselves as an expert, taking on the role of analysing the data. Others just tell a very dull story which has no people or places in it.' (Bradshaw 2015)*

And it makes for very dull stories because it forgets that one of journalism's major functions is to create a connection between the news and the people, which stories that contain human interest can do particularly effectively. 'Human interest stories have strong affective dimensions designed to provoke empathy and identification,' Judy Polumbaum (2009: 730, 732) contends. 'A human interest strategy can enhance understanding for widespread issues and problems by getting readers, listeners and viewers more fully engrossed, and thus empower them as citizens.' When added to a graph with just numbers and/or percentages therefore, a personal connection between the reader and the story is far more likely to be forged.

A story about an increase in infant deaths in hospitals due to failing hygiene standards, for example, could be put into context with a gripping case study of a mother who has lost her newborn child to infection. A reader is far more likely to realise the impact of the issue upon ordinary lives - and importantly, potentially theirs - if you illustrate it exactly.

I certainly found this to be the case when investigating a series on the decline of local newspapers for *The Media Briefing*. While the data I had showed that the local newspaper industry was in trouble and that journalists felt under pressure, the reality of the situation dawned on me the most when I went to a NUJ summit in Birmingham. My piece became more informed about the extended workload journalists have had to take on when I talked to attendees at the conference. As Bradshaw further notes:

> *'Journalism has to be different from an academic or government report. It has to tell a story, and on that front it helps to add quotes, background, colour and other details that bring it to life.'* (Bradshaw, 2015)

Conclusion

We are at a time when numbers have become exciting, and numbers have become sexy. Too sexy perhaps, as *The Times*' data editor Megan Lucero told journalists and developers at a Hacks/Hackers meeting in 2014 (Lucero, 2014). The overarching theme of all these mistakes would seem to be that it is easy to become wrapped up in the excitement of learning current and sought after skills and forget why you are doing it in the first place. Data journalists are here to tell stories that strive to move and appeal to people, as much as feature or comment writers - they just start with a different source. The journalism industry may have changed unrecognisably in the last decade with new technology and new ways of conveying information, but data journalism students must remember that its essential, informative storytelling function remains firmly in place.

References

ABC (2014) 'UK Regional Publications Interactive Report', *ABC*, December 2014, available at http://abc.fileburst.com/interactive/rp/main.php, accessed 1 June 2014

Bradshaw, Paul (2015) 'Is data journalism teaching repeating the same mistakes as online journalism teaching?' in *Online Journalism Blog*, 14 January, available at http://onlinejournalismblog.com/2015/01/14/data-journalism-teaching-should-learn-programming/, accessed 31 July 2015

Bradshaw, Paul (2015) Email conversation with author, July 2015. Personal correspondence.

British Newspapers Online (2014) *British Newspapers Online*, available at www.britishpapers.co.uk/, accessed 19 December 2014

Cairo, Alberto (2014) 'Alberto Cairo: Data journalism needs to up its own standards' in *NiemanLab*, 9 July, available online at www.niemanlab.org/2014/07/alberto-cairo-data-journalism-needs-to-up-its-own-standards, accessed 31 July 2015

Guibourg, Clara (2015) '4 mistakes in data journalism - and how to avoid them' Clara Guibourg blog, 7 May, available at https://cguibourg.wordpress.com/2015/05/07/4-mistakes-data-journalism-how-to-avoid-them, accessed 31 July 2015

Haile, Tony (2014) 'What you think you know about the web is wrong' in *Time*, 9 March, available at http://time.com/12933/what-you-think-you-know-about-the-web-is-wrong/, accessed 31 July 2015

Jicreg (2014) *Jiccreg*, available at http://jiab.jicreg.co.uk/#, accessed 19 December 2014

Lucero, Megan (2014) Speech presented at Hacks/Hackers meeting, October 2014

Office of National Statistics (2013) 'Population - ONS', *ONS*, available at http://ons.gov.uk/ons/taxonomy/index.html?nscl=Population#tab-data-tables, accessed 19 December 2014

Polumbaum, Judy (2009) 'Human Interest Journalism' in Sterling, Christopher H (ed), *Encyclopedia of Journalism*, California: Sage Publications, pp. 728-732

Scott, Patrick E. (2014), Interview with Andrew Hill data scientist at CartoDB, *Interhacktives*, January 2014, available at www.interhacktives.com/2014/01/17/interview-with-andrew-hill-of-cartodb, accessed 31 July 2015

Shackleton, Emily (2015) 'Map of UK's local newspapers and websites reveals London's news gap' in *Press Gazette*, 5 June 2014, available at www.pressgazette.co.uk/map-uks-local-newspapers-and-websites-reveals-london-news-gap, accessed 14 August 2015

Shackleton, Emily (2015) 'Twitter's swearing mapped: Which UK country is the most foul mouthed on social media?' in *The Independent*, 24 July 2015, available at www.independent.co.uk/life-style/gadgets-and-tech/news/twitters-swearing-mapped-which-uk-country-is-the-most-foulmouthed-on-social-media-10413091.html, accessed 14 August 2015

Student Learning Development, Numerical data, *University of Leicester website*, available online at www2.le.ac.uk/offices/ld/resources/numerical-data/, accessed 31 July 2015

Vigen, Tyler (2015) *Spurious Correlations*, US: Hachette Book. Website for project is also available at http://www.tylervigen.com/spurious-correlations, accessed 31 July 2015

Worral, Patrick (2015) 'FactCheck: the summer budget – what George Osborne isn't telling you', *Channel 4*, 9 July, available at http://blogs.channel4.com/factcheck/factcheck-summer-budget-george-osborne-telling/21257, accessed 31 July 2015

Data journalism: A-Z from pitch to delivery

Analysis of Local Government Pension Fund investment data brought to light ethical dilemmas, with councils seeking to make returns while at the same being arbiters on planning proposals in the nascent fracking industry, as Jan Goodey discovered

Introduction

As a teacher of journalism it's long been crucial for me to stay engaged in the field and what better way than to involve the students in a project and engage them at the same time. I had been running a National Council for the Training of Journalists (NCTJ) professional course at an FE college in Brighton, UK for seven years. Being a freelancer on environmental issues as well meant there was a sufficient, natural confluence when this particular project in fracking investments came up. At the time in 2013-14 my students were mostly 18-25 year-olds who understood the basics of news reporting and feature writing. The syllabus included data journalism theory but not much in the way of practicalities. We considered current good practice and looked at video clips of examples of how data journalism was being used in the field. These included a project mapping rainforest destruction in the Brazilian Amazon entitled 'Gustavo Faleiros: Spreading Data Journalism in Brazil' (Faleiros, 2012) and a look at some purely amazing flight infographics/visualisations from Stanford University (Koblin, 2010). We looked at websites from *the Guardian* Datablog through to trends mapping. And of course we appraised the various tools available: Google Fusion, Microsoft Excel etc. My own work in the fracking arena had included Freedom of Information Act (FOI) requests into drilling accidents and articles for The Ecologist website on the anti-fracking movement, including 'Anti-fracking special report: UK' (Cottrell and Goodey, 2013); and 'The UK's anti-fracking movement is growing' (Goodey, 2013).

Local Government Pension Fund (LGPF) investigation

In January 2013 a contact and anti-fracking campaigner, Will Cottrell, came up with the proposal for an investigation into public funding of fracking companies through local government pension funds. He had a contact, Ed Jones, who had spent a number of years looking into local government finances in general and had an extensive portfolio of research that included resultant articles that had appeared in national broadsheets. So the die was cast and an eighteen-month to two-year project began. Initial idea and strategy meetings between us took place weekly in which we came up with nailed down ideas, timelines and solutions as to how we would stand stories up. We started making initial contacts with councillors on relevant finance and planning committees up and down the country and press officers at key councils in order to see if there was a particular conflict of interest i.e. were there councillors who were members of the planning and pension fund committees, where the planning committee was to make a decision on a planning application for exploratory drilling and possible fracking?

Meanwhile back on my NCTJ fast track course (September 2013 to February 2014) and still looking at concrete ways to add this practical aspect to the data journalism theory we had covered on the course, I had the bare bones of an idea to get the students involved in an actual real time project. There was a mature student, Jennifer Kennedy, who had travelled widely in South America and contributed articles on human rights issues to respected international websites. Of the 11 students of 36 who showed enthusiasm in playing a part in this financial investigation, Jennifer took the ball and ran with it. So we had an improved project and team of four.

Teamwork between campaigners, journalists and students

We were fortunate to have a head start on a number of fronts. First in Ed Jones we had a first class researcher who had been immersed in the chicaneries of local government systems for eight or nine years. His wide reading and constant updating of current local government policies via various citations he would post from journals, newspapers, trade magazines and websites was invaluable. He knew how to approach council press officers and how to construct watertight FOI requests. He had also, during the course of the years, built up sound working relationships with a number of councillors.

Jennifer Kennedy, the youngest team member in her 20s, had the up-to-date academic skills and a keener eye for data and subsequent copy to attract a younger readership. She also had a phenomenal work rate, working on our time consuming project while in the space of two years holding down this high-pressure vocational journalism course followed by an extremely demanding job on the *Hastings Observer*, then a Masters at University College London (UCL).

Will Cottrell had a thorough knowledge of the fracking industry through campaigning work and a basic understanding of the financial markets we were looking into. As the founder of Brighton Energy Co-op, his knowledge of the geo-politics of the worldwide energy industries constantly in flux, gave us the over-arching perspective we required.

My own contribution was the piecing together of the puzzle in the drafting stages and final written submissions of copy for *The Independent* and the *i* newspaper (Milmo and Goodey, 2013), having previously put in place the commissions through successful pitching.

What systems do we put in place?

We had a job on our hands: 99 FOI requests to all the regional pension funds. There was a strict timeline to work to in order that we kept on top of replies and more importantly subsequent follow-ups and appeals to the Information Commissioner's Office (ICO) should the requisite information not be forthcoming. By Winter 2013 Ed Jones had completed two visiting lectures to my NCTJ students on the project and we had a group of volunteers who were going to take ownership of a number of FOI requests. Most of these were to be carried out using the public service website, WhatDoTheyKnow https://www.whatdotheyknow.com. The remaining requests were conducted privately so that any access issues to the full data set were dealt with comprehensively and any chance of our work being hijacked or compromised by aggregating our replies on WhatDoTheyKnow was obviated.

The template letter request we used included the following paragraphs to head off at the pass any time wasting which could result from a vague or unclear wish-list (always worth bearing in mind when you carry out FOIA requests for a data investigation):

> *I would like to request the following information:*
>
> 1) *The full details of what the X Council Pension Fund currently invests in, including the name and amounts of each asset class or investment being held. Ideally this information would be broken down into the different categories, including: index linked securities, unit trust property, cash instruments, unit trust equities, infrastructure, fixed interest securities, equities segregated unlisted, equities segregated UK, equities segregated foreign as well as any other investments that the Pension Fund holds.*
>
> 2) *A full list of all the companies that the Pension Fund currently invests in. This should be covered in the above question. This list should include the names of each company and the amount invested in each company.*
>
> 3) *The current yields of the different investments the pension fund holds. Can you clearly specify the total value of all investments that the Pension Fund holds.*
>
> 4) *I would like to receive this information in an unlocked Excel sheet without protext cells (.xls). If you have to password protect the Excel sheet, can you also provide the password to the Excel sheet. I would like to receive the information in electronic format if possible.*

If one part of the request can be answered sooner than others, please send that information first followed by any subsequent data. If you need further clarification, please contact me by email. Many public authorities release their contracts, minutes and other information of interactions with private vendors in line with the Freedom of Information Act. The exemption for commercial interest under the Act (section 43) is a qualified exemption, which means information can only be withheld if it is in the public's interest. The public have an interest in knowing what the Pension Fund is investing in, the terms of contracts and the minutes of meeting with public authorities, whether or not public money changes hands immediately. If you are relying on section 41 (the exemption for legal breach of confidence) then I would like to know the following:

- *When these confidentiality agreements were agreed?*
- *All correspondence and email in which these confidentiality agreements were discussed*
- *The precise wording of the confidentiality agreements*

I ask these questions because guidance issued by both the Lord Chancellor (draft guidance on FOI implementation) and the Office of Government Commerce (Model terms and conditions for goods and services) specifically state that public authorities should not enter into these types of agreements; they go directly against the spirit of the laws of disclosure. I would also point to the Information Commissioner's guidance on accepting blanket commercial confidentiality agreements: 'Unless confidentiality clauses are necessary or reasonable, there is a real risk that, in the event of a complaint, the Commissioner would order disclosure in any case.

Finally, within the law of confidence there is also a public interest test. Therefore, the information should be disclosed in full. If any parts are redacted they must be for information that can be proven to be a legal breach of confidence in court, and only then where secrecy can be shown to be in the public interest. These are difficult positions to argue when public money is at stake or where a public authority is offering a private company a monopoly to charge its stakeholders. I reserve the right to appeal against your decision to withhold any information or to charge excessive fees, and understand that under the Act, I am entitled to a response within 20 working days. I would be grateful if you could confirm in writing that you have received this request.

The next step was to set to work building databases using Google Drive as a hub as well as Dropbox and personal email accounts for sensitive, summative material. We had four master documents on Google Drive which were updated: an 'active' fracking sites list; a database of worldwide fracking companies, related industry partners and investment vehicles; a list of press contacts; and a national LGPF database checklist which enabled us to track accurately all incoming replies and outgoing responses. In Dropbox we had an 'original' data folder which contained the discrete 99 documents of LGPF raw data (some in annual report format, some in pdf and some in xls.) and a 'reformatted' data folder which held the 99 LGPF documents in a format we considered workable. These reformatted documents were all documents we had spent time and considerable effort converting into Excel spreadsheets with seven bar headings of: Asset; Value; Type; Holder; Sector; Date; Notes. An example is below:

Asset	Value	Type	Holder	Sector	Date	Notes
3I GROUP ORD GBP0.738636	710,494.12	Equities	Cardiff		9/30/2013	UK
ABERCROMBIE & FITCH CO CL A	181,181.31	Equities	Cardiff		9/30/2013	US
AMLIN ORD GBP0.28125	992,616.53	Equities	Cardiff		9/30/2013	UK
ASTRAZENECA ORD USD0.25	772,813.27	Equities	Cardiff		9/30/2013	UK

Table 2: An example of an investigative spreadsheet

Once we had close to the full dataset we were able to transfer all 99 separate spreadsheets to a giant master file that had upwards of 57,500 rows of data. This could then be sifted into various formats required for our subsequent stories (using Excel pivot tables) which as well as the fracking industry included an exposé of the tobacco world (Kennedy, Milmo and Goodey, 2014).

When I referred earlier to 'close to the full dataset', it is important to recognise as a journalist that you have to draw the line at some point and go with what you have. So (for example) on this occasion we had three or four regional LGPFs that were obdurate in their stance not to disclose and, despite appeals to the ICO, refused to give the full data we required. As we were nearing the end of the allocated time for research (Spring, 2014) going further in the appeals process wasn't viable and hence the data we had from these four regions was included as the 'headline figures' we were given: figures which were accurate but not broken down.

At this juncture we decided that a resource website that we could develop further even after the project would be a good idea. We set up Asset Tracker (asset-tracker.org) with the aim of pushing for greater transparency and accountability within the LGPF framework and supporting divestment campaigns from fossil fuels, tobacco and arms. Allied to this website was an Asset Tracker Twitter account @asset-tracker. We disseminated relevant articles and infographics including one that showed the links to a county council in the southeast and the UK fracking industry. See below:

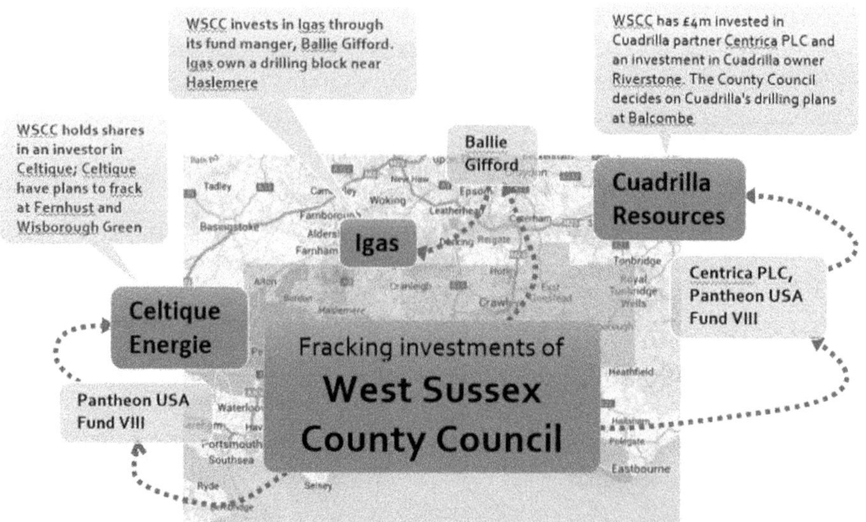

Figure 6: Graphic used in storytelling. *Courtesy asset-tracker.org*

Overall we came across some highly interesting investments with a systematic scouring of the data using our fracking company and 'active fracking site' databases, to cross check any connections to the original raw data. For example there was £1.9m held by Lincolnshire County Council's pension fund in Total, the French company that earlier that year (2014) became the first major oil company to have a foothold in the UK fracking industry, with a £30m stake in two exploration projects in the county at that time. Also West Sussex County Council had indirect holdings in Cuadrilla, which carried out controversial tests in the Sussex village of Balcombe in 2013. Furthermore we discovered that the same county council had investments worth £3.5m in Centrica, the parent company of British Gas – which in 2013 took a 25 per cent stake in a Lancashire frack site operated by Cuadrilla. Taking the time to speak with press officers and officials tasked with dealing with FOI requests was key as this occasionally landed us with extra unexpected, but extremely helpful data that had been handed out inadvertently.

Towards the end of the project Will and Ed had had to leave the team due to pressures of work and illness. Jennifer and I took on the laborious yet necessary task of making sure we had a 'clean' dataset. Missing just one entry in a column by incorrectly deleting, inserting or copying data led to hours of frantic, forensic checking. It is vital to adopt a rigid and thorough approach to the cleaning up of data with 100 per cent accuracy the aim. Being consistent and uniform in what you do is essential. When our pitches to national newspapers began to pay dividends (both *The Sunday Times* and *The Independent* showed interest) we had the data in a professional package that meant that when it was viewed for verification purposes there were no questions regarding its accuracy or provenance.

The importance of the data having impact

The impact we wanted from the discoveries we made and subsequent stories published was to feed into the movement of divestment from fossil fuels: Bill McKibben's *350.org* international awareness campaign of the need to decrease carbon dioxide concentration in the atmosphere to *350* parts per million; *the Guardian*'s subsequent drive to *Keep it in the ground.* Coming from an environmental background this was how we envisaged it. Our website picked up traction on the issue and we included 'extras': exclusive material that we had gleaned from the earlier data investigations but had not published anywhere previously. The impact of the national newspaper articles and the publication of background material on our website led to local paper reports from the *Argus* in Brighton to locals in London and the Midlands. Twitter contacts followed with other campaigning journalists and student journalists requesting data we had accrued for their own projects in their particular geographical area. To make greater use of the work we had done we decided to open-source the dataset via the not for profit website Corporate Watch with arms investment from LGPFs a possible avenue for staff there to explore.

Future data-mining and possible follow-ups

In terms of future plans we have a number of options in how to follow-up on this work, with possible further yearly trawls to come up with new full or partial datasets of LGPFs. If it were to be partial, we could take in certain regions covered in our previous national stories and analyse how investments in particular companies had risen or fallen. If it were to be the full dataset, we could see how overall totals had increased or not in different parts of the country and what that meant for different industries. By having the updated data to hand we could mine information that was topical to that particular timeframe. So for example are certain regional funds investing in suspect payday lending companies? Or are certain regions investing in companies that carry out animal testing? And were there to be a particular and obviously egregious conflict of interest, it could well narrow down the story to that one subject and one region with the impact being nevertheless explosive.

References

Cottrell, Will and Goodey, Jan (2013) 'Anti fracking special report: UK' in *The Ecologist*, 27 August, available at www.theecologist.org/News/news_analysis/2057777/anti_fracking_special_report_uk.html, accessed 25 August 2015

Faleiros, Gustavo (2012) 'Spreading data journalism in Brazil', YouTube video post, available at www.youtube.com/watch?v=QH9a6PIStw4, accessed 25 August 2015

Goodey, Jan (2013) 'The UK's anti-fracking movement is growing' in *The Ecologist*, 1 August, available at www.theecologist.org/News/news_analysis/2016997/the_uks_anti_fracking_movement_is_growing.html, accessed 25 August 2015

Kennedy, Jennifer and Milmo, Cahal and Goodey, Jan (2014) 'Councils paid to cut smoking, but have £2bn of tobacco shares' in *The Independent on Sunday*, 9 November, available at www.independent.co.uk/news/uk/politics/councils-paid-to-cut-smoking-but- have-2bn-of-tobacco-shares-9849300.html, accessed 25 August 2015

http://www.youtube.com/watch?v=QH9a6PIStw4Koblin, Aaron (2010) 'Journalism in the age of data. Ch. 1: Introduction' YouTube video post, available at available at http://www.youtube.com/watch?v=g_B7TyKcFT8, accessed 25 August 2015

Milmo, Cahal and Goodey, Jan (2014) 'Local authorities have "conflict of interest" on fracking investments' in *The Independent*, April 27, available at www.independent.co.uk/news/uk/politics/exclusive-local-authorities-have-conflict-of-interest-on-fracking-investments-9294590.html, accessed 25 August 2015

Montague, Brendan and Amin, Lucas (2012) *FOIA without a lawyer*. London: Centre for Investigative Journalism

Williams, Corin (2014) 'Resignation over pension tobacco investment,' in *Environmental Health News online*, July 16, available at www.ehn-online.com/news/article.aspx?id=12110&terms=tobacco, accessed 25 August 2015

Data journalism grows up

Data journalism has evolved partly out of computer-assisted reporting (CAR) in the USA, bolstered by freedom of information (FOI), open data and journalism education. Jonathan Hewett traces the development and teaching of data journalism in the UK

Introduction

'Data journalism is the future,' declared Tim Berners-Lee, the inventor of the world wide web, in 2010 (Arthur, 2010). But using the term 'data journalist' only a couple of years earlier would have produced puzzled faces in most newsrooms. 'Journalists like us who use data in our reporting, you mean?' may have been the reasonable retort from some reporters, such as finance news specialists. Others may have made a connection with spreadsheets, databases and computer-assisted reporting (CAR). At university journalism departments in the UK, the response would have been similar, I suspect. But a few years later, 'data journalism' was appearing in job advertisements, university courses, discussions about the future of journalism – and even in book titles.

Indeed, it has evolved and diversified so rapidly that data work is now found among local newspapers, hyperlocal bloggers, international news organisations, investigative and specialist journalists and beyond. While many publishers sought to integrate data within their existing strategy, some initiatives focused particularly on data. One high-profile example developed out of Nate Silver's statistical analysis of baseball, and for US election forecasts. His *FiveThirtyEight* became part of *The New York Times* and then launched as separate site, owned by television network ESPN. It grew from two full-time journalists to 20 (Silver, 2014). In the UK, where some newspapers and the BBC assembled data journalism teams, Trinity Mirror (TM) piloted a fresh approach to data journalism with its standalone *ampp3d* team. Responding quickly to news with a tabloid-style approach, using bold graphics and interactivity, and geared for access on mobile devices and social sharing, the site reached places that few data projects had tried to go. Although it closed after 18 months, *ampp3d*'s impact was felt widely (Bradshaw, 2015) and TM's separate data journalism unit continued.

Such projects may seem far removed from the roots of data journalism in CAR, going back to the 1960s in the USA. Even if they had heard of this computer-assisted reporting stuff, very few UK journalists were using spreadsheets for data analysis by (say) 2008 – outside of financial and business journalism, at least. Even fewer were actually teaching it.

Tough times for investigative work

One factor underlying this situation in the UK involved the challenges faced by investigative journalism – the main focus for CAR. 'Many would argue that the glory days of investigative journalism in the UK are well beyond us now,' Arjan Dasselaar suggested (2005: 221), attributing this to cuts in editorial budgets, fierce competition and legal liabilities. David Leigh, then investigations editor at *the Guardian*, bemoaned 'difficult and frustrating times for investigative journalism in Britain' (Meek, 2005).

Dasselaar's survey noted also 'some distrust towards new methods of information gathering, such as the Internet'. While the BBC's *Panorama* programme employed 'computer researchers, journalists seem to consider going out and talking to people as superior to using Google'. Others felt that 'information on the internet must be untrue, for otherwise it would have been picked up already' (ibid: 224) – a point well made, given recurring errors attributable to 'facts' taken from websites apparently without checking (Orlowski, 2007).

Signs of change were already evident in 2005, as more journalists grasped the opportunities offered by the internet, particularly financial reporters accessing records. 'The advent of the Internet has revolutionised this branch of journalism,' noted Dasselaar (op cit: 224). Even so, it was off the scale to anticipate the scale of a shift that five years later led to news organisations such as *the Guardian* dealing with huge volumes of data requiring detailed analysis. These included the Afghan war logs (92,201 rows of data), the Iraq war logs (391,000) and the US embassy cables (251,287) released through WikiLeaks (Rogers, 2013a: 71).

Nerds plus words add up in the USA

Journalists on the other side of the Atlantic were far ahead of their UK counterparts. Already by 1999, a growing network of reporters, editors and journalism educators could look back on substantial developments in CAR over the previous 10 years (Paul, 1999). *When Nerds and Words Collide* reviewed progress since the 1989 creation of the National Institute for Advanced Reporting and the Missouri Institute for Computer Assisted Reporting (which became NICAR, the National Institute for CAR). Education and training formed a recurring theme in that report: notably how to train practising journalists and integrate CAR into journalism education at universities.

The resistance to change in journalism education has been documented extensively (Hewett, 2015). It is linked to another long-standing debate on the stance of journalism education towards employers; some critics attribute a lack of innovation partly to it having been a 'handmaiden to industry, not its critic or visionary guide' (Dennis, 1983: 3). In any case it is hard to disagree with Folkerts that 'journalism education has, to a great degree, ignored the larger contours of the digital age' (2014: 63).

Even by the mid-2000s, the lack of UK networks such as NICAR in the USA for sharing ideas, skills and discussions was a pointed contrast with the situation not only across the Atlantic but also with many other European countries, such as the Netherlands, Denmark, Sweden and Germany. Again, this might have reflected the state of investigative journalism in the UK, which provided only 10 out of 450 delegates at the Global Investigative Journalism Conference in far-off Amsterdam in 2005 (Meek, 2005).

Some CAR training was taking place in the UK, however, particularly through the Centre for Investigative Journalism (CIJ). Established in 2003, it had close links with the USA – hardly surprising as it was founded by a journalist from the States. Gavin MacFadyen had worked as a producer of investigative documentaries on both sides of the Atlantic – including on *World in Action*, Granada Television's campaigning series – and became the CIJ's director. The CIJ's first summer school in July 2003 offered what may have been the first intensive training conference in the UK (albeit with participants from outside the UK, too) on investigative techniques for journalists. It included a half-day introductory CAR course, plus advanced classes, explaining:

> *'CAR is an increasingly important tool that enables journalists to add depth to their stories by accessing, making sense and presenting relevant government, financial, and social statistics,'* (CIJ, 2003).

Transatlantic training triumphs

The influence of US journalism's experience in CAR was clear from the seven trainers who led the CIJ sessions. They all came from or had close links with NICAR and/or its parent body, Investigative Reporters and Editors (IRE), and included already experienced data practitioners such as Brant Houston, Aron Pilhofer and Jennifer LaFleur. The leading role played by NICAR can be inferred from the 40 to 50 seminars a year it ran during 1994 to 1999, and the estimated 12,000 journalists who attended its 300 conferences and seminars in its first 10 years (Houston, 1999: 7).

Houston became managing director of NICAR in 1993 (before it gained that name), having been database editor at the *Hartford Courant* and won awards for his investigative work. His book *Computer Assisted Reporting: A Practical Guide*, into a third edition by 2003 (Houston, 2003), became a key resource, drawing on 'what many of us had learned about training' and providing 'at least one road map for classes in newsrooms and journalism schools' (Houston, 1999: 6).

Pilhofer was working as database editor at the Center for Public Integrity in Washington DC, and later led the development of data and interactive journalism at *The New York Times*. LaFleur had worked as database editor at the *San Jose Mercury News* before becoming IRE's first director of training. She went on to be CAR editor at the *Dallas Morning News* and director of CAR at non-profit investigative newsroom *ProPublica*. As early as 1989, she had analysed the use of computers as part of her master's degree at the University of Missouri School of Journalism (home to IRE and NICAR) (LaFleur, 1999: 25).

The beginner's CAR workshop at the 2003 CIJ summer school focused on 'more effective searching techniques, resources and data on the internet, downloading data, and doing basic analyses using spreadsheet software such as Microsoft Excel'. An 'intermediate track' involved moving 'from filtering and sorting data in Excel to calculating rates and ratios for news stories, cross-tabulating data and generating graphics' before 'showing how to select and filter information in a database manager and introducing users to summarising data effectively to find trends and story ideas' (CIJ, 2003). More complex techniques of data analysis were covered in an 'advanced track'.

Freedom of information, better journalism?

Such CAR training became a core feature of CIJ summer schools, along with another theme relevant to the emergence of data journalism: the use of freedom of information (FOI) legislation. Passed in 2000, the FOI Act came properly into force on 1 January 2005 and was fundamental to the development of data journalism in the UK. For the first time, journalists had a legal right to request information held by public bodies, which now had to respond (although not necessarily by providing the information requested). This was a huge advance on the preceding code of practice on access to government information, introduced in 1994 as an alternative to FOI legislation (Brooke, 2004). Drawing on her background as a reporter in the USA, Heather Brooke wrote an influential book on using FOI in the UK, *Your Right to Know*, partly out of her 'frustration with the relationship between the citizen and the state in Britain, which was not as egalitarian as in America' (Brooke, 2013). Primarily because a culture and legislative framework enabled access to information there, data and CAR techniques were becoming well-established among US investigative reporters in the 1990s, Brooke says:

> *'The main reason was that the datasets were available. A typical story was to get hold of a list of school bus drivers and cross-reference it with a list of sex offenders or other offences. They are both public records in America, with no privacy law, so you could find out whether any of the school bus drivers were paedophiles or had other convictions'* (ibid).

The appliance of science to reporting

In contrast to the UK – and its lack of public data – the US federal FOI Act had operated since 1967. The timing seems coincidental, but it was same year in which Philip Meyer and colleagues at the *Detroit Free Press* produced a Pulitzer Prize-winning investigation into the causes of riots in the city, often cited as the beginning of CAR. Meyer saw the potential to apply social science techniques to journalism, having studied them the previous year while on a Nieman fellowship at Harvard. A course he took there also introduced him to computing in the form of an IBM 7090 mainframe machine (Meyer, 1999: 4). In Detroit, Meyer deployed quantitative survey research, helped by two university professors, a team of 30 interviewers for fieldwork, and a computer programmer. (This was not the first use of computing in support of journalism – in 1952, a Remington Rand Univac machine was used to help US television network CBS predict election results (Chinoy, 2010).)

Having demonstrated 'the application of the scientific method to the practice of journalism' (Meyer, 1999: 4), he started to pass on his skills to other reporters in the same newspaper group as he developed his statistical and computing abilities. Published in 1973, his *Precision Journalism* (Meyer, 1973), and its 1991 successor became landmarks in CAR. Meyer did not use public records in his investigative journalism until 1972 (Meyer, 1999: 4) but his work converged with FOI in the use of computing tools and statistical techniques for analysis. As computers and software became more ubiquitous and easier for non-specialists to use, so US news organisations began to appoint dedicated database editors.

Grappling with hygienic spreadsheets

Interest in the UK seems to have remained very limited until more journalists began to realise the opportunities provided by FOI. From 2005, Heather Brooke trained hundreds of journalists in FOI techniques with the National Union of Journalists and elsewhere – and while she mentioned the value of obtaining information in the form of spreadsheets, she was not teaching analysis using them (Brooke, 2013). She was also putting FOI through its paces herself as a freelance journalist – and learning CAR techniques to deal with the resulting data. One striking success published during the first year of FOI was an investigation with *The Times*. The resulting 'justice by postcode' story, published on the front page, revealed huge disparities in conviction rates around the UK (O'Neill, Gibb and Brooke 2005). It also highlighted the greater experience in data analysis that journalists elsewhere in Europe had developed.

'I talked to the FoI officer at the Crown Prosecution Service about when they switched to electronic data. I got three years' worth of data in Excel spreadsheets – which was great, but it was 42 different sets of records from different CPS areas,' Brooke recalls (2013; O'Neill and Brooke, 2005). To help with the analysis, she turned to Tommy Kaas, who had run CAR training sessions at CIJ summer schools. He had set up the Danish International Center for Analytical Reporting (DICAR), which evolved from the Association of CAR in Denmark, set up in 1997 with other CAR pioneers such as Nils Mulvad, who taught CAR at the Danish School of Journalism.

A tipping point for CAR and UK data journalism

The fourth CIJ summer school (2006) was a turning point for CAR and data training. CIJ director Gavin MacFadyen noted a 'surge in interest in computing. The rooms where those skills were being taught were packed and that's the first time that's happened.... The whole landscape has changed and journalists see the value of using electronic tools that we've taken for granted and don't really know much about' (Brooke, 2006). CAR trainers at the summer school – mostly from the USA – were starting to use data about the UK, obtained from UK public bodies under UK FOI legislation, to demonstrate what could be done:

> *'One of my very first FOI requests was for London councils' inspection reports on restaurant hygiene. Most of them were electronic datasets, which I didn't really know how to handle properly. It was around that time that Aron Pilhofer was over, and I gave him my restaurant inspection data. "This is really great for teaching," he said. "I'm going to use this for our CAR classes in London." He showed us different ways of analysing it using Excel – but also what the limits where, and how you could switch over to Access and write SQL queries to drill down into the data and find out very specifically which were the dirtiest restaurants in London. I think that was a real transitional point because it was teaching using real data from this country rather than America, and obtained from FOI,'* (Brooke, 2013).

Another US CAR trainer, David Donald (then training director of IRE), was encouraged: 'I think you'll begin seeing many more in-depth investigative stories that will be based on using CAR,' he said (Brooke, 2006). To support that growth, and to share tips and ideas among interested journalists in the UK, a mailing list called BICAR emerged – inspired by the successful equivalents at DICAR in Denmark and NICAR in the USA. It was set up by Martin Stabe, then at journalism weekly *Press Gazette*, after post-CIJ summer school discussions in a pub with Brooke and freelance investigative journalist Stephen Grey. Alas, their enthusiasm seemed to outrun the wider interest among journalists for such a project, as Stabe recalls:

> *'It never really amounted to much – there were almost no messages and it fizzled out quickly. There just wasn't the volume of material or people to make that viable, and I seemed to spend more time administering the server it ran on than actually having any content. I like to think that it was just ahead of its time'* (Stabe 2013).

Journalism education and training

Data-related work was also developing at City University London, where the CIJ was based and Brooke had become involved in teaching. I introduced FOI as part of the postgraduate Newspaper Journalism course at City in 2005; every student researched an FOI project to generate their own original story for publication. Some City students also worked with Brooke on other FOI/data projects, too. They included Elena Egawhary (BBC *Newsnight* and *Panorama*), James Ball (later data editor at *the Guardian* and now at Buzzfeed), and Alex Wood (who worked as a data journalist at the BBC World Service).

FOI became important not only for the data it enabled journalists to access (for data journalism stories and projects); it also acted as a gateway for students – a valuable bridge from more conventional reporting to data journalism. Many characteristics of journalistic FOI work – from spreadsheets and the analysis of changes over time, to patterns and statistics – underlie data journalism, too. Arguably FOI serves as a useful introduction to computational thinking (Hewett, 2014a).

A stuffy computer room hosted a dozen or so participants for a key training event for UK data journalism in July 2007. Two hugely experienced trainers, Aron Pilhofer (then database editor at *The New York Times*) and David Donald (by then data editor at the Center for Public Integrity in Washington), ran an intensive three-day 'training the trainers' programme at City University London. Subtitled 'how to teach computer-assisted reporting', the course – arranged through MacFadyen and the CIJ – aimed to 'show how CAR is successfully taught so that more CAR training can take place here and more home-grown, UK-based journalists can take advantage of these skills'. An outline of the course noted not only the importance of CAR – but also the lack of training in data-related skills and stories in the UK:

> *'Computer-assisted reporting (CAR) has led many reporting advances the past 20 years in the United States, Europe and elsewhere. It's both a method to discover stories that otherwise would go unreported and a way of adding depth and context to existing stories. Historically, the United Kingdom has offered little training in these techniques for experienced journalists and novices alike,'* (CIJ 2007).

A number of key people subsequently involved in data journalism in the UK took part in that week's training sessions. Also that summer, two university courses for postgraduates were preparing to welcome their first investigative journalism students. Both included the use of CAR techniques, and elements – such as data-mining or scraping – of what one might now call data journalism, and were led by experienced investigative journalists (Waterhouse, 2011; O'Neill, 2011a). At the University of Strathclyde, in Glasgow, Eamonn O'Neill set up a MSc Investigative Journalism after studying the development of courses at universities in the USA. Investigative classes had been 'available on American campuses since at least the 1950s and possibly earlier' (O'Neill, 2011b).

The Investigative Journalism MA at City University London was run by Rosie Waterhouse, formerly with BBC *Newsnight* and *The Sunday Times*. She was able to build also on the teaching experience at City, including the CIJ and its director, Gavin MacFadyen; the investigations editor of *the Guardian*, David Leigh; David Lloyd, former head of news and current affairs at Channel Four, and Heather Brooke. While these two courses represented an important step in journalism education in UK universities, and were followed by a BA in Investigative Journalism at Lincoln, it would be misleading to suggest that investigative journalism had previously been absent from the curriculum.

At the University of Sheffield, for example, Mark Hanna had developed an investigative module for journalism undergraduates, the first to include a requirement to use FOI (Hanna, 2008). At City, some courses included investigative research techniques and FOI, and Leigh and MacFadyen had already run a specialist investigative option. But such developments were relatively recent; O'Neill suggests that the UK 'did not offer investigative journalism classes until the mid-late 1990s' (2011b). An earlier Investigative Journalism MA, at Nottingham Trent University, had been launched in 1997 (Hanna, 2000) but ran into difficulties. It ceased after a number of dissatisfied students left the course (Adams, 2001).

More online, more open data

Journalism education was also reflecting the industry's shift to the web, which was another factor that enabled data journalism to take off. Some courses focused specifically on online, such as the Online Journalism MA started by Paul Bradshaw in 2009 at Birmingham City University. He had noted data's significance for journalists, and had been teaching students to use Yahoo Pipes to aggregate, filter, mash and map since 2006. By 2010 he was also teaching data journalism to established reporters and news organisations' trainees (Bradshaw, 2013), and made an introduction to data part of the core MA journalism curriculum at City.

Did the timing help the later courses to fare better? Online tools and web publishing were making new forms of storytelling possible. FOI was becoming better established and continuing to help journalists break stories. It was also at the heart of one of the biggest stories of the period in 2009, on MPs' expenses, even though the core material was ultimately leaked before it was due to be released (with redactions) under FOI legislation.

Although the MPs' expenses files were obtained electronically, it was not a database that the *Telegraph* obtained – it was a mass of PDF files. That meant the investigating journalists 'could mostly still operate like old-style reporters', says Brooke (2013), cross-referencing names, addresses and other details – even if spreadsheets were involved (Winnett and Rayner, 2009: 220).

The open data movement was gathering pace, too, emphasising the importance of publishing data resulting from publicly funded work, and in accessible formats. Technology journalists Charles Arthur and Michael Cross had kicked off a 'Free Our Data' campaign aimed at changing government policy (Arthur and Cross, 2006). The data.gov.uk site eventually followed in January 2010, expanding to offer more than 9,000 datasets by October 2013. Spurred on also by the commercial possibilities, David Cameron made a series of commitments on open data after he became prime minister in May 2010 – complementing the momentum that FOI had provided for data journalism.

Dealing with data from FoI requests had been an essential part of James Ball's route towards data journalism in 2007 and 2008, when he worked with Brooke as a student on the pilot Investigative Journalism course at City:

> *'Lots of the early stuff I was doing was standardising FOI responses, getting them into a spreadsheet, and doing … doing everything the hard way actually, because I hadn't been taught lots of things that I would now do to make the process easier. … But this was before anyone was interested in data journalism,'* (Ball 2013).

WikiLeaks – and a journalism MA goes interactive

In 2010, the year after MPs' expenses, and more significantly for data journalism, came the huge WikiLeaks releases of war logs from Iraq and Afghanistan, and of cables from US embassies around the world. 'It was a big deal for us – and it also made newsrooms see data people differently,' says Simon Rogers, who had launched *the Guardian*'s data blog the previous year (Rogers, 2013b). Working on the war logs and cables also proved formative for Rogers' successor as data editor, Ball, first at the Bureau of Investigative Journalism and then at WikiLeaks (Ball, 2013).

Ball was soon teaching his successors at City University London, first on the MA Investigative Journalism. Data experience from the course helped Conrad Quilty-Harper gain a job at the *Telegraph* in 2010, where he became interactive news editor. The next step in data journalism at City was the MA Interactive Journalism, which I set up in 2011. This included a separate module dedicated to data journalism, led by Ball and Bradshaw, with input from Rogers – at the same time as his team grappled with data from the August riots that took place in London and other cities.

The Interactive Journalism course now has its fifth cohort of students (for 2015/16). Out of the first 36 graduates, 11 went on to work as data journalists, and a further eight in data-related roles (Hewett, 2014b). Employers of these alumni include the BBC, *The Times* and *The Sunday Times*, *the Guardian*, *The Daily Telegraph*, *Financial Times*, *Manchester Evening News*, *CityAM*, *Property Week*, investigative site *Exaro* and Trinity Mirror's data journalism team (set up in 2013 to work with its regional newspapers and the *Daily Mirror*). The course also includes a specialist module on strategic social media, community and online engagement, and many alumni are working in this area – where data is also relevant, eg in analytics – as well as in more traditional reporting or editing roles.

Although a growing number of university programmes in the UK and elsewhere have included data journalism in their curriculum, the picture is mixed. As recently as 2014, one journalism educator concluded that 'the route into data journalism is not an obvious one and a period of studying journalism at a UK university certainly doesn't seem to be part of that route' (Hannaford, 2014). Most journalism schools 'don't get it', according to the head of interactive news at the *Financial Times* (Tinworth, 2014). This may reflect the particular complexities of running data journalism courses, which include ensuring its currency; the 'million-dollar question' (McKerral, 2013) of who will teach it; technical and statistical demands; and – in a market-oriented HE system – the need to attract students who may not be familiar with data journalism (Hewett,

2015). At the same time, coding has been making its way into journalism programmes, at Cardiff, Goldsmiths and City, for example.

Conclusion

'The time has come to abandon "computer assisted reporting",' Meyer asserted in 1999. 'CAR is an embarrassing reminder that we are entering the 21st Century as the only profession in which computer users feel the need to call attention to themselves' (1999: 4). Eleven years later, when Tim Berners-Lee declared data journalism to be the future, the technology editor covering this wondered pertinently: 'how long will it take for the methods of data journalism [...] to filter through to everyday use in journalism?' (Arthur, 2010).

Data journalism draws on wider foundations and aspirations than CAR, and it now appears to be flourishing. Certainly it is in everyday use in some parts of journalism, although it takes many different forms and its practitioners vary from solo operators to large teams. Its spread, successes and diversity surely qualify data journalism to be a worthy successor to CAR.

References

Adams, Catherine (2001) 'Inside story', in *the Guardian*, 13 March, available at www.theguardian.com/education/2001/mar/13/highereducation.uk, accessed 30 October 2013

Arthur C (2010) 'Analysing data is the future for journalists, says Tim Berners-Lee' in *the Guardian*, available at www.guardian.co.uk/media/2010/nov/22/data-analysis-tim-berners-lee, accessed 3 September 2015

Arthur, Charles and Cross, Michael (2006) 'Give us back our crown jewels,' in *the Guardian*, 9 March, available at www.theguardian.com/technology/2006/mar/09/education.epublic, accessed 30 October 2013

Ball, James (2013) Interview with Jonathan Hewett, 25 October 2013, London

Bradshaw, Paul (2013) Interview with Jonathan Hewett, 14 October 2013, London

Bradshaw, Paul (2015) 'The legacy of Ampp3d, UsVsTh3m and Row Zed', 13 May, available at http://onlinejournalismblog.com/2015/05/13/the-legacy-of-ampp3d-usvsth3m-and-row-zed/, accessed 15 September 2015

Brooke, Heather (2004) *Your Right to Know*. London: Pluto Press

Brooke, Heather (2006) Investigate! *Journalist*, August/September, National Union of Journalists, available at http://heatherbrooke.org/2006/article-future-of-investigative-reporting, accessed 27 October 2013

Brooke, Heather (2013) Interview with Jonathan Hewett, 18 October 2013, London

Centre for Investigative Journalism (2003) 'Programme for CIJ Summer School', 18-20 July 2003, London

Centre for Investigative Journalism (2007) 'Programme for Training the trainers: How to teach computer-assisted reporting', 23-25 July 2007, London

Chinoy, Ira (2010). *Battle of the Brains: Election-Night Forecasting at the Dawn of the Computer Age*. Dissertation, University of Maryland

Dasselaar, Arjan (2005) 'United Kingdom', in Van Eijk, Dick (ed) *Investigative Journalism in Europe*, Amsterdam: Vereniging van Onderzoeksjournalisten pp 213-226

Dennis, Everette E. (1983) 'An exchange. Journalism education: failing grades from a Dean' in *Planning for Curricular Change in Journalism Education*. Eugene: School of Journalism, University of Oregon

Folkerts, Jean (2014) 'History of Journalism Education' in *Journalism & Communication Monographs*, SAGE Publications

Hanna, Mark (2000) 'British investigative journalism: protecting the continuity of talent through changing times'. Paper presented to the International Association for Media and Communication Research, Singapore, 18 July

Hanna, Mark (2008) 'Universities as evangelists of the watchdog role: Teaching investigative journalism to undergraduates' in De Burgh, Hugo (ed) *Investigative Journalism*, Abingdon and New York: Routledge (3rd edn) pp157-173

Hannaford, Liz (2014) 'Data Journalism - a modern day Bletchley Park?' available at www.lizhannaford.com/data-journalism/data-journalism-a-modern-day-bletchley-park, accessed 8 October 2014

Hewett, Jonathan (2014a) 'Engaging with data: reflections on developing a data journalism course'. Paper presented to Computation and Journalism symposium, October 24-25, New York

Hewett, Jonathan (2014b) 'Growing data journalism in the UK' in *American Journalism Review*, 13 November, available at http://ajr.org/2014/11/13/growing-data-journalism-uk, accessed 15 September 2015

Hewett, Jonathan (2015) 'Learning to teach data journalism: innovation, influence and constraints' in *Journalism* (in press)

Houston, Brant (1999) 'Changes in Attitudes, Changes in Latitudes' in Paul, Nora (ed) *When Nerds and Words Collide: Reflections on the Development of Computer Assisted Reporting*, St Petersburg, Florida: Poynter Institute for Media Studies, pp6-7

Houston, Brant (2003) *Computer Assisted Reporting: A Practical Guide*. Boston: Bedford/St Martin's (3rd edn)

LaFleur, Jennifer (1999) 'Evangelizing for CAR' in Paul, Nora (ed) *When Nerds and Words Collide: Reflections on the Development of Computer Assisted Reporting*. St Petersburg, Florida: Poynter Institute for Media Studies, pp25-27

McKerral, Mac (2013) 'Steering data journalism into the curriculum' in *Quill*, 101(4), p24

Meek, Colin (2005) 'Analysis: Computer-assisted reporting leaves UK journalists in the slow lane' in Journalism.co.uk, 5 October, available at www.journalism.co.uk/news/analysis-computer-assisted-reporting-leaves-uk-journalists-in-the-slow-lane/s2/a51543, accessed 25 October 2013

Meyer, Philip (1973) *Precision Journalism: A Reporter's Introduction to Social Science Methods*. Bloomington and London: Indiana University Press

Meyer, Philip (1991) *The New Precision Journalism*. Bloomington and Indianapolis: Indiana University Press

Meyer, Philip (1999) 'The Future of CAR: Declare Victory and Get Out' in Paul, Nora (ed) *When Nerds and Words Collide: Reflections on the Development of Computer Assisted Reporting*. St Petersburg, Florida: Poynter Institute for Media Studies, pp 4-5

O'Neill, Eamonn (2011a) 'Digging Deeper: Reflecting on the Development and Teaching of Investigative Journalism in a University Setting in the United Kingdom' in Mair, John and Keeble, Richard Lance (eds) *Investigative Journalism: Dead or Alive?* Bury St Edmunds: Abramis, pp291-307

O'Neill, Eamonn (2011b) 'Written evidence', in *The Future of Investigative Journalism.* London: House of Lords Select Committee on Communications, pp 425-429

O'Neill, Sean and Brooke, Heather (2005) 'Prosecutors in dock over disparity in convictions' in *The Times*, 23 November, p6

O'Neill, Sean, Gibb, Frances and Brooke, Heather (2005) 'Justice by postcode: the lottery revealed' in *The Times*, 23 November, p1

Orlowski, Andrew (2007) 'Braindead obituarists hoaxed by Wikipedia: only fools and journos' in *The Register*, 3 October, available at www.theregister.co.uk/2007/10/03/wikipedia_obituary_cut_and_paste, accessed 30 October 2013

Paul, Nora (ed) (1999) *When Nerds and Words Collide: Reflections on the Development of Computer Assisted Reporting.* St Petersburg, Florida: Poynter Institute for Media Studies

Rogers, Simon (2013a) *Facts are Sacred: The Power of Data.* London: Faber and Faber/Guardian Books

Rogers, Simon (2013b) Interview with Jonathan Hewett, 22 October 2013, San Francisco/London (via Skype)

Silver, Nate (2014) 'What the fox knows' in *FiveThirtyEight*, 17 March, available at http://fivethirtyeight.com/features/what-the-fox-knows, accessed 15 September 2015

Stabe, Martin (2013) Email exchange with Jonathan Hewett, 30 October 2013, London

Tinworth, Adam (2014) 'Data Journalism - buzzword or baseline skill?' available at www.onemanandhisblog.com/archives/2014/01/data_journalism_-_buzzword_or_baseline_s.html, accessed 8 October 2014

Waterhouse, Rosie (2011) 'Can you Teach Investigative Journalism? Methods and Sources, Old and New' in Mair, John and Keeble, Richard Lance (eds) *Investigative Journalism: Dead or Alive?* Bury St Edmunds: Abramis pp284-290

Winnett, Robert and Rayner, Gordon (2011) *No Expenses Spared*, London: Random House

To visualise is to dramatise: storytelling with data

Storytelling is a vexed subject in data visualisation but Adam Frost and Tobias Sturt argue not only is it inevitable but necessary for communicating with an audience, which means we have to understand storytelling as well as we understand our data

Introduction

The idea of storytelling in data visualisation is often viewed with suspicion. Scott Murray has talked of the 'toxic nature of the "storytelling" fad' (Murray, 2015) Moritz Stefaner warned on Twitter of the 'power and danger of storytelling' and Alberto Cairo replied: 'I sympathise with Moritz's uneasiness with storytelling'. These are some of data visualisation's leading lights: why are they so wary of stories? On one level, it's easy to see why. 'Storytelling' is a fashionable term, widely touted as a magic bullet for a diverse range of professions, from estate agents ('Show more than just boring pictures. Sell the story!' (Studeo, 2015) to architects ('Story telling is at the heart of great place-making.' The Architecture Foundation, 2015). Stefan Sagmeister recently ranted: 'I read an interview with somebody who designs roller coasters and he referred to himself as a storyteller. No, f**khead, you are not a storyteller, you're a roller coaster designer. And that's fantastic!' (Sagermeister, 2015)

When you're working with data, the concept of storytelling is doubly problematic. Data suggests objectivity, evidence, facts. Storytelling suggests subjectivity, bias, lies. As Edward Tufte says: 'Above all else, show the data' - not distracting verbal or visual flourishes. But it's worth returning to Alberto Cairo, who concluded his conversation with Moritz Stefaner with this statement: 'There isn't such a thing as a story-free vis, no matter how wary I am of storytelling' (Cairo, 2015). In other words, he believes that you don't have a choice. When you select a dataset, chart it, and make it visually engaging, you are storytelling whether you like it or not.

We agree with Alberto Cairo. But before pursuing this argument, let's define our terms. For us, a story is *a series of facts or incidents, structured into a narrative, that provokes an emotional and/or intellectual response in an audience.* Stories can be fact, fiction or a mixture of both (e.g. an anecdote) and their length, quality and format can vary hugely, depending on who is telling them. However what they all have in common is how they are put together. Most storytellers - regardless of their medium - use what might be called *selection* and *emphasis. Selection* is ensuring that you only put the most relevant and engaging elements in your story - removing all others. Emphasis is essentially your plot - arranging the incidents you've chosen into a logical sequence that keeps your audience's attention.

Selection and emphasis

Data visualisation is usually described along these lines: *the use of verbal and visual techniques to make data or information more comprehensible and memorable for your audience.* At first glance, it feels different to a story - there isn't the same emphasis on narrative momentum. But on closer inspection, there are similarities - we are combining verbal and visual techniques (as with a film or a comic strip), we are making dry or confusing information more memorable (as with a news report or a history book) and we are doing this not for our own benefit, but for a specific audience. Then there are the techniques we use. Like other narrative forms, data visualisation uses selection and emphasis, selecting the datasets that are most relevant for our audience and then emphasising some above others (in our information hierarchy) in order to provoke and sustain interest.

Sometimes, the kinship with storytelling is obvious. This is the first of a series of graphics we put together for *the Guardian*'s Datablog:

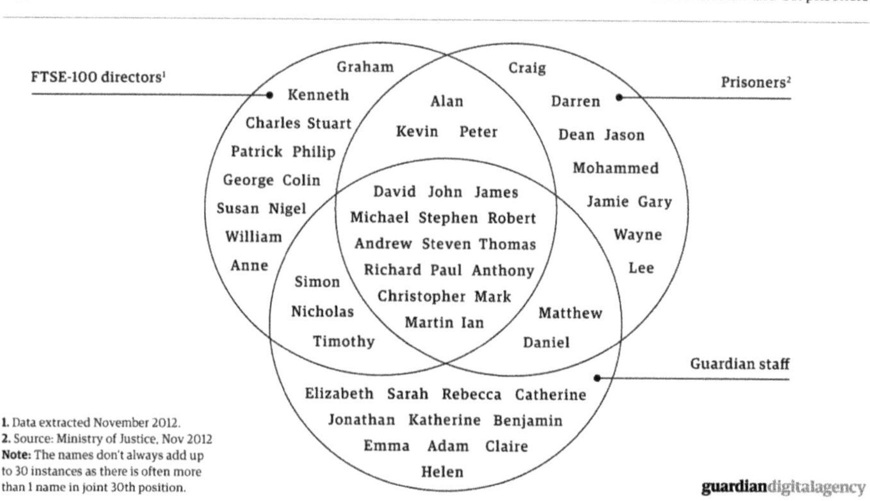

Figure 7. A Venn diagram of common forenames among company directors, prisoners and *Guardian* staff

We looked at the most popular first names of people in a number of key professions to see if there were any interesting correlations in terms of race, age, class and gender. It's fair to say that there were. On the first slide, we showed three of the most interestingly skewed professions: FTSE100 company board directors; UK prisoners; and *Guardian* staff. We chose the datasets and the chart type deliberately to dramatise our key story: that your background appears to determine your fate. We couldn't control the order in which the reader would work through the story - some might spot the male, working-class names in the 'prisoner-only' section first, others might start by realising that only two of the FTSE-company names are female. Everybody would hunt for their own name. But this didn't matter - there were only a limited number of permutations and none of them undermined our central narrative.

All the decisions we made were motivated by what worked for the story: top 10 names told a weaker story, top 50 became unreadable. Replacing FTSE-directors with doctors was less emotive. Swapping a Venn for a kind of parallel co-ordinate chart was less clear. Making the female names a different colour detracted from the other stories. So we stuck to the same colour for all the names. All the time we were trying to keep our reader's attention by packing our graphic with new or surprising information - just as a journalist would.

Sometimes it's less obvious that a story is being told. Here is a bar chart showing the percentage of the population of EU countries that have a positive view of the EU.

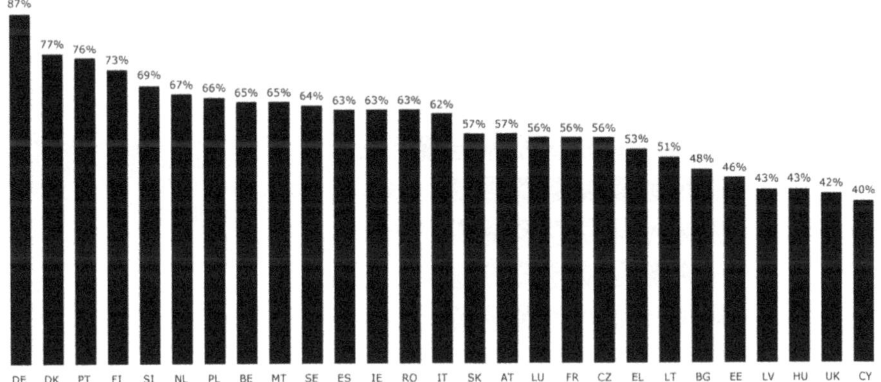

Figure 8: percentage of EU countries with a positive view of the EU (sample data)

The story here may be subtler, but it is no less present. For example, what if we re-order the chart, so the countries are in alphabetical order?

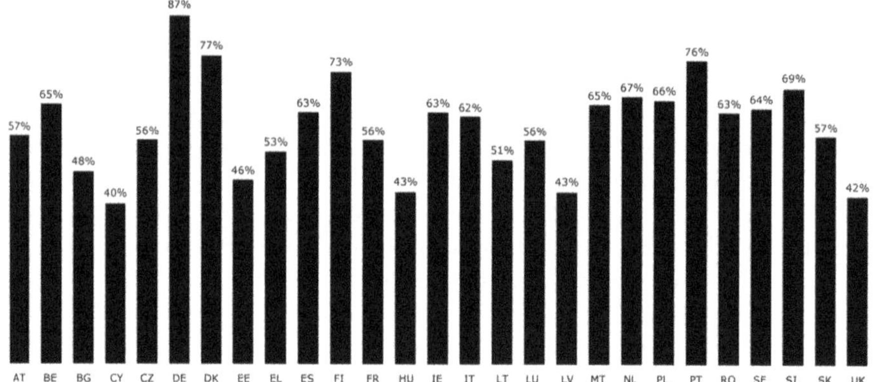

Figure 9: percentage of EU countries with a positive view of the EU (sample data) - ordered alphabetically

Now it is less obvious that this is a chart *about* positive views of the EU. It makes it harder for the reader to find the most and least positive countries, which implies that this is not what this chart is primarily *for*. It is more neutral. We could have made other decisions. We could have focussed on the top 10 most positive countries.

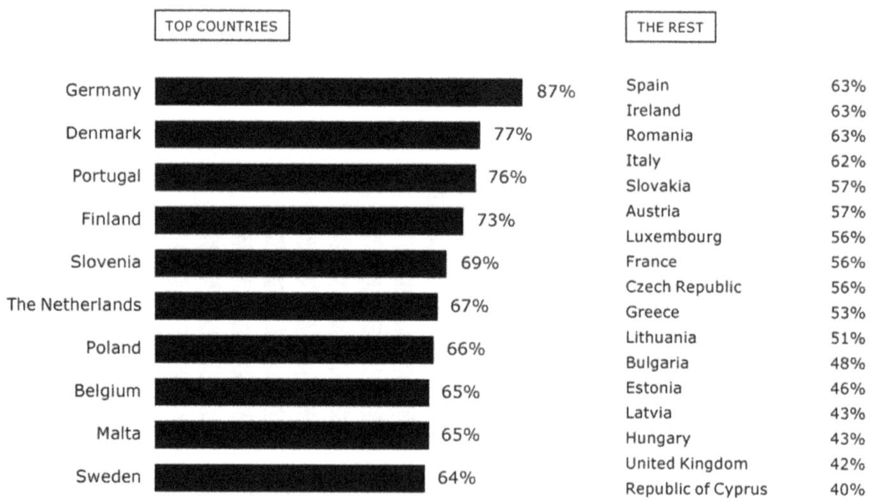

Figure 10: percentage of EU countries with a positive view of the EU (sample data) - emphasising top ten

This chart rewards the most positive countries with greater visual prominence. There is no question here that more positive is *more important* and less engaged is *less important* - and *less interesting*. Then again, we could dispense with bars altogether.

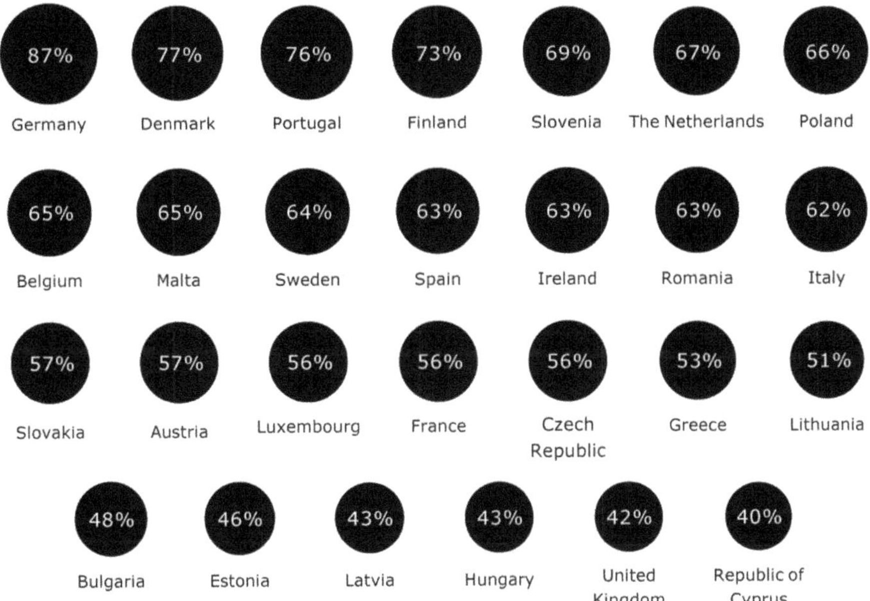

Figure 11: percentage of EU countries with a positive view of the EU (sample data) - as a bubble chart

Using circles changes the story once again. For a start, they are a more accessible shape - described as the perfect shape in classical antiquity and associated with divinity and holiness in the Renaissance. For most of us, they have positive associations, reminding us of human faces, the sun and the moon, clock faces, wheels. They aren't as easy to compare with each other - think about the clear, sharp distinctions we get in a bar chart. But maybe that doesn't matter. If our audience is not hugely interested in tiny distinctions between datapoints, then sacrificing detail for visual appeal could be the right choice. Furthermore, it could be that we want to suggest kinship between our European countries. Using circles suggests a continuity, a harmoniousness between our datapoints - which could be what we want to emphasise in our story. There's only one caveat here: circles should always be sized by area, then they can at least be fairly compared. Sizing by diameter grossly distorts the data.

Interpretations

There are other treatments we could try: a heatmap, a cartogram or a straightforward table of numbers. We could show rows of ten people, shaded to show levels of agreement - isotype-style. We could choose to visualise the negative views rather than the positive. We could choose to show both positive and negative in a stacked bar. What if we include the 'don't knows' as well? We could change the title from 'Percentage with a positive view of the European Union' to 'Which countries are the most pro-European?' or 'Does the EU have a future?' All of these decisions change the nature of our story and imply a different relationship to our audience.

So even if you are uncomfortable with the term 'story', we'd urge you to see yourself as an *author.* Because the decisions you are making are no different to those made by a journalist, historian or even novelist. You are trying to deliver *your interpretation* of the data to an audience so they stay to the end and remember it when it's over. Even when you are creating an interactive chart, which appears to give more freedom to the user, you are using the same techniques. For example, let's take the ultimate 'sandbox' interactive - Gapminder.

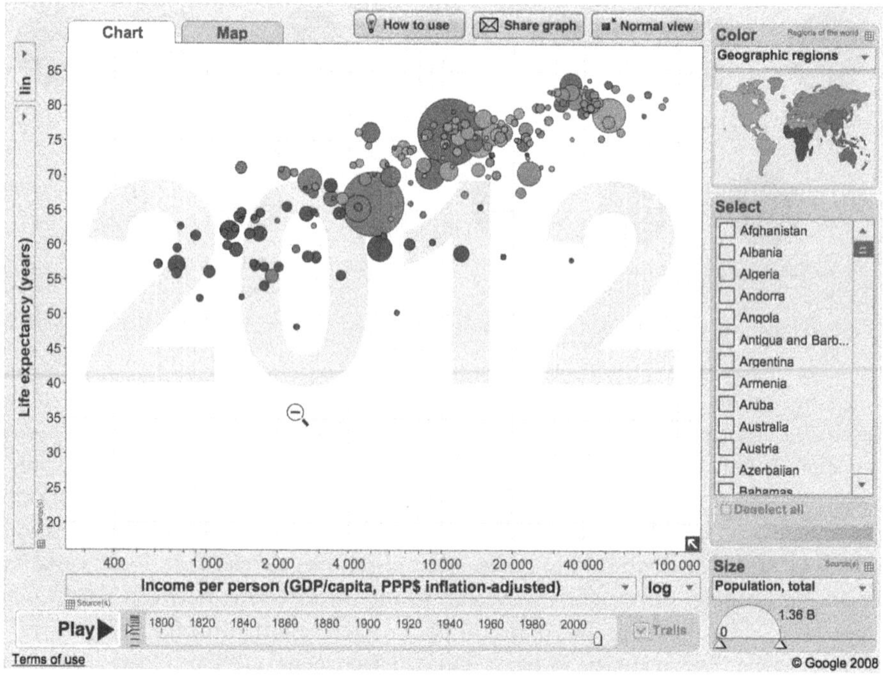

Figure 12: the Gapminder 'Trendalyser'

Gapminder allows the user to plot a huge range of data on a scatter plot. You can define the x and y axis in a multitude of ways. You can make colour mean geographic region, CO^2 emissions, mean years in school or any of the other indicators (there are hundreds). You can do the same with the size of each bubble. Then you can hit Play and watch the history of these indicators over the course of 200 years.

There's no story here surely? Isn't it all open-ended exploration? But even here, we are invited to foreground particular types of information. The default home screen shows income per person on the x axis and life expectancy on the y axis - the two most widely-accepted criteria of a 'successful nation'. We are encouraged to play with this first - the implication being that this is the optimum narrative for this interactive. We watch countries getting healthier and wealthier

- particularly as the Industrial Revolution gathers momentum and poorer countries gain independence.

This is reinforced by Hans Rosling's appearances at TED talks and on numerous TV shows, where he almost always uses this default narrative. Gapminder tells the story of western civilisation and how we should 'mind the gap' (the clue is in the title) between the developed and developing worlds. On closer inspection, this underlies all the choices the interactive allows us to make. The data we can load on to the screen is not 'every dataset in the world' - there is selection and emphasis here.

Rosling and his team have chosen the datasets that underline this story of two - or even three - types of society. We can look at employment rates, access to water, HIV rates - all of the ways in which countries define themselves as successful. Clearly decisions have been made about which data is relevant for the central story and which is not (we cannot plot, for example, percentage of the population on Facebook or the percentage who attend football matches). The number of choices must be controlled or users get swamped and the story gets lost.

But, more than this, Rosling has emphasised the most important datasets. Look at what happens when we click on the y axis. Five datasets are put outside of the folder structure.

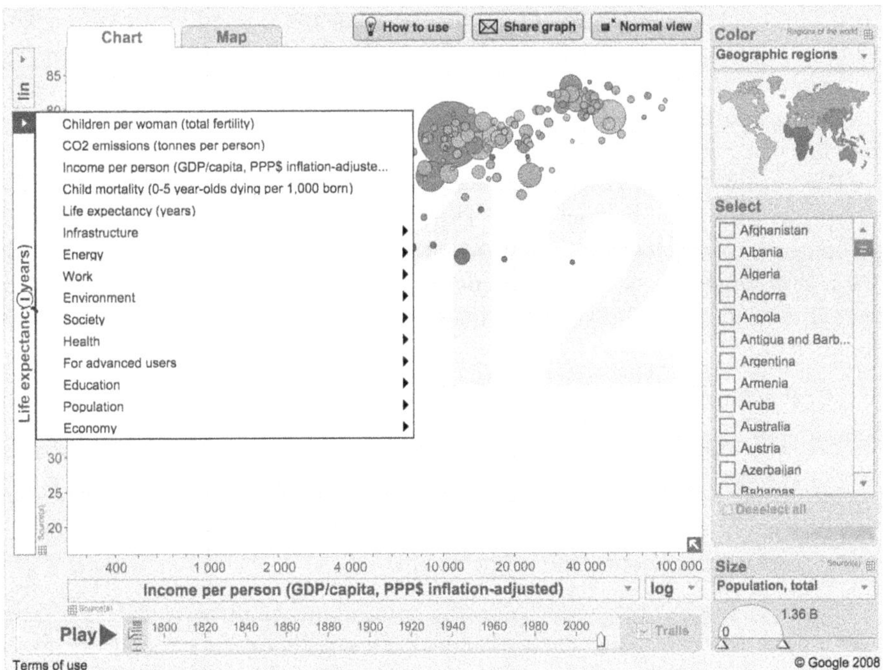

Figure 13: the Gapminder 'Trendalyser' - menu options

Children per woman, CO^2 emissions, income per person, child mortality and life expectancy are given particular emphasis. These - it is implied - are the most important datasets for this interactive. These are the stories that this tool is best placed to tell. So even here, in this most open-ended of tools, there is an author and a controlling intelligence. There is more freedom for the user than in a flat graphic, we are being told stories rather than a single story, but there is no question that Hans Rosling has selected his information and emphasised parts of it over others to create a sustained intellectual and emotional effect.

Design matters

But when we have devised and structured our story, are we finished? Does it matter what typeface we use, what colour palette, what font size? Looking at our Venn diagram of first names again, if we had set it all in Papyrus and made every circle luminous green, would it have mattered? The same information is displayed, after all. It sounds trivial but it couldn't be more important. In data visualisation, design is the equivalent of an author's *style.* Shakespeare is remembered because he wrote 'to be or not to be, that is the question', not 'should I kill myself or not?' 'Should I kill myself or not?' may be correct - in terms of the information conveyed - but it is flat and boring, it lacks soul and poetry, it is completely forgettable.

So design - like style - matters. The question is: how to approach it correctly. Scott McCloud offers one solution when he talks about good visual storytelling being a combination of *persuasion* and *clarity* (McCloud, 2006). In other words, you *persuade* your audience that you are worth their attention by looking interesting and then you repay that attention by telling your story with *clarity* so that they can understand and remember it.

Of course with data visualisation we add a third task: accuracy. We also have to represent the data with accuracy. The success of our communication lies not just in our audience being interested in our content and being able to understand it, but also being able to trust it, and decipher all of the detail. This means that in the practice of design in data visualisation, we're generally trying to do three things:

1. Represent the content, the data itself;
2. Help the audience understand that content, structuring it so that it is easy to comprehend and explore;
3. Present the content so that people *want* to comprehend and explore it, making it attractive and interesting.

The tricky thing is that we're generally trying to do all three at the same time. And it's not just a juggling act, although that would be tricky enough. It's more like one of those logic problems where you're trying to cross a river in a small boat with a sheep, a wolf and a chicken that tells very entertaining lies, because each of the three goals influences the others. They interlock with and influence each other, so that finding the right blend defies easy guidelines.

Typeface matters

The way we use text itself is a pretty good example of this. We rely on text, of course, to give us the granular detail - it is generally where we find the actual data points, the specifics that defy general visualisation - and that is its primary purpose. But it is doing so much more than just containing information. Famed documentary maker Errol Morris recently carried out an experiment in conjunction with *The New York Times* that appeared to suggest that people are most likely to believe a statement presented to them in Baskerville than in any other font (Morris, 2012).

Baskerville
From Wikipedia, the free encyclopedia
Baskerville is a serif typeface designed in 1757 by John Baskerville (1706 1775) in Birmingham, England and cut by John Handy. Baskerville is classified as a transitional typeface, a refinement of old style typefaces of the period, such as those of William Caslon. Compared to earlier designs, Baskerville increased the contrast between thick and thin strokes, making the serifs sharper and more tapered, and shifted the axis of rounded letters to a more vertical position. The curved strokes are more circular in shape, and the characters became more regular. These changes created a greater consistency in size and form.

Comic Sans
From Wikipedia, the free encyclopedia
Comic Sans MS, commonly referred to as Comic Sans, is a sans-serif casual script typeface designed by Vincent Connare and released in 1994 by Microsoft Corporation. It is classified as a casual, non-connecting script for use in informal documents inspired by comic book lettering.

Figure 14: Baskerville and Comic Sans fonts (text from the respective Wikipedia pages)

We might have guessed that a serif font would have such an effect - a font like Baskerville is a font of record, the voice of the broadsheet headline; the encyclopaedia entry; the sophisticated dinner invitation. It has a tone of the establishment, of authority and knowledge. Just as the voice of a font like Comic Sans has the opposite effect. Unlike Baskerville it was designed to sound friendly, approachable, informal. Originally intended to set speech bubbles in cartoons aimed at small children, it has an appropriate tone of voice that suits it well to Nursery School announcements, passive-aggressive notes on the shared fridge, the unconvincing bonhomie of an email from the CEO. In fact, now so many have learned to laugh at it, they may simply not bother to read it at all.

Indeed, in data visualisation either tone of voice might be a liability. The hectoring of an old-fashioned, stick-in-the-mud serif might look too opinionated; an illegible Zapfino, gurning Comic Sans or the half-hearted cosplay of Papyrus too shallow. Most work online is done with some sort of Sans Serif: a Helvetica or Gotham - something unobtrusive, well-mannered, nothing to impeach the impartiality of our data.

But as well as what it does to the accuracy of our data representation (larger than 6pt would be helpful) or our visual persuasiveness, it also affects the clarity of our communication, not just in matters of legibility, but in the impact it has on the structure of the content. The way that font is set - the size, the weight, the style, the colour, even its technical twitches, kerning and leading and spacing - all of these affect not just the visual persuasiveness of the text but also how we understand its importance and significance - its place in the information hierarchy.

Baskerville
From Wikipedia, the free encyclopedia
Baskerville is a serif typeface designed in 1757 by John Baskerville (1706–1775) in Birmingham, England and cut by John Handy. Baskerville is classified as a transitional typeface, a refinement of old style typefaces of the period, such as those of William Caslon. Compared to earlier designs, Baskerville increased the contrast between thick and thin strokes, making the serifs sharper and more tapered, and shifted the axis of rounded letters to a more vertical position. The curved strokes are more circular in shape, and the characters became more regular. These changes created a greater consistency in size and form.
Hot type versions
The following foundries offered versions of Baskerville:
The original matrices were sold by Baskerville's widow and eventually ended up in the possession of Deberny & Peignot, who then donated some to Cambridge University Press.
The Fry type foundry of Bristol cut its own version in the late eighteenth century, presumably by house designer Isaac Moore.
When Fry's successors closed, this version was acquired and issued (or possibly recut) in hot metal by Stephenson Blake under the name "Baskerville Old Face".
The Fry Foundry version was also sold by American Type Founders with an italic designed in 1915 by Morris Fuller Benton.
Linotype's Baskerville was cut in 1923 by George W. Jones, though it was subsequently re-cut in 1936. A bold version was cut by Chauncey H. Griffith in 1939.
Lanston Monotype's Baskerville was cut in 1923 under the direction of Stanley Morison. Italic and bold versions were cut by Sol Hess. These versions were modified slightly and then offered by Intertype.

Baskerville
From Wikipedia, the free encyclopedia

Baskerville is a serif typeface designed in 1757 by John Baskerville (1706–1775) in Birmingham, England and cut by John Handy. Baskerville is classified as a transitional typeface, a refinement of old style typefaces of the period, such as those of William Caslon. Compared to earlier designs, Baskerville increased the contrast between thick and thin strokes, making the serifs sharper and more tapered, and shifted the axis of rounded letters to a more vertical position. The curved strokes are more circular in shape, and the characters became more regular. These changes created a greater consistency in size and form.

Hot type versions

The following foundries offered versions of Baskerville:

The original matrices were sold by Baskerville's widow and eventually ended up in the possession of Deberny & Peignot, who then donated some to Cambridge University Press.

The Fry type foundry of Bristol cut its own version in the late eighteenth century, presumably by house designer Isaac Moore.

When Fry's successors closed, this version was acquired and issued (or possibly recut) in hot metal by Stephenson Blake under the name "Baskerville Old Face".

The Fry Foundry version was also sold by American Type Founders with an italic designed in 1915 by Morris Fuller Benton.

Linotype's Baskerville was cut in 1923 by George W. Jones, though it was subsequently re-cut in 1936. A bold version was cut by Chauncey H. Griffith in 1939.

Lanston Monotype's Baskerville was cut in 1923 under the direction of Stanley Morison. Italic and bold versions were cut by Sol Hess. These versions were modified slightly and then offered by Intertype.

Figure 15: Text from the Baskerville Wikipedia page in unstructured and structured formats

And this is vital because our story is structure, after all, which means that hierarchy or title and subtitle, label and highlight is necessary in making that structure visible and navigable by our audience. Done with consistency it not only shows them the outline of the structure, it instructs them how to read, relieving them of the work of puzzling out the information order and letting them concentrate on the information itself. So even the choice and setting of typeface involves that complex dance of accuracy, clarity and attraction, each of the three influencing the effectiveness of the others.

Charts and mapping

The same is true of charting. Accuracy, of course, tends to have primacy in our charting. But charts are not entirely about accuracy. In order to create a chart we have to structure and emphasise elements of the data to generate a visual analogy for the data, a pattern. If we were interested solely in accuracy we would show our audience a table of values, but we are interested in helping them understand that accuracy, to use it for themselves. We are using the pre-attentive, preconscious effect of visuals to give our audiences a broader view of the data that in turn helps them sharpen their granular understanding. Maps work the same way (they are, in effect, a specialised form of data visualisation); the grand presentation of the landscape helps us plan our detailed exploration. Like stout Cortez on a peak in Darien they may examine the chart in wild surmise before plunging down into the tangled data.

William Cleveland suggested the terms 'pattern perception' and 'table look-up' to describe this dual function of charts - use of shape and line to represent data in such a way that an audience can gain an immediate idea of its whole but also enabling close reading and the beginnings of exploration. In their paper 'Graphical Perception and Graphical Methods for Analysing Scientific Data', William Cleveland and Robert McGill (Cleveland & McGill, 1985) tested the effectiveness of charts, asking people to estimate values based on different kinds of charts, an effort that depends on the ability to see the whole and focus on individual elements, and arrived at a scale:

1. Position along a common scale (so scatter charts or William Cleveland's apparent favourite, the dot chart)
2. Position on identical but nonaligned scales (multiple scatter plots)
3. Length (bar charts and column charts)
4. Angle / Slope (pie charts and line charts)
5. Area (bubble charts and tree maps)
6. Volume / density / color saturation (heat maps)
7. Color hue (dot matrices and chloropleths)

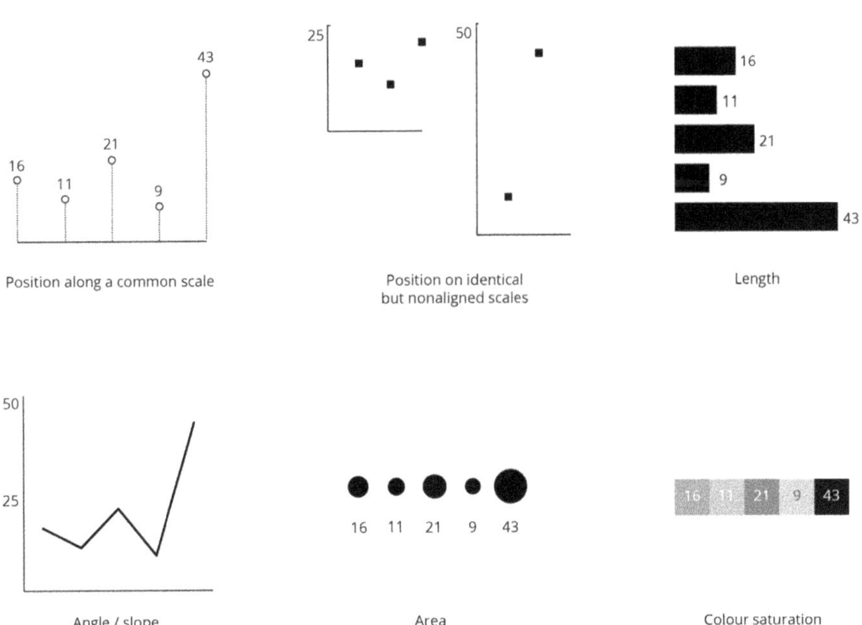

Figure 16: Charts illustrating the Cleveland McGill scale

But there is an important but easily overlooked clause in the title of McGill and Cleveland's paper: 'Graphical Perception and Graphical Methods for Analysing Scientific Data'. *Scientific data* - a very specific kind of data with specific goals. A traditional map of our town is extremely useful, but such a map of the featureless expanse of the Antarctic or the Pacific Ocean starts to become meaningless. Different kinds of data require different visualisations. The title also stipulates *analysing* data. While accuracy, of course, is paramount in analysis, when we are trying to understand our data and what it might be telling us, analysis is very different to communication. We have a very different intention. We can plot two crossing trends on a scatter plot, but doesn't a line chart make the change more obvious?

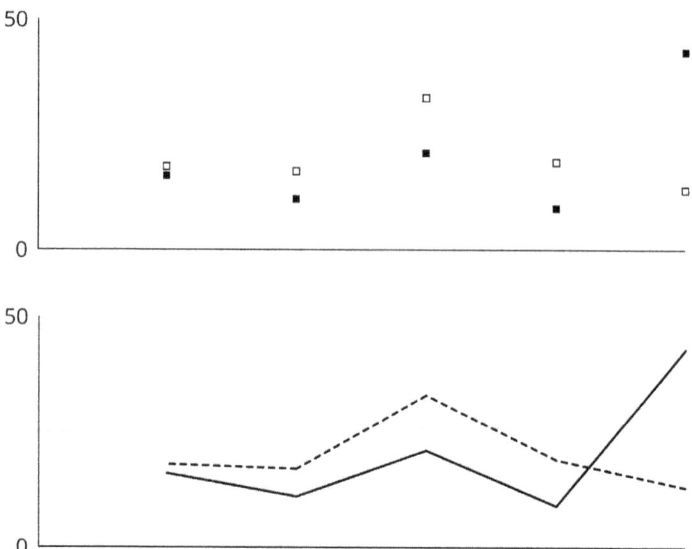

Figure 17: Trend data as a scatter plot and as a line chart - the lines illustrate the trend with far greater clarity

We can show the different opinions of a population on a dot chart, but might not a stacked bar or a pie chart do a better job of helping our audience understand how we are looking at the divisions of a complete data set?

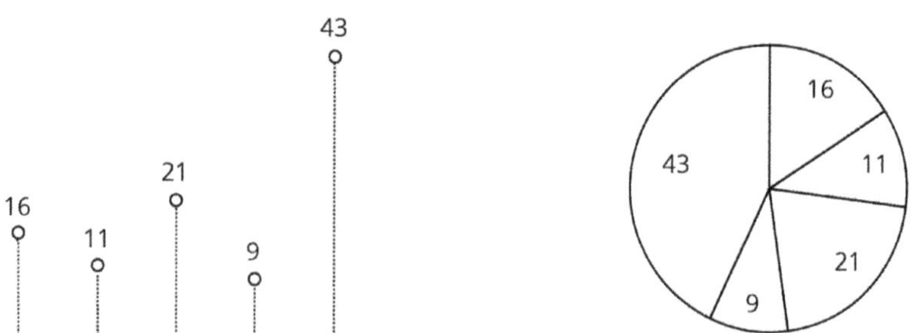

Figure 18: Compositional data in a dot chart and a pie chart - the pie is a clearer demonstration of a single dataset broken into constituent parts

Colour catches the eye

In fact, you will rarely see a scatter plot in a newspaper. It is not that our audience wouldn't understand them, but it might be that they might not want to. Just as chirpy old Comic Sans might make us suspect the depth of a piece of analysis, so might a white-coated and punctilious scatter plot make us wary of approaching something so forbidding and technical. Once again we have to consider the need to be visually interesting alongside our duty to be accurate.

Our use of colour is a good example of this. We can see from Cleveland and McGill's scale that colour is all but useless in representing data, but in catching our attention, it's priceless. Our reactions to colour can be atavistic, even irresistibly biological. The sight of red (the colour, of course, of visible, extra-corporal, oxidised blood) raises our blood pressure a little, puts us into a state of arousal, so what better way of catching our attention, as filmmakers such as Michael Powell or Martin Scorsese can attest.

But the same red against a palette of blues and greens will have a very different effect compared to a palette of oranges and pinks (unless, like a sizeable percentage of the male population, your audience is red/green colour blind, of course). Colour is defined by its relationships with other colours. Just as text cannot be styled arbitrarily without damaging the clarity of our information presentation, so we have to understand how our colour palettes affect the clarity of our communication.

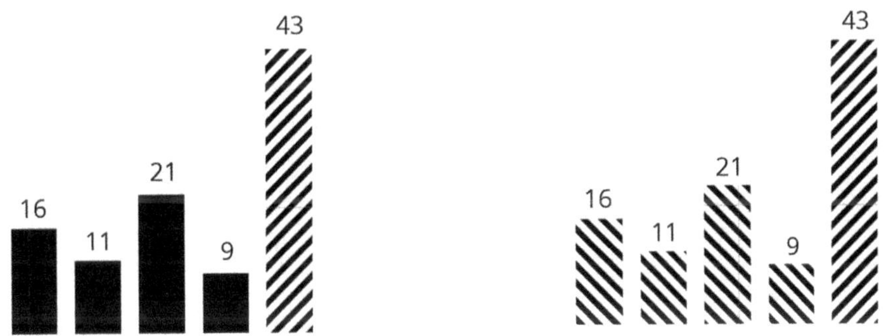

Figure 19: Visual contrast always works more effectively as a narrative tool in the context of visual consistency - the easiest way to be interesting is to surround yourself with boring people

Conclusion

In structuring and emphasising parts of our data to make a chart we are, by definition, telling a story about that data. The data we are working with may demand a kind of story just as the chart type we choose changes the story we are telling.

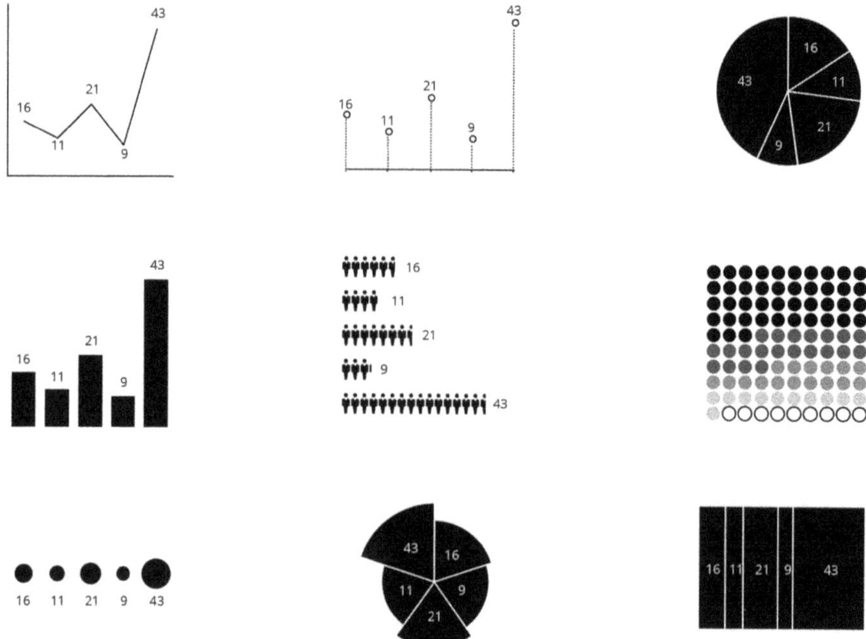

Figure 20: The same dataset charted in multiple ways - the right hand charts emphasise the dataset and its composition, for example. The line chart emphasises trend while the dot chart emphasises difference, the column and pictochart show comparison while the bubble chart tends to smooth it out.

In the balance between beauty, accuracy and clarity, the greatest of these is clarity. It is very hard to instruct people how to make beauty, but in the simplicity and directness that clarity requires we can find an elegant minimalism that is at once attractive and full of information. And it is only through the clarity of our communication that our audience will appreciate the accuracy of our data representation, because it only then that they will understand it well enough to use. In defining the structure of our story, we understand how to communicate it with clarity, and the layers of emphasis that we need to tell it effectively. By using the design elements of shape, line, colour, text and layout to express this story, we create a structure that enables our audience to discover and explore the data for themselves, to make it theirs, to make it useful. Both are essential. As with any kind of authorship, it is the combination of a great tale and a great teller that creates the most enduring work.

References

Burgoyne, Patrick (2014) 'Sagmeister and the "bullshit" around storytelling' at Creative Review online, available at www.creativereview.co.uk/cr-blog/2014/july/sagmeister-storytelling, accessed 25 August 2015

Cairo, Alberto, (2015) '@alignedleft @moritz_stefaner @datastories @eagereyes There isn't such a thing as a story-free vis, no matter how wary I am of storytelling' by @albertocairo on Twitter, available at https://mobile.twitter.com/albertocairo/status/550675058117447681?p=v, accessed 25 August 2015

Cleveland, William and McGill, Robert (1985) *Graphical Perception and Graphical Methods for Analysing Scientific Data.* Cleavland, OH: American Association for the Advancement of Science

McCloud, Scott (2006) *Making Comics.* New York, NY: William Morrow Paperbacks

Morris, Errol (2012) 'Hear, all ye people; hearken, O Earth' in *The New York Times* Opinator blog, available at http://opinionator.blogs.nytimes.com/2012/08/08/hear-all-ye-people-hearken-o-earth, accessed 25 August 2015

Stefaner (2015) '@serial - good entertainment but mostly damage to everyone actually involved? Power and danger of storytelling' by @Moritz_Stefaner on Twitter, available at https://mobile.twitter.com/moritz_stefaner/status/550607190378414080, accessed 25 August 2015

Studeo (2015) *Storytelling: A Real Estate Agent's Guide to Online Success in 2015*, available at http://studeohq.com/2015/04/30/storytelling-a-real-estate-agents-guide-to-online-success-in-2015, accessed 25 August 2015

The Architecture Foundation (2015) *Selling the Dream*, available at www.architecturefoundation.org.uk/programme/2015/selling-the-dream, accessed 25 August 2015

The future of data journalism is its past

Can data journalists of today learn lessons from history? The BBC's Bella Hurrell and John Walton look to early visualisations by Florence Nightingale and others to find out

Introduction

If you are new to data journalism or data visualisation it may come as a surprise that if we jump back in time to the 19th Century we can find many powerful examples of data-driven storytelling that can inspire us, teach us and give us some insight into where our discipline might go next. More than 150 years ago US newspaper man Horace Greeley was holding politicians to account over their travel expenses using data; Florence Nightingale, the nurse and media-savvy campaigner for better conditions for Britain's troops at war in the Crimea, was using statistics and the latest data visualisation techniques to forcefully make her case that too many servicemen were dying needlessly from poor sanitation and medical care. While the social reformer Charles Booth meticulously mapped 19th Century London to give us the first real picture capable of showing the full extent of poverty in the UK's capital.

Do their stories sound perhaps a little familiar? In Greeley we see echoes of the 2009 MPs expenses scandal; in Nightingale we have someone experimenting with design and presentation in a way reminiscent of current buzz around dataviz and in Booth we can see a distant ancestor of the ubiquitous interactive mapping that is now a staple of data journalism. Here we consider these three examples of data-led storytelling and use them to see how we might borrow from the past as we look towards the future.

Honest Abe

First let's take Horace Greeley, founder of the *New York Daily Tribune*. A man of intense beliefs he took politicians to task over their travel expenses in 1848, more than 150 years before MPs expenses became a big story in the UK thanks to the work of both Heather Brooke and *The Daily Telegraph*. Last year, Scott

Klein of ProPublica brought back from the archives this fascinating, previously little-known and slightly flawed example of data-journalism from the 1840s[1]. It touches on many modern themes, the familiar story of politicians in strife over public money, access to open data and the importance for journalists of getting your figures straight.

The focus of Greeley's ire happened to be the antiquated system by which Congressmen had their travel expenses paid for by the taxpayer as they journeyed from their home states to Washington DC. The travel allowance or mileage as it was called had been calculated at 40 cents a mile for more than 30 years. It was a system that had worked well enough until the proliferation of the railways and steamboats made it seem rather generous.

Freedom of Information legislation, the mainstay of journalist wanting to know more about government, was more than 100 years away and unavailable to Greeley. Luckily he had other means to access public documents - he became a Congressman himself, albeit very briefly. For three months he served as the representative for New York's 6th District - he was nominated to the post by the Whigs, a forerunner of today's Republican Party. Fittingly, bearing Greeley's campaigning zeal in mind, he was filling in as representative because his predecessor in the 6th District had been dismissed for electoral fraud.

Congressman Greeley's new job gave him access to precious data. He was now able to see the figures paid to the whole House of Representatives for their travel to Congress, although the figures were not obtained without 'considerable delay and difficulty'. He tasked one of his reporters with the job of working out the shortest route between each congressional district and Washington. They were then to work out the mileage and compare this to the public money awarded to each congressman. Greeley then published the difference between what congressmen were receiving and what he believed they should get.

One example springs off the page. According to Greeley a junior congressman from Illinois, Abraham Lincoln, was up on the deal to the tune of $676.80. Lincoln did not win re-election to the House - although that was more due to the future president's stance on the Mexican-American war rather than revelations over his expenses.

Pointing out possible flaws in your colleagues is never a recipe for popularity in the workplace, especially if you make those flaws public in one of the US's largest newspapers, as Greeley did, but many Congressmen also felt Greeley did not have his sums quite right. Greeley was taken to task by them for using the US mail route guides as the means of calculating the shortest route, while the law had stipulated the vaguer term 'the usually travelled route'. In any case Greeley insisted he was not trying to take his fellow politicians to task as individuals, but rather he was attacking the rules used to pay out their expenses. And in this he was successful. The law was changed and the per cent mileage rate was eventually reduced.

Hit them between the eyes

Greeley's data story was presented as a simple list, but the work of Florence Nightingale set out to achieve the most visual impact possible to drive home the message she hoped to convey. As she said herself her graphics were meant to 'affect through the eyes what we fail to convey to the public through their word-proof ears'.

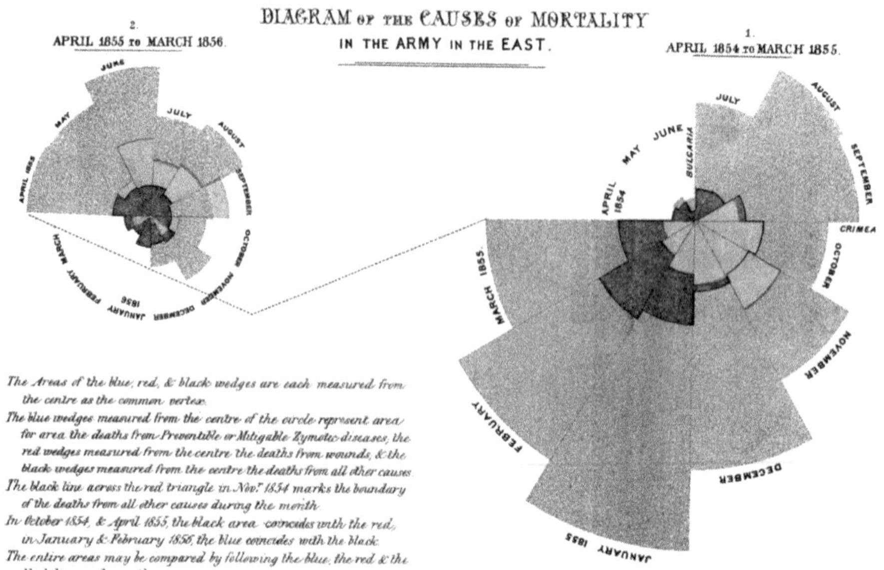

Figure 21: Graphic shows causes of mortality as described by Florence Nightingale. Source: Creative Commons/Wikipedia. Originally published in 'Notes on Matters Affecting the Health, Efficiency and Hospital Administration of the British Army' 1858.

So, what are they telling us? The two charts each show a year of British casualties in the Crimean war. The larger chart starts in April 1854, its companion on the left starts in April 1855. Blue is the colour that dominates. It is the colour of deaths from preventable disease, red shows deaths from wounds and black shows deaths from all other causes. So, in short, she is showing us that more soldiers are dying from preventable disease than anything else. It is not the fight with the Russians that is causing the deaths of so many servicemen but rather the poor care and insanitary conditions they experienced once injured.

What is also clear is that something happened after the end of the first year. The number of preventable deaths is way lower during the second 12-month period. It was the arrival of Sanitary Commission in 1855 that splits the 'before' and 'after' that the two charts are showing. The message is there – good sanitation, nutrition and proper care saves lives; hardly controversial now, but revolutionary then, at a time before the transmission of disease was entirely understood.

The design Nightingale chose is spare and minimal. The strong use of colour is striking - the unusual shape of the charts push the reader to find out exactly what story they seek to tell. The 'rose diagrams', as they are known after their petal like shape, look and feel surprisingly modern. Looking at the graphics more than 150 years later, the Swedish professor of public health, Hans Rosling, summed up their influence, estimating that the visualisations themselves probably saved more lives than Nightingale's nursing work in the Crimea. Rosling, like Nightingale, a public health practitioner with a flair for information graphics – most notably with his animated bubble charts – praised the clarity of their execution: 'Nightingale's graphics were so clear they were impossible to ignore.'[2]

Despite their rather flat title of 'Diagram of the Causes of Mortality in the Army in the East' the charts were produced as a dramatic call for change. They were intended to influence politicians and policy and so had to be focused and clear in their presentation. Surprisingly the charts do not show individual figures for lives lost by either cause or by monthly total. Instead they only give an impression of the overall problem being examined and do not blunt their message with too much detail.

Nightingale knew very well how to court public opinion; she hoped the charts would speak for themselves and enable a change in attitudes that could not just save lives in the military but could also save lives in society as a whole where many people, children in particular died early in the poor conditions in Britain's industrial towns in the 19th Century. This was something of which she was well aware: 'Let us now ask how it was that our noble army all but perished in the East? And we shall at the same time learn how it has happened that so many hundreds of millions of human race have by pestilence perished before their time' (Nightingale, 1859).

For data journalists working now the rose diagrams show the value of looking for fresh ways of presenting information, of honing a story or a message and making sure your choice of presentation supports the message you are trying to convey. The rose diagrams, also known as polar charts are now supported by several JavaScript libraries available for data visualisation work today and are also supported in Microsoft Excel. There have also been some wonderful attempts to re-imagine Nightingale's graphics for the present day, with interactive versions available at the Understanding Uncertainty website - http://understandinguncertainty.org.

Map it

One of the most significant data projects that helped to define the modern era of digital cartography was Adrian Holovaty's chicagocrime.org. A decade on, it is almost impossible to imagine how revolutionary Holovaty's daily plotting of Chicago Police Department crime reports on Google Maps was in a world before the Google mashup was ubiquitous. For the first time Holovaty's website made it possible for everyone to find out where the crime hotspots were –

which Chicago streets were worse for burglaries and which for street crime. It had a tremendous effect on how people perceived their city.

His work also encouraged Google to develop an API for their maps, making it easier for data journalists and others to follow in his footsteps. Today it is standard practice for police forces to visualise their crime data on maps made for the public to search by their postal code. But this kind of mapping has even deeper roots. In the same way that Holovaty's maps shed light on crime in the city of Chicago, over a century earlier Charles Booth's 'Life and Labour of the People' brought the real picture of poverty in London into startling focus. The report contained his now famous 'Maps Descriptive of London Poverty'. They paved the way for changes in social policy that would affect millions.

Booth was a businessman and philanthropist who took issue with the claims of the socialist Henry Hyndman that one-quarter of Londoners lived in abject poverty. Booth believed the figure to be lower and that these claims could encourage dangerous unrest among the working classes. As a businessman, he was used to making decisions based on quantitative data, and when he found census records to be unreliable he resolved to find out the true extent of poverty in London himself.

The result was Booth's three-year investigation first published in 1889. Using information gathered from school board reports – useful to Booth as school board members visited the families of school age children –, census data, and accounts by social researchers, Booth categorised the people of the East London into one of eight different social classes. The data was visualised using Stanford's maps of London, with streets coloured to indicate different levels of income. Later editions covered more of London with researchers accompanying police on their beats, taking into account crime reports – like Holovaty more than a century later – as well as measurements of income and occupation to create updated maps.

Booth's study received significant press coverage. He found that about 30 per cent of those in the East End lived in poverty, more than had been suspected. While his work was a snapshot of a changing Victorian London, it had a lasting legacy: firstly as a landmark scientific social survey, and secondly as one of the factors contributing to the development of the welfare state.

The key on Booth's maps can seem quaint and condescending from a modern perspective – with Victorian moral judgements seeping into both the colours used and the names for the social classes he described with his 'vicious and semi-criminal' class coloured blackest of all.

Figure 22: Booth's map of London poverty. *Courtesy London School of Economics Library Collection, Booth/E/1/1-12*

But while research methods and visualisation techniques have improved in the past century, Booth still has much to teach us. When he found the available data presented an incomplete picture, he searched for other reputable sources and also did his own research to create a new dataset. Although visualisations have lasting impact, Booth also realised that it was important to humanise the numbers and the maps. He included qualitative data in his reports, such as first-hand accounts of daily life among the poor, equivalent to a modern day data journalist's case study.

An ever changing toolkit

While the essence of what makes a good story does not change from one century to the next, the way we tell those stories does change. The relentless pace of technological innovation means there are now more tools available to journalists, democratising both the investigation and visualisation aspects of data journalism. Plus the dramatic rise in the use of smartphones has meant that our canvas for storytelling is evolving yet again.

What does this mean for the future of data journalism and data visualisation? This year's Reuters digital news report indicates the significance of the growth of the smartphone to news organisations. Of those audiences in the UK who use a digital device to access news, 27 per cent say the smartphone is now their main device, up from 15 per cent in 2013. That rises to almost 50 per cent in those aged 25-34. Smartphones present huge opportunities for delivering focussed personal data-led stories, delivering information based on the user's interests or location. The restrictions of the screen size in terms of visual storytelling are a challenge that information designers are already tackling. Many of the big data stories of the future will be designed to be consumed primarily on mobile phones.

Regarding the proliferation of tools that can automate processes for data analysis and visualisations, there is every indication that these will become even more common. News organisations – via joint hack days – are already collaborating on exploring how they can create a shared toolbox for journalists to use in their daily storytelling. This toolbox could simply aggregate the host of free tools now available on the web or, as is the case in the BBC, organisations may also create internal tools enabling all their journalists to make charts and other visualisations to their own specification.

Figure 23: The BBC's chart tool. *Courtesy BBC*

As all journalists, not just data journalists, become more sophisticated at using data so will our readers. They will routinely expect personally relevant data in addition to a national picture or general overview. Data apps or calculators produced by the BBC and others have already become the benchmark for public service data-led storytelling, enabling users to find out how they fit into a story. For example, the recent BBC care calculator made it easy for readers to find out how much they would have to pay under proposed government social care legislation.

The dream of an open data era where informed citizens would independently explore public datasets to find out what affects them is still a long way off for time-poor audiences. So in the future it will still fall to the data journalist – whether from a developer or journalism background – to use their ingenuity, skills and nose for a story to expose what matters. Publishing a scoop that exposes wrongdoing or by making an app that reveals how an individual is affected by the world around them are both valid ways of achieving this goal.

Notes

[1] Link to original article. (1848) The Mileage of Congress, *New York Daily Tribune*, 22 December http://chroniclingamerica.loc.gov/lccn/sn83030213/1848-12-22/ed-1/seq-2/

[2] Quote taken from 'The Joy of Stats', (2010) broadcast on BBC Four, 7 December

The dark side of data journalism: mapping for marketing

Data journalism is a fast growing domain with increasing employment opportunities. If media often look for experienced applicants, marketing offers good salary prospects to young graduates. Data journalist Isabelle Marchand compiles tricks and tips to help beginners creating advertising visualisations

Introduction

Each time I introduce myself as a data journalist, the following moments are generally filled with an awkward silence. 'What the hell is a data journalist?' is the question I often read in the blank expression of my interlocutor's eyes. 'Data journalist' seems a bit of a redundant expression, as every journalist technically handles data. The difference in my case is that instead of gathering information by interviewing people, I source it from Excel spreadsheets. The story emerges from a succession of numbers, irregularities, average or highest/lowest values. Boring, you may think. Fascinating, I would reply. Every one of us deal with statistics on a daily basis but usually, we let others tell us what they mean. People like politicians, professors, or… data journalists!

> *'There are three kinds of lies: lies, damned lies, and statistics'* - Prime Minister Benjamin Disraeli, 1868 (Best, 2012: 5).

The truth is, a number without context is meaningless. A loophole widely used in marketing, where the story is sourced from data but interpreted following an advertising intention. Where data visualisation provides 'a frame of reference to give the reader a way to understand the magnitude of the original number' (Krum, 2013: 19). Marketing orients that comparison in a beneficial way for the brand. A simple scheme illustrates the difference of reasoning between a data journalist working for a news outlet, and a data journalist employed in marketing:

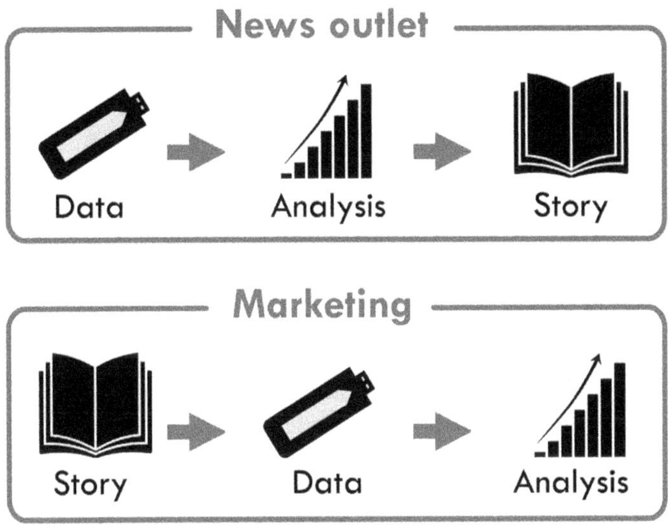

Figure 24: Processes involved for different outcomes.

Employed by a creative agency, my daily task is to produce visualisations for the Ford Motor Company. Therefore my first concern when investigating an Excel spreadsheet is to convey a positive message about the brand I represent.

For instance, following a mobility project issued by Ford, a survey has recently been released about commuting in five European cities: London, Paris, Madrid, Berlin and Rome. The desired outcome was to prove that commuting is difficult in major cities and to invest time and resources, as Ford does, into multiple transportation solutions, is essential. When analysing the survey's results, it is important to keep in mind the brand's intention: mobility projects are crucial step for future of cities. Hence the analysis of data should demonstrate how strenuous it is to commute.

Surveys stand for 'any research effort in which data is gathered systematically from a representative sample population,' (Tapan, 2006). They reveal to be excellent marketing tools as they offer the opportunity to define the initial variables (the questions) while providing data about topics that could not be gathered otherwise.

Audience targeting

The reasoning differs from journalism to marketing, as the output does. A data journalist directly reaches its audience, while in marketing pick-up by media are the marks of a successful visualisation.

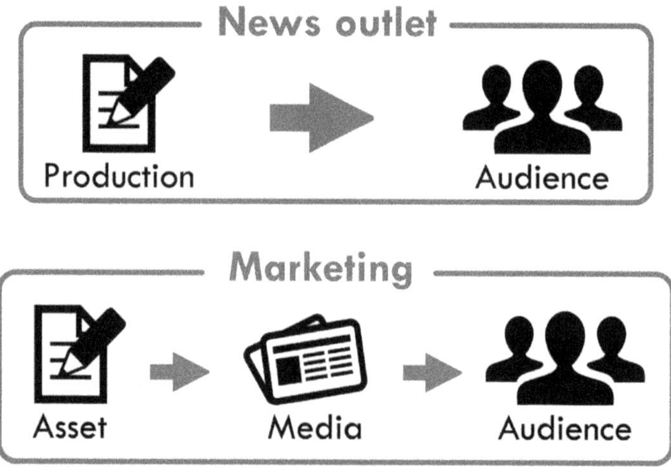

Figure 25: Different processes for newsrooms versus marketing departments

When both media and audience may share your work, your objective should be to maximise your impact for both categories. As for classical journalism, title matters, as does the hierarchy of the info. Good storytelling usually follows a simple scheme (Krum, 2013: 27):

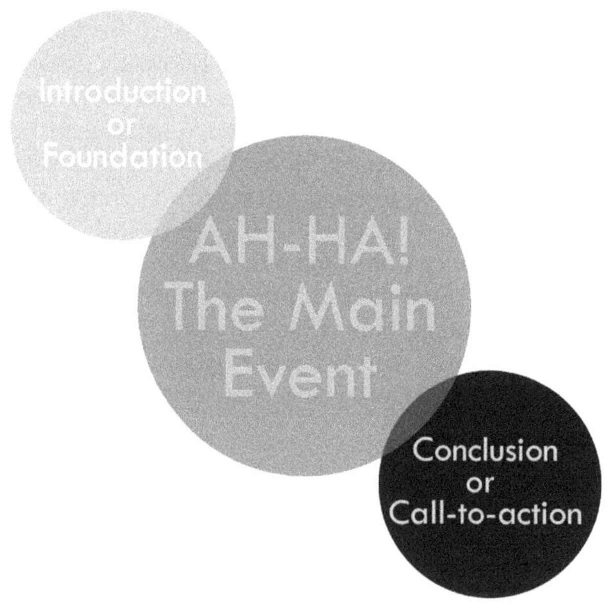

Figure 26: Storytelling according to Krum

A brief analysis of 2014 viral infographics shows that five of the top 10 have 'you' or 'we' in the title (Hines, 2014). It is not a rule applicable at all times, however employing personal pronouns helps developing a relationship with your audience (Harvard Business School, 2005). Following that rule, the aforementioned commuting infographic is titled 'Is yours the worst journey to work?'

Counter-intuitively, statistics that surface large quantities are not always impressive. '80 per cent of people have used their mobile phone when crossing the road' is not surprising. 'One out of three have watched a movie on their mobile phone when crossing the road' is more so. The second statement has a greater chance of pick-up by media.

Tips...

Don't sell it, prove it

Infographics available online can be classified in six main categories: informative; persuasive; visual explanations; advertisements; public relations infographics; and posters. Informative infographics are the most popular, and represent a golden opportunity for companies to reach an audience that would not normally expect to find their products or services of interest. For instance, the probability of you promoting an infographic about Ford's latest mobility solution is low. However, it could be tempting to share an infographic about commuting in your city, two variables part of your daily life. Informative infographics have been described as visualisations giving valuable information without an apparent sales pitch, often issued from extensive researches (Krum 2013). See the website Hongkiat's '50 Informative and Well-Designed Infographics' at www.hongkiat.com/blog/50-informative-and-well-designed-infographics for examples.

Spreadsheet programmes (Excel, Google Sheets, and others)

First thing to do is to check the file's formatting. When working on many worksheets with similar categories such as a list of countries, better be sure the same number of categories is present on each worksheet before copying the data from a page to another. When processing your worksheet, find a way to verify your results. For instance, add up all partial values to check if you reach the total value. When calculating percentages, do not be afraid to add them together and see if they add up to 100 per cent.

Do the maths

Most students get scared of data journalism because of statistics. The good news is that there is no obligation to be a maths genius to be a good data journalist. Software will do the calculation. However, being aware of formulas will help to produce relevant comparisons. Here are the formulas commonly used:

Percentages : Format cells... > Number > Percentage

Average: =AVERAGE(cell X:cell Y)

Quartile 1: =QUARTILE(cell X:cell Y,1)

Median: =MEDIAN(cell X:cell Y)

Quartile 3: =QUARTILE(cell X:cell Y,3)

Percentage of evolution (very useful): (Latest value – oldest value)/ oldest value x 100

For instance, in 2010 the rate of greenhouse emissions was 0.6g by car, and in 2015 it has been reduced to 0.3g, your calculation will be:

(0.3-0.6)/0.6 x 100 = - 50% greenhouse emissions by car in 5 years!

Keep it simple

Nathan Yau states: 'Chart and graph design isn't just about making statistical visualisations but also explaining what the visualisation shows,' (Yau, 2011), while Edward Tufte calls 'chartjunk' the 'interior decoration of graphics (…) that does not tell the viewer anything new' (Tufte, 1983). Both are statisticians and pioneers in the field of data visualisation, however their approaches are slightly different. Each data journalist develops his own balance between design and data, keeping in mind viewer's short attention span.

Inspiration, not imitation

Research existing infographics on the topic. Get inspiration, but do not try to adapt your data to a preformatted visualisation or you may have to drop important bits that don't fit in.

Choice of graphs

A good knowledge of graphs is important, as being familiar with their usage will increase your creativity. After a period of time using them, you should be able to analyse a spreadsheet and quickly make a selection of graphs that can suit your data. A very useful website that compiles most graphs is Datavizcatalogue.com

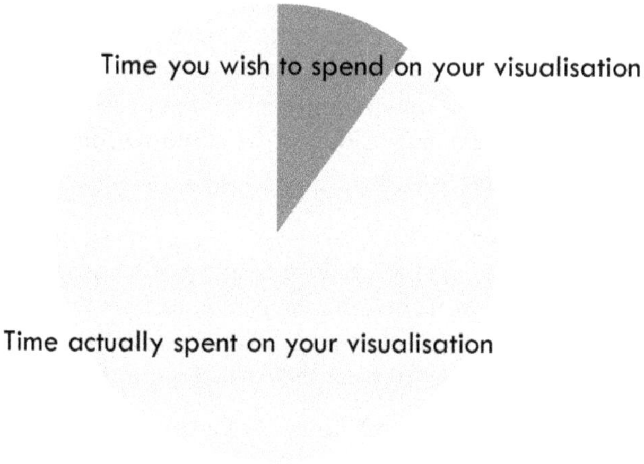

Figure 27: Time spent on visualisations

Pie charts are widespread, even if mostly decried by the statistician community as they prove to be difficult in discerning small values. However, they are useful to show contrasts.

Do not add extra useless information

Each graph should be a part of your argument. Ask yourself: 'will my visualisation still be clear without it?' If the answer is yes, get rid of it. Where, as in a press release, you can embellish a story with details and explanations, it is not possible with graphs. The visualisation itself proves the point. If statistics do not back up the message, adding a caption explaining why seems pointless.

Newbie common mistakes

When designing a proportional area chart (meaning using a shape area to represent the data), it is a common error to use the length of the shape to determine the shape's size. In order to avoid missing on proportionality, it is necessary to calculate the square root of the initial value and to define it as a length.

Let's say you want to show eight out of 10 people find commuting stressful. Instead of taking 8cm and 10cm as the length of your squares, calculate the square root of eight and 10, and use that number as a length. There's no reason to fear the calculation, it is a formula to enter in the spreadsheet and the software will do it for you. In Excel, enter =SQRT(number)

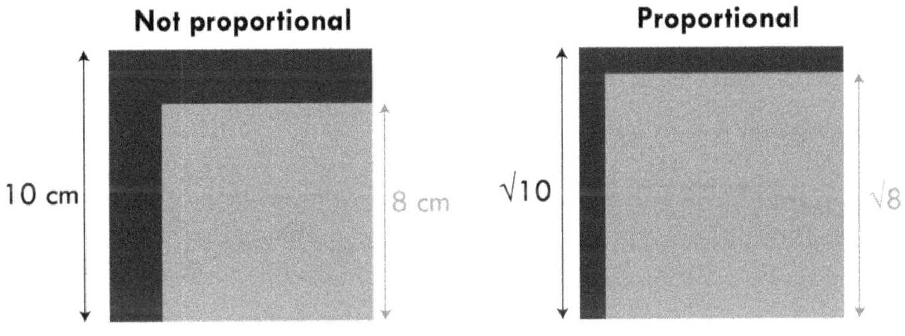

Figure 28: Proportional versus non-proportional visualisations

'Create your own visual style... Let it be unique for yourself and yet identifiable for others' - Orson Welles (Brower, 2012)

As part of the same culture, we have a common library of symbols. To use the most recognisable ones helps reaching a wider audience. From my experience homogeneity encourages visual attractiveness. To mix different icon styles may damage the general effect. Once set on a simplistic / complex design, keep it.

Figure 29: Using common symbols breeds familiarity with audiences

Do not get carried away

A successful visualisation is a subtle balance between an attractive design and selected content. Fall into one of those extremes and the general effect will be impaired. A beautiful visualisation with poor content is as ineffective as an appalling design with strong content.

Size matters

It gets easy to forget about proportions when designing with software such as Illustrator, where it is possible to zoom in and out. Your audience however may use a smaller screen than your. Export your work at various stages of the design process to check the text remains readable.

And tricks

Unfortunately, it also happens that the information retrieved does not fully back up the message you wish to convey. Tricks may apply. Don't get me wrong, there is no magical solution to transform a negative dataset into a positive one. However it is possible to set up a visualisation that reduces negative aspects. If your goal is to display an increase or a decrease over a long period of time but data shows small irregularities over time, you can group days, months and years together to extract the average or median until the curve proves your point.

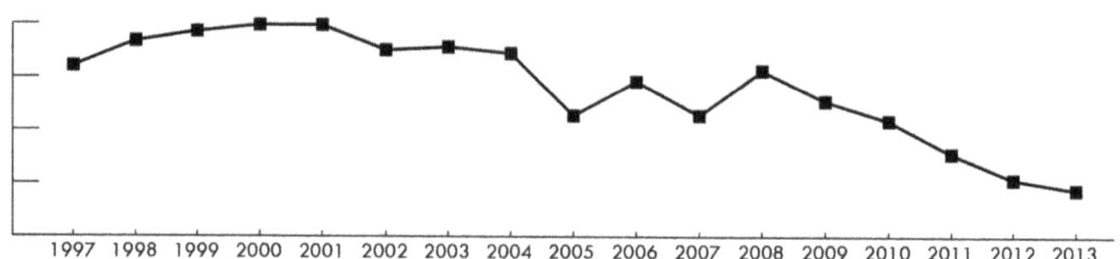

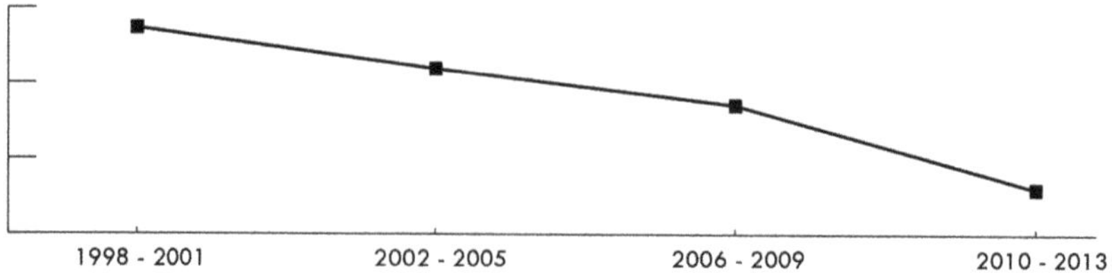

Figure 30: Examples of graphed visualisations

If the data is lacking, add projections to show what should happen following your forecast.

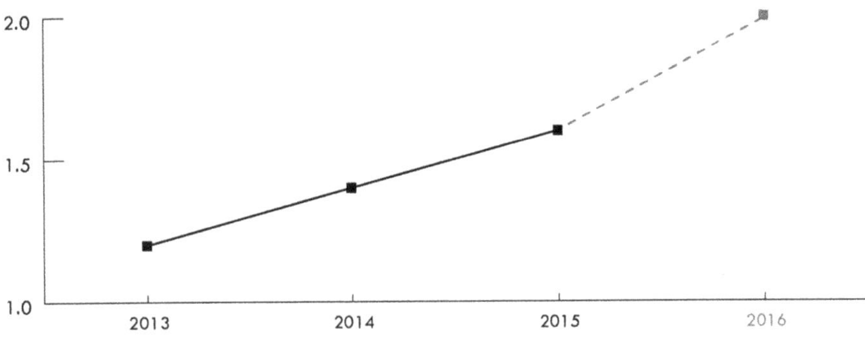

Figure 31: Time series graphed projections

Colours will help your audience to interpret the data in the way you would like them to. Red is bad, green is good.

Wording also counts. Captions should be positive or negative to back up the point made by the graph. Another example of this is how saying 'one out of 3' can have more impact than measuring by percentage and saying '30 per cent'.

What to know before submitting

What is obvious for you is not for everyone

On social networks there was a picture of Steven Spielberg sitting next to a dead dinosaur circulating. A bunch of people made comments, outraged that the director could 'slaughter such innocent animals' and boast about it. Following the event, my editor-in-chief told me something I will never forget: 'Remember that our readers believe dinosaurs are still alive!' He meant that we should never assume that everyone holds the same knowledge as we do.

> *'If confidence is one key to success, enjoying your work is another'*- John Hegarty (2014)

Journalists should be confident to stand by their articles. The same is true of data journalists and their visualisations. Usually the employer provides initial statistics. However, comparisons may be based on third party information. Consider the worst-case scenario where inquisitive media may question the work. Make sure sources are reliable.

The first shot is rarely the good one

With submitting a visualisation comes the never-ending approval process. You will have to modify parts of your work. Do not hesitate to explain why you have selected a graph instead of another when asked. However standing firm where changes bring a real possibility of improvement is not the wisest behaviour.

Hippos (highest paid person's opinion) are not an unusual phenomenon in the corporate world, patience and determination will be your best virtues.

Good luck!

Journalism is often synonymous with long hours, low pay and little recognition. The good news is that data journalism, especially related to communications, is a well-paid area, and it is in the interest of your employer to publicise your productions. Although there is no escaping the long hours, being familiar with graphs, comparisons and design software takes time. Data journalists such as Simon Rogers, who launched and edited *the Guardian*'s Datablog and Datastore, or David McCandless, author of *Information is Beautiful* (2010), have developed their own analysis and design styles. It is what is called 'voice' in written press. Failures are also part of the game, but can be avoided by relying on a team, or you may end up on websites such as http://viz.wtf/.

References

Best, Joel (2012) Damned lies and statistics: untangling numbers from the media, politicians and activists. Los Angeles, CA: University of California Press.

Brower, Steven (2012) 'A touch of Welles: Orson Welles, American comic books and pop culture' in *Steven Brower Writings* blog (quoting Welles), 25 January, available at https://stevenbrowerwritings.wordpress.com/2012/01/25/a-touch-of-welles-orson-welles-comic-books-and-pop-culture/, accessed 26 August 2015

Harvard Business School Press (2005) *Power, Influence, and Persuasion: Sell Your Ideas and Make Things Happen.* Boston, MA: Harvard Business Review Press

Hegarty, John (2014) *Hegarty on creativity: there are no rules.* London: Thames and Hudson

Hines, Kristi (2014) 'What you can learn from the top 50 infographics of 2014' in Piktochart blog, available at http://piktochart.com/what-you-can-learn-from-the-top-50-infographics-of-2014, accessed 26 August 2015

Krum, Randy (2013) Cool infographics: effective communication with data visualization and design. Indianapolis: John Wiley & Sons

McCandless, David (2012) *Information is beautiful.* New York: Harper Collins

Panda, Tapan K (2008) *Marketing Management.* New Delhi: Excel Books (2nd edn)

Tufte, Edward (1983) *The visual display of quantitative information.* 2nd ed.: Cheshire, CT: Graphics Press (2nd edn)

Yau, Nathan (2011) Visualize this: the flowing data guide to design, visualization, and statistics. Indianapolis: John Wiley & Sons

Section 2: General Election 2015: the big test

John Mair

The May 2015 General Election in the UK delivered many shocks. Not least of which was the unexpected (and unpredicted) return of David Cameron and the Conservatives with a clear Parliamentary majority. Until 9:59pm on Election night, 7 May, this scenario was out of the question. The opinion polls had predicted anything but this, yet the people had spoken.

Transition plans for the Miliband team and concession speeches by the Prime Minister had to be ripped up. The biggest casualties were the opinion pollsters who had read it wrong once, wrong twice and wrong thrice. They have now gone away to hang their heads in shame to come back with a more accurate dipstick next time round. Perhaps.

What of those whose visualisations in print and screen depended on their frankly duff data? Were they caught out too? Not if they were sassy – as Megan Lucero of *The Times* shows in this section. *The Times* rightly decided to mistrust the methodology of conventional opinion polling and evolve their own more robust version. And they were right, once, twice, thrice.

For the big broadcasters, Election Night is their factual Cup Final. They play three others and there is only one winner. *Sky News* and Nick Phipps can lay claim to capturing the silverware in May 2015. His team were often first with election news and certainly mounted the biggest ever outside broadcast presence. He plays well on the Election night / football metaphor:

> *"Unscripted drama" is the phrase the chief executive of the Premier League, Richard Scudamore, uses to describe his product's appeal. In my business, election night delivers the ultimate in unscripted drama, a Premier League decider and FA Cup Final rolled into one. The principles governing both are the same:*

-a pursuit, the aim of which is to win (football, democracy)

- rivals teams (Chelsea, the Conservatives)

- accepted rules (offside, First Past the Post)

- key players (Wayne Rooney, Ed Miliband)

- running statistics (goals scored, seats won)

'The Premier League and Election Night share another similarity. They have been utterly shaped by live television. Every editor asked to prepare their channel's election night programme knows that showbiz and spectacle are part of the DNA. Viewers brought up on a diet of "swingometers", cutting edge computing power and big building projections expect no less'.

Jonathan Spencer plays in a different part of that Cup Final. He is one of the creative geniuses behind the BBC's Election Night programme. Jonny is *the* graphics supremo. For 50 years, ornate (some say too ornate) television graphics have been the cornerstone of BBC Election shows. From cardboard to 2d to 3d to projections onto buildings, the BBC have led the way. Others have, sometimes, followed. In *Back to the Future (in praise of projectors)* Spencer discusses the behind-the-scenes efforts of the BBC in preparing to use an array of visualisations to tell the unfolding and unscripted drama of the 2015 Election Night results. This time round they used their own building – New Broadcasting House – and the piazza outside of that as the canvas on which to paint their visualisations:

'The centrepiece of the piazza graphics was the physical hex map on the ground….. The 650 parliamentary constituencies were shown as equal size, it was built in the piazza to a large scale and many party coloured hexagonal tiles ordered to cover every plausible election result. The map was coloured in with the 2010 result at the start of the night and the tiles were then removed to show the country without any MPs, as the 2015 results came in the tiles were added again to show the map filling up. It was a particular useful tool when showing the SNP landslide in Scotland.'

As ever Jonny Spencer and the BBC pulled it off, although in a later public Media Society 'Who won the TV election?' event, there was some cavilling (by this author!) at the sheer volume of graphics on the BBC. Too much visualisation, too many platforms, too little context.

In print and online, the competition to be first and best is as intense as on television. (Too) many newspapers used the flawed opinion poll data to speculate on what turned out simply to be fanciful scenarios. Acres of newsprint wasted on coalitions, minority governments and constitutional niceties. At *The Times*, Megan Lucero and her small team were more cautious – and right to be so. In *Election data v journalism basics* she explains how they went for trusted non polling stats and developed their own methodology from scratch. Let her take up the story :

'For all that came out of May 2015, our team was reminded that no matter how high the stakes are, the essence of journalism cannot be forgotten. We must critically examine what is trusted, investigate even when it is not easy and be honest about what we find. Yesterday, today and tomorrow, this will always be true.... Once ditching the prediction model, we pushed ourselves to only use data we could trust.

'Data led the coverage - data that was free of polling vice. The risk we took in holding our ground had paid off and we could proudly say that we helped The Times *retain its motto as "the paper of record".*

'Like in any kind of journalism, complacency is the enemy. The future of data journalism, and I believe journalism itself, is not about putting the story or the data on the internet, it is using the fabric of it to find stories. The election taught the journalism world this is needed. And now we know it can be done. This is just the start.'

Finally, to another new data innovation for this Election. Martin Moore of the Media Standards Trust cares about quality in the media. He and Gordon Ramsay looked towards social media in analysing the zeitgeist of this election. They developed a special tool and special software to analyse literally millions of tweets from MPs, wannabe MPs, and the most of the major political actors in the drama. This may not have been the 'Twitter election' predicted by the Twitterati but the presence and influence (positive and negative) of Twitter was clear from their 'Election Unspun' analysis:

'Twitter, while following rather than leading the campaign agenda, did to a large extent play a role in investigating factual claims by parties, news sources, and journalists. These observations have wide implications for British electoral politics for the next electoral cycle at the very least, and perhaps much longer. If social media continues to occupy a significant role in political communication, official claims by both parties and news outlets will be critiqued and – perhaps regularly – debunked, undermining trust and authority, but perhaps preventing the more transparent examples of spin. If political parties continue to view the expanded digital media landscape as necessitating damage limiting and risk-averse campaigning, a long procession of dull campaigns may lie before the British electorate.'

Overall, back to that soccer analogy: the end result on 8 May 2015 was Pollsters 0 - 1 Data journalism, but the real winner was the voting public and David Cameron.

Decision time: Sky News and the numbers that delivered an election night shock

Sky News editor Nick Phipps gives an insight into the hive of data analytics and visualisations in use at Sky News during the UK's 2015 General Election

Introduction

9.41pm, 7 May 2015.

I am sitting in my chair in the Sky News gallery when the phone rings. I'm expecting the call. 'Sky News?'

My colleague, managing editor Peter Lowe, is on the phone. 'I have the exit poll numbers, Nick' he says. 'Are you ready? Conservatives three one six. That's three… one… six…'

I nearly fall off my chair. Really. I feel like I've had a mild electric shock, the type you get from a farmer's fence, and lurch forward. I recall the times during our rehearsals when we worked through this scenario. I had dutifully included versions where a party was on the verge of victory, while accepting the campaign narrative that it was never going to happen. This poll would energise election night and I was one of the few people who knew it.

Nineteen minutes later, millions more would share my shock as the exit poll commissioned by Sky News, ITV News and the BBC was released. These numbers became a 'where were you when you heard?' moment and would define the election.

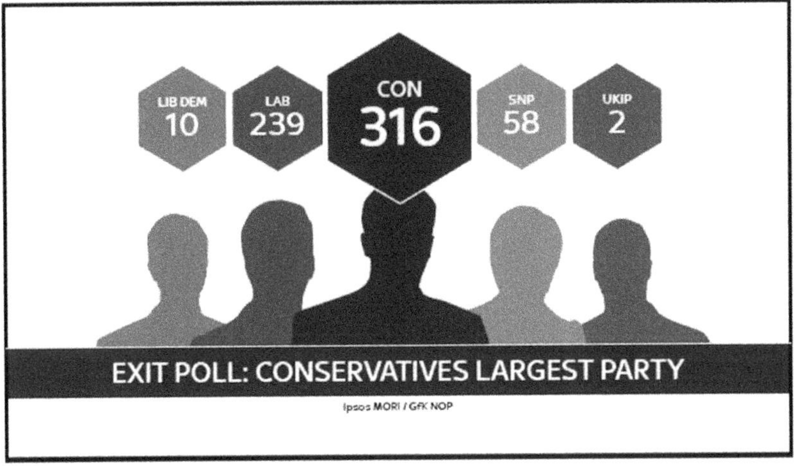

Figure 32: The news graphic used on election night to announce the exit poll. *Courtesy Sky News*

The FA Cup Final of News

'Unscripted drama' is the phrase the chief executive of the Premier League, Richard Scudamore, uses to describe his product's appeal. In my business, election night delivers the ultimate in unscripted drama, a Premier League decider and FA Cup Final rolled into one. The principles governing both are the same:

- a pursuit, the aim of which is to win (football, democracy)
- rivals teams (Chelsea, the Conservatives)
- accepted rules (offside, First Past the Post)
- key players (Wayne Rooney, Ed Miliband)
- running statistics (goals scored, seats won)

The Premier League and election night share another similarity. They have been utterly shaped by live television. Every editor asked to prepare their channel's election night programme knows that showbiz and spectacle are part of the DNA. Viewers brought up on a diet of 'swingometers', cutting edge computing power and big building projections expect no less. At Sky News, we included plenty of pizazz in our election night coverage. We delivered 138 live simultaneous video streams – an official Guinness World Record - filmed by our network of video stringers based at election night counts across the United Kingdom. An 'X marks the spot' light show lit up Sky headquarters. For our story-telling inspiration, though, we turned to the digital world.

TV = Mobile

Figure 33: How news looks via the mobile interface. *Courtesy Sky News*

Sky News' election planning began in late 2013. For the first time ever, we could be confident of the date of polling day. The Fixed Term Parliaments Act 2011 set the next election for 7 May 2015, and only the collapse of the coalition or a no confidence vote would change it.

Our inspiration was simple: to treat all our news consumers as equal citizens. The political world metamorphoses between elections, and so does media. News consumption had changed considerably since the previous election in 2010 and the key area of growth for Sky News' content was now mobile. We decided our election offering should be framed so as to treat our digital users as favourably as television viewers. This meant our content needed to be:

- interactive
- platform neutral
- informational

These are not vanilla requirements.

Interactive meant that users on all of our platforms needed to be able to drill into our results service. Our mobile users would search the data on their smartphone or tablet; our results presenters on TV would mirror the experience, using an iPad-based control interface to delve into the numbers.

Platform neutral required a fundamental reworking of our back-end results database and the creation of a single system to feed the latest election results data to all platforms simultaneously.

Informational inspired our design. Data rich yet imbued with simplicity and balance. On TV we would leave visual gimmicks and gags to our rivals, so no virtual House of Commons or projections onto Big Ben this time.

The run-up to the General Election included three very useful test beds for our ideas. At the local and European elections in May 2014, and the Scottish referendum in September, we rolled out coverage based on these principles. In May, we created a trial database that delivered live local and European election results on our digital platforms and a dummy version for an off-air TV channel. The Scottish referendum, a politically seismic but electorally straightforward vote, gave us the chance to test run our new combined database across all platforms. Its success gave us the confidence to roll out the new system in full at the General Election.

From 2D Swing to 3D Chess

> *'Election watchers normally talk about swing - the movement of voters from one party to another across consecutive elections... but the 2015 election is so unlike previous elections that such forecasting conventions should be abandoned. National polls are now too blunt to capture the undercurrents of electoral opinion. They fail to reflect the turbulence in Scotland following the referendum vote, differences across the English regions, and politics in individual constituencies,'* - Professor Michael Thrasher, Plymouth School of Government (January 2015).

Professor Thrasher has worked as the election analyst for Sky News since the channel was founded in 1989 and the issue he articulates – the challenge the 2015 General Election would present to forecasting conventions – shaped our thinking throughout the planning process. British elections have traditionally been seen as a straightforward battle between Labour and Conservative. This informed the central aspect of storytelling in television coverage, the legendary 'swingometer'. Seats were historically presented on a battleground defined by how safe they were, based on the percentage swing needed to flip party control, and then tracked as their results came in. There had been challenges to this model in the past, notably in 1983, when the Liberal/SDP Alliance polled 25.8 per cent of the vote but won just 23 seats (House of Commons Public Information Office, 1984). The convention had held though, and the Conservatives' success in becoming the largest party in 2010 was matched by a swing from Labour of 4.9 per cent (Parliament of the United Kingdom, 2010).

From early on in our planning process we debated the death of swing but the first solid sign that 2015 would require a different approach came from the consistently high polling of the UK Independence Party (UKIP). Early in 2014 the party was polling in the low teens nationally (UK Polling Report). By early May, that support had increased with one poll (Opinium, 8 May, 2014) placing UKIP on 20 per cent. The party's rise raised a key question for our planning of election graphics: should we elevate UKIP to 'primary' status and include them alongside Labour, the Conservatives and the Liberal Democrats in all graphical representations of the results?

The party's performance in the European elections helped make up our minds. UKIP polled 26.8 per cent of the vote across the UK (European Parliament, 2014) becoming the first party other than Labour or the Conservatives to top a national poll since 1906. In March 2015, the media regulator Ofcom was to decide that UKIP should indeed be designated a major party in England and Wales at the General Election (Ofcom, 2015). By that stage we had long planned to give the party equal billing in our graphics.

The second challenge to the election night convention was to come from the Scottish National Party (SNP). During discussions in early 2014 the party's inclusion in the front rank was not a foregone conclusion. In recent decades the Scottish electoral landscape, at general elections at least, had been placid. In 2010 every single seat went to the same party that had won it at the previous election. In our internal discussions at Sky News, and external discussions with our partners in the exit poll, the consequences of the September referendum were considered uncertain and so it was agreed we would assess the SNP's status post-referendum.

The first polling evidence of the change wrought on Scotland's political landscape came on 29 October 2014, when Ipsos MORI carried out a poll for STV that put the nationalists on 52 per cent. The SNP's consistent polling performance through late 2014 and early 2015 led us to conclude that Scotland's likely political earthquake needed to be brought to the fore of all graphics across Sky News platforms. Hence, for the first time at a general election, we decided to take the SNP's seat and vote count out of 'Other' and give the party a primary listing alongside the Conservatives, Labour, the Liberal Democrats and (for 2015) UKIP.

Thus the consequence of the twin UKIP/SNP surges for our viewers and users would be an increase in the number of 'primary' parties highlighted in results coverage. Rather than our traditional designation of four (Conservative, Labour, Liberal Democrat, Other), we would now have six (Conservative, Labour, Liberal Democrat, UKIP, SNP, Other). What had traditionally been a story of linear swing had developed multiple dimensions. In an interview with *the Guardian* in early May, the author described the prospect as 'like 3D chess… so multi-faceted' (*the Guardian*, 4 May, 2015). How we presented these numbers on screen was the next challenge.

Primary information: the 'Lower Third'

The multi-dimensional nature of the 2015 General Election forced us to prepare for many different outcomes and narratives of the night. We needed to be ready to explain outright victory, coalition and minority government, all in a variety of different party political colours. The key challenge, though, was ostensibly the most simple. What primary information should we deliver to our viewers and users? What combination of data and editorial would tell them, instantly and at any moment, the story of the election so far? For this, we developed our 'Lower Third'.

The Lower Third is so-named because it appears to TV viewers as if it takes up the lower third of the screen. It allows us to deliver information graphically while still bringing viewers the latest video or live reports from presenters and reporters. In deciding the design of the Lower Third, we considered first the key stages of the election narrative. We needed to be able to tell viewers the story at every stage. These stages (with approximate timings) were:

- The exit poll moment and aftermath (22:00-23:00)
- Early results (23:00-02:00)
- The results 'rush-hour' (02:00-06:00)
- The election outcome (06:00 onward)

To describe events during these stages, we split the Lower Third into four key areas, which we termed 'modules'. Each module could 'take over' the entire Lower Third area when needed.

Figure 34: Lower Third used on election night. *Courtesy Sky News.*

Table 3: Lower Third text explainers

Module	Normal state	Takeover state
Exit Poll	Primary description: 'Conservatives Largest Party'	Full numbers: Con 316, Lab 239, SNP 58, LD 10, UKIP 2, Other 25
Vidi Printer	Latest results: 'Lab Hold Blaenau Gwent'	Key result: 'Ed Balls loses seat'
Seat Counter	Totals so far for primary parties: MPs elected + change Share of vote + change	Final result: Con 330, Lab 232, LD 8, UKIP 1, SNP 56, Other 23
Top Snap	Breaking news: 'SNP gain Paisley & Renfrewshire South from Labour'	Major breaking news: 'Conservatives win election'

In designing our digital product, we followed the same modular approach. Each element was mirrored and surfaced at all times in the user's mobile and desktop experience.

Figure 35: The mobile app layout on election night. *Courtesy Sky News.*

Interactivity: The election toolkit

Our move away from the convention of linear Labour-Conservative swing in 2015 was wise, in the light of the election results. Seen purely through that traditional metric, Labour marginally *improved* its position compared to 2010 with a 0.4 per cent swing to the party from the Conservatives. The SNP's landslide in Scotland and the Liberal Democrat collapse, notably in its heartland of the South West of England, would deliver the unexpected Conservative victory but the picture could have been very different. We needed the tools to tell every conceivable story.

We devised sequences of graphics, all fed by live data, which could be presented through the Sky News studio 'big screen'. The big screen consists of 24 monitors, each 1x1.5m in size, fed by a 4K graphics engine. Our results presenters were able to direct the output of the screen using an iPad controller, allowing them to lead the viewer wherever the night's narrative was moving.

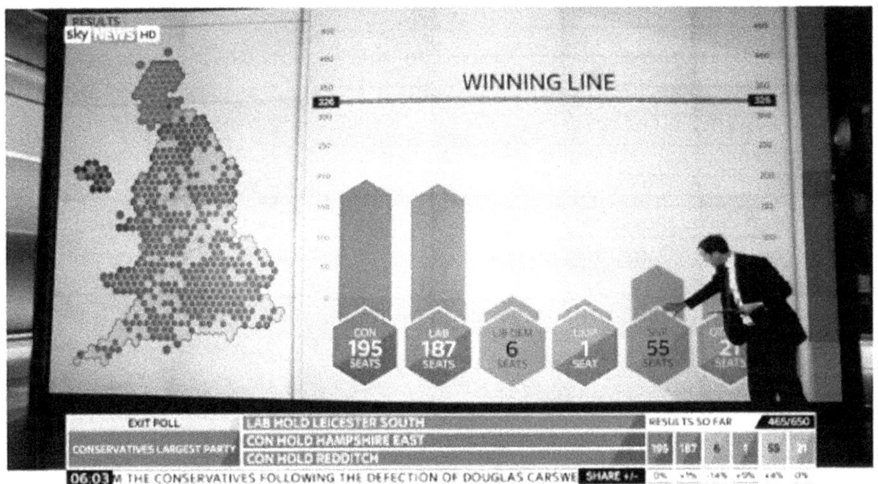

Figure 36: Screengrab from Sky News 'big screen' live on election night. *Courtesy Sky News.*

Screen option	What you see	What it helped us tell
Seat Map (pictured)	Every constituency represented by an equal sized hexagon	The geographical spread of results
Winning Line (pictured)	The totals for the major parties	Which party was in the lead
The Grid	All 650 seats listed alphabetically, coloured in live as they declare	How far through the night we were
Gains and Losses	Total gains and losses by party, with toggle to show which other parties the gains and losses have come from/gone to	The real battlegrounds of the night e.g. most Con gains coming from Lib Dems
Coalition Builder	A representation of the House of Commons and the parties' latest seat totals	By moving the parties around, we could build and break coalitions – as it turned out, not needed
Con/Lab battleground	Seats organised by per cent swing needed to flip control	Labour's failure to take key target seats e.g. Nuneaton
SNP Targets	Every Scottish seat sorted by per cent swing the SNP needed to take it	The SNP landslide
UKIP Targets	20 potential UKIP targets	UKIP's failure to break through
Lib Dem Seats	Lib Dem seats from most to least marginal	The Lib Dem collapse

Table 4: Explaining Sky News' 'Big Screen'

The result

Sky News coverage was widely praised in the aftermath of the election. In a review organised by the Media Society the BBC's election editor in 2001 and 2005, Alexandra Henderson, said 'Sky was fantastic, fleet of foot and had a feel of being where the action is' (Media Society, 2015). The 2020 election is currently a distant prospect, and the question over whether the conditions in which the 2015 election was fought will sustain is moot. What is clear is that viewer and user consumption of news will continue to change as usage increasingly moves onto mobile platforms. However the next election's results are consumed, numbers will be at their heart.

References

Conlan, Tara (2015) 'TV Companies vie for poll position in an election that no one can call', *the Guardian*, 4 May, available online at http://www.theguardian.com/media/2015/may/04/television-election-coverage-emily-maitlis-bbc-sky-itv , accessed 14 August 2015

Conway, Ed (2015) 'RIP Swingometer – a post-mortem', *Medium.com* for Sky News, 12 May, available online at https://medium.com/@edconwaysky/rip-swingometer-a-post-mortem-b716ba403cd2, accessed 14 August 2015

Thrasher, Michael (2015) 'Will there be another hung parliament in May?' Sky News, 27 January. Available online at http://news.sky.com/story/1415528/will-there-be-another-hung-parliament-in-may, accessed on 14 August 2015

Parliament of the United Kingdom (2010) 'General Election 2010: key issues for the 2010 Parliament', available online at http://www.parliament.uk/business/publications/research/key-issues-for-the-new-parliament/the-new-parliament/general-election/, accessed on 14 August 2015

Parliament of the United Kingdom (1984) 'General Election Results, 9 June 1983'. *House of Commons Public Information Office Factsheet No 22*, revised June 1984. Available online at http://www.parliament.uk/documents/commons-information-office/m09.pdf , accessed on 14 August 2015

European Parliament (2014) 'Results of the 2014 European elections', available online at http://www.europarl.europa.eu/elections2014-results/en/country-results-uk-2014.html#table02, accessed 14 August 2015

Ofcom (2015) 'Review of Ofcom list of major political parties for elections taking place on 7 May 2015, March 16, available online at http://stakeholders.ofcom.org.uk/binaries/consultations/major-parties-15/statement/Major_Parties_Statement.pdf, accessed 14 August 2015

IpsosMORI (2014) 'SNP open up significant lead ahead of general election vote', 29 October, available online at https://www.ipsos-mori.com/researchpublications/researcharchive/3469/SNP-open-up-significant-lead-ahead-of-General-Election-vote.aspx, accessed 14 August 2015

Opinium (2014) 'UKIP reach a 2014 high of 20 per cent while Labour and the Conservatives fall back, 8 May, available online at http://ourinsight.opinium.co.uk/survey-results/political-polling-6th-may-2014, accessed 14 August 2015

UK Polling Report (2015) 'Voting Intention since 2010', available online at http://ukpollingreport.co.uk/voting-intention-2, accessed on 14 August 2015

Media Society (2015) 'Who won the TV election?' 20 May. Remarks reported to author by event participant. Full list of event participants available online at http://www.themediasociety.com/20th-may-won-tv-election/, accessed 14 August 2015

Back to the Future (in praise of projectors)

Jonathan Spencer discusses the behind-the-scenes efforts of the BBC in preparing to use an array of visualisations to tell the unfolding drama of the 2015 General Election results night

Introduction

'Everything changes, but everything stays the same' and 'whoever you vote for, the government gets in' are refrains commonly heard around the country at election time: but one thing that was not the same was that due to the Fixed-term Parliaments Act of 2011 the date of the 2015 general election had been (barring unforeseen circumstances) known for years. Prior to this the BBC had depended on political intelligence to predict when the Prime Minister would call an election within a five-year window (traditionally the first Thursday in May, four years after the start of the previous parliament. A Prime Minister who took the full five years allowed would not look confident).

Foreknowledge of the date notwithstanding, in the case of the BBC's 2015 election programme the challenge stayed the same as always; to present the results in a timely and accurate manner so that the audience can clearly see who has won the election. The presenters broadly stayed the same, David Dimbleby, Huw Edwards, Jeremy Vine, Emily Maitlis, Laura Kuenssburg, Sophie Raworth etc, the basic studio set structure remained unchanged since 2010. It had been in store since 2010 in case the Conservative-Liberal Democrat coalition collapsed. Even the polls prior to the election stayed broadly the same too, predicting another hung parliament. Whilst the polls and opinion pieces may argue that one outcome is a forgone conclusion and the BBC production team were expecting much the same story, they plan for every possible permutation; and whilst the suite of graphics needed stayed much the same, the design team were looking further back for inspiration.

In a field such as graphic design which is heavily dependent on fashion, to know the direction of travel sometimes it is worth knowing where you have come from. In broadcast industry's crossover to digital from analogue in the 1990s there were a number of hybrid solutions. One of a graphic designer's duties during this period was to physically select images from the 35mm slides in the News Library in the basement of Television Centre and take them up to the transmission suite, where the slides would be loaded into a modified Kodak SAV2000 slide projector and colour corrected to be finally recorded as a digital still image for transmission by an operator. For a while, the Kodak SAV 2000 was a ubiquitous tool in the creative motion designer's armoury. For big presentations, at conferences and events, a number of projectors could be sequenced to sound with audio pulses recorded to magnetic tape. These methods were some of the first to be digitised with the introduction of computer graphics to create the images for the 35mm slides. At the height of this technique's popularity a single slide could cost a customer as much as £250, with 81 slots to be filled in a slide carousel and at least eight projectors needed for smooth motion, the rewards were considerable and ultimately unsustainable.

Since the 2010 general election the BBC had sold off Television Centre in west London, losing access to the cavernous TC1 studio – the previous home of election programmes. The nearest studio in the BBC estate big enough and close enough to Westminster to stage an election programme was (and is) at Elstree, the home of Eastenders. The BBC was also keen to show off its new central London HQ with an event in the piazza at W1. The concept was to use a traditional technique that had visual impact and have the exit poll projected onto the iconic prow of Old Broadcasting House in Regent Street. In order to achieve this the BBC had to seek planning permission from Westminster Council. If this had not been granted the BBC had a contingency plan for virtual projections. The planning application was supported by visuals, face-to-face meetings and site visits. Once we had the permission, work could commence, however with limited resources the BBC has to be careful with planning, and as the projections were non-essential they were fitted in late into the production cycle.

Scottish referendum 'shark tank' effect

Figure 37: A screengrab from the BBC Scottish referendum coverage, available at www.youtube.com/watch?v=GvmhMRzKjLg. *Courtesy BBC.*

The production cycle for the 2015 general election was complicated by the Scottish referendum in September 2014. The programme covering the referendum had been produced and transmitted from the BBC headquarters in Glasgow. The challenge for the graphics team in Glasgow was to create an environment for Jeremy Vine to provide his analysis without using a green CSO (colour separation overlay) space. This challenge was to allow both presenters to use the impressive atrium space of the building without an unsightly patch of CSO green in the wide establishing shots and to try something new. The production team decided to use one of the split level floors in the atrium of Pacific Quay to create a studio space for Jeremy. The BBC used a large real world screen to provide a graphic picture space behind Jeremy and then key foreground graphic elements in front of Jeremy. The trick used to add value to the big screen was to perspective correct the background scenes shown in the big screen for any live camera. The technique had been tested by the BBC and TV2 (Denmark) as part of a technical evaluation process in February 2011. TV2 went on to use this for their election coverage on the autumn 2011. The technique depends on the computer rendering the screen image knowing the position of the live camera and adjusting the view of the 3D graphic shown in the screen in real time as the live camera moves. This has the effect that the 3D graphics in the screen can be viewed from all sides and appear as an object behind the screen. The BBC calls the method 'shark tank' after Damien Hirst's 1991 artwork 'The Physical Impossibility of Death in the Mind of Someone Living'. Subsequently this Vine screen featured heavily in the BBC's winning Broadcast Design Award (Gold) of 2015 and gave the BBC the confidence to build an interactive screen with depth for the 2015 UK general election.

The General Election screen went through many design iterations, before delivery. The objective was to achieve a flat and clear design that would be relevant to the presenter's field of view on a very large and impressive screen. The further complication was that the buttons needed to be large enough for the presenter to hit without having to be too accurate. The trigger mechanism was an invisible sheet of laser light that reports the x and y position of an interruption – in this case a finger touching the screen behind the invisible sheet of laser light; from which the interface can infer which on-screen button has been pressed. Due to the nature of the studio build, the sheet of laser light was a couple of centimetres away from the screen surface. From the presenter's point of view this offset can cause the presenter's finger to intersect the laser above and on the presenter's side of a button, missing the button completely if it is too small. This and the scale of the proposed screen dictated a simple flat and clean design was an appropriate solution. The production team was very keen that a 1:1 scaling ratio was adopted between the computer render engine pixel sizes and the LED screen used in the studio. Testing had shown that this ratio would give a clearer and brighter image when shot on camera. Post render scaling of the image added anti-alising and blur, which was undesirable for a screen within a live studio. The unscaled LED pixels naturally anti-alias themselves because the intense light of an individual diode blends effectively with its neighbours. The presenter's narrative function is to relate the interesting constituency results as they come in to the studio anchor, the materials needed for this are a constituency map, a candidate photo, the result, the change for the previous general and the swing.

Having a solid set of designs agreed, the development team took over the delivery task. Flat and clean as the designs were, they were built in 3D, X and Y as normal and very minimal Z values. With this proviso the development team were confident that they could retro fit enough Z depth to the animations to make the 'shark tank' worthwhile. Once in the studio however the design of the rostra constricted the lateral movement of the pedestal cameras dedicated to shooting the screen; this meant that the only camera that could sweep the length of the screen was the crane which was always in demand for other shots. As a result the screen was shot on two pedestal cameras, one oblique and off to the side and one in front. As the 'shark tank' effect works best with one camera sweeping across the whole screen; the parallax effect was lost for the audience at home. For people in the studio the behaviour of the screen can look very odd if they are viewing off axis. The pedestal camera shot from the side exaggerated the size of the screen whereas the camera shot from the front cut the presenter out of the screen. Therefore during the course of the night it was difficult for the viewer to get a clear idea of the size of the screen or to perceive the depth.

These issues all point to the need for the BBC to use the type of pre-vis tools in use in the film industry and to the importance of studio directors in planning big graphic installations. It is vital for designers and developers to consider the final outcome of their work and the studio director is the final arbiter of that outcome for all studio and OB graphics.

Back-plates 'Road to Downing Street'

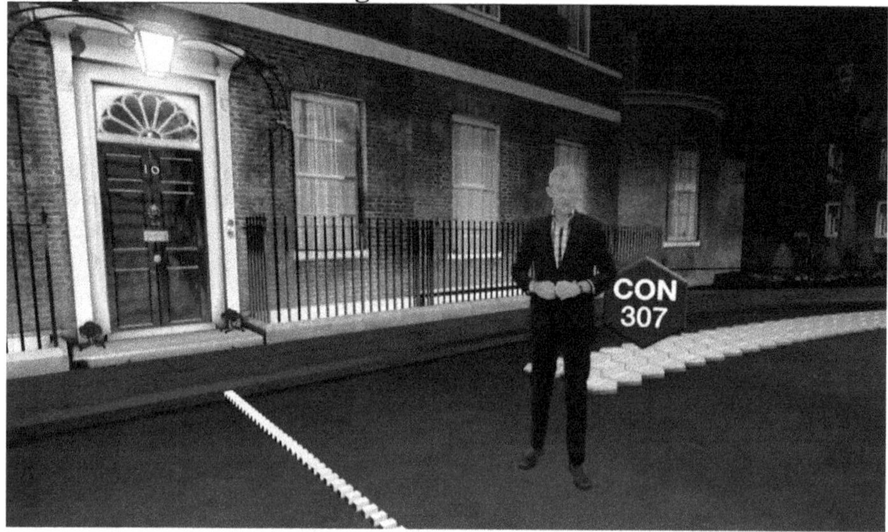

Figure 38: A screengrab from the BBC's 'virtual' Downing Street, available at www.youtube.com/watch?v=qBOdSXAnZDs. *Courtesy BBC.*

The 2015 election was an event where the BBC made extensive use of film techniques; two graphic sequences were dependent on pre-shot back-plates. One of the areas the BBC team was excited about was an opportunity to light and record a sequence of back-plates in Downing Street for Jeremy Vine's 'Road to Downing Street' graphics. The team was granted access to the street in early March. The brief was to light number 10 and 11 Downing street in a plausible and naturalistic manner. This was to help both the computer graphics and the lighting director in Elstree. Working backwards in the compositing chain, the lighting for the back-plate is defined by the need to get a good CSO green key. To do this the lighting director has to evenly light the whole green space around the subject without spilling any of this light over the subject. This means there will be a higher concentration of light around the subject than would be normally believable if Downing Street had been filmed in natural light.

As the result of the election is obviously unknown at the time of filming the back-plates, the BBC had to plan a number of scenarios where the shots would be used. The concept was that the coloured hexagons, each one representing a constituency would build up towards the door of number 10. The idea was at different times during the night Jeremy Vine could return to Downing Street to monitor the progress of the parties as represented by hexagons. Early in the night the hexagons would fall far short of the door and later on a position near the door and even a position past the door should one party achieve a landslide.

This meant laying a track so the crane could traverse the length of the building. The BBC also collected tracking data live from the crane and track to extrapolate the position of the virtual camera for the composite shot on the night. The positional data collected looked good, but once the shots were examined in post-production there was considerable camera shake due to the wind rocking the crane. The decision was made to stabilise the shots, as the same stabilisation algorithm cannot be applied to the video and the tracking data, the team lost the tracking data and had to re-track the shot post stabilisation. Again these decisions were dictated by the final output in that the video playback would be cut with studio shots, which by their nature tend towards the steady and stable.

The camera track is created by picking two or more points in the video and tracking their movement, from this the software is able to extrapolate the position of the camera that filmed the video. This post-produced camera track was used to create a virtual camera in the render engine that was synced to the back-plate. A piece of 3D geometry was then placed centrally in front of the door of Number 10 in the scene; we then moved this forward until it appeared comfortably in front of the door. We then filmed Vine live with a locked off studio camera, through the chroma-keyer and fed this signal into the render engine mapped and the video onto the 3D geometry; Vine appeared to be outside Downing Street as the camera moved.

The job of the lighting director is to light live Jeremy Vine so that he matches the per-recorded video back-plate and is still key-able off the green studio. Now that Vine is composited into the back-plate we were able to add any computer graphics to the 3D geometry on the back-plate render engine. This shot was cut into a sequence using a virtual model of Downing Street created with textures collected during the crane shoot. On transmission the match between the video and the virtual model was seamless. Whilst the technique lacked the 'wow' factor, it did allow the for what we had thought to be an impossible sequence, real location shot, seamlessly into VR on a studio camera, then spin round out of the green VR space to show the wider studio and a hand over to anchor David Dimbleby.

Exit poll graphics 'augmented reality'

Augmented reality graphics were used in Glasgow for the 2014 Scottish referendum and deployed again for the exit poll in the 2015 general election. This type of graphic is usually force keyed over the real world and as such do not need a green background, they are almost always in the foreground. The reveal of the exit poll is a key moment in the election programme. There have been reams written about how and why the polls in the campaign were so far adrift from the exit poll and the final result, suffice to say for the BBC election team no assumptions are ever made over the veracity of any polls taken before the count. For the 2015 election results programme the BBC was able to get the sitting Prime Minister into New Broadcasting House to pose for the House of

Commons graphic, once the Prime Minister had been in, the other party leaders followed and as a result we had video loops of them all. With this material we were able to create an augmented reality with all the key party leaders standing in the studio with their projected numbers.

Virtual reality

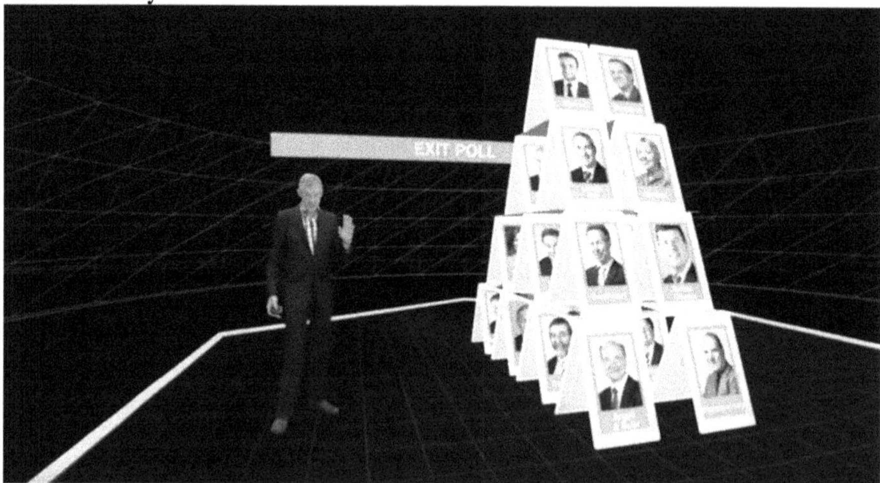

Figure 39: A screengrab from the BBC's Election night coverage, available here: www.youtube.com/watch?v=519nN9eqvqA. *Courtesy BBC.*

Virtual Reality graphics have for a long time been a key part of election night, an extensive list of commissions included:

- Battlegrounds: A staple of election graphics, a list of seats arranged by marginality. An important ability for this graphic is to update the list as results come in so the audience can follow the progress a party is making into another parties defence board. The semantics are important here as defence / attack boards are identical. The look is similar to a railway departure board.
- Swing-o-meter: A popular graphic device, particularly useful for simple two horse races. The design for the SNP versus Labour was recalibrated during the build to go to 30 per cent.
- Road to Downing Street: described previously.
- Parliament: The House of Commons, model populated with faux MPs as video textures
- House of Cards: The Lib Democrats electoral performance visualised as a House of Cards.

- UKIP: A House of Commons building site, a method of visualising support of UKIP in seats where they came second and could make gains in future election. The foundations and lower floors built up the better they did.
- History: A graphic set in the House of Commons lobby, with past Prime Ministers and their share of the vote.

Drones and projectors

Figure 40: A Screengrab from the BBC's election night coverage, available at www.youtube.com/watch?v=UvsMege-LVo. Others are available at www.youtube.com/watch?v=SkNcNkp0dJ8; www.youtube.com/watch?v=A9bbGKPpZsQ; and www.youtube.com/watch?v=t_oGw-OTNFE. *Courtesy BBC.*

An area the BBC has been experimenting with since 2014 is the use of pre-recorded unmanned aerial vehicles (UAV) shots combined with live data. In part it is this experience that gave the Visual Journalism CGI and Real Time Development Group the confidence to try the Downing Street shoot. The current kit needed to track the exact position of the UAV camera in relation to its target is too heavy for the current generation of civilian UAVs so the BBC collected the shots then stabilised and tracked them on the ground. In the case of the House of Commons shoot there were a number of understandable bureaucratic hoops to be jumped through with wanting to fly a drone (UAV) in a sensitive area. The initial feeling was that the project would be impossible to achieve, but working with the House of Commons, the BBC was able to answer all the relevant authorities' concerns. The House of Commons gave the BBC access to the Terrace to fly a UAV to collect the shots needed. On the initial reconnaissance, the creative director was disappointed to see that a substantial proportion of the roof of the House was covered with scaffolding and tarpaulins. Subsequently the BBC's creative team realised this was a gift as it gave a framework and context to build a virtual scaffolding cinema screen on which to add virtual projections. The team flew at first light to get a shot that could be treated to give a night-time look, and again later in the morning to get daytime shots. The process of tracking was similar to the Downing Street workflow, but simplified by the lack of a live presenter. The faux projections worked well with numbers driven by live data.

Once the key graphics needed for the main results programme had been designed and handed over to the in-house development team, the designers could start to revisit the initial visualisations (pre-vis) created to support the planning application for the external Broadcasting House projections. Once the project had moved from the theoretical to the practical, the team had to research the best way of realising the polished visuals shown. The relationship between pre-visualisation and the production process is one of the more paradoxical areas of design. The usual aim of pre-vis is to sell a particular concept regardless of the complexities of actual delivery, whereas the production phase is always about problem solving.

The first step was to seek a suitable external technology partner who had experience for this type of installation. The BBC was fortunate to find a company with former BBC staff who had produced a number of successful large-scale architectural projections. The best two areas for projection were mapped out. The BBC's initial model had been made from collaging a huge number of photos shot specifically and supplemented with images from the internet and extrapolating a point cloud from the resulting collage. This model was too data heavy to be useful, so a simpler one was built by hand using the point cloud as a 3D reference. This was a useful tool, but the creative teams did not have sufficient faith in the accuracy of the model. The decision was made to scan the building. The production team had sensibly opted for the stonework on the prow rather than the internal curved glass walls above the main entrance to New Broadcasting House, which would have to have been covered. The ratio between using all the available pixels at 16x9 and filling the target area meant that the faces of the party leaders and fonts had to be scaled precisely before being sent to the projectors. The faces were cropped very close and had a slow zoom, so that any key features distorted by the building would not stay distorted for long. The idea was to keep all aspects of the graphics moving at all times, to get the best effect the BBC decided to limit the use of colour to party colours only and using big monochrome high contrast images gave the most legible graphics. A lot of consideration was given to the non-live data side of the projection, with one of the BBC's Computer Graphics specialists being given a month to devise and create architectural special effects. These were pre-rendered and a producer could use a wipe to get from the data driven graphics to full scale animated special effects loop, this was essential as if there had there be a glitch in the results system the producer could take the live data driven graphics off the front of the building and replace them with the attractive effects loop.

The centrepiece of the piazza graphics was the physical hex map on the ground. This is a graphic that came from the 2010 election and was re-versioned without alterations to the artwork because the geographical boundaries of the constituencies had not changed in the interim. The 650 parliamentary constituencies were shown as equal size, it was built in the piazza to a large scale and many party coloured hexagonal tiles ordered to cover every plausible election result. The map was coloured in with the 2010 result at the start of the night and the tiles were then removed to show the country without any MPs, as the results 2015 results came in the tiles were added again to show the map filling up. It was a particular useful tool when showing the SNP landslide in Scotland.

Conclusion

The BBC was very satisfied with the suite of graphics broadcast during the 2015 general election; but there are areas that can be improved in the future. It is interesting to note that the image that was picked up by newspapers and websites around the world was the exit poll projections on the prow of Broadcasting House. Design and build team (not all staff full-time on the project) included Julie Tritton, Mark Edwards, Jonathan Barrett, Caroline Pitt, Joanne McDonald, George Spencer, Tony Sinclair, David Hughes, Martin Ayub, Steve Mantz, Max Blaber and the author.

References

Holovaty, Adrian, (2005) 'Announcing chicagocrime.org', 18 May, available at http://www.holovaty.com/writing/chicagocrime.org-launch, accessed 18 August 2015

Klein, Scott (2015) 'Antebellum Data Journalism: Or, how big data busted Abe Lincoln', *ProPublica*, 17 March, available at https://www.propublica.org/nerds/item/antebellum-data-journalism-busted-abe-lincoln, accessed 18 August 2015

Newman, Nic and Levy, David and Nielsen, Rasmus Kleis (2015) *Reuters Institute Digital News Report 2015*. Oxford: Reuters Institute for the Study of Journalism, University of Oxford, available at http://www.digitalnewsreport.org/, accessed 18 August 2015

Rogers, Simon (2013) *Facts are Sacred.* London: Faber and Faber

Nightingale, Florence (1859) A Contribution to the sanitary history of the British Army during the late war with Russia. London: John W Parker & Son

Unknown Author (2002) 'Charles Booth and the survey into life and labour in London (1886-1903)', *Charles Booth Online Archive.* London School of Economics, available at http://booth.lse.ac.uk/, accessed 18 August 2015

Data journalism and the 2015 UK General Election: media content analysis for a digital age

Martin Moore and Gordon Ramsay discuss how they monitored dozens of media outlets, thousands of candidates, hundreds of thousands of news articles and millions of social media engagements using a specially designed data monitor during the General Election campaign

Introduction

Over the course of the 2015 General Election campaign, from Monday 30 March to polling day on Thursday 7 May, 497 Conservative candidates published 68,974 tweets. Some 18,843 contained references to political or policy issues, of which 56 per cent (10,491) were about the economy. The next most tweeted policy area by Conservative candidates was health, at only 13 per cent. This strong focus on the economy matched the agenda set by the party leadership on Twitter. We are able to say this because we analysed more than one million tweets during the campaign. Likewise, we were able to see that from January to April 2015, as the long election campaign gathered momentum, around half of the UK's 650 parliamentary constituencies received almost no coverage in the national broadcast and print news media – 326 constituencies featured in five or fewer news articles during the 15-week period (54 received no coverage at all). We were able to say this because we were analysing around 30,000 online news articles each week for the 18 weeks prior to polling day.

This chapter explains how we set up and managed 'Election Unspun', an experimental content analysis project using software we developed expressly for the purpose. It was a project conceived in the light of the enormous possibilities for large-scale news analysis offered by advances in processing power, data storage, analytical tools, and the explosion of information in a digital age. With a relatively small team, modest resources, and some programming expertise, it is now possible to undertake news analysis projects on a scale unimaginable a just a few years ago. By explaining Election Unspun, we hope to show how new researchers might experiment with new methods of content analysis on large digital datasets.

Content analysis: analogue to digital

News content analysis used to be, and in many cases still is, a very time-consuming process. In the days of print-only newspapers – and today still, in non-digitised archives – it could mean spending weeks in a newspaper library poring over kilometres of microfiche. Video or audio analysis could involve spooling through piles of VHS tapes, audio cassettes, or delicate (and sometimes disintegrating) reel-to-reel film. Before the use of spreadsheet and statistical analysis packages, results would need to be hand-calculated. The usual constraints of time and money ensured that such content analysis projects were either limited in scope, or very expensive and required a small army of researchers. More recently, print news content analysis has been made somewhat easier by the collections of commercial companies like Factiva or Gorkana, but again large-scale analyses using these resources require a lot of manual counting and transferring of data to (e.g.) SPSS for analysis (Ramsay 2014), and charge expensive subscriptions. Though source material is far easier to collate using these techniques, analysis can still be extremely time-consuming.

There is something a little incongruous about manually counting digital information and going through several stages of gathering and preparing data to transfer to Excel or SPSS before even rudimentary quantitative analysis can be done. We set out to develop a more efficient and flexible way of doing news content analysis, building on our previous experience of creating digital tools such as Journalisted.com and Churnalism.com. Unable to find any equivalent open-source software to do the job, we built our own digital news content analysis tool, Steno. Named in honour of Nicholas Steno, a 17th Century geologist who, amongst other things, discovered that fossils did not fall from the sky (as many of his contemporaries believed), but were instead the accretion of once-living organisms. As Nicholas Steno made discoveries in layers of rock laid down over millennia, so – our thinking went – Steno the research tool would discover patterns in layers of news articles laid down day after day.

Part content collector, and part analytical tool, Steno can be aimed at news websites, from which it will collect every article published, as well as logging important metadata about each article – who wrote it, when it was published, the headline and URL, and so on. This content is then stored in a structured database for retrieval. Provide Steno with the dates you would like to analyse, and it will provide every news article published by your chosen news sources on each chosen date. A desktop application then allows researchers to perform queries on the resulting sample of articles.

Ultimately, Steno is intended for targeted analysis of news coverage of specific policy areas. However, since the 2015 General Election campaign provided a unique opportunity to see whether a small research team using Steno could deal with the complexities of monitoring the entire range of party policy platforms, we decided not just to cover the election as a whole, but to analyse election coverage on an ongoing week-by-week basis, making all the findings and data available online (via www.electionunspun.net). Once we knew that our analysis worked on our sample of mainstream media outlets, we decided to add a Twitter analysis component and started collecting every tweet from more than 3,000 political actors and influencers.

Doing Election Unspun taught us a lot. For example, we learned about the dynamics of the relationship between parties, press, Twitter and broadcast news – particularly the intimate relationship Twitter has with broadcasting. We learnt about the bizarre inefficiencies of online publishing – for instance that a shortlink in a tweet can link to up to 10 different shortlinks before reaching the original URL. We also learned that, before we begin any future similar project, we need to answer five questions.

Question 1: What news content should we analyse?

In a world where everyone can do journalism and publish news – and many do – establishing the boundaries of digital news content analysis is the fundamental first step. Even when fast and easy-to-use tools make analysis of large datasets possible, a realistic and justifiable sample is essential.

We began by focusing on articles published online by national newspapers (*The Times*, *the Guardian*, the *Daily Mirror*, etc), but quickly saw that it would be insufficient to exclude the BBC's news website and – consequently – the websites of *ITV News*, *Sky News* and *Channel 4 News*. Conscious that the period between the 2010 and 2015 General Elections has seen the growth of serious online-only news publishers, we added the UK versions of *The Huffington Post* and *Buzzfeed Politics*. We could have gone further; weekly journals like *The Spectator* and *New Statesman* were publishing election campaign news and opinion daily, as were spin-off election sites like www.may2015.com.

Selecting a sample of Twitter accounts to analyse proved a greater challenge. Generating representative samples is a key concern in any analysis of Twitter (Bruns and Liang 2012, Gaffney and Puschmann 2014). Given that we were interested in understanding the dynamics of political influence and agenda-setting, we decided to focus on a selection of political actors and political influencers. Of the two groups, political actors were fairly easy to identify. We followed 2,412 Parliamentary candidates with personal Twitter accounts. Identifying political influencers was more difficult. We used a combination of criteria – number of followers, number of profiles the account follows, Klout score, and the frequency and type of tweet content – to capture one group of general political influencers, and two groups of specialist policy influencers (Moore et al, 2015).

Question 2: How should we collect the news content?

There are various ways to collect news content, some commercial and some non-commercial. We chose to develop software to do it ourselves by building

Steno. This allows for the collection of very large amounts of information, and the subsequent analysis of that data through relatively straightforward tools. Steno is written in 'Go', an open source programming language developed by Google (it could just as well have been written in Python, Ruby, C++, Javascript or PHP). It consists of a server-side set of programmes that collect the textual content and metadata from each URL, and a client-side graphical user interface (GUI) desktop application for performing analysis. The server side runs continuously to collect news articles from a set of target sites. These articles are stored in a database, ready for later collection and analysis. Using the GUI application, the researcher can pull in articles (and/or tweets) from one or more servers. Once downloaded, the user can access and analyse them via a simple Excel-like window on the desktop. In the window are tools for tagging and untagging articles, and a simple scripting language to help automate this. The whole system is modular – different servers can be configured to collect different data, and the server Application Programme Interface (API) for extracting articles can be used by other tools, not just the GUI application.

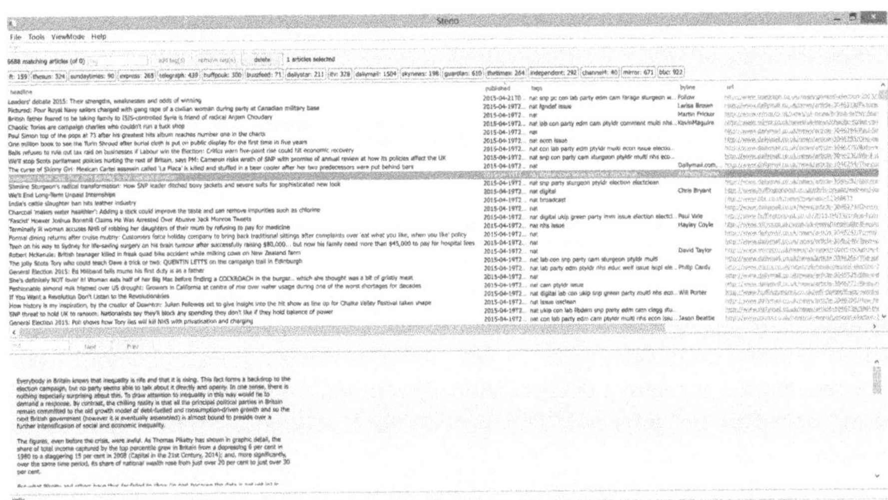

Figure 41: A screenshot of the application

Question 3: How should we index the news content?

The key to analysing bulk media content is applying effective methods of filtering and classification. For example, to find the proportion of news articles that contain references to political party leaders, one had to find all the articles that contain references to one or more leader. Steno does this by 'tagging' – in other words by adding descriptors to content to explain what it is or what it contains. Tagging is done through matching strings of text within articles, or on the basis of metadata attached to certain articles (i.e. text of byline or headline). Like keywords within news websites, each article could have a large number of tags attached.

Relatively simple tagging – marking all articles containing references to Nigel Farage, for example –was fairly straightforward. We used a 'Party Leaders' tagging script, which automatically tagged relevant articles according to whether it mentioned each leader. The 'Nigel Farage' script fragment was: '"Nigel Farage" OR Farage OR "Farage's" => TAG farage'. We also used more complex tagging, for example to study specific policy issues like health or welfare. Basing our definition of policy issues on the Ipsos-MORI Issues Index, we separated out fourteen areas of public policy and wrote scripts to capture all references to each of these areas. For something like defence and foreign policy, we identified a number of recurring terms, such as 'Trident', 'Ministry of Defence', 'foreign office', to indicate that the article was about defence or foreign policy. Tags were not mutually exclusive; many articles referenced multiple areas of policy. For Twitter we added abbreviations and hashtags to the tagging script. In this case, examples included #tridentrenewal and #scraptrident.

Question 4: Is the data clean?

No large data set will start out clean. Unexpected content will accidentally be included, and content incorrectly tagged. For our news content, we cleaned the data in two stages. First, we took out all the articles that had nothing to do with politics (sport, lifestyle, fashion, entertainment) by automatically tagging them, usually on the basis of URL content (e.g. /sport/), and deleting. This left us with the 'core' of political news articles that we conducted our analysis on, typically 7,000 – 8,000 articles each week. Second, we scanned through the lists of the lists of articles tagged for each policy issue in order to see if any had been tagged incorrectly. Some policy tags, we found, were highly accurate – immigration and housing, for example, could be tagged by a number of words and phrases that were fairly unambiguous. Certain other policy areas – particularly education and crime, policing and justice policy – were associated with more ambiguous terms (e.g. 'sentence', 'academy') that occasionally resulted in mis-tagged articles, which then needed to be untagged. This process took around 2-3 hours per weekly sample.

Question 5: What will the data tell us?

Large data sets, particularly of news content, can seem overwhelming. By developing hypotheses, and assessing the extent to which the data can provide the answer to these hypotheses, the initial stages of analysis become much more manageable. Having devised methods to collect, tag and clean the data we came up with a series of hypotheses to test. These were partly based on findings from previous studies of media and Twitter in election campaigns, and partly from our own experience of monitoring news sources and Twitter. For parliamentary candidates on Twitter, for example, we wanted to see if candidates used the platform for dialogue or, as found in previous studies, for broadcast (Graham, Jackson and Broersma, 2014). We wanted to discover what political issues candidates were tweeting about and the extent to which they were 'on message'.

We were keen to explore where candidates linked to from Twitter, and whether mainstream news media sources were their chief sources of authority.

What did Election Unspun 2015 discover?

Despite the plethora of media platforms available – or perhaps in response to the abundance of media – 2015 was a top down, stage-managed campaign. From the statements, tweets and party political material published by the parties, the party leaders, and the candidates it was clear what they wanted the campaign to be about. Both the Conservatives and Labour were eager to talk about the economy.

What was *not* being talked about was also interesting. Some 4 per cent of mainstream news coverage was about the environment. Low as this was, it was even lower on Twitter, where less than 3 per cent of tweets from political actors and influencers were about the environment. Not even the Green Party leader, Natalie Bennett, was closely associated with the environment. In the press, Bennett was associated with the environment less than she was with health, immigration, defence, or education.

Parliamentary candidates used Twitter during the campaign, but not as a way of creating more openness and dialogue with the public. They used it as a broadcast campaign platform. 59 per cent of candidates' tweets were re-tweets, generally of tweets by the party leader, the party press office or a senior party figure. When not re-tweeting, the candidates were telling followers that they were out campaigning: 'My pedometer says I walked 10.1 miles campaigning up and down in Islington and Battersea. Tired today *pours third cup of tea*', Emily Thornberry (@EmilyThornberry) tweeted on 22 April.

Certain politicians came out of the media campaign better than others. George Osborne had a highly successful election in media terms. More than a thousand articles in the mainstream media referenced Osborne (1,069). Many, particularly those published by newspapers, wrote about the Chancellor and the economy over which he presided in glowing terms. In a *Telegraph* article entitled 'George Osborne's "housing revolution" election pledge' the paper asked 'does the Chancellor agree with Mr Cameron that he would make a fine leader of the party and PM one day?' (Ross 2015).

By contrast Ed Miliband was lambasted and lampooned in much of the press. He was called a shameless hypocrite, a land-grabber, a tax avoider, a puppet of the unions and the SNP, and a flop, amongst other things. Some 5,374 articles were published in the mainstream press referencing Ed Miliband. Yet, there were also 46,756 tweets referring to the Labour leader, many of which reacted against the press coverage. Political influencers enjoyed and in some cases adopted the brief #milifandom craze and #JeSuisEd.

Beyond the politicking of the campaign itself, our data analysis also illuminated the relationship between different media platforms. By comparing the extent of coverage of issues over time, for example, it showed the symbiotic relationship between broadcast and Twitter. During each televised election debate, notably during the leaders' debate of 2 April, the challengers' debate of 16 April, and the *Question Time* of 30 April, political activity on Twitter shot up. The number of tweets published by political actors and influencers almost doubled on Thursday 2 April compared to the week previously – from an average of 23,000 to just under 45,000. Similar, if not quite as extreme, jumps happened on 16 and 30 April.

This intimate relationship between broadcast and Twitter is also apparent, to a lesser degree, on radio. When the Defence Secretary Michael Fallon re-asserted his claim that Ed Miliband would would 'stab Britain in the back' over Trident on BBC Radio 4's *Today* programme on Thursday 9 April, defence tweets more than tripled amongst political actors and influencers (2,034 tweets, compared to average 590 tweets per day).

Overall, the data we generated during the Election Unspun project, as well as giving us concrete information on certain quantitative measures (mentions of parties and their leaders, policy issues covered, and so on), also allowed us to draw some broader conclusions about the 2015 General Election campaign as a whole. First and foremost, 2015 was an extremely risk-averse campaign. Candidates on social media were on a very tight rein, and the major parties at various times restricted journalistic, never mind public, access to their walkabouts, photo-ops and factory visits. Second, the dominance of the economy as the main policy issue across all news outlets benefited the Conservatives, whose party messages (posters, interviews, official Twitter feeds) were very keen to remain focused on that issue.

Periodic swings of attention towards the NHS and housing were exceptions to the rule, while news coverage of immigration was curiously muted. The relatively small amount of coverage of immigration (despite some very high-profile incidents during the campaign) demonstrated another theme: the news issue agenda, itself very close to the parties' campaigning agenda, did not match public opinion during the campaign. Ipsos MORI's Issues Index, conducted throughout the campaign found the public viewed immigration as the first or second most important issue facing the country. In news coverage, it was fifth. The campaign was extremely personalised, with vicious criticism against the party leaders. Ed Miliband's treatment at the hands of *The Sun* and *The Daily Mail*, amongst others, was matched to an extent by *The Daily Mirror*'s personal attacks on Cameron. Even the party press offices' Twitter accounts indulged in taunting and insulting other party leaders.

Twitter, while following rather than leading the campaign agenda, did to a large extent play a role in investigating factual claims by parties, news sources, and journalists. These observations have wide implications for British electoral politics for the next electoral cycle at the very least, and perhaps much longer. If social media continues to occupy a significant role in political communication, official claims by both parties and news outlets will be critiqued and – perhaps regularly – debunked, undermining trust and authority, but perhaps preventing the more transparent examples of spin. If political parties continue to view the expanded digital media landscape as necessitating damage-limiting and risk-averse campaigning, a long procession of dull campaigns may lie before the British electorate. Regardless, there will be a continuing need to monitor how politics, the media and the electorate interact in British politics, and emerging practices of digital news analysis – such as that we employed in the Election Unspun project – will play a vital role.

Where next?

During the course of the General Election campaign we analysed more than 250,000 news articles and more than one million tweets. We could not have done this without digital analytics tools. The amount of digital content is only increasing. Whereas today we can justifiably still focus on national news sites and a sample of Twitter users, at the 2020 election there are likely to be many more platforms and channels we need to take into account.

We can build on our research model and start applying it to other elections within the UK and internationally, and specific policies, and other issues. How will the UK press cover the build-up to the UK's European referendum? How will the future of the BBC be shaped by political actors and influencers in the lead up to Charter Renewal in 2016? Perhaps, if we can enhance the software enough, we could even take a shot at analysing the media and the November 2016 US elections.

References

Bruns, Axel and Liang, Yuxian E (2012) 'Tools and methods for capturing Twitter data during natural disasters' in *First Monday*, Vol. 17/4, available at http://firstmonday.org/htbin/cgiwrap/bin/ojs/index.php/fm/article/view/3937/3193, accessed 24 July 2015

Gaffney, Devin and Puschmann, Cornelius (2014) 'Data collection on Twitter' in Weller et al (eds) *Twitter and Society*. New York: Peter Lang Publishing

Graham, Todd, Jackson, Dan and Broersma, Marcel (2014) 'New platform, old habits? Candidates' use of Twitter during the 2010 British and Dutch general election campaigns' in *New Media and Society*, August 2014, available at http://nms.sagepub.com/content/16/3/434.full.pdf+html, accessed 18 August 2015

Moore, Martin et al (2015) *Election Unspun: Political Parties, the Press, and Twitter During the 2015 UK Election Campaign*. London: Media Standards Trust, available at http://mediastandardstrust.org/wp-content/uploads/2015/07/Election_Unspun_July_20151.pdf, accessed 18 August 2015

Ramsay, Gordon (2014) *How Newspapers Covered Press Regulation after Leveson*. London: Media Standards Trust, available at http://mediastandardstrust.org/wp-content/uploads/2014/09/Final-Draft-v1-040914.pdf, accessed 28 July 2015

Ross, Tim, (2015) 'George Osborne's "housing revolution" election pledge', in *The Daily Telegraph*, 4 April, available at http://www.telegraph.co.uk/news/general-election-2015/11515683/George-Osbornes-housing-revolution-election-pledge.html, accessed 15 July 2015

Election data v journalism basics

A cardinal rule of journalism is to always trust your source. No less is true of data journalism, writes Megan Lucero of *The Times*, who ignored data from unreliable polls and explained the election using trusted data instead

Introduction

'I don't trust the polls,' he said. 'There is no way anyone should be making seat projections from this data.' This is the start of a conversation that would come to play over and over in my head in the wake of the Conservative victory in the last General Election. As we know now, the polls had prepared the public to expect Labour and the Conservatives to be neck-and-neck. Although shocked like everyone else in the newsroom, my shock was of a different nature. I turned to my team, 'we were right,' I said. Still in disbelief, this phrase kept repeating within our team, 'we were right.'

That initial conversation started to play in my memory. It was four months before the election. My small team was sat together making plans for 7 May. In the room were Stefano Ceccon, machine learning and data mining PhD, Nicola Hughes, programmer / journalist, myself, and my election hire Zsolt Kiss, formerly of NatCen. We had a decision to make about our model. It had already been worked on for several months and was extensive. To build it we put together survey data, constituency characteristics, even local election data in order to predict the election outcome. However it became clear that our prediction model – like others – was centred around intention data. The team discussed how the samples were small, confidence intervals were wide and the skewed predictions at constituency level were alarming. Stefano and Zsolt, the architects of the model, said it plain and simple: we cannot continue with such uncertainty and we certainly can't make seat projections.

Building a new model

The decision was easy to make but immediately forced us to change our approach. We had been regularly using polling data for analysis ahead of the election since the summer of 2014. Voter intention data was a large part of our trend analysis. In November 2014 we were able to report an unprecedented shift in party allegiance. We revealed that 44 per cent of Britain's voters did not plan to vote for the same party as they did in 2010. We detailed where the rising Ukip voters were coming from and where the Lib Dem exodus was going.

Sticking to our decision meant analyses like this would be the furthest extent of our use of polling data. Anything beyond big picture analysis was just out of the question. While we knew we didn't trust the polls at constituency level, we knew there was a chance the election could end up playing out in line with them. Across the industry, interactives with the polls were already being published and many had started making seat projections.

There was a great deal of pressure for us to compete with other papers. Yet the team didn't doubt Stefano and Zsolt – not even for a moment. We stood by the statistics and we stood by their judgement. Right then and there, we decided we would not make seat projections, we would find another way to cover this election.

For all that came out of May 2015, our team was reminded that no matter how high the stakes, the essence of journalism cannot be forgotten. We must critically examine what is trusted; investigate even when it is not easy; and be honest about what we find. Yesterday, today and tomorrow, this will always be true. The difficulties in the data challenged us to be creative about how to cover and explain the election after the results came in. Once we ditched the prediction model, we pushed ourselves to only use data we could trust.

By stepping back and relying on this basic guide, we realised the solution was very simple, almost too simple. Publicly available information about constituencies – actual results and data coming from the Census and Labour Force Survey – was all we trusted but it was all we needed. We realised we could use this data to explain what kinds of people made up the constituencies that go to one party versus another.

We knew it was far simpler than our planned prediction model but it was something no one had done before. To do this, we decided to use a statistical technique called a 'classification tree' – a machine-learning model that looks for the best predictors of a certain outcome.

In our case, we would be looking for the factors that influenced the winning party in each constituency. The predictors we selected for the algorithm to choose from included education level, unemployment rate, region, gender and age distributions, density, household tenure, ethnicity, size and number of businesses. We tested the algorithm on previous results to create a mock tree in order to see what we could expect on the night. With this simple preparation, all that was left was to drop in the actual results and let the algorithm do the work.

We got to the office at 10pm on election day, just as the exit poll was released. We had planned to find a story on the viable coalition possibilities while we were waiting for actual results. That was before the exit poll of course; before we felt the weight of that decision we made months ago. Now all that mattered was to focus on the work we prepared – work that didn't involve polling data, work that would be crucial in telling a distinct picture of this election.

We stayed up throughout the night and ran the tree as the results came in. We watched the tree grow as Scotland finished announcing results and marginal seats were held or swung. While the shock of such unexpected results swept the newsroom, our classification tree held strong and calculated the factors that influenced the seats, unchanged by inaccurate polling or predictions. We edited the tree, designed it and published it within half an hour after the final results.

This was a huge win for us. For the very first time in the history of the paper, we used computing to produce a first analysis of the election ahead of our renowned columnists. Data led the coverage; data that was free of polling vice. The risk we took in holding our ground had paid off and we could proudly say that we helped *The Times* retain its motto as 'the paper of record'.

We found that in the fight to win constituencies, the real battle came down to housing. The saying 'an Englishman's house is his castle' comes to mind here. The vast majority of constituencies with low levels of council housing went to the Conservatives. In the remaining constituencies, Labour won seats in areas of high unemployment and lower education levels. Conservatives took the rest – except in Scotland where the SNP now dominates.

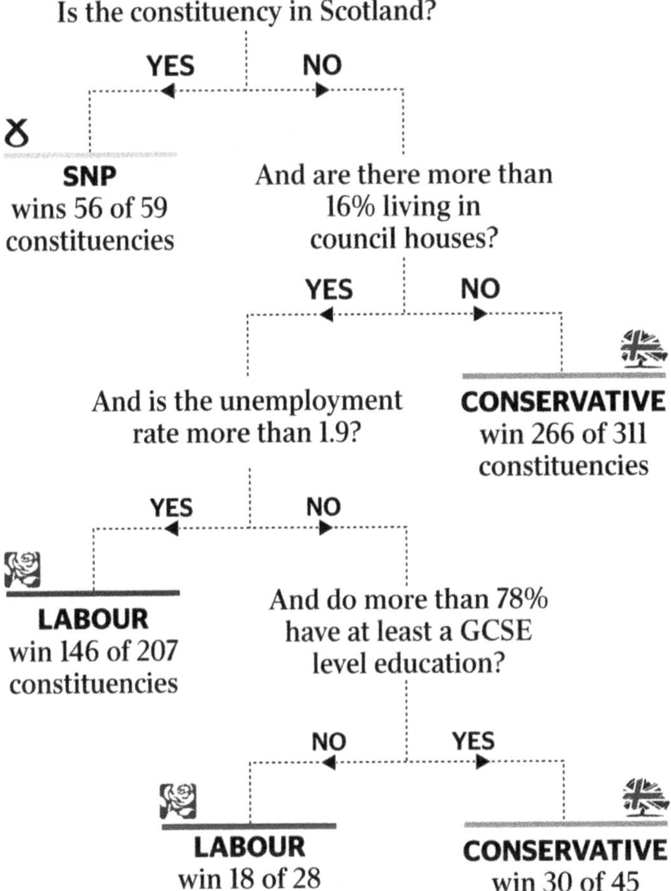

Figure 42: The UK Divided. Sources: Census, Nomis and National Records of Scotland. Elections results via The Press Association. *Courtesy* The Times *Data Team.*

Swing seats

We decided to look into the swing seats as well, yet the only party with an interesting swing dynamic was the Liberal Democrats. While Labour lost Scotland to the SNP and the Conservatives barely moved, the Lib Dems were decimated. We ran the same model but in this case only looked at 2010 Lib Dem constituencies and then looked at which were held or swung. They lost their Scottish seats to the SNP, their younger constituencies to Labour and their older seats with more big businesses to the Conservatives.

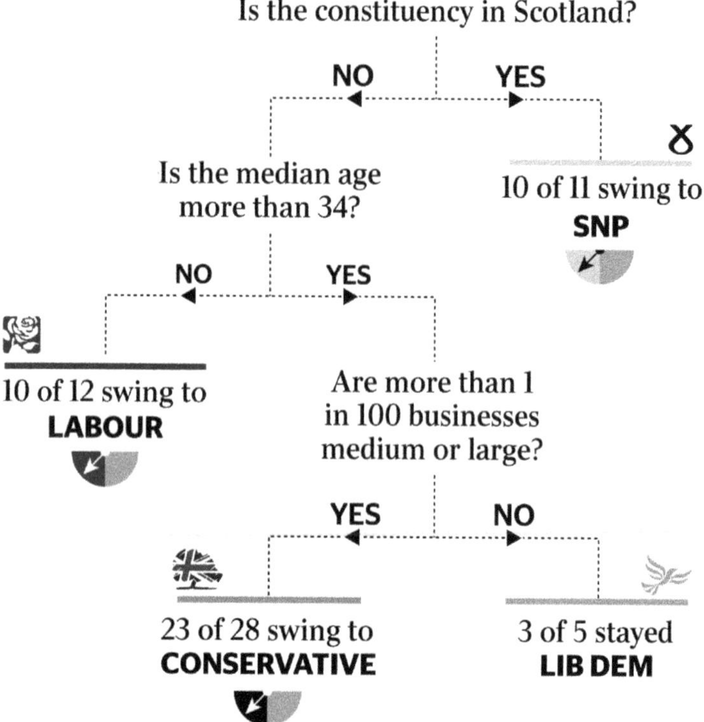

Figure 43: Liberal Democrat seats lost and held. Sources: Census, Nomis and National Records of Scotland. Elections results via The Press Association. *Courtesy* The Times *Data Team.*

All our data parsing and prototyping was written in R Software, using the 'rpart' library for building the tree and the 'rpart.plot' library for visualising the output. *The Times* graphics team then adjusted the R output to *Times* style to produce static graphics.

We made the bold decision to publish static graphics during the election while everyone else had interactives. The focus was on getting the content out quickly and simply rather than making it move. In this case, as in many, making it clickable would not make it any more insightful. Whenever we communicate data, the ultimate goal is to make the complex simple for the reader. To us, this is data journalism in its truest form. This is how we do data journalism at *The Times.*

Nothing new

Data journalism is nothing new. It's been around since John Snow's London cholera revelations and Florence Nightingale's presentation of data that changed hospital sanitation after the Crimean War. It also has a long history at *The Times* as well. One of my favourite pieces from *The Times* archive is a piece published in 1868, where the paper contextualised the Census. None of this is new. Making sense of complicated strings of information for readers is as old as journalism itself.

Conclusion

For many, the result of the election, and the shock of the polls, was unsettling. Data journalism is the new wave right? How did it fail us? The truth is, it didn't. Humans did and can and will in the future if we don't lend an analytical eye to our work. The polling industry erred in their calculations but more importantly, humans erred in blindly trusting them. Data journalism is not moving graphics, it is not every press release thrown into a chart, it is the use of data in journalism – an industry that must scrutinise, investigative and strive for truth. Like in any kind of journalism, complacency is the enemy.

When the team started at *The Times* in 2013, we decided to challenge the 'data journalism is nothing new' motto. We as a team decided we wanted to reinvent it. We knew we wanted to use data in a way that had never been done before for a newspaper. We wanted to integrate computing into the investigation process in order to find and chase stories in a way a human could never do without a computer. Armed with a statistician, a programmer, a data visualiser and a journalist, this is how *The Times* and *The Sunday Times* plan to face the future. Nicola Hughes, a former data journalist for this team, most aptly coined our work when saying the data journalism we do is not 'on the web' but instead is 'of the web'. The future of data journalism, and I believe journalism itself, is not about putting the story or the data on the internet, it is using the fabric of it to find stories.

The election taught the journalism world this is needed. And now we know it can be done. This is just the start.

Section 3: Meeting points

Tom Felle

For some newsrooms the transition to digital represents the beginning of the end. A perfect storm of collapsing circulation, decreasing advertising and an inability to compete online means they are (*if* they are even still printing) simply managing decline. For a few nimble innovators, however, we are just at the end of the beginning of the first wave of digital innovation in journalism. But getting traditional news hounds to work collaboratively with developers, statisticians and other tech-savvy gurus from very different workplace cultures doesn't always succeed. Likewise, getting developers and non-journalists to understand newsroom culture – and deadlines – can also prove challenging as well all know.

In *So you found a unicorn – now what?* Zara Rahman writes that a major culture change is needed in newsrooms to fully integrate digital and data-driven teams. Equally, news managers need to understand the processes involved in data-driven reporting, visualisation and development. As she says:

> *'Realistic expectations need to be set for what different people with varying skill sets can and can't do. Giving someone a big dataset and asking them to 'find a story' might be fruitful, or it might take a long time, and have very little outcome. Equally, a dataset needs to be in a certain state before it can be analysed, and depending on its size, this can take a long time. On both sides of the equation, what might seem to be a small task can take a frustratingly long time, and understanding and being prepared for this can be a big help.'*

Kathryn Corrick gives a fascinating insight into the power of open data and websites that aggregate financial and company information when investigating company finances and government spending. Her not-to-be-missed chapter – *Follow the money: investigative journalism using data* – offers some really useful tips for would-be investigative data journalists. While tracking down corporate information is never a walk in the park, she lists a number of digital tools to make the job easier. As she writes:

> *'...much work has been done for understanding and making UK government spending data more usable in five years. And if open data keeps gathering pace globally, as we have begun to see, then we might expect similar tools to be appearing elsewhere. Whilst the stories such data potentially stores may not be as big as Watergate or Edward Snowden's leaks, the ability to use company, government and spending data to fact check and make straightforward investigations, without the need for specialist data or coding skills, is now easier than ever. Similar moves are also happening in the non-governmental organisation and third sectors, where organisations such as IATI, USAID, DfID, the World Bank, OpenBRF and Publish What You Fund are leading the way in aid and sustainable development spending transparency. But data by itself is never the story, only with context can it be used to create information, insight and may be that scoop.'*

Her simple advice: follow the money!

In *Recalculating the newsroom: the rise of the journo-coder?* Liz Hannaford's original research looks at how digital teams operate in two case studies at the BBC and the *Financial Times*. Journalists working in digital teams at these news organisations are highly specialised, she found, with most possessing some coding skills though journalists and developers see themselves as separate from each other (unlike in the US where journalist-coders are common) though things may be changing, as she notes:

> *'Programmers and journalists see themselves as having separate roles and skills - albeit with some overlap. But it seems likely that as more journalism courses teach computational and coding skills more young journalists with these technical skills will be working in newsrooms and could challenge existing models and work practices. We might also see more students with a technology background undertaking journalism training in order to gain jobs in a newsroom. Certainly, the developers interviewed for this study described newsroom jobs as more 'fun' than traditional programming roles in, for example, banks. It is worth noting that only a minority of the developers interviewed for this study had a computer science degree. The others had arts or humanities degrees (like the journalists) but had developed a passion for programming that they had nurtured informally.... Perhaps the barrier between journalist and technologist is not as solid as we might think.'*

The theme of collaboration between developer coders and reporters is again taken up by *the Guardian*'s data projects editor Helena Bengtsson in *The difficult art of collaborating*. Bengtsson is a self-taught data pioneer who worked for Sweden's national broadcaster before her move to London. Simple practicalities like getting digital teams of journalists and developers to sit together – rather than journalists in newsrooms and developers in IT departments – is a first step, she says.

'So, for me, my life as a data journalist has very much changed the last couple of years. Collaboration is needed for both visualising and analysis, and the key point is that access is crucial. In my experience, I have to be able to lift my head and talk to the person I'm working with. It can't be somebody at a different department, in a different place, he/she has to be right there, following in the daily work.'

Finally, while newsrooms are going to increasingly need to look beyond shorthand and owning a bicycle as essential qualities in a would-be apprentices, the Pulitzer Prize winning journalist-turned-journalism professor Steve Doig warns against journalism graduates turning into developers. Sure, digital skillsets are important, but the basics of journalism – a nose for a good story and a little literary ability – still go a long way. As he says in his contribution *To code or not to code?*, newsrooms need a variety of skillsets – including traditional reporting skills:

'The ability to write useful computer code is a special skill that is critically needed in modern multimedia news organizations. Journalism students need to know that such tools exist and that the ability to use them is valuable. Journalism programs with the right instructors should offer advanced data journalism courses as electives, or at least aim interested students at courses in the computer science department. But I believe that the argument that all journalists need to be coders is utopian at best and arguably unfair to the majority of students who want to develop other kinds of story-telling skills. Every newsroom needs people like me. But a newsroom filled with people like me couldn't function.'

Well said Steve.

So you found a unicorn – now what?

News organisations need to consider how to integrate data reporters, developers and coders - who often come from a very different culture - into their 'traditional' newsrooms if they want to succeed, writes Zara Rahman

Introduction

The rise of data-driven journalism is relatively well-charted. Major newsrooms all around the world boast 'data journalists', 'journo-coders', and/or major graphics and design departments. But how does this change in the way stories can be found and put together integrate within the traditional newsroom? Here, I argue that a major cultural shift in how those working in a newsroom perceive technology is necessary to successfully integrate data-driven storytelling into a newsroom's repertoire.

So you have a data team – now what?

Earlier this year, I attended the International Journalism Festival in Perugia, Italy. School of Data, in collaboration with the European Journalism Centre, have been running the data journalism track of the IJF for the past four years, and similar to previous years, the sessions were popular among those wanting to boost their data skills. But it felt like the community weren't there so much to hear technical explanations of how to use certain tools in their reporting, or how to tell their first data-driven story. Conversations centred more on **what comes next**. Once the data team have been hired (under whatever label) – how do these newcomers to the newsroom actually support better journalism?

The step of truly integrating technical approaches together with what might be known as more 'traditional' journalism is the one that seems to be causing the most hurdles. Put more simply: it is asking a set of people who have a completely different skill set to ones that are usually found in a newsroom to enter this challenging environment, and somehow integrate with their peers.

New workflows are needed, new forms of collaboration, and, in a way, new sets of values around what makes 'good' journalism.

Managing expectations

In traditional journalism courses, data skills have not been taught, and this means that most (but by no means all) journalists have relatively low levels of data literacy. This is changing; more and more universities, especially those in the US, have been starting to have dedicated courses on 'computational journalism', or computer-assisted reporting, for example. One of the most fundamental issues that arises with those with low levels of data literacy is **not knowing what is possible** – and this lack of understanding of how data-driven approaches can complement or support work naturally presents some communications issues. Sometimes this can be in terms of technical requirements given that are wildly unrealistic, or people not knowing what to actually ask for when making technical requests.

In all respects realistic expectations need to be set for what different people with varying skill sets can and can't do. Giving someone a big dataset and asking them to 'find a story' might be fruitful, or it might take a long time, and have very little outcome. Equally, a dataset needs to be in a certain state before it can be analysed, and depending on its size, this can take a long time. On both sides of the equation, what might seem to be a small task can take a frustratingly long time, and understanding and being prepared for this can be a big help.

Journalists who code, or coders who tell stories?

Building a team with a diverse set of skillsets and perspectives can be a huge boost to supporting new forms of storytelling. People with high levels of technical understanding may well not be the best people to communicate a story that they have found – and this is where the 'traditional' journalists come in. Similarly, someone with a low level of data literacy is unlikely to be the most efficient person to gain insights from a large dataset, even though they might be willing to learn. Pairing up these varying personas – a storyteller and an analyst for example – can bring new perspectives to a story. Finding people who are accustomed to working with people from different backgrounds to their own might facilitate this process, indicating that they are more accustomed to working with people not like themselves; just another reason for building a diverse team.

An indicator of how these roles have been mixed can be observed through groups focused much more on the data and technology side of things who have moved into more data journalism related work. Take, for example, Code for South Africa (Code4SA), an organisation of civic coders, aimed at 'connecting people to government' through effective use of technology, and supporting civil society. They boast an impressive repertoire of data journalism related projects such as the 'Living Wage Calculator' (2015), which allows the user to input the amount that they are paying their domestic worker and see how it compares to the living wage for that individual. From its launch in April 2015 to the time of writing in July 2015, more than 12,000 people completed their survey, and thus created the biggest dataset ever on this topic; perhaps, then, providing fodder for further in-depth stories on the topic.

Code4SA are just one example of how previously distinct roles of journalist and technologist have merged, and there are many more. There has been a big rise in recent years of initiatives aimed at teaching journalists how to code or use data more effectively in their work, but alongside this, effective collaborations between those with strong writing and storytelling skills and those with coders or data analysts are also needed.

Success stories

There seem to be a few common trends among successfully integrated teams. Firstly, an acknowledgement at all levels within the newsroom that technical literacy and technical skills can open the door to new forms of storytelling. This could manifest itself in ways such as the data team being invited to regular editorial meetings, just as the 'traditional' journalists are – or even in the way that they are referred to, with 'journalist' in their job title.

Secondly, newsroom managers need to recognise that the data journalists aren't there to solve everyday technical issues, even though their technical know-how might mean that they are able to. Nowadays, a newsroom has all sorts of digital demands that add an extra layer of technical complexity to a regular organisation, such as publishing online, or having a suitable content management system (CMS). In addition to that, there might be other more regular technical issues that arise – from digital security practices to websites going down, or bugs appearing.

In most cases, though, addressing these issues simply doesn't lie within the mandate of a data journalist – and though it might be quicker if they're sitting at the desk just round the corner, this can seriously undermine their journalistic responsibilities. In much the same way that any random native English speaker wouldn't be asked to copy edit a piece before publishing purely on merit of their language skills, an individual who has a certain technical skill set is not necessarily the go-to person for all of the problems that involve digital technologies. Respecting the diversity of skills that lie within digital technologies is crucial for many reasons. For the data journalist or team in question, it gives them the time and space they need to do the job they signed up to do – telling stories with data. For their peers, it can send a clear signal that the data journalists are not simply the IT department or the system administrators with a different name, but that they are peers in the field of journalism. Knowing that they are there to go to with ideas or questions can (and should) bring up all sorts of collaborations that can make a story that much stronger.

Thirdly, news organisations need to prioritise communication, and understand that it might not be that easy. For those who aren't sure what benefits data-driven journalism could bring to a story they are working on, flagging it up as early as possible with the data or graphics team leaves space for new approaches to the story. For those with technical skills, sharing knowledge can be a good way of flagging to colleagues areas that they are interested in, as well as bringing the broader benefit of boosting data literacy across the newsroom.

Avoiding jargon in communication can be important too, and providing spaces where questions are welcomed rather than seen as a sign of a lack of knowledge. One example of this can be seen in the regular 'learning lunches' that Noah Veltman, a developer placed within the BBC for a year as part of the Knight-Mozilla OpenNews fellowship, held on a regular basis (Veltman, 2013). His colleagues were invited to drop in and learn about technical topics they might have heard referred to, and the sessions were well-documented for future reference.

To a degree, this means that those who really do understand the benefits of a data-driven approach are left with the task of advocating internally within their own newsrooms to make changes to age-old processes, and incorporate new forms of storytelling into their work. While perhaps the onus shouldn't necessarily be on them to change these practices, pragmatically speaking, they are most likely to be the best placed to do this job, and the outcomes will, ultimately, benefit their positions as well as the newsroom culture as a whole.

Getting some help from the outside

Relying on all of these changes to be internal can be hard, though, and this has been recognised on a number of external levels. One common way of boosting a newsroom's technical literacy, especially with regards to data-driven stories, has been through fellowships. Typically, fellowships provide funding for an individual (or a number of individuals) to work in an environment they wouldn't otherwise have access to – and vice versa. It puts someone into a workplace environment unused to their set of skills.

One example is the Knight-Mozilla OpenNews fellowships (OpenNews, 2015), which have been running since 2012, and as a result, to date 26 fellows have been placed within newsrooms around the world. They've built up an established and well-reputed online and offline home, too, with data journalists and coders from around the 'news nerd' community sharing lessons, tools, and writing detailed explainer posts on technology implemented in newsrooms on their online blog, Source (https://source.opennews.org). Tellingly, many of the biggest and most successful newsrooms who are integrating data-driven storytelling into their work, often encourage their coders to write blog posts on the platform. Offline, they run a small, US-based conference called SRCCON (SRCCON 2015), which brings together said news nerds for a two day, in person event. Their work spans providing targeted individual support to the fellows, alongside building and supporting the overall community.

Their efforts at making the fellowships a viable work opportunity for people from all sorts of backgrounds, as well as a variety of skill sets, really speaks to their overall mandate of 'amplifying journalism code'. Unlike many other fellowship programmes, they provide monetary supplements for child care, housing, and health insurance, thus opening up the space for people who would otherwise be excluded from such an opportunity. Crucially, they recognise that **diversity of all kinds can hugely benefit newsrooms**, bringing a more intersectional understanding that goes beyond simply skill sets, or professional experience.

Another external initiative aimed at bringing together communities of journalism and coders is the international 'Hacks Hackers' network, a 'grassroots network of journalists and technologists, brought together to rethink the future of news and information' (HacksHackers.com, 2015). Hacks Hackers chapters all over the world organise regular in-person meet ups and events to bring these communities together to learn from each other and build connections that otherwise might be difficult to do internally. Hacks Hackers meet ups also provide fertile ground for recruitment, providing an accessible 'way in' for those who otherwise might not come into contact with journalists to such a degree. At Hacks Hackers Berlin, for example, a job presentation section forms a regular part of the meet up, and many people have found new positions through coming to the meet ups.

If the 'unicorns' in a newsroom are struggling to do the job they signed up to do, encouraging them to spend time with others in similar positions in other newsrooms can provide a strong sense of community that will undoubtedly help address theses issues. Similarly, providing a space where journalists who have not been exposed to so many data-driven stories can go and meet the people behind successful collaborations might also provide inspiration for their work. If those in a newsroom are serious about integrating data-driven storytelling within their work, contributing as active members of this growing community is crucial.

It's not the technology, it's the people

On a more general level, there needs to be a basic understanding that what we're moving towards here is a major cultural shift in the way that journalism has been done. Though the inherent goal of journalism has stayed the same, the methods have changed. This means that people with different skillsets and areas of expertise are coming to the sector, and that the sector (and those in it) need to adjust to welcome and really integrate them into the storytelling process.

Even the most technically skilled individuals in the world aren't going to be able to make a difference in a newsroom if their work isn't valued within the newsroom culture. Data journalism is made up of a diverse set of skills, from expert designers, to statisticians, to coders and more. We're beyond the point at which someone can be labelled as 'technical' and tasked with 'technology' in the newsroom. We need to recognise that there are varying levels of technological and data-related skills needed for any newsroom to keep up in the digital world, and embrace those changes.

References

Code for South Africa, available online at http://code4sa.org, accessed on 29 July 2015

Knight-Mozilla OpenNews, available online at http://opennews.org/, accessed on 29 July 2015

Living Wage Calculator, built by Code4SA, available online at http://living-wage.co.za/, accessed on 29 July 2015

SRCCON, available online at http://srccon.org/, accessed on 29 July 2015

Veltman, Noah (2013) 'Learning Lunches', available online at http://schoolofdata.org/learning-lunches/, accessed on 29 July 2015

Follow the money: investigative journalism using data

Kathryn Corrick assesses the power of open data and websites that aggregate financial and company information when investigating company finances and government spending, and offers some useful tips for would-be investigative data journalists

Introduction

When Ben Bradlee, executive editor of *The Washington Post* from 1968 to 1991, was asked of the lasting legacy for Watergate, he replied: 'Follow the money' (*The New York Times*, 1997). The phrase, made famous by the 1974 film *All The President's Men* telling the story of the Nixon Presidential scandal, has been a rally cry and methodology for investigative journalists from there on in. But it's not just investigative journalists who need to understand where money and the relationships between business, government, third sector organisations or individuals lie. Often the most straightforward articles require basic information or facts about a business to give context.

Over the last five years a large amount of government, company and spending data has become openly available globally and a number useful tools and services to access this data have come online. What's more some of these services have begun doing some investigative journalism themselves to show what's possible or to scratch an itch. Company website, LinkedIn and Wikipedia searches are useful but they do not always reveal key data or enable systematic data queries. National governments hold registers of companies for tax and other purposes. Wikipedia has a list of 197 country company registers at https://en.wikipedia.org/wiki/List_of_company_registers.

In the UK Companies House holds this data. Its database holds more than 170 million records (Companies House, 2015), which can be explored, for free at https://beta.companieshouse.gov.uk/ or via their API at https://developer.companieshouse.gov.uk/api/docs/. Companies House data includes a filing history, where appointments and terminations of directors, full accounts and annual reports are available to download as PDFs. As an example, PDFs of Marks and Spencer PLC's submitted files can be downloaded for free currently back to March 1995: https://beta.companieshouse.gov.uk/company/00214436/filing-history.

Electronic data of filed accounts is available as a daily download at http://download.companieshouse.gov.uk/en_accountsdata.html formatted as XBRL or iXBRL (eXtensible Business Reporting Language is a freely available and global standard for exchanging business information). XBRL allows the expression of semantic meaning commonly required in business reporting. Currently about 60 per cent of Companies House filed accounts are submitted electronically (Companies House, 2015).

Whilst searching the national company registers may be an obvious place to start, many countries have not made this data freely available, and not all companies are named in ways you'd expect, or have multiple holdings and subsidiaries across jurisdictions. Registers can sometimes be held at state rather than national level - as with the US and Mexico. Even if the register is publicly available it may not include data such as directors, latest accounts or shareholders. One way to check if a national government has made company data available publicly is to go to http://registries.opencorporates.com. Those researching companies in the UK, Denmark and Norway are the most likely to find information they are looking for.

Where else to begin?

Founded by former journalist Chris Taggart, OpenCorporates.com have an open database of more than 85 million companies in the world, which is continually being updated and added to. You can access the data via their online search engine, or through their API at http://opencorporates.com. Data can be searched by company name, address, number or director's name and filtered by fields such as jurisdiction, company status and company type. Similarly named companies and both active and inactive directors are also listed and many pieces of data are links which can be used for cross-referencing or further exploration.

Crucially, where data is available, search results show how a company connects to a wider corporate grouping. Such a group will highlight holdings, non-profit companies, subsidiaries and offices in different jurisdictions. A list of corporate groupings collected to date can be found at https://opencorporates.com/corporate_groupings. For example, Google's corporate grouping has 60 companies known by OpenCorporates (Open Corporates, 2015), which include Base Steel Ltd in the UK, Get Found on Google Inc. in Michigan and Google Energy Private Ltd in India. Disney, by comparison, has 667 companies listed in its grouping (Open Corporates, 2015). Such relationships are often complex and obscure how citizens often understand a corporation as a single entity.

For example, Amazon paid £11.9m in UK tax in 2014 from a recorded profit of £34.4m of its British-based Amazon.co.uk limited subsidiary. Yet the

Amazon group posted a strong UK sales performance with overall takings rising 14 per cent to £5.3bn representing 9.4 per cent of its global sales. As *the Guardian* explained:

> *'As in previous years, the UK accounts make clear Amazon.co.uk Limited claims not to sell to British online shoppers: instead the group's Luxembourg arm fulfils that role. Amazon.co.uk Limited's much more modest turnover of £679m comes from providing "fulfilment and corporate support services" to Luxembourg'* (*the Guardian*, 2015).

Amazon's UK sales, as well as those from Germany, France and other European countries, are taken through its Luxemburg company Amazon EU Sarl. Confusingly, Amazon EU Sarl reported a loss last year through the use of other company structures to move profits from Amazon EU Sarl back to the US (Guardian, 2015). As this shows, beginning to gather data on these subsidiaries and their relationships (and there is a long way to go in doing so) makes it a little easier to follow the money.

To show the power of this data OpenCorporates worked with data visualisation company Kiln to produce an online interactive map showing a selection of corporations (Open Corporates, 2015).

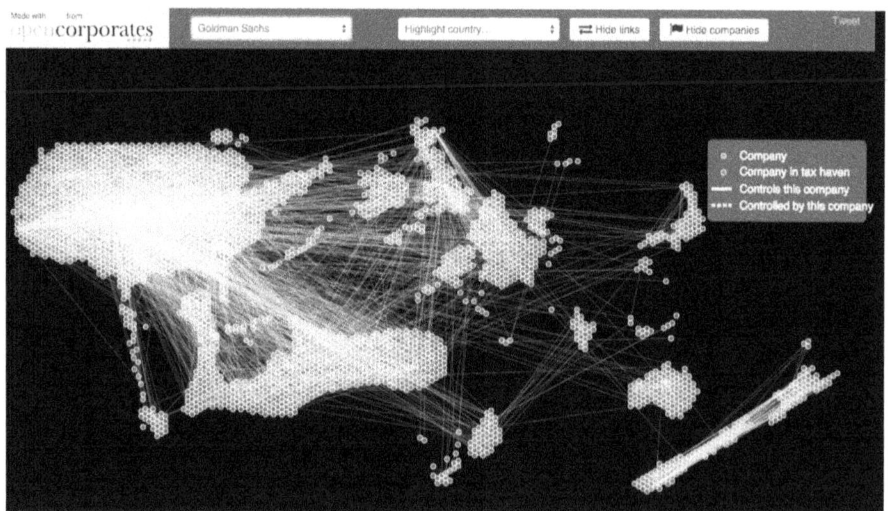

Figure 44: Source: Data visualisation of Goldman Sachs company holdings by location, and chains of control, screen shot, Open Corporates, 2015, https://opencorporates.com/viz/financial/index.html#goldman

Companies in the investigation included Goldman Sachs, Morgan Stanley and JP Morgan. The visualisation gave a point on a map for each holding, which could then be hovered over to see its relationship (chain of control) and connections with the rest of the group and with its headquartered offices. OpenCorporates differentiated companies located in tax havens as well as who controlled each company. The map for Goldman Sachs, for example, showed that the number of subsidiaries Goldman had registered in the tax haven of the

Cayman Islands - population 58,435 – was more than any other country outside the US and only half that of their subsidiaries registered in the US – population 318.9 million. Additionally the control chain of companies was sometimes found to be 15 deep.

Less sophisticated network and tree maps are available for a number of company groupings, such as this tree map of The Gap's known companies: https://opencorporates.com/companies/us_de/2157877/network. To take this further OpenCorporates launched Map The Banks (http://mapthebanks.com/) - a global data collection and crowd sourced project to collect, publish and link banking regulator data with company data on banks. Their rationale: 'The financial crisis cost society over $10tn. Before we can disrupt the industry, we need to understand what it looks like.' (Map the Banks, 2015)

As these visualisations of financial firms begins to show, tax is only one issue such company group data helps reveal. It can also show the nature of a less well-known company's business and understand the real scale of a corporation's activities. This may seem rather innocuous and abstract until applied to an industry such as oil, where ownership and management of land and resources, the environment as well as the value chain, national economies and politics are combined.

Consultancy and publisher, OpenOil aims to make 'the world's oil contracts available at a click' (Open Oil, 2015). They have so far collected 732 contracts across 72 countries, which can be searched and downloaded using their wiki at http://repository.openoil.net. In partnership with OpenCorporates, they have investigated the network of oil companies and contracts in Nigeria and BP's corporate network (Open Oil 2015). Their Nigeria network map (Open Oil, 2015) shows primary production contracts awarded to oil companies by the government, secondary service contracts awarded to producing companies to service companies and companies involved in the oil industry in Nigeria. For each data point in this network they provide a reference to the data source. This can either be a website link to a company report, government website or media article; or a link to a document they have extracted from the Nigerian company register.

For contracts on which they have data they include: the dollar value of the contract; the field and license area relevant to the contract; the announcement date; and duration of the contract. For production sharing contracts they also include the percentage share of the contract held by each company (Open Oil, 2015) OpenOil have released some of their data (which goes beyond BP and Nigeria) as an API (Open Oil, 2015), which could be used for further investigations, to answer questions like: 'who holds exploration licenses in Brazil?' Another data source for those looking to follow the money within the extractive industries is Resource Contracts (beta) http://www.resourcecontracts.org/#documents which has 374 documents (mostly contracts) across 53 countries. Whilst less extensive than OpenOil, some of the documents date back to 1958.

These contracts remind us that the biggest relationships companies often have is with government, and that citizens taxes go to provide services, supplied by both the public and private sector. But before putting in a Freedom of Information request to understand a national government's spending or budget it's, again, worth discovering if this data is already available.

Since 2013 the Web Foundation have annually surveyed 86 countries on their publishing of open data. You can view country summaries as an interactive graphic at http://www.opendatabarometer.org/report/analysis/explorer.html where, amongst other indicators, it shows whether budget, spending and company data are available.

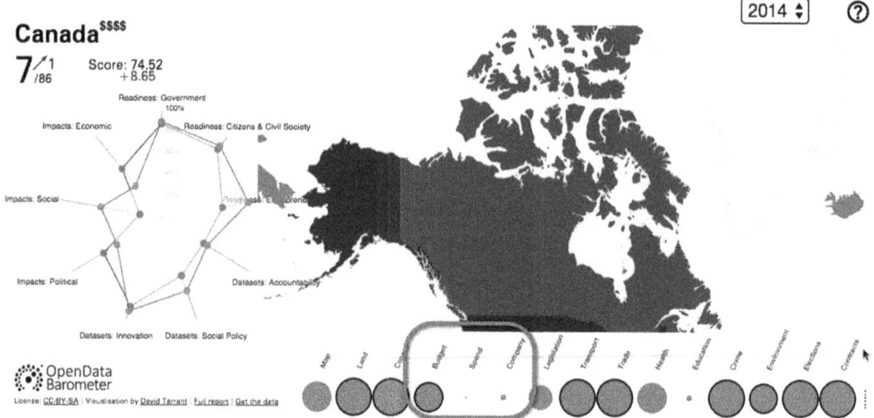

Figure 45: Graphic shows Open Data Barometer Country Explorer for Canada, source: www.opendatabarometer.org/report/analysis/explorer.html, David Tarrant, Creative Commons, Share Alike (CC-BY-SA)

In the UK, a prime ministerial letter in May 2010 outlined requirements for the publication of expenditure as open data (Cameron, 2010). As well as the publication of all new items of central government spending over £25,000 and all items of local government spending over £500, it included the request to publish contracts and tenders. But be warned, how such data should be published was not part of the requirements. This has meant that publication and format vary by authority and department from PDFs through to machine-readable data. One of the first sites to exploit the release of spending data in the UK was a project called 'Where Does My Money Go?' in 2010 (Where Does My Money Go?, 2015), run by the Open Knowledge Foundation and supported by Channel 4's digital investment fund, 4IP. The project visualised macro departmental and regional spending, as well as calculating roughly how much an individual's income went on tax and where it was proportionally spent.

WHERE DOES MY MONEY GO?

Showing you where your taxes get spent

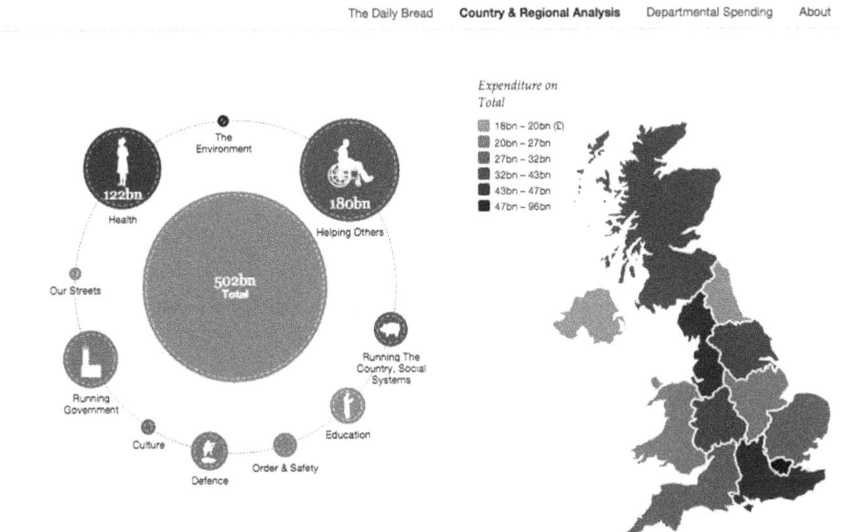

Figure 46: UK country and regional spending analysis. Source: Where Does My Money Go, http://wheredoesmymoneygo.org/bubbletree-map.html#/~/total, Creative Commons license CC-BY 3.0

The project proved to be popular globally and morphed into the larger grassroots site OpenSpending.org, again run by the Open Knowledge Foundation. It believes that 'by understanding how governments spend money in our name can we have a say in how that money will affect our own lives' (OpenSpending, 2015). Run by volunteers and crowd sourcing, its focus is on data collection and cataloguing rather than visualisations, and houses 1,064 spending datasets from 75 countries in 36 languages. Highlights include 395 datasets for Japan – the highest for any country listed; Albanian election spending; EU Commission grants; and commitments for Greece.

The publication of spending data isn't always about what is said, but what is not said, what isn't revealed at a granular level – none more the case than budgets for secret services. The US administration's 'Black Budget' (OpenSpending, 2015) – its secret service operations budget – was leaked by Edward Snowden, and published by *The Washington Post* in August 2013 (*Washington Post*, 2013). As journalists Barton Gellman and Greg Miller reminded readers, that whilst the US government has annually released its overall level of intelligence spending since 2007, 'it has not divulged how it uses the money or how it performs against the goals set by the president and Congress.' (*Washington Post*, 2013) *The Washington Post*'s visualisation of the data (*Washington Post*, 2013) reveals for the fiscal year 2013 a US$52.6bn (£34bn) spend on covert action, surveillance and counter-intelligence across 13 US government agencies that included the Departments of Justice, Energy and Treasury, as well as the CIA and NSA. Data collection costs, topped a number of agencies' spend with the CIA's totalling US$11.5bn (£7.4bn), not including their US$387.3m (£250bn) spend on data processing and exploitation and $1.1bn on data analysis. For spending comparison, the UK spends £2bn in total across the three security intelligence services of GCHQ, MI5 and MI6. This is provided from the Single Intelligence Account and the National Cyber Security Programme (MI5, 2015). *The Washington Post*'s report or leaked documentation (*Washington Post*, 2013) does not however reveal how spending is apportioned to private sector contracts and to whom.

Whilst SpendNetwork (www.spendnetwork.com) can't solve this challenge, it aims to make UK government spending and contracts data easier to use. Their target audience isn't journalists but companies wanting to supply government. Their data so far comes from UK central government, English regions and Wales, but does not include Scotland or Northern Ireland. For a journalist with a local, business or government beat it could be of particular value.

Their main free tool currently has two types of searches – one for buyer/supplier data and the other for EU tenders. On entering a supplier in the buyer/supplier search users are shown a graph of revenue over time, the number of transactions, who made the transaction, the amount each transaction was worth, the date of each transaction and a link through to further details for each transaction. The data can also be filtered by buyer, listing all those who purchased a supplier's services. For example, there are 11,476 transactions listed under 'British Telecom' by 83 buyers since 2011. Northumberland Unitary Authority spent the most, purchasing £7.95m of services on 356 transactions (SpendNetwork, 2015). Hillingdon Council have made the highest number of transactions to British Telecom with 1,854 and East Sussex County Council have paid the highest single transaction to British Telecom where their Economy, Transport and Environmental department spent £1.6m in December 2014 (SpendNetwork, 2015).

On entering a buyer, such as a government department, users are shown the reverse face of the supplier data – the buyer's spending transactions, their worth, date and a link to further details. These can be filtered highest/lowest, most/least recent. Separately, entity data is also available, which brings together spend, tenders, contracts and suppliers, such as for the Cabinet Office here: https://www.spendnetwork.com/entity_spend/CAB010_CO_gov.

Using this spending data and - once again - OpenCorporates data, SpendNetwork worked with the think tank, Centre for Entrepreneurs, to investigate how much English and Welsh local authorities spent using small companies between 2011 and 2014 (Spend Small, 2014). At a time where government is claiming to want to support small businesses and to encourage local entrepreneurship, they found that of the £89.1bn spent on 42 million transactions by local authorities with companies only 12.5 per cent (£11.1bn) was spent with small companies. Monmouthshire County Council spent the highest proportion of its budget with small companies at 25.6 per cent and

Barnsley Metropolitan Borough Council the least at 4.17 per cent (Spend Small, 2014).

Conclusion

From the macro picture of Where Does My Money Go? to the more micro transaction data now available via SpendNetwork, much work has been done for understanding and making UK government spending data more usable in five years. And if open data keeps gathering pace globally, as we have begun to see, then we might expect similar tools to be appearing elsewhere. Whilst the stories such data potentially stores may not be as big as Watergate or Edward Snowden's leaks, the ability to use company, government and spending data to fact check and make straightforward investigations, without the need for specialist data or coding skills, is now easier than ever.

Similar moves are also happening in the non-governmental organisation and third sectors, where organisations such as IATI, USAID, DfID, the World Bank, OpenBRF and Publish What You Fund are leading the way in aid and sustainable development spending transparency. But data by itself is never the story, only with context can it be used to create information, insight and may be that scoop.

Follow that money…

References

Bowers, Simon (2015) 'Amazon's UK business paid just £11.9m in tax last year' in *the Guardian*, 24 June, available at http://www.theguardian.com/technology/2015/jun/24/amazons-uk-business-paid-119m-tax-last-year, accessed 17 July 2015

Cameron, David (2010) 'Letter to government departments on opening up data' gov.uk, available at https://www.gov.uk/government/news/letter-to-government-departments-on-opening-up-data, accessed 27 July 2015

Companies House (ND) 'Free Accounts Data Product' available at http://download.companieshouse.gov.uk/en_accountsdata.html, accessed 13 July 2015

Companies House (2015) 'Launch of the new Companies House public service beta' available at https://www.gov.uk/government/news/launch-of-the-new-companies-house-public-beta-service, accessed 17 July 2015

Gellman, Barton and Miller, Greg (2013) '"Black budget" summary details US spy network's successes, failures and objectives' in *The Washington Post*, 29 August, available at https://www.washingtonpost.com/world/national-security/black-budget-summary-details-us-spy-networks-successes-failures-and-objectives/2013/08/29/7e57bb78-10ab-11e3-8cdd-bcdc09410972_story.html, accessed 27 July 2015

Map the Banks (ND) available at http://mapthebanks.com, accessed 27 July 2015

MI5 (2015) 'Funding and resource allocation' available at https://www.mi5.gov.uk/home/about-us/who-we-are/funding.html, accessed 27 July 2015

Open Corporates (Nd) 'Google search' available at https://opencorporates.com/companies?jurisdiction_code=&q=Google, Accessed 17 July 2015

Open Corporates (ND) 'Disney search' https://opencorporates.com/corporate_groupings/Disney, accessed 17 July 2015

Open Corporates (ND) 'How complex are international corporate structures' https://opencorporates.com/viz/financial/index.html#goldman, accessed 17 July 2015

Open Oil (ND) http://openoil.net, accessed 27 July 2015

Open Oil (ND) 'BP Corporate Network', available at http://openoil.net/corporate-networks/bp-corporate-network, accessed 20 July 2015

Open Oil (ND) 'Nigeria Corporate Network', available at http://openoil.net/corporate-networks/nigeria-corporate-network, accessed on 27 July 2015

Open Oil (ND) 'Open Oil API', available at http://openoil.net/openoil-api, accessed 20 July 2015

Open Oil (ND) 'Main Page', available at http://repository.openoil.net/wiki/Main_Page, accessed 27 July 2015

Open Oil (ND) 'Nigeria National Petroleum Corporation', available at https://data.openoil.net/#nigeria_production, accessed 20 July 2015

OpenSpending (2015) available at https://openspending.org, accessed 27 July 2015

OpenSpending (2015) 'Black Budget' available at https://openspending.org/black-budget, accessed 27 July 2015

Safire, William (1997), 'Follow the proffering duck', in *The New York Times*, 3 August, available at http://www.nytimes.com/1997/08/03/magazine/follow-the-proffering-duck.html, accessed on 13 July 2015

Spend Small (2014) http://spendsmall.org, accessed 27 July 2015

SpendNetwork (2015) 'British Telecom', available at http://www.spendnetwork.com/topBuyersBySupplier/01626499_com# accessed 27 July 2015

SpendNetwork (2015) 'Transaction – East Sussex County Council / British Telecom plc', available at http://www.spendnetwork.com/transaction_detail/E1421_ESCC_gov_2014_12_496, accessed 27 July 2015

Unnamed author (2013) 'Inside the 2013 US intelligence "black budget"' in *The Washington Post*, 29 August, available at http://apps.washingtonpost.com/g/page/national/inside-the-2013-us-intelligence-black-budget/420/ accessed 27 July 2015

Unnamed author (2013) '$52.6 billion: The Black Budget' (visualization) in *The Washington Post*, 29 August, available at http://www.washingtonpost.com/wp-srv/special/national/black-budget, accessed 27 July 2015

Where Does My Money Go (ND) available at http://wheredoesmymoneygo.org, accessed 27 July 2015

Recalculating the newsroom: the rise of the journo-coder?

Liz Hannaford investigates the development of digital skillsets in UK newsrooms and asks if it's time to ditch shorthand in favour of coding

Introduction

Data-driven journalism has become increasingly democratised as new tools enable anyone to start crunching numbers and producing basic visualisations. But there comes a point when these free tools are no longer enough. News organisations are going much further and producing interactive maps, multimedia stories, news apps to explore databases and even creating online news games. These kinds of innovative news products require some real computer programming skills. But how are newsrooms doing that? Do they now need journalists who can also code? Or are they bringing in programmers to replace journalists? What's the effect of bringing programmers out of the IT department and into the heart of the newsroom? Or can we create a hybrid who is proficient in both journalism and programming?

Journo-coder, programmer-journalist, hacker-journalist, journo-programmer – the terminology is undecided (Pilhofer, 2010) – but certainly there is excited talk in the United States about bringing these two roles together. 'Why all your students must be programmers' was the provocative title of one of the liveliest panel discussions at the August 2013 Conference for the Association for Education in Journalism and Mass Communication in Washington, DC. It was dubbed the #AEJMCBattleRoyale on Twitter (Hernandez, 2013). The panellists talked passionately about how their programming skills enabled them to take their journalism to a whole new level – interrogating data to find the stories nobody else could or turning static, text-based web pages into dynamic, interactive tools. There was less agreement about what level of 'programming' knowledge is actually useful to a journalist. There was even less agreement about how to teach it to students in an already tightly-packed course schedule. What do you throw out?

A number of universities in the States are responding to these developments by offering joint journalism and computer science programmes (Cohen, Hamilton and Turner, 2011). Notable amongst these is the Columbia University Graduate School of Journalism (together with the Tow Center for Digital Journalism), which offers a dual degree in Journalism and Computer Science the stated goal of which 'is for its graduates to help redefine journalism in a fast-changing digital media environment' (Columbia Journalism School, 2014). Here in the UK, some of the top journalism schools have also introduced computing into their courses. Most recently, the University of Cardiff launched a Masters in Computational Journalism in 2014 (Cardiff School of Journalism, 2014). But what is it that our newsrooms actually want? Is it time for journalism students to ditch shorthand and learn to code instead?!

This chapter draws on a recent study carried out by the author at the BBC and *Financial Times* to try to answer these questions in the context of current literature on computational journalism.

Newsroom dynamics

First of all, we need to think about how newsrooms work and what drives them to make changes when new technology comes along. There have been two conflicting theoretical frameworks for explaining this. The first is a determinist approach, as emphasised by Pavlik (2000), who wrote that 'journalism has always been shaped by technology' (Pavlik, 2000: 229). A similar technological determinism is suggested by McNair (1998) who writes that 'the form and content of journalism is crucially determined by the available technology of newsgathering, production and dissemination' (McNair, 1998: 125). But this determinism has been dismissed by others as an overly simplistic way of explaining technological change in the newsroom (Cottle and Ashton, 1999; Örnebring, 2010). Instead, we need to understand that newsrooms are complex organisational structures. This viewpoint has been strongly influenced by the work of Michael Schudson. His 'Sociology of News Production,' first published in 1989 and revised several times since then, argues that change in the newsroom is driven by politics; economics; organisational structure; and culture (Schudson, 1989, 2005). This sociological framework has been taken further by Pablo J. Boczkowski who carried out a comprehensive study into three online newsrooms in the United States (Boczkowski, 2004). He focused on the process of adopting new technologies and identified three factors which influence this:

1. organisational structures;
2. work practices; and
3. representations of the end-user (ibid).

So by understanding the newsroom as a complex socio-organisational structure with an audience at the end of it, we can start to understand the variations that exist around the world as journalism evolves and adapts to computational journalism (Anderson, 2013).

Computational journalism in newsrooms

Computational journalism is itself, of course, a contested term (Coddington, 2015). Whilst it is undoubtedly important to understand the subtle differences between data-driven journalism, computer-assisted reporting (CAR) and computational journalism, the latter term will be used for convenience in this chapter in the broadest sense of its meaning to cover all journalistic work done in the 'intersection between journalism and computing' (Karlsen and Stavelin, 2013).

Although there has been academic interest in computational journalism for some years, there have been very few empirical studies of journalists and programmers working in newsrooms in this field (Anderson, 2011). Those studies that do exist tend to suggest that the hybrid model of people combining journalism and programming skills in some way is the ideal and the one to be emulated.

The earliest example of such a study is Cindy Royal's 2010 case study of the Interactive News Technology Department at *The New York Times* led at the time by Aron Pilhofer, currently at *the Guardian* in London (Royal, 2010). The NYT, she wrote, is particularly innovative in producing interactive maps, timelines and graphics to engage the user. Royal's research found that those working in the department were technologists and developers hired because they could also demonstrate a passion for journalism and storytelling. In fact, the developers she interviewed identified their work as journalistic with a strong editorial element – 'as fluent in journalism as they were in coding' (Royal, 2010: 3) - suggesting they saw their role as a hybrid one combining both skill sets. When she asked them how they had acquired their technical skills, most of them said they were 'self-taught' (ibid).

Sylvain Parasie and Eric Dagiral looked at what they term 'programmer-journalists' in the city of Chicago, hired by newsrooms to design data-driven news projects (Parasie and Dagiral, 2012). They found that bringing these programmers into the newsrooms had profound implications because the programmers' ideas about what to do with data differed from more traditional journalists' ideas – especially those journalists from the CAR tradition. The programmers tended to come from the open-source/hacker community and they wanted to create tools that enabled the user/audience to access granular data for their own personal information – how much crime is happening on my block, for example. Journalists traditionally have a different idea of constructing facts and knowledge (epistemology) and want to use data to disclose public issues, set the political agenda and create narratives (Parasie and Dagiral, 2012). So although these newsroom workers identified as hybrid programmer-journalists, the data-driven products they produce perhaps stretch the definition of journalism a long way from the profession's traditional concepts with programmer-journalists driven primarily to create software rather than journalism (Coddington, 2015; Lewis and Usher, 2013).

Wibke Weber and Hannes Rall (2013) share Royal's (2010) belief that the NYT model whereby programmers consider themselves to be also journalists is a 'key success factor' in computational journalism (Weber and Rall, 2013: 170). They contrast this with examples of newsrooms in Germany and Switzerland where journalists and programmers/designers had clearly separated roles and identities and they suggest this is a weaker model. However, the authors' hypothesis rests on an assumption that *The New York Times* does indeed represent best practice and a role model without explaining how this is the case. In such a small study, it seems simplistic to make such a strong claim.

A European example is investigated by Joakim Karlsen and Eirik Stavelin who conducted a small study into computational journalism in Norwegian newsrooms (Karlsen and Stavelin, 2014). The authors use the terms 'journalist,' 'programmer' and 'journalist-programmers,' to describe those workers they interviewed for the study (Karlsen and Stavelin, 2014: 37) because they have focused on 'computational journalism' as a craft rather than the professional identities of the craftsmen themselves so it is difficult to compare directly with other studies. However, the authors do argue that everyone working in this field needs to understand how technology and journalism fit together and have a 'pragmatic relationship to technology' with the ability to learn new skills readily (Karlsen and Stavelin, 2014: 42). The authors insist that journalism must always come before programming and computational journalists – whatever their background – should distance themselves from the IT department and fully belong to the newsroom.

Computational journalism in the BBC and *Financial Times*

Having looked at some of the relevant literature in the field, we can now look at data gathered here in the UK between July 2013 and May 2014. This data comes from interviews with staff at the BBC's Visual Journalism unit including the team leader, Andrew Leimdorfer, and the *Financial Times*' Interactive News team, led by Martin Stabe. Both of these teams are primarily producing data-driven, multimedia, interactive features, visualisations and dynamic maps. Ten interviews were conducted in all for this study. The team leaders were asked to describe the organisational model for computational journalism in their newsrooms.

Organisational model – the team approach

In contrast to much of the literature based on US examples, the hybrid, programmer-journalist model (Parasie and Dagiral, 2012; Royal, 2010; Weber and Rall, 2013) is strongly rejected in the two news organisations studied in the UK and instead a team approach has been adopted whereby journalists, programmers and designers work closely together to produce the interactive, data-driven news products (see Figure 1).

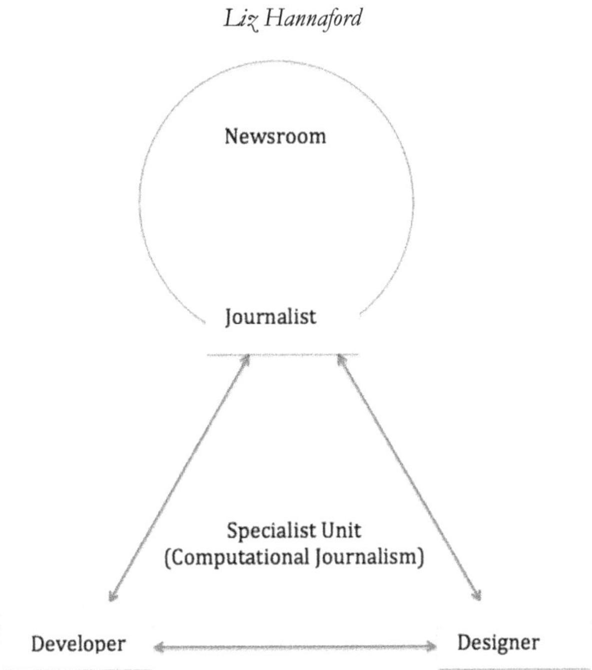

Figure 47: The newsroom triangle

Martin Stabe argues that truly hybrid journo-coders or programmer-journalists do not currently exist in the UK.

> *'We've decided at the FT that the only way to bring those skills into the newsroom is to create a team that has people who come from both those backgrounds, plus designers. You really need a numerate journalist, a developer who can work on deadlines, and a designer who understands technology. If you have those three people working together, you have a journalist-coder'* (Stabe, 2013).

The same approach is taken at the BBC and seems similar to that identified by Weber and Rall (2013) in their German and Swiss examples. In this team model, the news product is driven and managed primarily by the journalist, which ensures that the story and the journalism are always centre stage. It is usually the journalist who finds the new dataset and carries out the initial analysis in order to find the story angle and ideas for how to present it to the end-user – the audience. Having carried out this preliminary work, the journalist then works with the developer (and designer) to create the news product - be it an interactive map, calculator or multimedia story. But the journalist never leaves the project. They remain as a sort of project manager ensuring that the user experience is suitable for the journalistic aim of the story. This model differs significantly from that described by Parasie and Dagiral (2012) in Chicago and Royal (2010) at the NYT where the programmer-journalists were more concerned with innovation than the traditional boundaries and conventions of journalism (Karlsen and Stavelin, 2014).

However, the triangular model at the BBC and *Financial Times* only works if the journalists on the teams have the appropriate skills to at least understand what is technically possible and '…who can write just enough code to understand what the developers are doing, who can do good data management and the data sourcing aspect of the interactive, investigative project' (Stabe, 2013). So it is clear that we are not talking about a conventional newsroom journalist here but a rather more specialist journalism role which includes some computational skills which we shall return to later in the chapter.

As well as being part of the triangle with the developer and designer, the journalist in these teams is also part of the organisations' wider newsroom (see Figure 1). So as well as generating their own story ideas, these journalists might be the point of contact for, say, the business or health desk if they have a dataset they want analysed and visualised.

The developers on the team, however, were still officially part of the IT department even though they were based in the newsroom. The FT's Martin Stabe explained that this was to preserve their career path as technologists rather than editorial staff. This shows that there are significant organisational and human resource issues in large newsrooms that play a role in determining how work roles evolve and become defined. New people with new skillsets entering newsrooms may well have to fit in with existing work structures with implications for the way in which computational journalism develops.

Computational Journalism Skills

Having established an organisational model for computational journalism teams at the BBC and *Financial Times*, we can now consider the skills and attitudes of the people who work in these teams, specifically the journalists and programmers. Firstly, the interviewees were asked to list their key technical skills and these have been categorised in Table 1.

	Developers	**Journalists**
Front End (User Interface)	HTML/CSS	
	JavaScript	
Back End (support systems eg database management)	Python	
	PHP	
	Ruby	
	SQL	
	UNIX	
Data-analysis/presentation		Excel
	MPS	
	SPSS	
	GIS mapping software	GIS mapping software
		Tableau
	R	R

Table 5: Key skillsets of developers and journalists

The table shows a clear distinction between the journalists' skills and the programmers' skills. None of the journalists claimed to have programming as a skill but instead said their skills were in data analysis, primarily Excel spreadsheets. Mapping software and the data visualisation tool, Tableau, were mentioned by journalists but only as a way of analysing data. The journalists did not produce the maps and visualisations that appeared on the final online product; that was the job of the developers and designers.

But during the interviews, a more nuanced picture emerged. Although the journalists categorically denied they had programming or coding skills - or the need for them - they did admit to some "basic" knowledge that enabled them to, for example, write a simple programming script in Python to scrape data from a website and store it in a spreadsheet. That might be trivial for a developer, but for a journalist that is still an exceptional skill. However, the journalists interviewed at the BBC and FT did not consider their level of skill to be high enough to merit the term 'programming' or 'coding' because it was so far down the spectrum compared to the experienced developers they worked alongside.

Acquiring Skills

All the interviewees – journalists and developers alike – agreed that learning new skills was a big part of their job and took up to 25 per cent of their time each week.

> *'Every year there's a different way of doing things, producing graphic or interactive, so you have to constantly look at what you know about how to do your job,'* (journalist).

> *'You learn by always coding at the edge of your understanding....It's about constantly throwing yourself into a slightly uncomfortable situation then learning your way out of it,'* (developer).

> *'I don't think you can do this role without the attitude and willingness to learn new skills all the time and I think the point at which you stop learning is probably the point you're not at the top of your game any more,'* (journalist).

However, hardly any of this learning is done formally on courses or from text books. Instead, it is informal and self-directed. The main sources of learning mentioned were:

- Newsroom colleagues
- Online resources
- Meet-ups (eg Hacks/Hackers)
- Online communities (eg NICAR, CIJ)
- Other journalists
- Other news organisations' code

This culture of constantly pushing boundaries, updating skills, learning from a community of fellow practitioners and sharing knowledge transparently owes more to the open-source/hacker culture than traditional journalism (Lewis and Usher, 2013). It values innovation, tinkering and collaboration and has been observed in other studies of computational journalism in the newsroom (Karlsen and Stavelin, 2014; Royal, 2010).

Hybrids or specialists?

We have already seen that the BBC and *Financial Times* examples in this study strongly reject the hybrid model of journo-coders and have put in place a team model in which specialists work closely together on collaborative projects. So how do the journalists and developers working in these teams view their roles and describe themselves? Only one of the interviewees – a developer - described himself as a 'journo-coder' or any of the other hybrid job descriptions, commenting 'I'd like to think that any developer that works on any journalism team is a journalist," (developer). This interviewee believed that any work that involved building something to tell a story for an audience was 'journalism.' However, this response was in stark contrast to all the others from this study where interviewees identified strongly as either developers or journalists and were, indeed, sceptical about the possibility of combining both skillsets in one person in any meaningful way.

> *'I've never met a journalist who is particularly adept at coding in my fairly limited pool"* (developer)
>
> *'I just say I'm a journalist who specialises in maps and charts,'* (journalist).
>
> *'I don't think a person can straddle both. To make an interactive requires so many different areas of knowledge, you need years of experience just doing that. And journalism is a whole other area of expertise so you'd be lacking in focus on one side,'* (developer).
>
> *'I think it's great that we have crossover in our world - a bit like a Venn diagram - but I think I'm never going to be at the level that (a developer) is at and I think my time is better spent doing the more journalistic part of the work'* (journalist).
>
> *'I'm an expert in my field, the journalist is an expert in their field and together we get things done. There's a huge amount I don't need to know - law, editorial guidelines, style - I just don't get that involved in that kind of thing,'* (developer).

The programmers interviewed did not feel competent finding news stories or writing copy and relied on the journalists for this aspect of the projects. However, all programmers did say they had acquired some understanding of the journalistic process – the need for a news angle, hitting deadlines, understanding the audience – which they felt distinguished them from programmers working in the IT department. Thus, given this strong belief in clearly-defined, separate roles, collaboration becomes a key component of the attitude to work where members of the teams are, in the words of one interviewee, constantly 'bouncing bits of knowledge off each other.' This requires an understanding of each other's sphere of expertise leading to what Andrew Leimdorfer at the BBC has described elsewhere as a need for a new generation of 'tech-savvy journalists and news-savvy technologists' (Leimdorfer, cited in Herrman, 2011).

Conclusion

Understanding newsrooms as complex socio-organisational structures with different types of audience enables us to better understand the constraints and drivers that lead to different models of computational journalism. But it seems likely these models will evolve over time and it will be important to investigate these developments longitudinally because of their implication for the education of future generations of journalists.

Currently in the UK newsrooms investigated for this study, programmers and journalists see themselves as having separate roles and skills - albeit with some overlap. But it seems likely that as more journalism courses teach computational and coding skills more young journalists with these technical skills will be working in newsrooms and could challenge existing models and work practices. We might also see more students with a technology background undertaking journalism training in order to gain jobs in a newsroom. Certainly, the developers interviewed for this study described newsroom jobs as more 'fun' than traditional programming roles in, for example, banks. It is worth noting that only a minority of the developers interviewed for this study had a computer science degree. The others had arts or humanities degrees (like the journalists) but had developed a passion for programming that they had nurtured informally. This is consistent with Cindy Royal's findings in the NYT newsroom (Royal, 2010). Perhaps the barrier between journalist and technologist is not as solid as we might think.

Furthermore, there are now journalism jobs being advertised in the UK that specifically require at least a basic understanding of HTML and even JavaScript (Hannaford, 2015). Recently, a number of major news organisations in the UK have offered journalism trainee schemes which specifically mention coding and data analysis skills in the list of criteria suggesting news organisations may be increasingly confident of finding graduates with this skillset and nurturing it in their newsrooms – for example, *the Guardian*'s 2013 Digital Trainee scheme, the Reuters Journalism Programme (Thomson Reuters 2014), the *Financial Times*' 2015 scheme (*Financial Times*, 2014), the Telegraph Media Group's Editorial Graduate Programme 2015 (Telegraph Media Group, 2014).

Finally, there is debate about the impact of bringing developers from the open source/hacker culture into the newsroom with their emphasis on innovation and software and challenging the existing ideas of what constitutes journalism (Karlsen and Stavelin, 2014; Parasie and Dagiral, 2012; Royal, 2010). It is not without implications for the future of journalism practice and there are even signs of diverging practice between US and European newsrooms. Much more research is needed in this exciting, evolving field. The need for longitudinal studies of particular newsrooms was mentioned earlier but we also need cross-national comparisons to better understand how computational journalism is being done in newsrooms around the world – and who exactly is doing it. Then we can decide if journalism students really should think about ditching shorthand and learning to code instead.

References

Anderson, CW (2013) 'Towards a sociology of computational and algorithmic journalism' in *New Media & Society*, Vol. 15, No. 7) pp 1005-1021

Boczkowski, Pablo J (2004) 'The processes of adopting multimedia and interactivity in three online newsrooms' in *Journal of Communication*, Vol. 54, No. 2, pp 197-213

Cardiff School of Journalism (2014) 'MSc Computational Journalism', available online at: http://www.cardiff.ac.uk/jomec/degreeprogrammes/pgmasters/msc_computational_journalism/, accessed 12 September 2014

Coddington, Mark (2015) 'Clarifying Journalism's Quantitative Turn: A typology for evaluating data journalism, computational journalism, and computer-assisted reporting' in *Digital Journalism*, Vol. 3, No. 3, pp 331-348

Cohen, Sarah, Hamilton, James T and Turner, Fred (2011) 'Computational journalism' *Communications of the ACM*, Vol. 54, No. 10, pp 66-71

Columbia Journalism School (2014) 'Dual Degree: Journalism and Computer Science' available online at: http://www.journalism.columbia.edu/page/276-dualdegree-journalism-computer-science/279, accessed 12 September 2014

Cottle, Simon, and Ashton, Mark (1999) 'From BBC newsroom to BBC newscentre: On changing technology and journalist practices' *Convergence*, Vol. 5, No. 3, pp 22-43

Financial Times (2014) 'Join the FT as a graduate trainee,' available online at http://aboutus.ft.com/careers/graduates/#axzz3OWf9dy5q, accessed 8 January 2015

Hannaford, Liz (2015) 'Computational Journalism: hybrids or specialists?' in *Journalism Education* Vol.4, No. 1, pp 6-21

Hernandez, Robert (2013) '"Why All Your Students Must Be Programmers" – The #AEJMCBattleRoyale,' *Web Journalist Blog*, available online at http://blog.webjournalist.org/2013/08/, accessed 26 August 2013

Herrmann, Steve (2011) 'Knight Mozilla and BBC News' *BBC News - The Editors*, Available online at http://www.bbc.co.uk/blogs/theeditors/2011/11/welcoming_a_knight-mozilla_fel.html, accessed 26 August 2013

Karlsen, Joakim, and Stavelin, Eirik (2014) 'Computational journalism in Norwegian newsrooms' *Journalism Practice*, Vol. 8, No. 1, pp 34-48

Lewis, Seth C, and Usher, Nikki (2013) 'Open source and journalism: toward new frameworks for imagining news innovation' *Media, Culture & Society*, Vol. 35, No. 5, pp 602-619

Lewis, Seth C, and Usher, Nikki (2014) 'Code, Collaboration, And The Future Of Journalism: A case study of the Hacks/Hackers global network' *Digital Journalism* Vol.2, No. 3, pp 383-393

McNair, Brian (1998) *The sociology of journalism.* Arnold: London

Örnebring, Henrik (2010) 'Technology and journalism-as-labour: Historical perspectives' *Journalism*, Vol. 11, No. 1, pp 57-74

Parasie, Sylvain and Dagiral, Eric (2012) 'Data-driven journalism and the public good: "Computer-assisted-reporters" and "programmer-journalists" in Chicago', *New Media and Society.* Vol. 15, No. 6, pp 853-871

Pavlik, John (2000) 'The impact of technology on journalism' *Journalism Studies*, Vol. 1, No. 2, pp 229-237

Pilhofer, Aron (2010) 'Programmer-Journalist? Hacker-Journalist? Our Identity Crisis', *Media Shift – Idea Lab.* Available online at http://www.pbs.org/idealab/2010/04/programmer-journalist-hacker-journalist-our-identity-crisis107, accessed 15 September 2014

Royal, Cindy (2010). 'The journalist as programmer: A case study of the New York Times interactive news technology department,' paper presented at the Anais do International Symposium in Online Journalism, The University of Texas at Austin, Austin, TX, USA

Schudson, Michael (1989) 'The sociology of news production' *Media, culture and society*, Vol. 11, No. 3, pp 263-282

Schudson, Michael (2005) 'Four approaches to the sociology of news' in Curran, James and Gurevitch, Michael (eds) *Mass Media and Society*, London: Hodder Arnold, pp 172–197

Telegraph Media Group (2014) Editorial Graduate Programme 2015, available online at http://www.telegraph.co.uk/sponsored/telegraphcareers/10520003/TMG-Careers.html?ETREC107GF.open?VACANCY_ID=92647722Q4, accessed 11 January 2015

Thomson Reuters (2014) 'Reuters Journalism Programme,' available online at http://careers.thomsonreuters.com/Students/Bachelors/Europe/Reuters-Journalism-Program/, accessed 11 January 2015

Weber, Wibke and Rall, Hannes (2013) '"We are journalists" Production Practices, Attitudes and a Case Study of the New York Times Newsroom,' in Weber, Wibke, Burmester, Michael and Tille, Ralph (eds) *Interaktive Infografiken* Berlin Heidelberg: Springer pp 161-172

The difficult art of collaborating

***The Guardian*'s data projects editor Helena Bengtsson gets to the root of the issues of working with developers on data projects**

Introduction

When I started out in data journalism, long before it was called data journalism, you were supposed to do everything by yourself. In fact, you had to do everything by yourself. That meant gathering the data, cleaning the data and then analysing it, of course. And with that analysis, go out to interview people and write the story. But it also meant doing your own visualizing, programming your own website and publishing your own interactive databases. On your own website? Yes, most data journalists, if they wanted to publish something more than text and a picture, had to publish their databases and visuals on a parallel website. Usually run by the data journalist him/herself and usually on an old discarded machine under his/her desk. So, I taught myself how to use Excel and Access and I went to the NICAR conference in the US and learned about mapping and programming in Perl. And we all talked about how we needed to do everything by ourselves – and how it seemed like IT-departments of media companies around the world had a secret understanding to make sure to never let the data journalist do any kind of work on the company website.

Before there was only you

An example of that is a story I've actually done several times when I worked at SVT, the national broadcasting company in Sweden. The first time that story was done it was done completely by hand. We wanted to take a look at how the Swedish members of the European Parliament voted. In Sweden party loyalty is essential. It's almost never heard of that a member of a party should go against his/her party when voting in the national parliament. So, what happens when they go to Brussels and Strasbourg? Do they follow party lines?

As I said, the first time we did it all manually. Printed all the voting records from the EU parliament and went through them by hand using a yellow marker to keep track of all the Swedes. The whole office was filled with stacks of paper. The story took a couple of months to do, but it finally came out, showing that the parliamentarians acted very differently in the European Parliament compared to the Swedish one.

A couple of years later, we decided to repeat the story. This time, I wanted to try a more technical approach, trying to do the analysis programmatically. But, my knowledge of programming was very limited. For one thing I didn't know how to scrape a website so instead I downloaded all the documents by hand. Whenever I had a moment to spare, waiting on the phone or similar, I would go to the website and download a couple of voting records. The records were all Microsoft Word documents so the next step was to transform the text in the document into data. After a lot of trial and error I managed to write a small script to extract the information from all the documents. But there was still a lot of manual labour cleaning the data and getting it into an Access database so that I could do the analysis and find the story. I would estimate that the work took almost as long as it had when we did it all manually – and the end result was two small news segments on the national news broadcast. There was not even a thought of doing something else for the web – I didn't have the knowledge to do that. And for a long time that was how projects were done – with limited knowledge about the techniques needed, doing the best I could – and not even really aware of the fact that there was actually people out there who had all the skills and knowledge that I lacked.

Something changed

But, a couple of years ago, something changed. One of the more obvious signs was that the NICAR conference grew from around 300 to 400 persons to 1,000 to 1,200. And not all of them were journalists. They were graphical artists and graphic editors, they were applications developers and website designers. And they all did data journalism. So, something had changed. From the lone ranger who did all the work him/herself to a team of people, each doing what they were best at.

Another sign was that I found myself working at a project were three of the members were developers from my company's own team. And I was supposed to collaborate with them, not just tell them what to do. This was in 2010, at SVT, the national broadcaster of Sweden, and we were building an interactive database of 54,000 candidates in the national, regional and local elections that fall. My job was to gather and clean all the data around the candidates. Their job was to present it on the web. Very soon I realised that we talked a very different language and had very different goals. I wanted to shovel everything I found into my database and then start cleaning and checking for duplicates and all that. They wanted to put in a lot of constraints so that it would be impossible to enter a person twice or let a candidate have two income figures for the same year. And we clashed.

But, since we were sitting next to each other we had to solve that clash – and the ones that came after that. I learned a little bit more about keeping your databases secure, and they learned a little bit more about journalism. And the crucial thing was that we were working together, collaborating. I wasn't making a request of the IT department: we sat there together every day, changing the project and the goals as the project changed. And in my experience this is what makes the difference. The fact that I can lift my head and say 'I've been thinking that we need to add another variable in the database' – or they say, 'in order to display this we need to clean all the postcodes and make sure they are correct'. It's the daily communicating that makes the projects so much better.

Fixing the errors

Another example was when we had worked on a huge project about schools, building a database of all schools in Sweden, the number of pupils, the number of teachers, the result of the standardised tests and the grade point average. We were on our way to release the whole project and as usual we did a pre-release. We launched the website and started spreading the word through Facebook and Twitter. That's what we did when we had a big project lined up, first a pre-release and then, a couple of days later, an official release with stories in the news broadcast and a big article on the news site. So, the interactive database of all schools in Sweden was out, with number of students and teachers, test scores and average grades. And then a very angry principal called. This thing that you have published is all wrong. Our test scores are way higher that what your website states, she said.

So, the project manager called me and I went into the database and compared it to the data that we had downloaded from the Swedish National Agency for Education. And it turned out that the principal was right – and we were wrong. We had used our own system for storing the information when a school's results were deducted. If there were less than ten students taking the test or if the school hadn't reported the result, the data on their website contained one or two dots, . or ..

Since you can't store one or two dots in a numerical field in a database we had replaced the dots with -1 and -2. That was fine until we started calculating the average result for all tests and forgot about our own system. So, we had to fix this and quick. By this time we had worked together, journalists and developers, for a couple of years so the work went so smoothly. I checked the database and Fredrik Stålnacke, the developer, fixed the code. In less than half an hour we'd found the error and launched a new version of the database.

I can only imagine how it would have been if we had not been sitting side by side working together, and instead I had to make a request to the IT department, and they had built the database and the website. To start with I wouldn't even have known whom to call – and there would have been a lot of accusations of who did what and who didn't, and the simple problem would have taken days to solve.

New tools create awareness

You could argue that all the new tools for visualisations, Google Fusion, Tableau, CartoDB, Infogr.am and others have helped the lonely journalist to continue working on his/her own, but in one way I think that those tools have increased the collaborations between the data journalist and developers, graphical artists and designers. The tools helped journalists to realise that a story does not necessarily have to be a headline, picture and text, but you could actually tell a story in a lot of different ways. And once they realised that, they also realised that yes, the easy tools were good for those first stories, but very soon they wanted more: more and better interactive graphics, and they realised that there were people out there who actually knew how to tell stories in other ways.

An example is the project with property prices that *the Guardian* did during the summer of 2015. It started with a database. And that is, for me, an unusual way of starting a story. Usually you have a story idea and then you set out to find data that will help you with that idea. In this case, we had the data, and wanted to find the stories. The data is a public dataset, found here: https://www.gov.uk/government/statistical-data-sets/price-paid-data-downloads. It contains of 19 million records of property sales in England and Wales from 1995 onwards. The dataset had been used before, mostly by commercial sites for finding properties for sale or for rent. They had chosen to display the latest sales for each area, so that was not something we wanted to do. Instead we realised the potential in having all the data from 1995 – we could really tell a story about how house prices have developed over the years. You could argue that there is nothing new there: prices have gone up, we know that.

Collaboration helps develop stories

My job at *the Guardian* is to collaborate. In the work description it even says that I and my team should be 'aggressively collaborative' with the news desk, graphics, the interactive team and so on. So, in this case, I lifted my head and started talking to the interactive team right away. But it wasn't until I also talked to one of the reporters that I realized what the story was. He had an idea of writing about a family in Islington, London, where the parents had bought an apartment when they were young and just starting a family. And now when their children wanted to do the same thing, they couldn't afford a single apartment in London. So, we joked that they would have to move to the northern parts of England, because we assumed that flats would be cheaper there.

I then go the idea to compare the median price with the median income over the years and asked the HMRC for data by region from 1995 and forward. So, for the different regions in England and Wales I could do a comparison that showed that in 1995 the median price for a property was between 3 and 4 times the median income for that region. So, London was most expensive then too, with 4.4 times and the North West was the least expensive with 3.2 times. But, when I looked at the latest data available, I got a surprise. London had of course risen the most, to 12 times the median income, but even in the North West you had to pay 6 times the median income for the median house. So, if there is an old rule that says that banks will lend you 3-4 times your income, it's not possible to buy a property anywhere. And with that information, the story got a new angle – and we could start sketching on an interactive visualisation.

So, I prepared the data and put it into a PostgreSQL database and our interactive team started to work. But, the great thing is that both them, and me, can lift our heads at any time saying, 'could we add a field with postcode district?' or, 'I've managed to find about 24,000 of the 30,000 missing postcodes, you can now re-run your script.'

To be able to work together has improved the project immensely and we can see how the story angle changes because of the interactive, as well as the other way around. You can see the final outcome on *the Guardian*'s website here: www.theguardian.com/ society/ng-interactive/2015/sep/02/unaffordable-country-where-can-you-afford-to-buy-a-house

Big stories – and small

Yet another, less complicated example is this story on MPs who earn money from renting out properties: http://www.theguardian.com/politics/2015/may/06/number-of-mps-who-earn-from-renting-out-property-rises-by-a-third. Just before the election an idea came from one of the reporters at the paper: let's look at the property owned by the MPs, and let's especially look at those who own property for renting. Another publication had done a straightforward story about how much they own right now, and I was wondering how to do a better story. MPs are obligated to disclose a lot of different financial interests once they are elected. Property is just one of a number of items disclosed at the Register of Members' Financial Interests found online at http://www.publications.parliament.uk/pa/cm/cmregmem.htm.

There is one disclosure document for every month – so for this five-year session we were looking at 82 documents. We had done several attempts to scrape the information, attempts that failed because the documents aren't very consistent and applying programming rules didn't work that well. Just to mention one problem with the data, the information for each item is duplicated every time they do a filing – and then suddenly it's taken off. That makes it hard to make sure that you are not counting every unique property more than once.

To make it easier I knew that I only wanted the property information, item 8 for each member and in each document. So, I lifted my head and said to Will Franklin, the developer: "Will, could you help me scrape this down? But, we're just going to do this…" And, then he wrote a script that just copied down the documents in its most raw form. I got a zip-file of 82 files and went through them picking out just item 8. After that I put them all in Excel and removed the duplicates. By doing that, I could actually look at every single filing that every MP had done for each year and that made it easy to go through them all. Since the data is so fuzzy I knew I had to look at every unique filing to make sure that I wasn't doing anything wrong.

While cleaning the data I saw that there were several MPs that started out with none or just one property and then as the years went by I noticed that they were adding on to their ownership, one property at a time. And that was actually the story we went with. Of course I could have downloaded the 82 documents myself and done the first cleaning, but by getting the help to write the script, much faster and more efficient than any script that I could write, I could focus on the thing that I'm better at. Which is analysing data and finding the story.

So, for me, my life as a data journalist has very much changed the last couple of years. Collaboration is needed for both visualising and analysis, and the key point is that access is crucial. In my experience, I have to be able to lift my head and talk to the person I'm working with. It can't be somebody at a different department, in a different place, he/she has to be right there, following in the daily work.

To code or not to code?

Pulitzer Prize winning journalist turned journalism professor Steve Doig makes the case for strong data journalism skills in newly minted journalism graduates, but argues that not all of them need to learn to code

I wrote my first computer program nearly 50 years ago, when I was a freshman in college in 1966. The language was Dartmouth BASIC, and the sole purpose of the program was to wow my Winter Carnival date with how I could tell a machine to print out her name 100 times. Mission accomplished! After I finally graduated with a degree in government, I began a productive couple of decades as a reporter and editor for the *Miami Herald*, where I stumbled into becoming one of the pioneers of what was called computer assisted reporting (CAR). I started down that then non-existent career path of data journalist when I brought home an Atari 800 computer in 1982. I bought it as a hobby, but quickly realised that maybe I could use computer programming to help me do my reporting job better and thereby stand out in the highly competitive *Herald* newsroom.

Before long, I had progressed on my own from simple FOR--NEXT loops in BASIC on my 16kb Atari to writing increasingly powerful data analysis programs in SAS, a major statistical language used by big business and governments, on the *Herald* mainframe. As Louis Pasteur noted on several occasions, 'chance favours the prepared mind' (Vallery-Radot, 1902: 99). So my mind was prepared when Hurricane Andrew trashed South Florida in 1992. I used SAS to analyse the damage patterns from the storm and help prove that weakened building codes magnified the scale of the disaster. The attention paid to that Pulitzer-winning project and some other data-heavy investigations on which I worked ultimately led to me becoming a university professor of data journalism in 1996.

Clearly, I owe much of my career success to my ability to program in computer code. And I'm not alone in this – today there are hundreds of code-competent data journalists working in news organisations around the world, and there are plenty of good job openings for lots more of them. So surely I must be among those journalism educators who believe that all our students need to learn to write computer code in order to succeed in today's multimedia market.

Well, I'm not. In fact, I can think of many arguments against attempting to turn all journalism students into programmers. But before I make those arguments here, let me raise a problem of definition: What exactly is 'data journalism'? As a term, data journalism has expanded over the years to cover a pretty big area, a broad collection of functions and the skills necessary to accomplish those functions. Up until the mid-1990s I could say I knew how to do *everything* that was being done in data journalism. But about then people started creating newsroom intranets, and then newspapers began creating websites, and so on. Today data journalism covers a wide spectrum ranging from acquiring data and analysing it to presenting the findings on websites or mobile devices in increasingly interactive ways.

This raises the first big question facing the educator who thinks students need to learn to write code: what kind of work will the program they learn be used to accomplish? Is it to handle mindless repetitive tasks like scraping millions of records from a government website? Is it to analyse a dataset for the frequencies and patterns that reveal a story? Is it to do statistical tests on the data? Is it to standardise a messy dataset? Is it to link two or more datasets together by a common variable? Is it to publish the words of a story on a web page? Is it to make a dataset searchable on the web by news consumers? Is it to display the patterns in the data as interactive maps or charts?

All these and more are necessary data journalism tasks – but most of these are accomplished using very different programming languages. And that's a core problem for the students-must-program advocates: what language should be taught?

Programmer Paul Ford wrote a marvelous 38,000-word explainer titled 'What is Code?' for Bloomberg's BusinessWeek (Ford, 2015). In it he notes that more than 1,700 computer languages have been created over the decades. Data journalists today use only a few of those, but the real problem is that the languages and tools being used come into fashion and then go out as they are replaced by newer ones.

A fine example of this is the history arc of Adobe Flash, a tool with its own programming language used to create animated graphics on websites. Widely used by news websites in the early 2000s, Flash began to disappear when Apple decided not to support it on iPads and iPhones, using HTML5 instead to accomplish the same thing. Journalism professor Mindy McAdams wrote an excellent text called *Flash Journalism: How to Create Multimedia News Packages* (McAdams, 2005); it was obsolete within a couple of years.

Similar lifecycles of programming languages and tools can be seen in the archives of NICAR-L, the listserv of choice for data journalists of all skill levels (join at http://ire.org/resource-center/listservs/subscribe-nicar-l/). Graybeards who were discussing XDB queries in the 1980s and FoxPro in the early 1990s and then perhaps Microsoft Access now are writing structured query language for MySQL or SQL Server or Postgres. Those who do web development are split into camps that use Ruby on Rails or Python on Django. Data analysis types who use SPSS for statistical work are being wooed over to using R, a free tool with powerful features but an opaque syntax and a steep learning curve. And so it goes.

Another fact of data journalism is that accomplishing some of those tasks gets easier as new non-programming tools are built. I learned this early in my data journalism career. In about 1983 when I was covering state government, I spent a couple of weeks writing and debugging a program in BASIC that would analyse legislative roll call votes. It would allow me to quickly enter in the yes and no votes and then it would print out crosstabs showing how the vote broke down not just by party registration, but also by other political demographics such as geography, race, gender, leadership versus rank-and-file, etc; it even wrote the agate type listing of who voted which way. Great idea, but I soon realised that building such a thing could be done even back then in minutes, not weeks, using off-the-shelf tools like Lotus 1-2-3 or dBase.

Today there are web services, many at low or no cost, that will scrape data, clean it, do a statistical analysis of the data, map it, make charts of it, and allow you to embed the graphics as interactive elements of your news web page. It is true that you have much more control of all that if you can program such things yourself, but in a deadline-driven newsroom 'good enough for now' often is more important than 'much better a few days later'.

Another reality for the every-student-must-code enthusiasts to consider is that the vast majority of journalism students simply aren't interested in being high-level data journalists. I am blessed with really smart students, many of whom are in our joint Bachelors/Masters degree program. But it has been my experience in teaching hundreds of these students over the years that maybe one or two in each class of 20 might go on to do data journalism at a level beyond simple spreadsheet work.

I've thought a lot about why so few journalists want to do the kind of data work that drives major investigative projects or that powers immersive web presentations. The problem, I believe, is that most journalism students are self-selected to avoid anything that looks like maths. At some point during their pre-college education they hit a bad maths teacher, and since then have convinced themselves they must be a 'word person' and not a 'numbers person'. Frankly, I'm not sure it's a good idea to have journalists who struggle to calculate percentage change operating even light data machinery like Excel spreadsheets. Back in the old days it would take several keystrokes on a calculator to make a maths mistake; thanks to computers, it's now possible to instantly make millions of mistakes that way.

These days, students who arrive in college with good maths skills and natural intuition about data are more likely to gravitate to majors in computer science or engineering. In fact, that's where newsrooms eager to hire web developers should be recruiting. 'I used to believe it was better to teach journalists to program,' says *The Washington Post* projects editor Greg Linch, 'but in the last couple of years I've realised it's easier to teach programmers journalism' (Spinner, 2014).

So am I a militant anti-coder? Absolutely not. In my classes, students study journalism projects that require computer code to accomplish, and they learn where it was used. I teach them to write Excel functions that create new variables or use logical operators. I introduce them to slick data graphics tools like Google Fusion Tables and Tableau Public. They also learn basics of web page design and HTML in other classes they take at our school. Those who express real interest in going beyond spreadsheet skills are encouraged to explore coding themselves with such resources as Paul Bradshaw's *Scraping for Journalists* e-book (Bradshaw, 2013) or *Learn Python the Hard Way* by Zed A. Shaw (Shaw, 2014).

In sum, the ability to write useful computer code is a special skill that is critically needed in modern multimedia news organizations. Journalism students need to know that such tools exist and that the ability to use them is valuable. Journalism programs with the right instructors should offer advanced data journalism courses as electives, or at least aim interested students at courses in the computer science department. But I believe that the argument that all journalists need to be coders is utopian at best and arguably unfair to the majority of students who want to develop other kinds of story-telling skills. Every newsroom needs people like me. But a newsroom filled with people like me couldn't function.

References

Bradshaw, Paul (2013) *Scraping for Journalists*, e-book available at http://leanpub.com/scrapingforjournalists, accessed 18 August 2015

Ford, Paul (2015) 'What is code?' in Bloomberg.com, available at www.bloomberg.com/graphics/2015-paul-ford-what-is-code, accessed 7 August 2015

McAdams, Mindy (2005) Flash Journalism: How to Create Multimedia News Packages. Waltham, MA: Focal Press/Elsevier

Shaw, Zed A. (2014) *Learn Python the Hard Way*, e-book available at http://learnpythonthehardway.org, accessed 18 August 2015

Spinner, Jackie (2014) 'The big conundrum: should journalists learn code?' in *American Journalism Review*, 24 September, available at http://ajr.org/2014/09/24/should-journalists-learn-code, accessed 18 August, 2015

Vallery-Radot, Rene (1902) *The Life of Pasteur, Vol. 1*, translated by R.L. Devonshire. New York: McClure, Phillips and Co

Section 4:
Data journalism in action

Tom Felle

With all our pontificating on the importance of data driven reporting, this 'Data journalism in action' section takes readers into the newsroom to examine what's really going on on the front lines. The area is fast becoming a sub-genre of journalism itself with specialised skillsets developing, and highly creative teams of journalists, statisticians, developers and visual designers working collaboratively to report on everything from tennis to the latest refugee crisis. In short, these new digital teams are establishing a whole new beachhead for journalism itself: stories are being told that simply could never be reported on by any other means.

In his contribution, Gavin Freeguard, senior researcher at the Institute for Government, discusses the Whitehall Monitor project and how organisations such as theirs can engage with data journalism effectively to keep an eye on government. Freeguard offers an interesting insight into the work of the think tank, and argues that the fourth estate function of holding government to account (and reporting on what those in power do) is not a function solely of the press. As he writes:

> *'Traditional journalism – especially at a local level – is not in the best state, partly because of a failure to adapt to the digital age. A strong fourth estate should not be used an excuse for government to stop using this data itself, or to abolish scrutiny institutions (as it did with the Audit Commission – Timmins and Gash, 2014). Talented data journalism graduates are still likely to look to news organisations not think tanks. Civil society organisations may come to data journalism with their own agenda (though so do traditional news organisations). Explanatory data journalism can only do so much –*

investigative journalism, still largely the preserve of news organisations, is still necessary to hold government to account.'

This author took to the telephone to interview a selection of data journalists in leading newspapers and news magazines, broadcasters and online only publications worldwide. In my contribution, 'Accountability meets engagement: data journalism's watchdog role', I argue that in an era of increased celebrity and infotainment, championing the traditional fourth estate function of the news media has been taken up by data journalists. Data gurus – often using social science techniques – are publishing investigations that previously could not be undertaken to report on issues of public importance. Engagement with stories is also increasing as a result of data visualisation. However it is niche ABC1 publications, and not mass-market tabloids, that are leading the charge – with the danger that data journalism is creating – as Andy Dickinson and others have characterised elsewhere – technologically literate elites.

'Increased audience engagement with interactive news, in particular via news apps that allow interactivity and individualisation, may point towards a future direction in the development of news. In an era of declining audiences, engagement can be considered a "holy grail" for journalism, and storytelling approaches that increase engagement, such as data journalism, are important.... [But] by virtue of the fact that news organisations that conduct substantial data journalism are in the main ABC1 circulation publications or broadcasters with niche audiences, it is reasonable to argue that data journalism is still accessed primarily by those "quality" audiences who are already engaged, rather than reaching people from all socio-economic backgrounds. In short, while digital data reporting has the potential to increase audience engagement in both size and substance, it might also be contributing to the creation of data elites... and reinforcing the current socioeconomic structure of news audiences.'

Journalist, trainer and this book's co-editor Damian Radcliffe offers an insightful look at the use of data by hyperlocal and local newsrooms in storytelling. A combination of factors has lead to a dearth of data journalism output from locals, however some niche sites and hyperlocals have trailblazed. As ever, training, time constraints and a lack of access to high quality datasets has contributed to the many problems faced by these pioneers. He writes:

'...the importance of both local journalism – and local data journalism – should not be overlooked. After all, this type of reporting may provide more meaningful insights for the day-to-day lives of readers than many of the stories covered by national media. However, in the data space, the creation of in-depth localised content is not always easy to produce. Datasets are generally smaller, potentially making the stories within them less obvious; and most local newsrooms operate with considerably fewer resources than their national – and international – counterparts.'

In Jonathan Stoneman's humorously titled chapter 'Open data and journalism – a case for relationship counselling?' the former BBC journalist summarises the frustrations of many data journalists with the glacial pace of the much vaulted data revolution promised by the UK Government. Datasets are, well, pretty useless if they are not up to date as many reporters will testify – and that is all too often the case with official data released by government departments, councils, and other bodies and agencies. Public bodies are suspicious of journalists who only report 'bad' news, rather than holistically looking at datasets. As he writes:

> *'Open data and journalism should be natural partners – a marriage made in heaven, one might say. Open data needs public exposure, journalists need easily accessible, raw, facts without spin by politicians or press officers. But this marriage – if it is to be one – is like Romeo and Juliet: the two families have different cultures and treat each other with mutual suspicion (at best!) Each side sees the other as distorting facts for their own ends, dealing in half-truths, and doing whatever is needed to tell the story their way.... This natural state of affairs is not necessarily causing governments to withhold data, but it does make their data publishers more cautious.'*

Will machines one-day rise up and rule the world? Andy Dickinson doesn't offer a view on that, but he does gives us a fascinating insight into a different take on data journalism – using sensors to track everything from populations to bugs, creating masses of data that can be mined by news media to report on stories – and even be automated to create alerts. He offers interesting examples such as air quality assurances given by the Chinese government being unspun by Associated Press and the BBC in advance of the Beijing Olympics. Sensor journalism, as he refers to it, has had a number of successes but it is still in its infancy. He writes:

> *'Despite its successes, sensor journalism is still a developing area and it is not yet clear if it will see any growth beyond the environmental issues that drive many of the examples presented here. Like data journalism, much of the discussion around the field focuses on the new opportunities it presents. These often intersect with equally nascent but seductive ideas such as drone journalism.... As journalism follows the mechanisms of the institutions we are meant to hold to account into the digital space, it is perhaps a chance to think about how it can move beyond simply building capacity within the industry, providing useful case studies.'*

Technology expert Gabriel Keeble-Gagnère makes the case for journalists becoming security experts. He argues that following the Snowden exposé in 2013, journalists, especially those dealing with sensitive topics, should become familiar with encryption techniques. If they don't, he warns, in an increasingly digital world where national security organisations like the NSA in the US and GCHQ in the UK may have access to emails and other digital communications, whistleblowers may be unwilling to engage with journalists.

> *In short, journalists can no longer rely on internet companies, commercial software, or even the rule of law to protect them or their data. Especially at risk are those who work with whistleblowers – as Julian Assange and Glenn Greenwald are perhaps the most aware. It goes without saying that whistleblowers themselves must be especially careful, even more so than the journalists they work with; the experiences of Bradley/Chelsea Manning and Edward Snowden have made this clear. Indeed, following an initial (encrypted) exchange with Snowden (who had not revealed his identity at the time), Laura Poitras was given 'instructions for creating an even more secure system to protect their exchanges'. Snowden had already contacted Greenwald anonymously, with instructions on how to use encryption, but had been ignored (Mass 2013). In the future, unless journalists have a working knowledge of cryptographic techniques, whistleblowers will, rightly, be unwilling to approach them.*

He also provides a useful overview of the methods reporters can use to protect themselves from the snoopers. A chapter not to be missed.

Finally, Ændrew Rininsland, who is a newsroom developer on the digital desk at *The Times* and *The Sunday Times*, discusses the development of coding tools in data journalism and offers tips and advice for would-be developer journalists. He investigates the differences between exploratory and explanatory approaches to data storytelling. He argues that coding using explanatory approaches with languages such as 'D3' offers far more exciting possibilities for developer journalists (and, we might assume, better engagement experiences for readers):

> *'D3 really shines when used to create visualisations that highlight the most important pieces of data. D3's speed and utility have made it the de-facto standard for web-based data visualisation for news, with the D3 community leveraging some of the most exciting trends and best practises in web programming. This makes D3 proficiency a valuable skill for aspiring data journalists, newsroom developers, visualisation artists and journo-coders.'*

Charting government: doing data journalism as a think tank

Gavin Freeguard, senior researcher at the Institute for Government, discusses the Whitehall Monitor project and how Think Tanks can engage with data journalism effectively to keep an eye on government

Introduction

It's shortly after 10pm on Thursday 7 May 2015, and the only chart that matters is the one being projected onto BBC Broadcasting House. The exit poll for the 2015 General Election has just rendered weeks of hung parliament speculation pointless, Harriet Harman's party lines obsolete and Paddy Ashdown's hat edible: the Tories are on course for a workable minority, Labour for a disaster, the Lib Dems for near wipe-out, and the pollsters for some psephological soul-searching. My editor calls: he's seen this before. The result is only going in one direction – a Tory majority. Without the luxury of a couple of weeks of coalition negotiation, me and my team will be live-blogging the formation of the next government rather earlier than expected and will need to prepare for an early morning.

As David Cameron leaves Buckingham Palace at around 1pm the next day, Prime Minister with a Conservative majority, we get to work. For three solid days, we analyse the ministerial moves as Coalition gives way to Conservative government in real time. But there are two unusual things about our live-blogging exploits. The first is that we're doing the whole thing in charts – 225 of them, around nine an hour – all of them in Excel and many updated instantly as ministers move into – or out of – government. The second is that it wasn't my editor that called, but our deputy director. We don't have an editor, because we are not a news organisation. We are the Institute for Government. And we are a think tank.

Charting government – the Whitehall Monitor project

The Institute for Government is an independent charity, a stone's throw away from both Westminster and Whitehall, that aims to help make government more effective. One of the ways we do this – alongside various research projects, public events and development work with politicians and civil servants – is through our *Whitehall Monitor* project. *Whitehall Monitor* is essentially data journalism – we take data published by and about government to build up a picture (literally) of the size, shape and performance of government. We publish an annual report, regular blogposts and occasional special reports (Freeguard et al 2014; Freeguard et al 2015; Freeguard, Munro and Andrews 2015). We aim to improve the way government uses and publishes data, as well as increasing understanding of what government currently looks like.

This matters. When people think of government departments (if they think of them at all), it is probably what they have in common that stands out – the department of this or the ministry of that, based somewhere in London SW1, funded by our taxes with a minister around the Cabinet table. But departments vary hugely in what they are, what they do, how they do it and how well they do it, something we hope our work will help politicians, civil servants, journalists, civil society and the wider public appreciate.

Live-blogging government reshuffles is something of a speciality for us – we did it in July 2014 as well as the three days in May 2015. It's a fantastic opportunity to use the political drama of election results and ministerial moves to interest people in everything from the importance of ministerial stability (moving junior ministers around can affect whether policies are actually implemented) to how much departments have changed since 2010 (a lot, in some cases). Our most retweeted graphic was one on the disparity between vote share and seat share:

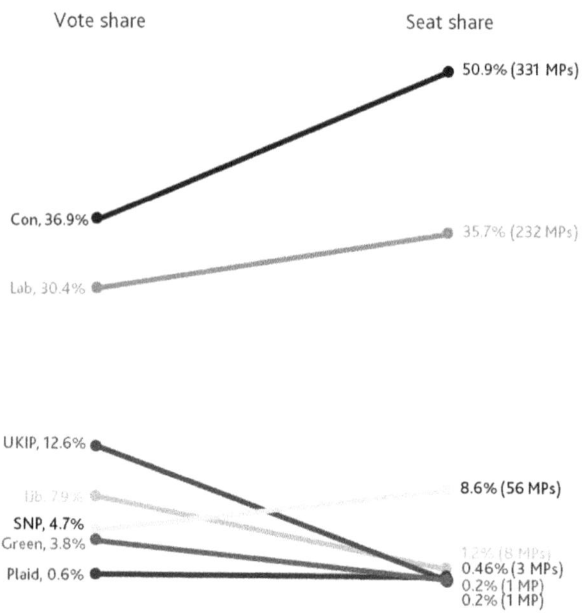

Figure 48: Vote share and seat share in the UK's 2015 General Election. Source: Institute for Government analysis of election results

But much of the content on the blog used ministerial appointments to highlight the challenges the ministers running their new departments would face, and what the departments they were inheriting looked like.

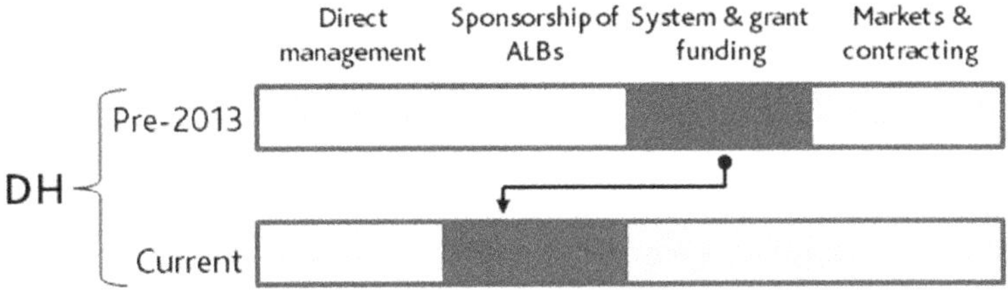

The Health and Social Care Act 2012 fundamentally changed how the Department of Health relates to the National Health Service. From April 2013, responsibility for managing the health service and the public health system moved to NHS England and Public Health England, respectively – both arm's-length bodies. The department itself has moved to an assurance role: rather than directly managing and shaping the health system, it specifies strategic goals in framework agreements with these bodies.

Figure 49: Change in resource management: Department of Health before and after NHS reforms. Source: Institute for Government analysis of DH annual accounts. Indicative of around 80 per cent of department spend. Text from Whitehall Monitor 2014

Think tanks and data journalism

In a sense, what we are doing is what think tanks have always done: conducting quantitative research and publishing it. But after releasing *Whitehall Monitor 2013*, we looked at the wealth of data and analysis in it and wondered what else we could to ensure it reached a wide audience and had some impact (Stephen, Bouchal and Bull 2013). We wanted our work to be not just on the web, but of the web. We spoke to a lot of people working with data. One remarked that what we were trying to do was akin to what 'some of the better newspapers are doing', and from then on, we consciously started to refer to what we did as 'data journalism'.

The Guardian and the *FT* already had notable data journalism output. *Ampp3d* was pioneering punchy tabloid data journalism. Full Fact was charting as well as checking data. Buzzfeed was combining images with punchy titles and comment. In the US, Nate Silver's FiveThirtyEight, Ezra Klein's Vox, the *Washington Post*'s Wonkblog and *New York Times*' The Upshot had a strong focus on data-driven 'explanatory' journalism.

Seeing what we were doing as 'data journalism' meant something different. It meant leading with some of the visuals and seeing them as stories in their own right rather than burying them deep in reports. It meant adopting more journalistic practices, such as working at speed and reacting to events. It meant connecting directly with the public, especially over social media, and aiming for more than just press coverage. And it meant shifting our entire organisational focus towards frequent and engaging blog posts rather than PDF reports (although hard copy annual reports can still reach an audience blog posts can't).

'Data journalism' wasn't without its critics. The US sites in particular faced criticism (some of it warranted) – a downside to the Upshot, if not unbridled FiveThirtyHate or a pox on Vox (for example, Ball 2014). But some of the problems they faced – caught between being too specialist (and therefore superficial to experts) or not specialist enough, the journalism being explanatory rather than investigative and proactive – were potentially advantages for us: we have an institutional expertise in the functions of government, and so much basic information about government was not being presented to a wider public. We also faced a possible internal problem: working in a different rhythm and using different skills to other projects in the Institute could have shut us off from colleagues. But our colleagues became really interested in what we'd done, and wanted to apply many of the same principles to their own work. We've now started rolling out data analysis and visualisation training across the Institute.

In September 2014, *The Economist* noted that think tanks, 'the semi-academic institutions that come up with ideas for politicians', were increasingly 'doing journalism' (Economist, 2014). But it felt this was 'more to promote ideas than to inform the public or expose wrongdoing', and noted that 'their policy papers are meant to be dry'. There's no reason why any of that should be true. Indeed, a number of think tanks – such as Policy Exchange, The King's Fund, the Resolution Foundation and the Institute for Fiscal Studies in the UK, and the Pew Center and Urban Institute in the US – have been increasingly using visuals to inform the public, as well as presenting and promoting their work, to great effect. These organisations may not see what they do quite so explicitly as 'data journalism' – but many of the practices are similar.

Armchair auditors, the fourth estate and ecosystems

Different think tanks will use different data sources and maybe create their own. We use open data from government (and the Office for National Statistics) for most of our work, helped by successive UK governments wanting to be a world leader in opening up data. Before he became Prime Minister, David Cameron looked forward to the 'army of armchair auditors' that would engage with expenses and government finances, and march towards a more transparent government and society (Cameron, 2009). But, for the most part, the armchair auditors haven't enlisted (Radcliffe, 2014; Worthy, 2013). Although it is a worthy aspiration that data should be published in a format anyone can use, there is no Excel field of dreams; you can build the spreadsheet, but they won't necessarily come.

A better model would be to think of a new 'fourth estate', wider than just the press. The digital revolution has provided a far greater range of individuals and organisations with the opportunity and the tools to publish and do 'journalism' – it is no longer confined to those working for news organisations (Brock, 2013). Good journalism requires expertise, resources and time – something that think tanks and other civil society organisations (as well as some individuals) can bring to particular subjects, as well as journalism organisations.

It would be easy to get carried away with this idea. Traditional journalism – especially at a local level – is not in the best state, partly because of a failure to adapt to the digital age. A strong fourth estate should not be used an excuse for government to stop using this data itself, or to abolish scrutiny institutions (as it did with the Audit Commission – Timmins and Gash, 2014). Talented data journalism graduates are still likely to look to news organisations not think tanks. Civil society organisations may come to data journalism with their own agenda (though so do traditional news organisations). Explanatory data journalism can only do so much – investigative journalism, still largely the preserve of news organisations, is still necessary to hold government to account.

And for all the creative opportunities – what Simon Rogers has likened to punk – there is a risk that those without the requisite expertise will produce work lacking in meaning and rigour (Rogers, 2014; Burn-Murdoch, 2014). We are lucky at the Institute for Government to have built up a wealth of knowledge and understanding of government, which we can link to and draw upon, and ensure we ask the right questions of the data. Without asking the right questions and simply aggregating numbers to draw pretty but meaningless graphs, data journalism can be the plural of anecdote journalism. And even though most of our work is done through widely-available Excel and we build our spreadsheets to turn around analysis as quickly as possible, cleaning and checking the data can still take time. Data journalism may be easier than ever before, but it's still not easy.

Nonetheless, there is now more data and more people and organisations with the expertise to do something with it. The right way of thinking about all this might be as an ecosystem – competitive and collaborative, with the different actors feeding off one another's work and constant conversation about how to publish, visualise and use data. A government department might publish the data; a think tank may do something with it and publish it directly to the public; a news organisation might pick up something directly from the department or think tank; members of the public or other organisations may find things to improve; and so on.

Data, information and evidence

At the heart of our data ecosystem is the data published by government. The Coalition prioritised open data publication for three broad reasons – government accountability to citizens, improving public services and catalysing economic and social growth (Maltby, 2013) – and it is the first that we have been most interested in (though with obvious implications for the second). We've started to think about it in three ways: data as data (the raw material), data as information (turned into something meaningful) and data as evidence (actually using it for something). Using those headings gives a sense of where things currently are, how we feel our work relates to it, and where others may also be able to learn and contribute.

Data as data

The UK government is seen as a world leader in open data, and is publishing more data than ever before. The number of datasets published by data.gov.uk has increased from 9,498 in June 2013 to 19,834 in March 2015 (Freeguard, Munro and Andrews, 2015). We wouldn't be able to produce a 150-page annual report without it. Even where the quality of the data leaves something to be desired, it is still better that it is published at all, and will hopefully improve with use. The new Minister for the Cabinet Office, Matt Hancock, has suggested the agenda will continue, saying that 'without [open data] governments bury their heads in the sand' (Hancock, 2015). However, there are definitely improvements that can, and should, be made.

More data could be published – for example, around contracts between government and independent providers of goods and services and around why departments' spending plans have changed (Wajzer 2014; Freeguard et al, 2014). The quality of data can often be improved, such as the data on Civil Service professions. The lack of unique identifiers for things like government departments, or a 'canonical register' in the current Government Digital Service lexicon, makes data work much more difficult than it should be (Howard, 2015). There are still accessibility problems – for example, too much data is still being published in PDF (aka Pretty Damn Frustrating) rather than in spreadsheets. Important data should be available to all users and not just the most technically-proficient ones – to those who think .json sang with Kylie, and that 'scraping' is something think tank researchers do to the barrel of bad jokes in writing book chapters on data journalism.

Running above all of this is how government organises the open data agenda. The appointment of Mike Bracken as the first chief data officer provides some opportunity to get this right (Cabinet Office, 2015). Continued political will is also vital. However, as Giuseppe Sollazzo, a former member of the Open Data User Group, has pointed out, the reduction in the number of open data advisory boards from four to zero over the last couple of years is not so positive – one hopes it is an outlier, rather than a trend (Sollazzo, 2015).

As well as holding government to account for how it publishes data, we also need to think about how we do it ourselves. Many data journalism sites have been criticised for their lack of transparency and not publishing their data (Bouchal, 2015). We say that government should show their working, make their data more accessible and easier for others to use and generate their own insights, and publish so that others might improve the quality of it – we should practice what we preach.

We try to ensure our own data is open, reproducible, usable, updatable (i.e. ready to receive the latest data quickly), consistent, and portable. But most importantly, it should be published; to paraphrase George Orwell's sixth rule of writing, break any of the above rules rather than doing something outright barbarous, which would not be publishing at all (Orwell 1946). No doubt we fall short of this on occasions and we could do more, but in bringing our own data out of the bunker we hope to encourage others to do so and improve the data we use.

A final point on open data. Data is not naturally occurring – when someone produces a dataset, they have chosen which data to collect and how to collect it. It will have inherent biases and limitations. So even though open data being published proactively is to be welcomed, it cannot replace people – whether journalists, academics or other organisations – going out to collect their own data to test hypotheses, or reactive requests, such as those under the Freedom of Information Act (FOI). Recent developments on Freedom of Information – the announcement of a review, and the transfer of the policy to the Cabinet Office – should therefore concern those who care about accountability and transparency. It is to be hoped the Cabinet Office does not become a FOI extinguisher.

Data as information

Publishing lots of data is one thing – making it mean something, quite another. In an age of 'infobesity', with so much data being published, it is possible for things to be hidden in plain sight. What is needed is for data – the raw material – to be converted into information – something that actually means something. For our purposes, turning data into information usually means turning it into a data visualisation. Data visualisation matters. It can bring to life important numbers and trends that would otherwise have remained hidden in the main text or ignored in data tables. Visualising the data is often the best way of telling the story. As William Playfair, a founding father of modern data visualisation, noted, numbers in a table are often like 'a figure imprinted on sand… soon totally erased' while charts ensure 'a sufficiently distinct impression will be made, to remain unimpaired for a considerable time, and the idea which does remain will be simple and complete' (Tufte, 2001).

But throwing numbers into an Excel spreadsheet and generating a random chart isn't good enough, any more than throwing a random selection of letters onto a page would qualify as a rigorous, well-written research report. Bad data visualisation can – unintentionally, as well as intentionally – distort, mislead, obscure, confuse and force the reader to do much more work than they should have to.

As a result, we've spent a lot of time refining our practices into an Institute for Government style guide, an evolving document setting out standards and practices for data visualisation across the organisation. It is necessary both for branding – it's important our images are consistent and easily identifiable as ours – and for understanding – our graphs should be telling their stories as clearly and accurately as possible, and all of the design choices involved in a chart can help or hinder this. When we talk about 'telling a story', we don't, of course, mean fiction – our style guide balances simplicity and clarity with accuracy and integrity.

According to one study, the average reader online will spend around 15 seconds on a page (Haile, 2014). Simplicity and clarity should therefore allow a reader who spends 15 seconds looking at one of our graphs to understand it. A good 'Twitter test' is whether the image, tweeted out and divorced from any deeper analysis, would make sense to a reader all by itself. This (usually) means only showing or telling one clear story per graph. For example, rather than trying to show both current position and change over time in the same clustered bar chart:

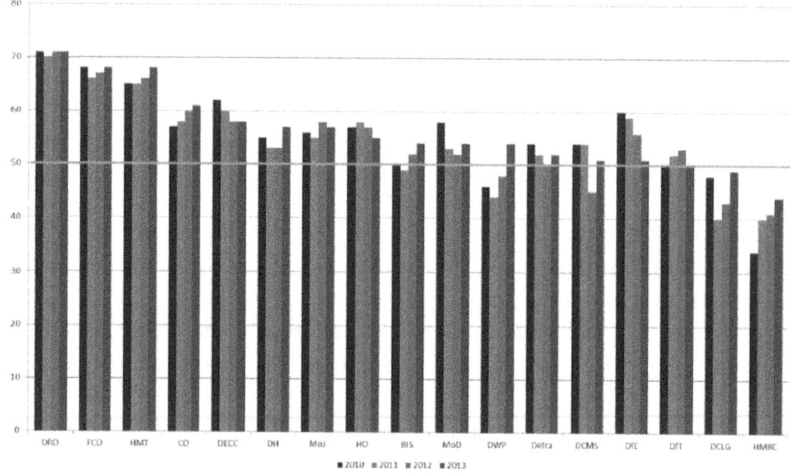

Figure 50: Engagement index by department, 2010-2013. Source: Institute for Government analysis of Civil Service People Survey, 2010-2013

We would show the current score in a bar chart, and the change over time in a separate 'coloured spaghetti' chart drawing out some key stories:

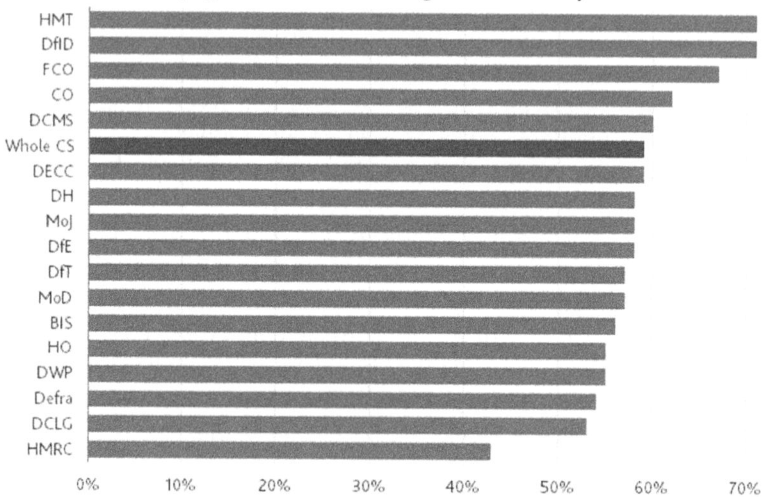

Figure 51: Civil service engagement by department, 2014. Source Institute for Government analysis of Civil Service People Survey, 2009-2014

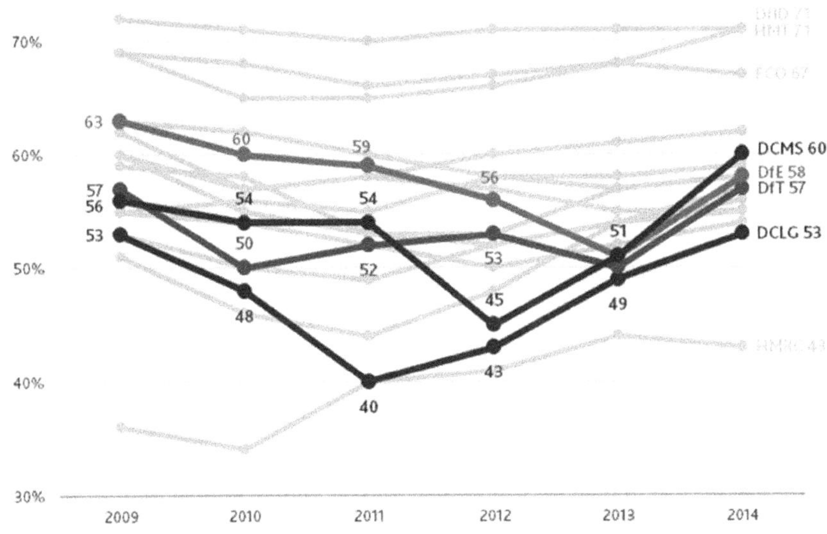

Figure 52: Civil service Engagement Index, 2009-2014). Source Institute for Government analysis of Civil Service People Survey, 2009-2014

Everything on the chart should aid the story, from the way the data is ordered (e.g. largest to smallest bar), to the title, to the minimising of gridlines, labels and other clutter. We try to let the data breathe – as Edward Tufte writes, 'Above all else, show the data' (Tufte, 2001). Data visualisation shouldn't be about showing off the fancy things your computer can do, showing off your intelligence to your reader or neglecting the data at the expense of making something beautiful but meaningless. You want your reader to understand you – data visualisation is, in Alberto Cairo's expression, a 'functional art'.

Another of Orwell's six golden rules for writing was to avoid cliché (Orwell, 1946). Data visualisation often benefits from the opposite – conventional presentations, such as bar or line charts, are easily understood. But there are exceptions. Not all conventions should hold – if pie charts are the answer, you're usually asking the wrong question (unless the question is 'what form of chart is overused, often distorts the data and can usually be replaced by something more useful?'). And using an unconventional and arresting chart can make most subjects engaging. Our most retweeted graphic is one on job grades in various government departments – the unconventional visualisation catches a reader's attention and draws them in:

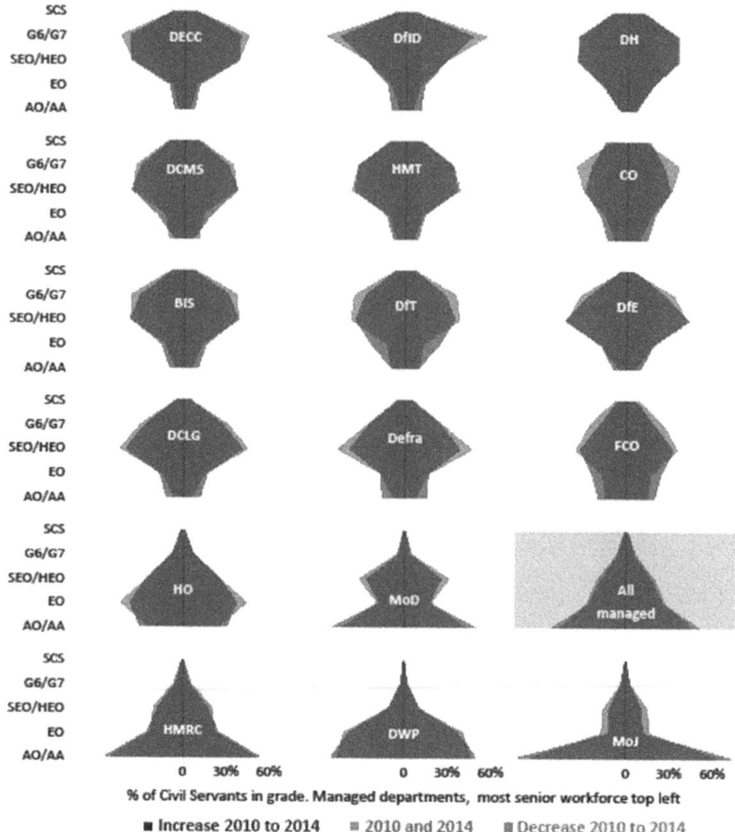

Figure 53: Grade composition by government departments, 2010 and 2014 (headcount). Source Institute for Government analysis of ONS annual Civil Service Employment Survey, 2010-2014

As for accuracy and integrity: the IfG has worked hard to develop a reputation for rigour, and a serious error could threaten this. We check our work as thoroughly as possible to avoid this – following data points from charts all the way back to the source, developing a list of 'gotchas' or common pitfalls to watch out for, publishing all of our working and being clear about any caveats. Where the data we are working with has problems (e.g. gaps or unreliability), that becomes part of the story. Data should not be distorted – whether intentionally to fit predetermined narratives, or unintentionally through bad design. We also have a 'Twitter test' for this: if the chart were retweeted without any further context, would it stand, accurately, by itself?

When we get all of this right, the data is turned into something meaningful. This can require a lot of work – thinking about what visuals are likely to work before a data release, making sure our spreadsheets are set up in a way to generate them quickly, and iterating to see what works and what doesn't. In our reshuffle live-blogs, for example, we made sure data could be updated and the right graphs produced instantaneously, as well as having prepared lots of graphics – on previous ministries and giving context on individual departments – in advance.

But there is a further step that can make data – and data journalism – even more powerful.

Data as evidence

The 'stat' or 'performance stat' model of government, associated with politicians like Maryland's former Governor, Martin O'Malley, has become popular in the United States (Freeguard and Gold, 2015). This has involved counties, cities and even states using data to understand what's going on, to set benchmarks, baselines and targets for public services, and to hold people to account, as a basis for running their administration. Data collection and publication is not just a 'dog and pony' show for the sake of it, but is actually used to govern. Data is only powerful when it is actually used – something which doesn't always happen in the UK. In our work, we have used data to go beyond the explanatory in a number of ways. For example, we can see whether the government is on course to meet its 'expectation' in reducing Civil Service staff numbers:

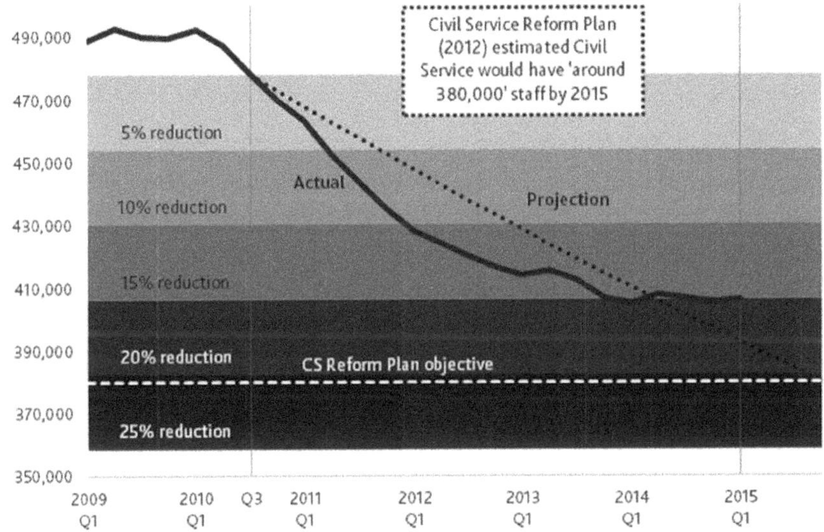

Figure 54: Civil service staff numbers, March 2009 to March 2015. Source Institute for Government analysis of ONS Public Sector Employment Data (Table 9), Q1 2009 to Q1 2015

It isn't, which surely signals the difficulty ahead in reducing the size of the state further.

We've also used government data to try to work out the impact that government departments had on important policy areas between 2010 and 2015 according to their own 'impact indicators' (Freeguard, Munro and Andrews, 2015) – had they moved in the right direction?

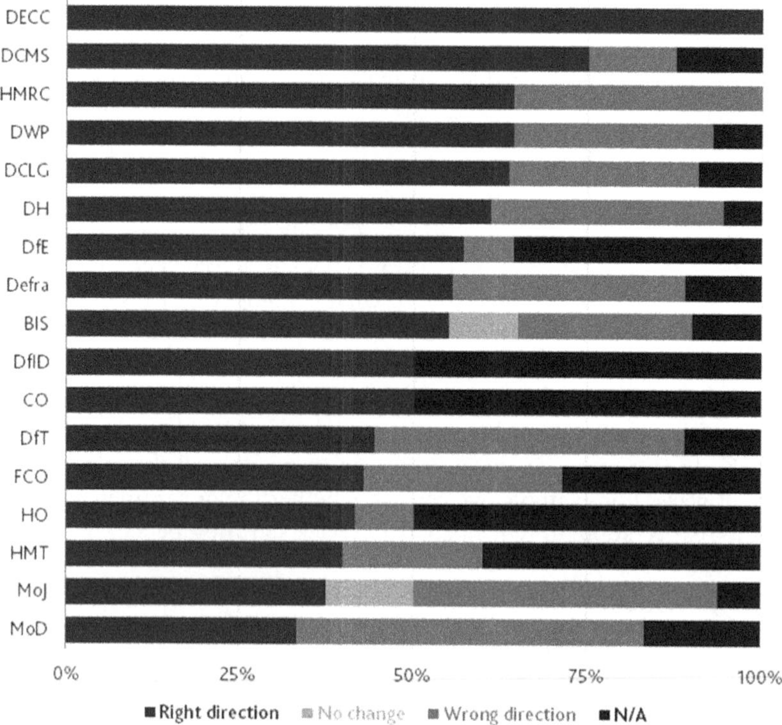

Figure 55: Movement in impact indicators, 2010-2015. Source Institute for Government analysis of impact indicators – multiple sources, Whitehall Monitor: Deep Impact 17 (2015)

We found that for some departments (like Energy and Climate Change), they had – for others (like Defence), they hadn't. But the bigger discovery was that, given the quality of much of the data (where it was published at all) and the lack of baselines and benchmarks, it was highly unlikely that government was actually using the data to hold departments to account. This highlights not only that government could be using data in a much more powerful way, but also the benefits of data journalism in holding government to account.

Over the next few years, we hope to use data – and data journalism – much more in this way, and to encourage government to improve how it publishes and uses data to make government more effective. Hopefully, by the time we have to live-blog after the next General Election, we'll have much more evidence of how government is performing and more evidence that it is using data to drive improvement.

Conversely, and for all the excitement about producing data journalism as a think tank, we might also hope that we're not talking about either data journalism or think tank data journalism as such an innovation. Hopefully, data journalism will be simply part of regular journalism – and journalism something that is much more mainstream for organisations like ours.

References

Ball, James (2014) 'The Upshot, Vox and *FiveThirtyEight*: data journalism's golden age, or TMI?' in *the Guardian*, 22 April, available at http://www.theguardian.com/commentisfree/2014/apr/22/upshot-vox-fivethirtyeight-data-journalism-golden-age, accessed 25 August 2015

Bouchal, Petr (2015) 'Bringing thinktank data out of the bunker', Institute for Government, 29 January, available at http://www.instituteforgovernment.org.uk/blog/10206/bringing-thinktank-data-out-of-the-bunker/

Brock, George (2013) Out of Print: Newspapers, Journalism and the Business of News in the Digital Age. London: Kogan Page

Burn-Murdoch, John (2014), 'The advent of the statistician journalist', Mair, John and Keeble, Richard Lance (eds) with Bradshaw, Paul and Beleaga, Teodora, *Data Journalism: Mapping the Future*. Bury St Edmunds: Abramis

Cabinet Office (2015) 'Local authorities setting standards as Open Data Champions', GOV.UK, 24 March, available at www.gov.uk/government/news/local-authorities-setting-standards-as-open-data-champions, accessed 25 August 2015

Cairo, Alberto (2012) The Functional Art: An Introduction to Information Graphics and Visualization, San Francisco: New Riders

Cameron, David (2009) 'Fixing Broken Politics', 29 March, available at http://conservative-speeches.sayit.mysociety.org/speech/601355, accessed 25 August 2015

Economist, The (2014) 'Think-tanks and journalism: Making the headlines', 20 September, available at http://www.economist.com/news/international/21618824-divide-between-having-ideas-and-reporting-them-dissolving-making-headlines, accessed 25 August 2015

Freeguard, Gavin; Bouchal, Petr; Munro, Robyn; Nimmo, Caragh and McCrae, Julian (2014) *Whitehall Monitor 2014*, Institute for Government, available at http://www.instituteforgovernment.org.uk/publications/whitehall-monitor-2014, accessed 25 August 2015

Freeguard, Gavin; Munro, Robyn and Andrews, Emily (2015), *Whitehall Monitor: Deep Impact? How government departments measured their impact, 2010-15*, Institute for Government, available at http://www.instituteforgovernment.org.uk/sites/default/files/publications/Deep%20Impact%20-%20FINAL.pdf and http://www.instituteforgovernment.org.uk/publication/how-government-measures-its-impact, accessed 25 August 2015

Freeguard, Gavin; Andrews, Emily; Bouchal, Petr; Devine, Daniel; Munro, Robyn; Nimmo, Caragh; Randall, Joe; Rutter, Jill and White, Hannah (2015) assorted *Whitehall Monitor* blogposts 2014 and 2015, Institute for Government, available at http://www.instituteforgovernment.org.uk/blog/author/the-whitehall-monitor, and via http://www.instituteforgovernment.org.uk/publication/whitehall-monitor-2014, accessed 25 August 2015

Freeguard, Gavin and Gold, Jen (2015) *Data-Driven Delivery: Lessons from the O'Malley Administration of Maryland*, Institute for Government, available at http://www.instituteforgovernment.org.uk/publications/data-driven-delivery-lessons-o%E2%80%99malley-administration-maryland, accessed 25 August 2015

Haile, Tony (2014) 'What You Think You Know About the Web Is Wrong', *TIME*, 9 March, available at http://time.com/12933/what-you-think-you-know-about-the-web-is-wrong, accessed 25 August 2015

Hancock, Matthew (2015) 'Open Government Partnership: UK national action plan 2015 launch', Cabinet Office, 13 July, available at https://www.gov.uk/government/speeches/open-government-partnership-uk-national-action-plan-2015-launch, accessed 25 August 2015

Howard, Alex (2015) 'UK's first chief data officer to focus on making data a public asset', TechRepublic, 27 March, available at www.techrepublic.com/article/uks-first-chief-data-officer-to-focus-on-making-data-a-public-asset, accessed 25 August 2015

Maltby, Paul (2013) 'What did open data ever do for us?' in data.gov.uk, 29 October, available at http://data.gov.uk/blog/what-did-open-data-ever-do-us, accessed 25 August 2015

Orwell, George (1946) 'Politics and the English Language', *Horizon*, April, available at http://theorwellprize.co.uk/george-orwell/by-orwell/essays-and-other-works/politics-and-the-english-language, accessed 25 August 2015

Radcliffe, Damian (2014) 'Hyperlocal media and data journalism', Mair, John and Keeble, Richard Lance (eds) with Bradshaw, Paul and Beleaga, Teodora, *Data Journalism: Mapping the Future.* Bury St Edmunds: Abramis

Rogers, Simon (2014) 'Why data journalism is the new punk', Mair, John and Keeble, Richard Lance (eds) with Bradshaw, Paul and Beleaga, Teodora, *Data Journalism: Mapping the Future.* Bury St Edmunds: Abramis

Sollazzo, Giuseppe (2015) 'Not an obituary: ODUG, three years at the heart of Open Data', Medium, 1 June, available at https://medium.com/@puntofisso/not-an-obituary-odug-three-years-at-the-heart-of-open-data-9ddc4ba23904, accessed 25 August 2015

Stephen, Justine; Bouchal, Petr and Bull, David (2013) *Whitehall Monitor 2013*, Institute for Government, available at http://www.instituteforgovernment.org.uk/publications/whitehall-monitor-2013, accessed 25 August 2015

Timmins, Nicholas and Gash, Tom (2014) *Dying to Improve: The Demise of the Audit Commission and Other Improvement Agencies*, Institute for Government, available at http://www.instituteforgovernment.org.uk/publications/dying-improve, accessed 25 August 2015

Tufte, Edward (2001) *The Visual Display of Quantitative Information*, Cheshire, Connecticut: Graphics Press USA (2nd edn)

Wajzer, Chris (2014) 'Taking transparency to taskforce', Institute for Government, 19 November, available at www.instituteforgovernment.org.uk/blog/9445/taking-transparency-to-taskforce, accessed 25 August 2015

Worthy, Ben (2013), 'Where are the Armchair Auditors?', Open Data Institute, 1 June, available at http://theodi.org/blog/guest-blog-where-are-armchair-auditors, accessed 25 August 2015

Accountability meets engagement: data journalism's watchdog role

Data reporting has an important contribution to make to accountability and in fulfilling journalism's fourth estate function, however the failure of popular 'tabloid' titles to engage with data means many are being left behind, writes Tom Felle

Introduction

In advanced democratic societies, the differing branches of government – an executive that is separate from the legislature and the judiciary – are set up to ensure checks and balances. The news media, in carrying out an investigating and reporting function, essentially keep an eye on the government and the elected office holders. They thus have often been labelled the 'fourth estate', a term that was first espoused by Edmund Burke (Schultz, 1998: 14). While most news organisations (except the BBC, some similar national state broadcasters and a minority of trust-owned newspapers) are commercial enterprises, journalists rarely see the pursuit of profit for their owners as their primary motivation. Most would agree that journalism has an explicit public-interest function, regardless of platforms (Galtung and Ruge, 1965).

The role of journalism as the fourth estate is so important that a number of states, including the United States, offer some privilege and protection to those working in the media. The First Amendment to the US constitution states that 'Congress shall make no law … abridging freedom of the press' (Government of the United States of America, 1787). No such explicit protection is offered elsewhere, but almost all advanced democracies recognise the right of journalists to investigate and criticize government and have adopted transparency legislation such as Freedom of Information (FOI) (Felle and Mair, 2015). The right to free expression and an implicit right to be informed are stipulated in the European Convention on Human Rights (Council of Europe, 1950) and the UN Convention on Civil and Political Rights (United Nations, 1966).

There are, of course, numerous cases where the media do not perform well as the fourth estate. Most news organisations in the United States and the United Kingdom, for instance, failed to question the validity of the American and the British governments' claims that Iraq had weapons of mass destruction in 2003 (Kumar, 2006: 48–69). In a number of Eurozone countries, including Spain, Greece and Ireland, the media collectively failed to seriously question their governments' economic policies in the mid-2000s (Schechter, 2009). The economies of these countries later collapsed with severe social and financial consequences for citizens.

However, despite falling short on occasion, the news media in advanced democracies have developed sophisticated mechanisms to serve as public watchdogs. Although it might be an idealistic notion, most journalists espouse to this fourth estate function. Even in the United Kingdom, where the role of the journalist and the news media might be said to be to entertain and to titillate people with entertainment scoops, sports and gossip, their mission to inform, engage, analyse, uncover, report events and issues of public interest and to hold power to account is still apparent and undeniable. Not all journalism brings down governments, but exposing the impact of health cuts, or uncovering favoured treatment or sharp practice in the awarding of public contracts, is every bit as valuable to citizens as investigations that lead to political resignations or sackings. Such serious consequences might not occur on a frequent basis but many stories uncovering bureaucratic incompetence and/or political corruption may still be embarrassing, highlight hypocrisy, feather-bedding or pork-barrelling or generate healthy public debate on the merits and demerits of policy decisions.

CAR, digital data journalism and the fourth estate

In the fulfilment of journalism's fourth estate function, the use of statistical data is longstanding. Newspapers and broadcasting organisations have always reported on the latest official statistics from state agencies. Business news has contained charts and graphs to tell the financial stories of the day. Editors have commonly used graphics to display rising house prices. Reprinting a table of figures may be unintelligible for audiences, so journalists have traditionally acted – or at least tried to act – as translators and story-tellers, reporting the figures contemporaneously, analysing what they mean and giving context to help audiences better understand them.

The use of data for journalistic purposes reached a new era with the intrusion of computer assisted reporting, or CAR as it became known. CAR was first used by the US television network, Columbia Broadcasting System (CBS), in 1952 to predict the outcome of the US presidential election (Bounegru, 2012: 18–20). For more than 60 years, journalists have compiled their own databases or sought to use official data when conducting investigations. Rather than simply report on what a government press release says, or on 'spin' from private corporations, many have sought to independently verify facts and reveal truths, often with the help of social science methods and computers. It is noteworthy that this branch of journalism became known as a form of 'public service' journalism (Bounegru, 2012: 18–20).

Recent years have seen the emergence of a newer form of data reporting with the advent of digital journalism, under the generic name of digital data journalism. Digital data reporting, loosely defined, acts both as an investigative and a storytelling tool for journalists. Greater and more powerful computers and software have allowed journalists to operate far more effectively in sourcing and investigating stories. Large and complex datasets can be mined and cross-referenced as rich news sources, especially since the development of application programme interface (API) that allows users to query and manipulate data.

But unlike CAR, which was mostly an investigative tool, digital data journalism also concerns storytelling. The rich visual tools and interactivity features made possible by online journalism may equate to a new form of storytelling. Visualisation software, such as Tableau and geo-coding with Google Maps, allows for far greater interaction between the story and the audience and therefore has the potential to increase public engagement with stories. As Lorenz (2012) and others have argued, such tools make journalism more personally engaging. Whereas a newspaper traditionally reports the headline figures, interactive data stories allow readers to drill right down to the individual or the local level.

Digital data journalism, like CAR, has an important part to play in helping journalists to fulfil their key role as the public's watchdog on democratic powers and processes. Increasingly, governments throughout the world have moved away from paper-based bureaucracy and hold far more information in electronic forms. Access to large datasets is increasingly being made available as an outcome of a general move towards open government (Frey, 2014; Maude, 2012). O'Murchu (2012) argues that a central mission for journalists in this new open space is to become able to operate effectively as digital data reporters who can investigate and report published data, independently verify stories and 'scrutinise the world and hold the powers that be to account' (p. 10). The 'fourth estate' role is heightened, with open data creating new possibilities to uncover and tell important stories and user-friendly software allowing journalists to find connections between data for far more complex investigations. Previously, these stories might not be told fully or may never be uncovered at all (Bradshaw, 2012: 2).

However, there is a potential risk. In order for data journalism to well serve democratic processes, it needs to have an engaged and wide audience. There has been some criticism, however, that data reporting is fast becoming an exclusive domain for the technologically literate. Journalism scholars, such as Dickinson (2014), have asked if data journalism is really producing tools that the majority of people can use in the democratic process:

> *'Does making a spreadsheet available to users really democratize information? Does making something searchable by postcode really make it more useful on the ground? Isn't*

> *it just creating a small, equally uncountable, data elite? Is it really just a good way to reposition (consolidate) journalism as gatekeepers?'* (Dickinson, 2014: 122)

This issue becomes more pertinent in the context that media outlets with the heaviest investment in and strongest record of data journalism so far are among the least popular titles that serve elite niche audiences, rather than those with lower socio-economic status and most likely to be disengaged from politics (Hansard Society, 2012: 4). For example, *the Guardian* and *The Times* are among the most pronounced media organisations with a significant digital data reporting presence in the United Kingdom. But *the Guardian*'s combined print and online UK readership in February 2015 was 5.2 million, while that of *The Times* was only 4.5 million. The readership of both newspapers is overwhelmingly in the ABC1 category. Meanwhile, some 25.4 million readers read either *The Sun* or the *Daily Mail* during the same month; neither of these regularly deploys digital data methods in their reporting (Hollander, 2015). There have been some examples of tabloid mass market publications engaging with data-driven journalism, though none have sustained. Trinity Mirror's *Ampp3d* – a niche site focussing on data – was widely acclaimed and attracted significant traffic, though it was expensive to run. *The Guardian* reported in May 2015 that Trinity Mirror planned to close the site in favour of targeting resources at a US news operation instead (Jackson and Sweney, 2015).

Ampp3d aside, few other examples of tabloid or mass-market data-driven reporting exist. In that sense, rather than acting as a watchdog on behalf of all citizens, data journalism might well be creating a wider gap between those that can afford to be engaged and large tranches of society that are becoming completely disengaged from the wider political process, and thus effectively opting out of society. If this is the case, it is significant.

In order to test these hypotheses, interviews were conducted with a number of leading data journalists in leading media organisations. Some 26 participants from 17 countries in Europe, the Americas, Australasia and Africa participated in semi-structured interviews. Answers to questions were coded and key themes identified. Findings are outlined below.

A new form of accountability journalism?

It is argued that digital data reporting has a central role to play in holding power to account and allowing journalists to strengthen the 'fourth estate'. Although the reality is perhaps more nuanced (in that digital data reporting is used to tell stories of pitches and plays in sports games as much as it is to report on government), the interviewed digital data reporters strongly identified themselves with the role of an agent of democratic accountability.

There was universal agreement of the role of journalism in general, and of digital data reporting in particular, as a watchdog on democracy. Respondents also unanimously agreed that their work should be considered a new form of accountability journalism that would be impossible without the availability of datasets and the digital tools to analyse and present them. Accountability journalism, as understood in this context, is investigative journalism with a specific public-interest role of holding those in power to account, not the sort of 'investigative journalism' into sordid details of the personal lives of celebrities and the like.

Respondents cited numerous examples of this new method of accountability journalism in action such as election coverage using digital data methodologies in European countries, a great deal of political coverage in Canada and public-interest investigations by media organisations in the United States, the United Kingdom and Europe. Some pointed to the work by Australian data journalist Craig Butt at the Melbourne-based *The Age* newspaper as robust evidence of accountability journalism in action using digital data reporting methods. An investigation by *The Age* into poker machine usage used datasets on household income and spending by neighbourhood to show gambling addiction in socially deprived areas of Melbourne. The story was front-page news in the newspaper, complemented by an interactive dataset online (Butt, 2012b). Respondents also pointed to the work of journalist Kathryn Torney of the non-profit investigative news service, theDetail.tv, in Northern Ireland. In one investigation, Torney examined religious segregation in education and found a large per cent of schoolchildren went to schools where their peer group was either predominantly Catholic or Protestant (Torney, 2012). Such works were 'textbook examples of investigative journalism in the public interest', according to one respondent from a US newspaper.

Better storytelling, more engaging journalism

It should also be noted that CAR was always an investigative tool, never a storytelling tool. In digital data reporting, however, these two cannot be considered separately – both the investigative method and its ensuing visual and interactive storytelling allow for greater accountability. Respondents cited a number of excellent examples to make this point such as National Public Radio's (NPR) 'State Impact' series on companies engaged in fracking in Pennsylvania (NPR, 2012a) and its 'Playgrounds for Everyone' series (NPR, 2012b).

Significant audience engagement with journalism is a relatively new phenomenon. Online journalism allows for interactivity and engagement through various methods such as the use of user-generated content, social media, audience comments and sharable links. Digital data reporting engages audiences mainly through the use of interactive maps and graphics and applications on news websites that allow for audience choice (such as address or age) to tailor stories to users based on answers to pre-set choices. All respondents agreed that storytelling was enhanced with digital data journalism. New tools have allowed reporters as well as audiences to interpret, contextualise, examine and analyse news in quite different ways. Some respondents suggested that this amounted to both a new method of engaging with audiences (readership) and a new method of storytelling.

Audience engagement was cited as important for respondents, although their experiences of audience engagement varied considerably, with respondents from US-based media organisations reporting far greater levels of engagement than those from other regions. Notable use of digital data journalism as a new method of engagement included a number of considerably successful reports by the US-based NPR. When publishing a series on disability accessible playgrounds, for example, the broadcaster admitted that it was unfinished and invited listeners to visit the site and fill in the gaps, including adding their local playground to the map and listing whether it was accessible or not. The story proved extremely popular with audiences (NPR, 2012b). In Australia, *The Age* ran a series on bicycle accidents, using official statistics to map accident black spots as well as asking readers to add to the map their own stories and experiences (Butt, 2012a). In the United Kingdom, *the Guardian* successfully crowd-sourced on a number of major data stories, the most famous being its readers sifting through thousands of documents on expenses claimed by their Members of Parliament (Rogers, 2009).

Despite *the Guardian*'s successes, the bulk of European and Australasian respondents had mixed success with crowd-sourced stories, with inconsistent results. Respondents suggested that engagement often depended on the story. In some stories such as political campaigns, spending and elections, although the issues were worthy and in the public interest, engagement tended to be low. In other cases, especially stories that personally impacted on audiences, engagement tended to be higher. Respondents reported a number of occasions when analytics showed that audiences were engaging by reading stories and/or interacting with visualisations, but editors were reluctant to respond to such analytics or to make use of user-generated content. Crime, health, schools and personal finances/taxes were among the oft-mentioned areas that attracted most engagement, along with local angles to major national stories. German and Canadian interviewees reported more often than those from elsewhere that politics elicited stronger engagement. However, elections were reported to tend to engage audiences everywhere, and data series that focussed on election results ranked among 'most visited' on many respondents' websites.

Visualisation successes

Visualisation, such as mapping, when combined with interactivity tools can allow a potentially limitless number of stories to be told. Respondents generally agreed that the way stories are presented played a significant role in determining the extent to which readers are engaged with stories, with visualisations making stories easier to read and understand. For example, large and complex datasets could be displayed in an interactive fashion using visualisation tools to help readers to look at both the big story (overall picture) and individual (local) stories. While a newspaper might be interested in telling overall crime figure stories, readers are likely to be much more interested in the crime figures for their local area, which an interactive graphic on crime statistics would allow them to explore. *The Irish Times* (Lally, 2012), for example, told the 'macro' story of national crime figures in the print edition but allowed readers to engage at the local level of each police station in their online data series. A similar approach has been used by NPR with its 'State Impact' fracking series (NPR, 2012a), as well as various data stories published by *Der Spiegel* (2013) online and by *Le Monde* (Léchenet, 2012). Respondents observed that such stories tended to have a far longer shelf life, with repeated visits for weeks and months after the original story has been published.

Journalism has always sought to engage audiences through various means such as letters to the editor pages and writing competitions. With the advent of social media, engagement – through new means such as shares, likes and re-tweets – is now a regularly measured and closely monitored metric in newsrooms. It is reasonable to posit that digital data reporting that uses interactivity has also become a new method of engaging with audiences. Such engagement was impossible before the advent of online journalism and the development of software applications that allow interactivity. Although the reporting – finding a story, fact checking and sourcing and attribution – has not fundamentally changed, it is argued that there has been a fundamental change in how stories are read and understood as a result of how they are digitally visualised, which may be interpreted as a new method of storytelling.

Technologically literate data elites

As discussed earlier, there is, perhaps with some justification, a perception that digital data journalism is for the elite. Media organisations that have a solid reputation for publishing data related stories tend to be ABC1 circulation publications, rather than 'low-brow' tabloids. Praiseworthy investigations concerning African governments' spending and mineral wealth by the Open Knowledge Foundation (Chambers, 2013) or *the Guardian*'s UK riot data series (Rogers, 2012), for example, may never be read by many people directly or indirectly affected by those stories. Equally, stories on social disadvantage or inequality may only ever be read by those who are already likely to be from an affluent demographic, given the nature of the audiences of news organisations that are reporting these stories. Is that creating a technologically informed elite? Almost all respondents strongly disagree. Some argued that, if we followed the logic of the argument that their reporting was elitist, the corollary of that would be to not report the stories at all.

Many pointed out that all media organisations within a given region have a certain market share of the audience and do not reach everyone via traditional methods. Some also noted that the Internet had made their reporting accessible to a far wider audience worldwide than was historically the case. Rrespondents also noted that news and data apps on mobile devices have made data journalism accessible for far greater audiences from a much wider demographic than would have traditionally been the case with newspaper readers.

Conclusion

As societies transition to digitalisation, more and more data are available in electronic forms. The role of journalism in the digital era must still be to report and to investigate in the public interest, but in order to do so it must deploy new methods. Digital data reporting is playing an increasingly important role in journalism both as an investigative method and an approach to engage audiences. The findings of this research suggest that digital data reporting is a significant resource for journalists in carrying out a democratic 'fourth estate' role as a watchdog on those in power – both elected government and bureaucracy. The study lends support to the argument that the accountability role of journalists is strengthened by the use of data reporting methodologies to investigate and to tell stories in public interest. However, the journalists participating in this study do not necessarily see the use and manipulation of datasets for news as something that amounts, in and of itself, to a new method of investigation.

While such reporting may not be seen as a new form of investigation, it cannot be considered solely as the evolution of CAR because digital data reporting includes both investigation and storytelling. As little scholarly research has been focussed on the implications for journalism of the use of digital data engagement tools, the views of the interviewed news professionals are interesting and noteworthy for future in-depth investigations. In the main, they – and the examples they cited – demonstrate a highly significant amount of engagement in their reporting. Increased audience engagement with interactive news, in particular via news apps that allow interactivity and individualisation, may point towards a future direction in the development of news. In an era of declining audiences, engagement can be considered a 'holy grail' for journalism, and storytelling approaches that increase engagement, such as data journalism, are important. This is an area worthy of further inquiry.

While interviewed journalists – all of who are from quality, broadsheet-style news outlets – did not agree that data journalism is elitist and is creating a new technologically literate class of readers, there is still cause for concern. By virtue of the fact that news organisations that conduct substantial data journalism are in the main ABC1 circulation publications or broadcasters with niche audiences, it is reasonable to argue that data journalism is still accessed primarily by those 'quality audiences' who are already engaged, rather than reaching people from all socio-economic backgrounds.

In short, while digital data reporting has the potential to increase audience engagement in both size and substance, it might also be contributing to the creation of 'data elites' as espoused by Dickinson (2014: 122), and reinforcing the current socio-economic structure of news audiences.

- *This is an extract from 'Digital watchdogs? Data reporting and the news media's traditional "fourth estate" function' published in* Journalism: Theory, Practice and Criticism, 2015.

References

Bounegru L (2012) 'Data journalism in perspectivei in: Gray J, Bounegru L and Chambers L (eds) *The Data Journalism Handbook*. Sebastopol, CA: O'Reilly Media, pp17-22

Bradshaw P (2012) 'What is data journalism' in: Gray J, Bounegru L and Chambers L (eds) *The Data Journalism Handbook*. Sebastopol, CA: O'Reilly Media, pp2-3

Butt C (2012a) Our killer roads. The Age. Available at: http://www.theage.com.au/victoria/roadtoll (accessed 12 September 2013).

Butt C (2012b) Pokies hit city's poorest. The Age, 1 August. Available at: http://www.theage.com.au/victoria/pokies-hit-citys-poorest-20120731-23d89.html (accessed 12 September 2013).

Chambers L (2013) 'African spending – Monitoring the money in Africa' in: Open Knowledge Foundation blog, 18 March, available at http://blog.okfn.org/2013/03/18/africanspending-monitoring-the-money-in-africa, accessed 26 September 2013

Council of Europe (1950) Convention for the Protection of Human Rights and Fundamental Freedoms. Strasbourg: Council of Europe.

Der Spiegel (2013) Available at: http://www.spiegel.de

Dickinson A (2014) Does data journalism help democracy? In: Mair J and Keeble R (eds) Data Journalism: Mapping the Future. Bury St Edmunds: Abramis, pp91-98.

Felle T and Mair J (eds) (2015) *FOI 10 Years on: Freedom Fighters or Lazy Journalism?* Bury St Edmonds: Abramis.

Frey L (2014) *Open government partnership four-year strategy 2015–2018*, available at www.opengovpartnership.org/sites/default/files/attachments/4YearAP-Online.pdf, accessed 19 January 2015

Galtung J and Ruge MH (1965) 'The structure of foreign news: The presentation of the Congo, Cuba and Cyprus crises in four Norwegian newspapers' in *Journal of Peace Research* 2(1): 64–90

Government of the United States of America (1787) *Constitution of the United States of America*. Washington, DC: US Government Printing Office

Hansard Society (2012) 'Audit of Political Engagement 9. The 2012 Report Part 2: Media and Politics' London: House of Commons.

Hollander G (2015) 'UK newspapers ranked by total circulation (print and online)' *Press Gazette*, available at www.pressgazette.co.uk/uk-newspapers-ranked-total-readership-print-and-online, accessed 30 March 2015

Jackson, Jasper and Sweney, Mark (2015) 'Trinity Mirror's *UsVsTh3m* and *Ampp3d* thought to be facing axe as jobs set to go' in *the Guardian*, 15 May, available at www.theguardian.com/ media/2015/may/13/trinity-mirrors-usvsth3m-and-ampp3d-thought-to-be-facing-axe-as-jobs-set-to-go, accessed 11 August 2015

Kumar D (2006) 'Media, war and propaganda: Strategies of information management during the 2003 Iraq war' in *Communication and Critical Cultural Studies* 3(1): 48–69.

Lally C (2012) 'Crime in a recession' in *The Irish Times*, 24 August, available at www.irishtimes.com/debate/crime-in-a-recession-1.542359, accessed 12 September 2013

Léchenet A (2012) 'Enquete sur ces consultations au prixfort' in *Le Monde*, 10 April available at www.lemonde.fr/sante/article/2012/04/10/enquete-sur-ces-consultations-au-prix-fort_1682940_1651302.html, accessed 20 September 2013

Lorenz R (2012) 'Why journalists should use data' in Gray J, Bounegru L and Chambers L (eds) *The Data Journalism Handbook*. Sebastopol, CA: O'Reilly Media, pp3-6

Maude F (2012) Open Data White Paper: Unleashing the Potential. London: House of Commons

National Public Radio (NPR) (2012a) 'Playgrounds for everyone (data series)' available at http://apps.npr.org/playgrounds, accessed 17 September 2013

National Public Radio (NPR) (2012b) 'StateImpact (Pennsylvania fracking database)', available at http://stateimpact.npr.org/pennsylvania/drilling, accessed 17 September 2013

O Murchu C (2012) 'An essential part of the journalists toolkit' in Gray J, Bounegru L and Chambers L (eds) *The Data Journalism Handbook*. Sebastopol, CA: O'Reilly Media, pp9-10

Rogers S (2009) 'How to crowd source MPs expenses' in *the Guardian*, 18 June, available at www.theguardian.com/news/datablog/2009/jun/18/mps-expenses-houseofcommons, accessed 31 August 2014

Rogers S (2012) 'Riots broken down: Who was in court and what's happened to them?' in *the Guardian*, 4 July, available at www.theguardian.com/news/datablog+uk/london-riots, accessed 26 September 2013

Schechter D (2009) 'Credit crisis, how did we miss it' in *British Journalism Review* 20(1): 19–26

Schultz J (1998) *Reviving the Fourth Estate*. Cambridge: Cambridge University Press

Torney K (2012) 'How integrated are schools where you live' in thedetail.tv, 23 November, available at www.thedetail.tv/issues/150/religioninschools/how-integrated-are-schools-where-you-live, accessed 21 September 2013

United Nations (1966) *International Covenant on Civil and Political Rights*. Geneva: United Nations Publications

The importance of little data: creating an impact at a local level

Data journalism can have a real impact at a local level, argues Damian Radcliffe, and although this type of reporting is less mainstream than it is nationally, examples and opportunities for best practise do exist

Introduction

Data is everywhere. Big data. Little data. Hyperlocal data. The amount of information being created – and increasingly published – about us and our environment is growing at an exponential rate. Government agencies, as well as commercial companies such as retailors, search engines and social networks, now generate – and have access to – substantial amounts of valuable data about our behaviours, preferences and geographic locality. The implications of this for citizens and consumers are considerable, but for journalists this volume of data generation is a potential boon; creating opportunities for storytelling and public scrutiny at a level not previously possible.

Typically, many of these data driven efforts have a strong international or national dimension, with publications such as *the Guardian* and *ProPublica* being among the best exemplars for investigations, visualisations and data originated content. Yet, at the same time, as a recent University of Westminster project exploring media power and plurality has noted: '...it is at the local level that the vast majority of citizens interact with hospitals, schools, transport systems, the police and elected council representatives ' (University of Westminster, ND).

As a result, the importance of both local journalism – and local data journalism – should not be overlooked. After all, this type of reporting may provide more meaningful insights for the day-to-day lives of readers than many of the stories covered by national media. However, in the data space, the creation of in-depth localised content is not always easy to produce. Datasets are generally smaller, potentially making the stories within them less obvious; and most local newsrooms operate with considerably fewer resources than their national – and international – counterparts. Both of these factors help explain why we tend to see less data journalism at the local level; and why most of the analysis of this activity – from both academics and practitioners – predominantly focuses on national data journalism efforts.

Nonetheless, when done well, the journalistic, public and civic value that local data journalism can deliver is discernible. As a result, I hope that this type of data driven output becomes more prevalent in the near future. With that objective in mind, this chapter contains a number of short case studies – as well as several general principles – designed to help aid and inspire J-School students, local journalists, community publishers and hyperlocal media practitioners in making local data journalism a more mainstream reality.

Hyperlocal data journalism: five case studies from the USA and UK

Much of the US media has well-established local and regional roots. Therefore, it's no surprise that a number of US based websites have deployed data journalism to help tell the stories of the local communities they serve. Historically this has primarily focussed on the use of public statistics to help tell stories related to popular local news beats such as crime, public health and education. This approach remains widespread, but increasingly we're also seeing publishers branching out into more sophisticated uses of data, as mapping, crowdsourcing and other visualisation efforts become ever more common.

Bay Citizen Bike Tracker[1]

In California, *The Bay Citizen*, a non-profit, non-partisan, member-supported news organisation covering the San Francisco Bay area, successfully used public data to produce a potentially lifesaving bike accident tracker. Published in 2011, their interactive microsite used five years of data to show the location of bike accidents across the entire Bay area. In doing this, their map harnessed information from 14,113 separate incidents that took place between January 2005 and December 2009; enabling cyclists to determine the safest routes to use, and the ones to avoid.

Alongside the presentation of top-level accident findings, users of this service could also filter the data by road conditions, lighting and other requirements such as 'who is at fault', thereby producing a more nuanced look at the causes of these accidents. The site also enables cyclists or motorists to submit their own crash data; an important addition to this data mix, as the police only produce accident reports if an ambulance is called. According to Zusha Elinson, one of the reporters on the project:

'Our hope is that this, combined with statistics from the police, will provide a better idea of where and why crashes are taking place,' (Elinson, 2011).

Blogger and keen cyclist, Steven Vance, is just one person who was inspired by *The Bay Citizen*'s approach and he used their model to produce a similar map for Chicago; charting the 4,931 bicycle crashes reported to the Illinois Department of Transportation in the City of Chicago from 2007 to 2009, including 12 fatalities.[2] Other areas where similar interactive services have been created include Boston, London, Los Angeles, New York City and Seattle.

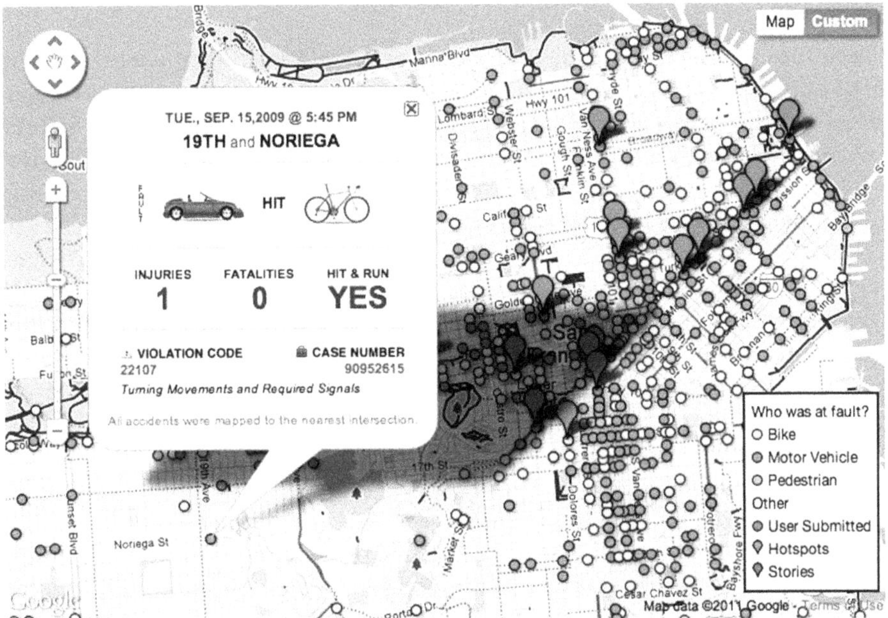

Figure 56: Screenshot from the Bike Tracker. Source: http://media.baycitizen.org/uploaded/images/2011/2/bike-app-ss/original/BIKE%20APP%20SS.jpg

San Jose Streetlight Shutoff Program

San Jose based *NeighborWebSJ* is also home to a range of data driven output. Although the site is currently mothballed – with no new activity since May 2014 – it previously used digital maps to report on the 'Streetlight Shutoff Program', a cost-saving initiative from City Hall that sought to permanently switch off certain lights across the town. The proposal was part of a wider effort to reduce the city's USD$90m (STG£58m) budget shortfall, and was anticipated to reduce the annual electric bill for streetlights by USD$77,000 (STG£50,000) against a total annual electric bill for streetlights of USD$3.5m (STG£2.27m).

Despite the need for cost savings, many residents and businesses campaigned against the scheme, arguing that it increased the risk of crime. On just one road, Alum Rock Avenue, a resident complained that lights were out at 13 bus stops, thereby increasing the vulnerability of passengers. In response to these community concerns, the website included a Google map to indicate where lights were out across the city, as well as information on how to contact the authorities about the issue (Rombeck, ND a). This combination of reporting and community facilitation helped to identify that some lights had been turned off by accident, while others were turned back on again as a result of public pressure; including the bus stops on Alum Rock Avenue. In February 2013 the city agreed to reconnect 900 of the streetlights that had been previously shut off as part of the budget cuts in 2008 and 2009 (Rombeck, ND b).

Homicide Watch

The team at *NeighborWebSJ* also produced a Google map identifying all of the 2012 homicides in San Jose, using data from police press releases, and links to other media.[3] Crime reporting has always been a journalistic staple, but the fusion of data with interactive online publishing tools has taken it to the next level; even spawning its own genre with specialist homicide websites springing up in a number of major US cities.

Of these, arguably the best known was *Homicide Watch DC*, which covered every murder in the District of Columbia. Although the site closed on 31 December 2014, it had previously spent the past four years blending data with 'original reporting, court documents, social media, and the help of victims' and suspects' friends, family, neighbours and others in an effort to 'cover every homicide from crime to conviction' (Homicide Watch, DC). It was awarded the Knight Public Service Award by the Online News Association in 2012 (ONA, 2012) in recognition of its efforts to explore a single issue in a single geographic area, and inspired a series of copycat services such as *Homicide Watch Trenton* and *Homicide Watch Chicago* and The Counted, a crowd-sourced – and more clearly data-driven – project by *the Guardian* 'working to count the number of people killed by police and other law enforcement agencies in the United States throughout 2015, to monitor their demographics and to tell the stories of how they died' (*the Guardian*, 2015).

Gritting routes in Bournville

That valuable sites like *Homicide Watch DC* – along with several others cited here – have closed reflects the harsh economic reality that many media operations continue to face, especially at a local level. Making journalism pay is a challenge for many publishers, even when they are clearly delivering public value and content that informs communities, and that can make a difference. There are few outlets that are immune to these pressures, although some hyperlocal websites, particularly those run by volunteers, are not always impacted in the same way. Alongside original content, these ultra-local channels can also help to generate value by taking information that is already in the public domain and repurposing it so that it is more useful for local audiences. This approach can be particularly useful for health, crime and transport data; with the latter consistently being a key driver for local media consumption.

One person who recognised this potential is the UK academic and hyperlocal publisher Dave Harte. In 2010 he produced a map of gritting routes for Bournville[4], taking publicly available information but presenting it in a more user-friendly format. On his blog he explained the 'tedious process of creating the map and why this hyperlocal blogging thing is doomed to failure unless we get a rich supply of local data to feed off' (Harte, 2010). But despite this tediousness, he also understood that such output could also be beneficial for his audience:

'I thought the potential grit shortage might mean that some roads would stop getting gritted should the cold spell continue and knowing which roads were meant to be gritted would be useful knowledge. "Will my road get gritted?" is an easy question to answer since the City Council has an alphabetical list of all the roads that are gritted in order of priority' (ibid).

Later in the year, James Cousins, a Conservative councillor for the Shaftesbury Ward in Wandsworth, London, did something similar: plotting the location of all grit bins in the borough on a Google map and posting this on his blog[5]. The data, previously only available in a text format – and four clicks deep – on the council website, was now potentially a lot more accessible and valuable to local audiences (Dale, 2011).

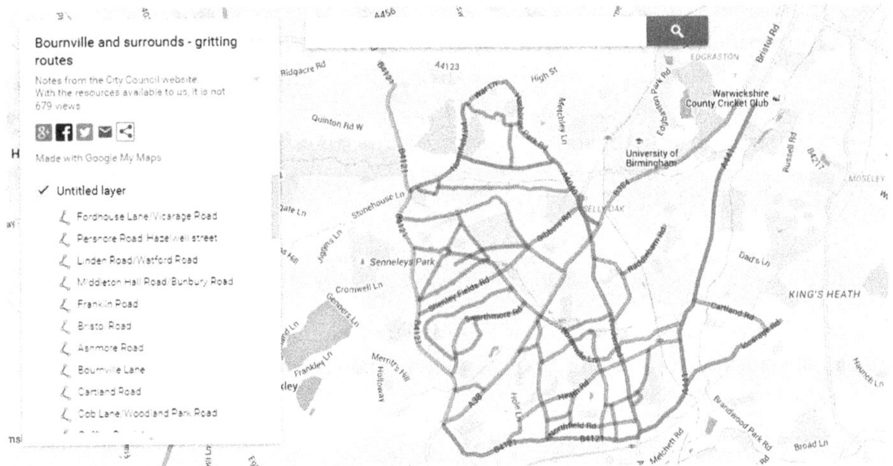

Figure 57: Dave Harte's gritting map for Bournville.

Tackling accident black spots in Bramcote

Alongside presenting existing data in new and creative ways, hyperlocal and geographically focussed community websites can also encourage the creation of new datasets: covering subjects where existing data either does not exist, or it fails to provide the level of detail that communities and local decision makers need. This type of crowdsourcing was manifest in *NeighborWebSJ*'s response to San Jose's Streetlight Shutoff Program, and also in the opportunity for audiences to contribute to *The Bay Citizen*'s Bike Accident Tracker. It is an approach that was also manifest in *Bramcote Today*'s response to online discussions about Hillside Road (Johnson, 2011a) – a notorious accident black spot on the outskirts of Nottingham. As a result of these online conversations, the county council installed equipment to monitor the number and speed of vehicles, later sharing the results (Johnson, 2011b) with *Bramcote Today* readers and involving them in a discussion around potential solutions; such as a community speed watch scheme (Austin, 2011). A number of these measures were successfully implemented.

This result was very much in line with the hyperlocal ethos of *Talk About Local* founder William Perrin. His company had supported residents in Bramcote to create their own website, and they've worked with other communities to produce similar outputs. A passionate advocate for hyperlocal media and community journalism, Perrin has described his ambition to:

> '*... use the web to drive people into local democratic avenues to get things to change.... [The websites are] there to augment real human engagement in the political process. You need representatives to make decisions ... but the web can help them understand better what those issues should be... we help augment traditional community action*' (cited in Beckett, 2010).

Data journalism: five tips, tricks and core considerations

As we have seen, data journalism – from the capturing of new data to the presentation of existing information in new and creative ways – can provide communities with valuable content that informs their day-to-day lives. Here are five areas for local journalists to reflect on, in order to determine the best way to use data (if at all) in their work.

1. Is it right for you, both personally and in terms of the story?

Data journalism is an increasingly high profile component of the journalist's playbook; being used as a tool for both storytelling and story gathering. But although data journalism can help to deliver valuable output, it's not always an easy area to engage with.

> '*... you need to be a particular type of person. Politically, you need to be engaged and interested in local government, understand how local government works and have a driving reason to dedicate yourself to it. To have all these traits in combination is rare* (Worthy, 2013).

Particular barriers pertinent – but not solely applicable – to local publishers include time; skills; and the format in which the data is available (Wheeler, 2012). Time is a particularly important consideration for hyperlocal publishers given that these sites are seldom run full-time (many successful practitioners hold down separate day jobs). Meanwhile, journalists at many local publications find themselves under increased pressure to produce an ever-greater volume of stories on a daily/weekly basis. As a result, journalists and publishers may come to the conclusion that they cannot cover everything (Jones, 2011) and that their limited time is better served focusing on delivering content that is quicker (and often easier) to produce. Journalists should, of course, not be adverse to hard work, but they also need to ask themselves if a data driven approach is the right one and, if it is, how to use it effectively.

2. Can I use an "off-the-shelf" solution?

One way that local publishers can help to make things easier for themselves is by using off-the-shelf resources – such as mySociety's 'FixMyStreet' widget (www.fixmystreet.com) – to help them produce data driven content. This online tool allows people to 'report, view, or discuss local problems like graffiti, fly tipping, broken paving slabs or street lighting' and websites in the UK and elsewhere have benefitted from this app and online plugin. Since it launched in early February 2007, more than 700,000 incident reports[6] have been generated through this service in the UK alone (FixMyStreet, 2013). MySociety has reported that more than 50 per cent of users have never contacted their local council before (ibid), showing that the tool can play a role in promoting active citizenship as well as being a fertile source for a variety of journalistic endeavours.

Some US hyperlocals use a similar tool, SeeClickFix (en.seeclickfix.com) to create content and community action around issues that matter to their audience. The data captured by these services can highlight problems, generate stories and promote discussion. It's 'an example of community news that doesn't necessarily come packaged in story form' (Gahran, 2012), but one that nevertheless provides actionable insights into the concerns of local communities.

3. Remember that data alone is not enough

Although tools like SeeClickFix and FixMyStreet – as well as public open data platforms – are incredibly useful resources for journalists, they only do half a job. Data on its own doesn't tell a story: we still need journalists to decide how to arrange, analyse and visualise data, as well as provide appropriate context and interpretation. These are important considerations for publishers, and the initial failure of the EveryBlock – a US-based website that aggregated local information produced by government and state agencies – merely reinforces this point. The site, which offered a data-centric approach to hyperlocal, launched in 2008 and was bought by MNBC in 2009. However, in February 2013, the site was closed after NBC decided that they 'didn't see a strategic fit for EveryBlock within the [NBC News Digital] portfolio' (Schiller, cited in Sonderman, 2013). In January 2014, with the EveryBlock brand and service now owned by Comcast – following their acquisition of NBCUniversal – the site was relaunched in Chicago; with Philadelphia following in late August (Wright 2014). Since then, Houston, Boston and Denver have been added to this list of active operations.[7]

One of EveryBlock's original problems, as Steve Johnson, Assistant Professor of Electronic Journalism at Montclair State University, noted was that: 'Readers don't care about the raw data. They want the story within the data' (Johnson, 2013). To illustrate this, he explained what happened when he explored data related to lower Manhattan:

> *'There were reports on what graffiti the city said it had erased each month, by neighborhoods. But what was missing was context, and photos. If I'm a reporter doing a*

story on graffiti, I want to show before and after photos, AND, more importantly, I want to know whether the city is successfully fighting the graffiti artists, i.e., who is winning. The raw data didn't provide that' (ibid).

This lack of context is, perhaps, one of the reasons why the site originally failed to resonate sufficiently with audiences or advertisers to survive. Despite its recent resurrection, this sobering experience offers valuable lessons for publishers.

4. The value of networked journalism

To some extent, the EveryBlock team acknowledged the shortcomings of their data-first approach when, in 2011, the site moved in a new direction, telling their audience:

'As valuable as automated updates of crime, media mentions, and other EveryBlock news are, contributions from your fellow neighbors are significantly more meaningful and useful. While we're not removing our existing aggregation of public records and other neighborhood information (more on this in a bit), we've come to realize that human participation is essential, not only as a layer on top but as the bedrock of the site, (Holovaty, 2011).

Prior to its 2014 revival by Comcast, this pivot was initially unsuccessful, highlighting the importance – when producing community news and information – of involving and engaging the community in this process from the outset. Techniques to do this include crowdsourcing information; fact checking; and tapping into the specific expertise of your audience, as the Birmingham based UK website Help Me Investigate (hempmeinvestigate.com) did on a case-by-case basis.

Working in this way may require a change of approach for some publishers. But, as Professor Jeff Jarvis has argued:

'Professional and amateur, journalist and citizen may now work together to gather and share more news in more ways to more people than was ever possible before. Networked journalism is founded on a simple, self-evident and self-interested truth: we can do more together than we can apart .... This, I believe, is the natural state of media: two-way and collaborative' (Jarvis, 2008).

5. Determine your approach on a case-by-case basis

Data Journalism may be in vogue at present, but its usage needs to be assessed like any other potential editorial approach; with journalists determining if, when, and how, usage of data journalism tools and techniques add value to the stories being told. This sentiment is just as applicable in the local news and information space as it is when covering elections, reporting on public spending, or holding national bodies to account. When used well, local media can harness data driven journalism to inform audiences, support campaigns and garner fresh insights into the concerns of their audiences.

In doing this, many publishers are making extensive use of maps and mapping tools, embracing off-the-shelf widgets and capturing data that helps to inform their reporting and campaigning. They are also increasingly presenting data in visually arresting ways – see, for example, DNAinfo.com, New York's use of maps and infographics to help demonstrate their analysis of the city's 2011 stop and frisk numbers (Colvin and Harris, 2012). In line with audience preferences for more visual content, media companies are also creating more data driven apps and microsites, providing a more detailed immersive experience into topics such as bike accidents, expenditure by public bodies, or cuts to the public sector (Watt, 2010), than might previously have been the case. That each story can be told in a different way is a valuable reminder that not all journalism can be produced with boilerplates.

As Simon Rogers has argued, due to its nascent nature 'data journalism is a great leveller… many media groups are starting with as much prior knowledge and expertise as someone hacking away from their bedroom' (2012). This is particularly true in the 'little data' space where there is considerable scope for more data-led reporting, as well as increased levels of innovation and creativity. Approaches to this should depend on a combination of the story being told, the skills of the journalists involved, what audiences want/need, as well as the mediums being used. As this paper shows there's lots of potential ways to do this; it's now up to local publishers and journalists to make it happen.

Notes

[1] *Bay Citizen* bicycle tracker is available at www.baycitizen.org/data/bikes/bike-accident-tracker

[2] Steve Vance's crash site is available at www.stevevance.net/crashportal/?page=bikecrash

[3] San Jose's homicides map is available at www.google.com/maps/d/viewer?ll=37.321732%2C-121.875501&spn=0.171191%2C0.205865&hl=en&t=m&msa=0&source=embed&ie=UTF8&mid=z41BAUCJvuoU.kSltz3XWQv30

[4] Gritting routes for Bournville is available at www.google.com/maps/d/viewer?mid=zFcpZs47iTHE.kpKEXjMO-pYw&hl=en

[5] James Cousins' grit bins map is available at http://jamescousins.com/2010/12/gritting-wandsworth

[6] A live incident counter for the UK is available at www.fixmystreet.com/

[7] Details for EveryBlock usage is available at www.everyblock.com/faq/

References

Austin, Steve (2011) 'Hillside Road Proposals' in *Bramcote Today*, 4 April, available at http://bramcotetoday.org.uk/2011/04/04/hillside-road/, accessed 6 October 2013

Beckett, Charlie (2010) 'Grassroots networked journalism key to future of local news, says Polis director' in Journalism.co.uk, 7 June, available at www.journalism.co.uk/news-features/grassroots-networked-journalism-key-to-future-of-local-news-says-polis-director/s5/a539020/, accessed 6 October 2013

Bradshaw, Paul (2011) 'Announcing Help Me Investigate: Networks' in Online Journalism Blog, 7 November, available at http://onlinejournalismblog.com/2011/11/07/announcing-help-me-investigate-networks/, accessed 6 October 2013

Colvin, Jill and Davis, Paul (2012) 'Port Authority is top stop-and-frisk hotspot regardless of race', in DNAinfo, New York, 4 June, available at www.dnainfo.com/new-york/20120604/new-york-city/port-authority-is-top-stop-and-frisk-hotspot-regardless-of-race#ixzz1wrTXMVW5, accessed 6 October 2013

Dale, Robert (2011) 'Engaging the local population – online' in BBC Online, 19 October, available at www.bbc.co.uk/blogs/blogcollegeofjournalism/posts/engaging_the_local_population, accessed 6 October 2013

Elinson, Zusha (2011) 'Police refuse to write reports for many San Francisco bike crashes', in *The Bay Citizen*, 9 February, available at www.baycitizen.org/news/bikes/police-refuse-reports-bike-accidents, accessed 14 September 2015

FixMyStreet (2013) 'FixMyStreet – press use', available at www.mysociety.org/press-area/fixmystreet, accessed 6 October 2013

Gahran, Amy (2012) 'SeeClickFix: Crowdsourced local problem reporting as community news', in Knight Digital Media Center, 19 September, available at www.knightdigitalmediacenter.org/blogs/agahran/2012/09/seeclickfix-crowdsourced-local-problem-reporting-community-news, accessed 6 October 2013

Harte, David (2010) 'Data is the New Grit', in daveharte.com blog, 14 January, available at http://daveharte.com/bournville/data-is-the-new-grit, accessed 6 October 2013

Holovaty, Adrian (2011) 'EveryBlock's first major redesign', EveryBlock blog, 21 March, available at http://blog.everyblock.com/2011/mar/21/redesign, accessed 6 October 2013

Homicide Watch DC, available at http://homicidewatch.org/, accessed 14 September 2015

House of Commons Culture, Media and Sport Committee (2010) *Future for local and regional media*, House of Commons, London, 24 March, available at www.publications.parliament.uk /pa/cm200910/cmselect/cmcumeds/43/4302.htm, accessed 6 October 2013

Jarvis, Jeff (2008) 'Supermedia: Saving Journalism So It Can Save the World' in BuzzMachine, 6 June, available at http://buzzmachine.com/2008/06/06/supermedia, accessed 6 October 2013

Johnson, Mike (2011a) 'Accidents on Hillside Road', in *Bramcote Today*, 14 March, available http://bramcotetoday.org.uk/2011/03/14/accidents-on-hillside-road, accessed 6 October 2013

Johnson, Mike (2011b) 'Accidents on Hillside Road – Traffic Survey Results', in *Bramcote Today*, 29 March, available http://bramcotetoday.org.uk/2011/03/29/hillside-road-survey-results-2, accessed 6 October 2013

Johnson, Steve (2013) 'Sorry EveryBlock, you never learned how to write a headline', *in Hudson Eclectic*, 8 February, available at http://hudsoneclectic.com/2013/02/08/sorry-everyblock-you-never-learned-how-to-write-a-headline, accessed 6 October 2013

Jones, Richard (2011) 'Thirteen lessons I've learned from running a hyperlocal site', in *The Richard Jones Journalism Blog*, 5 October, available at http://richardjonesjournalist.com/ 2011/10/05/thirteen-lessons-ive-learned-from-running-a-hyperlocal-site, accessed 6 October 2013

Online News Association (2012) '2012 Online Journalism Awards Winners Announced' available at http://journalists.org/2012/09/24/2012-online-journalism-award-winners-announced, accessed 14 September 2015

Rogers, Simon (2012) 'Anyone can do it: data journalism is the new punk' in *the Guardian* Datablog, 24 May, available at www.theguardian.com/news/datablog/2012/may/24/data-journalism-punk, accessed 14 September 2015

Rombeck, Janice (ND a) 'Shutoff streetlights worry SJ neighborhoods', in NeighborWebSJ, available at www.neighborwebsj.com/shutoff-streetlights-worry-sj-residents, accessed 6 October 2013

Rombeck, Janice (ND b) '900 streetlights shut off to save energy costs will shine again starting in March', in NeighborWebSJ, available at www.neighborwebsj.com/900-streetlights-shut-off-to-save-energy-costs-will-shine-again-starting-in-march, accessed 6 October 2013

Sonderman, Jeff (2013) 'NBC closes hyperlocal, data-driven publishing pioneer', in Poynter, February 7, available at www.poynter.org/latest-news/top-stories/203437/nbc-closes-hyperlocal-pioneer-everyblock, accessed 6 October 2013

the Guardian (2015) 'The Counted: About the project' available at www.theguardian.com/us-news/ng-interactive/2015/jun/01/about-the-counted accessed 14 September 2015

University of Westminster (ND) 'Local and Hyperlocal' blog, available at http://www.mediaplurality.com/local-and-hyperlocal, accessed 14 September 2014

Watt, Andrew (2010) 'Birmingham budget cuts ... The story so far', in Watt's Going On, 20 November, available at http://watts-going-on.blogspot.com/2010/11/birmingham-budget-cuts-story-so-far.html, accessed 6 October 2013

Wheeler, Brian (2012) 'Government online data ignored by "armchair auditors"', BBC News, 9 November, available at www.bbc.co.uk/news/uk-politics-20221398, accessed 6 October 2013

Wright, Paul (2014) 'EveryBlock: the online community for your neighborhood' Comcast Voices, 26 August, available at http://corporate.comcast.com/comcast-voices/everyblock-the-online-community-for-your-neighborhood, accessed 15 September 2015

Worthy, Ben (2013) 'Where are the armchair auditors?' Open Data Institute, 3 June, available at www.theodi.org/blog/guest-blog-where-are-armchair-auditors, accessed 6 October 2013

Open data and journalism – a case for relationship counselling?

Open data offers a myriad of possibilities for journalists and great benefits for civil society, but the gatekeepers of data – governments – are laggards when it comes to releasing useful datasets, writes Jonathan Stoneman

Introduction

Picture this: you've been on a data journalism course, and you're keen to do your first data-driven story. You visit data.gov.uk, the UK government's open data portal. After all, the UK is repeatedly touted as topping the international league for open data. Where to start? The most popular dataset perhaps? At the time of writing, road safety data heads the list of datasets in order of popularity. It's a huge database of car accidents on Britain's roads since 1979 – with records of cars involved, exact places, roads, traffic conditions, council jurisdiction, police service jurisdiction, purpose of journey, age of driver, vehicle, and so on. The data is ripe for mapping and visualisation in a host of different ways. There is only one problem. At the time of writing, the last dataset dates from 2013. More than halfway through 2015, 2014 has yet to appear. Any serious analysis of this data is more suited to historians than journalists. You move on.

As you look around, you will become aware that many datasets are out of date: for all their usefulness as sources of stories, they are just too old for anyone working in daily, weekly, or monthly journalism.

Who is opening up key data?

It is not just Britain whose data lags behind in this way. The Open Knowledge Foundation conducts its own survey of datasets on government portals around the world. In one part of its website OKFN shows results for the availability of 10 key datasets, covering Open Data on national budgets, registered companies, elections, emissions, legislation, mapping, postcodes, public spending, statistics, and transport timetables. Reviewers have submitted results from 97 countries.

Of the possible 970 datasets that would exist if each of the countries surveyed had all 10, some 837 are shown to exist: 86 per cent. Not bad. However, this drops to 106 (11 per cent) when limited to datasets that are open to all. If filtered by 'up-to-date' the total falls further, to 96, just under 10 per cent.

	Budgets	Companies	Elections	Emissions	Legislation	Maps	Postcodes	Spending	Statistics	Transport timetables	Total
UK		1	1		1	1	1	1		1	7
France	1		1	1		1	1		1		6
Germany	1		1	1	1	1			1		6
Norway		1	1	1		1			1		5
N Zealand	1		1		1	1			1		5
India	1	1		1	1				1		5
Australia	1		1			1			1		4
Netherlands	1					1	1		1		4
United States	1				1	1			1		4
Denmark	1		1			1	1				4
Romania		1	1			1				1	4
Finland			1			1			1	1	4
Uruguay	1						1		1	1	4
Sweden			1	1					1		3
Colombia						1			1	1	3
Iceland						1	1			1	3
Canada	1		1			1					3
Italy	1		1						1		3
Austria			1			1					2
Chile	1									1	2
Czech Rep			1			1					2
Switzerland										1	1
Mexico	1										1
Japan							1				1
Greece								1			1
Virgin Islands						1					1
Brazil	1										1
Taiwan										1	1
Ivory coast									1		1
Isle of Man	1										1
Portugal						1					1
Costa Rica									1		1
Argentina			1								1
Indonesia	1										1

Table 6: Countries with commitment to open data. Source: Open Knowledge Foundation, Global Open Data Index (http://index.okfn.org/place)

Journalists are not considered end-users

Open data was not conceived, nor is it published, with journalists in mind. No government declaration of commitment to open data ever mentions journalists among the target end-users. The US government portal, Data.gov has this rationale: 'Open government data is important because the more accessible, discoverable, and usable data is the more impact it can have. These impacts include, but are not limited to: cost savings, efficiency, fuel for business, improved civic services, informed policy, performance planning, research and scientific discoveries, transparency and accountability, and increased public participation in the democratic dialogue' (Data.gov).

The birth of the 'armchair auditor'

In the British Conservative Party's 2010 manifesto, the party had this to say: 'Drawing inspiration from administrations around the world which have shown that being transparent can transform the effectiveness of government, we will create a powerful new right to government data, enabling the public to request – and receive – government datasets in an open and standardised format'. In May 2010, soon after taking over as Prime Minister, David Cameron promised an open data revolution, 'with a whole army of effective armchair auditors looking over the books, ministers in this government are not going to be able to get away with all the waste, the expensive vanity projects and pointless schemes that we've had in the past'. (data.gov.uk, 2010). It is not clear who the 'armchair auditors' are, or how they should report their findings. Do investigative journalists count as armchair auditors?

Some armchair auditing has been carried out by NGOs and pressure groups. One frequently cited example is Prescribing Analytics, which describes itself on its website as 'a joint venture of a group of UK technologists and NHS doctors, who believe in the power of data and technology to help the NHS'. Prescribing Analytics mapped use of proprietary statins in the UK from 2011 to 2012, where, it says, the prescription of unbranded statins would have saved the National Health Service around £200m. There is no indication that the NHS has taken action on this recommendation; reporting of the analysis in the media concentrates on the technical aspect of the research – the ability of data analysis to spot things like inefficient spending patterns or postcode lotteries for cancer treatment – rather than the impact it has had.

A marriage made in heaven?

Open data and journalism should be natural partners – a marriage made in heaven, one might say. Open data needs public exposure, journalists need easily accessible, raw, facts without spin by politicians or press officers. But this marriage – if it is to be one – is like Romeo and Juliet: the two families have different cultures and treat each other with mutual suspicion (at best!) Each side sees the other as distorting facts for their own ends, dealing in half-truths, and doing whatever is needed to tell the story their way.

Of course journalists don't report dogs biting humans, or tens of thousands of aircraft landing safely, or hundreds of thousands of people not being the victims of crime. They report dogs being attacked by humans, planes that crash or have near misses in the sky, and people being victims of crime. So, when the Food Standards Agency publishes data about hygiene inspections in the UK, (subdivided locally and regionally, with no consolidated national picture) the declared intent is that people should use the data to look for the best, the restaurants and caterers with five stars. Journalists naturally look for dirty establishments, the ones that have repeatedly failed inspections.

The government publishes statistics on education and healthcare, wanting the public to see good performance statistics and good news stories; journalists look for the outliers – the worst performances, the bad news, which will make headlines. This natural state of affairs is not necessarily causing governments to withhold data, but it does make their data publishers more cautious.

A fire hose – of filtered water!

In theory, many datasets could be a sort of 'fire hose' – raw data being sprayed onto the web in real time. Very few datasets are emerging at that rate. Instead, governments are being much more cautious, having data checked and double checked before release, or committing to, say, an annual release only when all the data is ready. There are some instances of the 'fire hose' of data being turned on, in the USA in particular. But these examples are relatively rare, and provide only patchy coverage that varies in quality and completeness from state to state, city to city, complicating comparative analysis. Finding the datasets is not too difficult, but the spotty nature of the data being released does not inspire confidence, and anyway, one might reason, why 'do a story' just because the data is available, surely news is what 'they' don't want you to know: the equivalent of choosing whether to interview someone just because they are available, or to track down someone who does not want to face questions. The data journalist moves on to get unpublished data, and uses Freedom of Information legislation to get it – taking more time, and energy, and further reducing the impact of open data.

Openness in the real world

As one descends the league table of open data, and the missing datasets begin to outnumber the available ones, a question about the link between levels of openness and corruption suggests itself: perhaps the governments committing themselves to openness are not the ones we should be looking at? Let us compare the Open Data Barometer with the Corruption Perception Index, published by Transparency International. The Corruption Perception Index is based on people's responses to the question 'how far do you think the public sector in your country is corrupt'. The mean response is 4.1. On the Open Data Barometer, the maximum 'open data readiness' score is 100. Dividing this OD Readiness score by the Corruption Perception Index score, a country with maximum readiness for open data, and average corruption perception would score 23.4.

> The Open Data Barometer lists 86 countries rated according to whether they have: '*established open data policies, generally with strong political backing; a culture of open data out beyond a single government department, with open data practices adopted in different government agencies, and increasingly at a local government level. These countries tend to adopt similar approaches to open data, incorporating key principles of the open definition, and emphasising issues of open data licensing. They have government, civil society and private sector capacity to benefit from open data,' (Open Data Barometer, 2015).*

Transparency International rates 107 countries. 75 countries are listed on both tables. The top 50 countries are shown below for 2013, that being the most recent year for which both sets of figures are available. The higher the coefficient, the more open and 'un-corrupt' the country, with 23.4 as 'par':

Country	**2013 ODB**	**2013 corruption**	**2013 O/C**
Sweden	85.75	2.6	32.98
Denmark	71.78	2.2	32.63
United Kingdom	100	3.7	27.03
United States	93.38	4	23.35
Norway	71.86	3.1	23.18
New Zealand	74.34	3.3	22.53
France	63.92	3.1	20.62
Australia	67.68	3.6	18.80
Canada	65.87	3.7	17.80
Finland	49.44	2.9	17.05
Germany	65.01	3.9	16.67
Switzerland	43.24	2.7	16.01
Netherlands	63.66	4.5	14.15
Iceland	51.01	3.8	13.42
Estonia	49.45	3.7	13.36
Austria	46.03	3.6	12.79
Korea	54.21	4.3	12.61
Rwanda	24.27	2	12.14
Japan	49.17	4.2	11.71
Spain	48.19	4.5	10.71
Israel	45.58	4.3	10.60
Italy	45.3	4.4	10.30
Kenya	43.06	4.3	10.01
Czech Republic	43.18	4.4	9.81
Ecuador	21.12	2.2	9.60
Russia	44.79	4.7	9.53
Chile	40.11	4.3	9.33
Belgium	34.8	3.9	8.92
Singapore	36.29	4.1	8.85

Ireland	35.76	4.1	8.72
Uruguay	33.04	3.8	8.69
Thailand	35.33	4.1	8.62
Mexico	40.3	4.7	8.57
Portugal	38.63	4.6	8.40
Brazil	36.83	4.6	8.01
India	33.38	4.2	7.95
Argentina	35	4.5	7.78
Costa Rica	31.21	4.4	7.09
Kazakhstan	27.61	3.9	7.08
Turkey	27.58	4	6.90
Hungary	26.09	3.8	6.87
Colombia	26.71	4.4	6.07
Mauritius	26.08	4.3	6.07
Greece	27.59	4.6	6.00
Morocco	27.24	4.6	5.92
Jamaica	22.69	4.4	5.16
Bahrain	18.18	3.6	5.05
Philippines	21.91	4.4	4.98
Ghana	21.6	4.4	4.91

Table 7: Countries' open data readiness and corruption percetions. Sources: Open Data Barometer, Corruption Perception Index

One important proviso about the scoring methodology: Transparency International's questionnaire simply asks: 'On a scale of 1-5, how corrupt do you think the public sector is in your country?' But the Corruption Perception Index does not distinguish between a response based on the exposure of corruption by investigative journalists, and a response based on the person's own experience of corruption, which prompts them to say it's a problem, without the media ever reporting it as such.

The table quantifies the feeling that in some countries those who control the fire hose of open data are reluctant to open the tap. At the top of the table, Sweden and Denmark are known to have cultures of openness – everything is open by default. While in the UK, openness is not a natural tradition for civil servants. And elsewhere there is even greater concern that the public will look at the data, and especially that journalists will be among the keenest end users. In Kenya, for example, the national open data initiative was launched in 2011. Four years later the initiative is seen as stalling by many observers. In a blog entry on the Code4Kenya website in 2013, Nick Hargreaves said: 'Today the portal has less than 3,000 datasets with the latest one uploaded on December 12, 2012. Most of the data is from 2007 to 2011.' In June 2015 the Kenyan data catalogue listed 257 datasets. The most recently updated were GDP figures and price index data up to 2009, although there were a few recent datasets, such as petrol prices from 2015, and HIV infection data for 2014.

Hargreaves continues:

> *'There's hardly any interaction on the portal anymore in terms of dataset suggestions and creation of visualisations. Only 12 apps are listed under community apps and the mainstream media seems to have moved on, as it does when a story becomes stale. When the portal was launched, what was envisioned by most was better provision and access of services and accountability of government departments. Yet 2 years after the ribbon was cut and the champagne bottled popped we seem to be stuck at the beginning. What went wrong?* (Hargreaves, 2013).

He answers his own question, and comes to this conclusion: 'Open data is a pretty new concept and beyond the suspicions the government workers will have when you ask for the data, there's also the fact that they haven't been properly trained on it' (ibid). Even where training is sufficient, indeed, where it is being snapped up eagerly, data journalism is having only a minor impact on journalism as a whole.

'We can be the bridge'

In his *Guardian*, e-book *Facts are Sacred*, Simon Rogers notes:

> *'There are still reporters out there who don't know what all the fuss is about, who really don't want to know about maths or spreadsheets. But for others, this new wave represents a way to save journalism. A new role for journalists as a bridge and guide between those in power who have the data (and are rubbish at explaining it) and the public who desperately want to understand the data and access it but need help. We can be that bridge,* (Rogers, 2011).

Being that 'bridge' needs more work. Especially when it comes to open data. True openness is not just a 'nice to have' add-on; it is fundamental to society in all manner of ways. Yet the failure of governments to make relevant and meaningful data available in real time, or near real time, is rarely if ever discussed. Stories based on open data are not always making the impact they should. There are two main factors – the natural reluctance of journalists to reveal their sources, and the way data-driven stories are published, with a tendency of editors and journalists to link data-driven stories to visualisations such as graphics, maps, and interactives.

Does the audience use infographics?

Unfortunately, much of the effort expended on visualisations appears to be wasted. In its Digital News Report, 2014, the Reuters Institute noted:

> *'Over the last year newspapers, broadcasters, and digital pure players have been producing more visual content, pictures, data-rich charts, animated gifs, and video itself. This is partly because of the multimedia capabilities of new devices, partly because distinctive visual content works well in social media – but also for commercial reasons. Video in particular is attracting much higher advertising premiums. Despite this, our research shows that, for the moment at least, most users remain wedded to words*

(traditional articles and lists), though we do find that pictures and videos are relatively more important in the US, Brazil, and southern European countries like Italy and Spain, (Newman, 2015).

Breaking the responses into groups by country, and type of content, the disparity between news consumption through 'words' and through 'graphics' is all too clear:

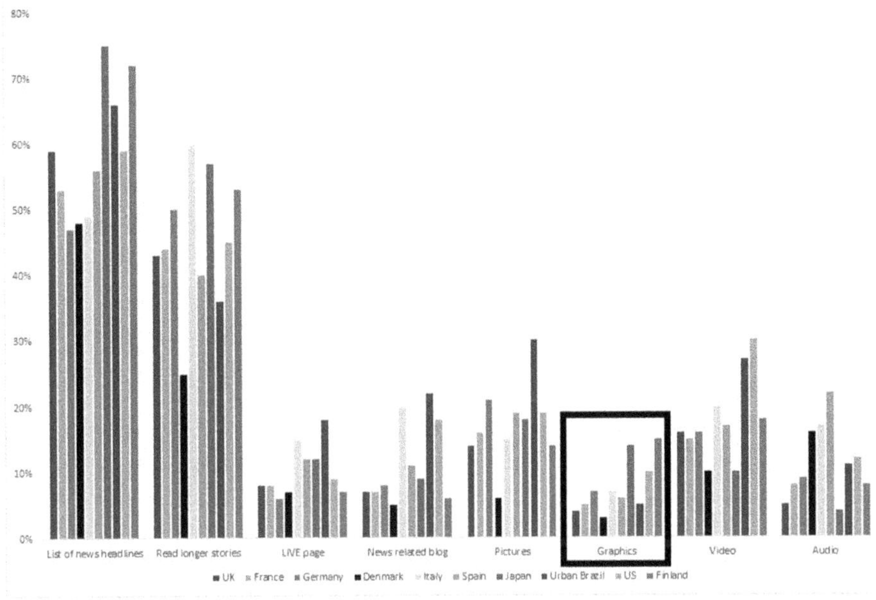

Figure 58: News consumptions across various visuals. Source: Reuters Institute Digital News Report 2014, (Newman, 2015).

The countries surveyed by the Reuters Institute were UK, France, Germany, Denmark, Italy, Spain, Japan, urban Brazil, the USA, and Finland. The two national peaks within the (ringed) graphics group are Japan and Finland, but it's clear that no country's consumption of graphics comes close even to the lowest consumption of headlines and stories (the leftmost two groups.) The implication is clear – turning data into graphics or tables is much less likely to make an impact on the audience than headlines and words.

This is not to argue that these figures mean data journalism is a complete waste of time – online graphics derived from datasets tend to be 'sticky': web analytics show users staying longer on those pages, making use of the interactive elements. For those who like those elements, there is satisfaction to be gained in being allowed to 'play' with the data, put it in one's own context, and look for patterns.

Data as a 'source'

There is an obstacle in the way journalists and their audience seem to associate 'data' with 'statistics'. Data is a source like any other – knowing how to interrogate a dataset is as important as knowing how to ask questions of a senior official, an expert, a whistleblower. Automatically turning a dataset into a complex interactive visualisation is rather like publishing an interview with a French-speaking source, verbatim, in French. Like any source, a dataset is not something one should only turn into statistics or charts. The information lead to another source, a piece of text, or it may provide the substance of a question to be asked of a human interviewee.

Journalists live and die by their sources, and rightly protect their identities where necessary, but where data is openly available, this needs to be reflected in the resulting story. Only a minority of publishers acknowledge or make available the data they used in researching the story. Readers need to be able to see the source material whenever possible. Openness needs to breed openness.

Conclusion

Open data needs to be a story in its own right. When governments fail to live up to their promises of openness this should be reported. Where there are holes in the data, missing datasets, out of date datasets, this is part of the story. Where open data initiatives stall, this is a story too. Leaving journalism out of the case for openness is short-sighted. Those responsible for open data at a policy level should be talking to journalists and trying to meet their needs in terms of availability, formats, relevance, and timeliness. If governments do not meet these needs, then open data will remain a sideshow, something for the 'Technorati' – developers and coders, rather than the public at large. Open data needs journalism, and journalism needs open data. The two will get together eventually, and the two families need to accept this and work together to make it happen. Both need to find new ways of working with each other: if they don't, open data initiatives will simply wither away.

References

Conservative Party (2010) 'Invitation to Join the Government of Britain', available at https://www.conservatives.com/~/media/files/activist%20centre/press%20and%20policy/manifestos/manifesto2010, accessed 25 August, 2015

Data.gov (ND) available at www.data.gov

Government of the United Kingdom (2010) *PM's podcast on transparency*, available at https://www.gov.uk/government/news/pms-podcast-on-transparency, accessed 25 August 2015

Hargreaves, N (2013) 'The missing link in Kenya's open data story', in Code4Kenya, available at www.code4kenya.org/?author=2, accessed 25 August 2015

Nic Newman, DL (2015) *Digital News Report 2015*. Oxford: Reuters Institute for the Study of Journalism, available at www.digitalnewsreport.org, accessed 25 August 2015

Newman, L (2015) *Digital News Report 2014*. Oxford: Reuters Institute for the Study of Journalism, available at www.digitalnewsreport.org/survey/2014, accessed 25 August 2015

Open Data Barometer (2015) *Open Data Barometer*, available at http://barometer.opendataresearch.org, accessed 25 August 2015

Open Knowledge Foundation (2015) *Global Open Data Index*, available at http://index.okfn.org/place, accessed 25 August 2015

Rogers, Simon (2011) *Facts are Sacred*. London: Guardian Books

Transparency International (2015) *Corruption Perceptions Index 2014*, available at www.transparency.org/cpi2014, accessed 25 August 2015

Making data journalism real

Sensor journalism and other digital tools can bridge the divide between data and the public, allowing news organisations to involve communities in storytelling, writes Andy Dickinson

Introduction: clean air, clean data

During the 2008 summer Olympics, the Beijing Air Track project[1] took a team of photographers from Associated Press and used them to smuggle hand-held pollution sensors in to Beijing. Using their press access to the Olympic venues, they gathered pollution readings to test the Chinese government's data that showed a series of extreme emergency measures put in place in the run-up to the games had improved the city's notoriously poor air quality. They were not the only organisation to use sensors in this way. The BBC's Beijing office also used a hand-held sensor to test air pollution gathering data that appeared in a number of reports during the games (BBC News, 2008).

The Air Track project and AP's interactive report (Associated Press, 2008) are now cited as a 'prime example of how sensors, data journalism, and old-fashioned, on-the-ground reporting can be combined to shine a new level of accountability on official reports' (Howard 2013). In contrast to the Chinese data, the level of transparency displayed in the way the data was collected[2] illustrates how sensors can play a part in reinforcing data journalism role in the process of accountability.

Testing the context, provenance and ownership – where our data comes from and why – is a fundamental part of the data journalism process. If we aren't critical of the data we use (and those that provide it), we risk a breathless trust (Rogers, 2012) that undermines our credibility with data 'churnalism' or worse still data 'porn'! (Oliver, 2010). So, as data journalism practice evolves, whilst the basic critical skills will remain fundamental, it would seem logical to explore ways that we reduce our dependency on other sources altogether.

The Beijing project, with its use of sensors, offers a compelling solution. As Javaun Moradi, product manager for NPR digital, succinctly put it: 'If stage one of data journalism was "find and scrape data", then stage two was "ask government agencies to release data" in easy to use formats. Stage three is going to be "make your own data"' (Moradi, 2011).

The sensors used by the AP team were specialist air pollution sensors that cost in excess of US$400 – an expensive way for cash-strapped newsrooms to counter dodgy data. Since 2008 however, the price has dropped and the growing availability of cheap computing devices such as Raspberry Pi and Arduino (Allan, 2013), advances in smartphone technology, and the collaborative and open source ethic of the hacker and maker communities, have lowered the barriers to entry. Now sensors, and the crowd they attract, are a serious option for developing data driven reporting.

Hunting for (real) bugs with data

In 2013, New York braced itself for an invasion. Every 17 years a giant swarm of cicadas descend on the east coast. The problem is that exactly when in the year the insects will appear is less predictable. The best indicator of the emergence of the mega-swarm (as many as a billion cicadas in a square mile) seems to be when the temperature eight inches below the ground reaches 640 Fahrenheit (180 Centigrade). So when John Keefe, WNYC's senior editor for data news and journalism technology, met with news teams to look at ways to cover the story, he thought of the tinkering he had done with Arduinos and Raspberry Pis (Waite, 2013). He thought of sensors.

Keefe could not find a data source that offered any level of local detail across the whole of New York. He took the problem of how to collect the data to a local hackathon, organised by the station's popular science show Radiolab, who helped create a 'recipe' for an affordable, easy to make temperature sensor that listeners could build and send results back to a website (New York Public Radio, 2013) where they would map the information (Alba, 2014).

Developing collaboration

Whilst sensors play an enabling role in both examples, underpinning both the Beijing AirTrack and Cicada projects is the idea of collaboration. The Beijing project was originally developed by a team from the Spatial Information Lab at Columbia University. Combining the access of the media with the academic process and expertise of the lab gave the project a much bigger reach and authority. It's a form of institutional collaboration that echoes in a small way in more recent projects such as 2012's Reading the riots (*the Guardian*, 2012). The cicada project, on the other hand, offers an insight into a kind of community-driven collaboration that reflects the broader trend of online networks and the dynamic way groups form.

Safecast and the Fukushima nuclear crisis

On 9 March 2011, Joichi Ito was in Cambridge Massachusetts. He had travelled from Japan for an interview to become head of MIT's prestigious Media Lab. The same day a massive underwater earthquake off the coast of Japan caused a devastating tsunami and triggered a meltdown at the Fukushima Dai-ichi nuclear plant, starting the worst nuclear crisis since Chernobyl in 1986. Ito, like many others, turned to the web and social media to find out if family and friends were safe and gather as much information as he could about the risk from radiation (Kalin, 2012).

At the same time as Ito was searching for news about his family, US web developer Marcelino Alvarez was in Portland scouring the web for information about the possible impact of the radiation on the US west coast. He decided to channel his 'paranoia' and within 72 hours his company had created RDTN.org, a website aggregating and mapping information about the level of radiation (Alvarez, 2011).

For Alvarez and Ito the hunt for information soon developed into an effort to source Geiger counters to send to Japan to help people monitor radiation. Within a week of the disaster, the two had been introduced and RDTN.org became part of project that would later become Safecast.org. As demand outstripped supply, their efforts to buy good quality Geiger counters quickly transformed into a community driven effort to design and build cheap, accurate sensors that could be deployed quickly to gather up-to-date information.

Solving problems: useful data

Examples such as WNYC's cicada project show how a strong base of community engagement can help enable data driven projects. But the Safecast network wasn't planned, it grew 'from purposed conversations among friends to [a] full-time organisation gradually over a period of time,' (Safecast, 2013). There was no news conference to decide the when and the how it would respond or attempt to target contributors. It was a complex, self-selecting mix of different motivations and passions that coalesced into a coherent response to solve a problem. It's a level of responsiveness and scale of coverage that news organisations would struggle to match on their own. In that context, Moradi believes that journalism has a different role to play:

> *'Whether they know it or not, they do need an objective third party to validate their work and give it authenticity. News organisations are uniquely positioned to serve as ethical overseers, moderators between antagonistic parties, or facilitators of open public dialogue,'* (Moradi 2011).

Building bridges

Taking a position as a focal point for those with the data and resources and a bridge to 'the public who desperately want to understand the data and access it but need help' (Rogers, 2011) is a new reading of what many would recognise as a fundamental part of journalism's process and identity. The alignment of data journalism with the core principles of accountability and the purpose of investigative journalism in particular, makes for a near perfect meeting point for the dynamic mix of like-minded hacks, academics and hackers, motivated not just by transparency and accountability. It also taps into a desire not just to highlight issues, rather to begin to put in place solutions to problems (Skoll World Forum, 2012). This mix of ideologies, as examples like the WikiLeaks story shows (Ellison, 2012), can be explosive but the output has proved invaluable in helping (re)establish the role of journalism in the digital space. Whether it is a catalyst to bring groups together, engage and amplify the work of others or a way to 'advance the cause of journalism by means other than reporting' (Moradi 2011), sensor journalism seems to be an effective gateway to exploring these new opportunities.

It's no surprise, then, that many journalists take advantage of sensors and their associated communities to take abstract concepts like open government and 'make them tangible, relevant and useful to real live humans in our communities' (Sopher, 2013). But a majority of the successful data journalism projects funded by organisations such as the Knight Foundation[3] have outputs that are almost exclusively digital; apps or data dashboards. As much as they might rely on the physical to gather data, the results remain resolutely trapped in the digital space.

The digital divide

As far back as 2009, the UK Government's *Digital Britain* report warned: 'We are at a tipping point in relation to the online world. It is moving from conferring advantage on those who are in it to conferring active disadvantage on those who are without,' (BIS, 2009: 11). The solution to this digital divide is to focus on getting those who are not online connected. As positive as this is, it's a predictably technological deterministic solution to the problem that critics say conflates digital inclusion with social inclusion (Livingstone and Lunt, 2012). For journalism, and data journalism in particular, it raises an interesting challenge to claims of 'combating information asymmetry' and increasing the data literacy of their readers on a mass scale (Gray et al, 2012).

Insight journalism: journalism as data

In the same year as the *Digital Britain* report appeared, the Bespoke project dived into the digital divide by exploring ways to create real objects that could act as interfaces to the online world. The project took residents from the Callon and Fishwick areas in Preston, Lancashire, recognised as some of the most deprived areas in the UK, and trained them as community journalists who contributed to a hyper-local newspaper that was distributed round the estate. The paper also served as a way of collecting 'data' for designers who developed digitally connected objects aimed at solving problems identified by the journalists; a process the team dubbed insight journalism (Blum-Ross et al, 2013). One example, the 'Wayfinder', was a digital display and a moving arrow that users could text to point to events happening in the local area. Another, 'Viewpoint'

(Taylor et al. 2012), was a kiosk, placed in local shops, that allowed users to vote on questions from other residents, the council and other interested parties. The questioner had to agree that they would act on the responses they got – a promise that was scrutinised by the journalists.

The idea was developed during the 2012 Unbox festival in India, when a group of designers and journalists applied the model of insight journalism to the issue of sexual harassment on the streets of New Delhi. The solution, share the stare (Eggleston, 2014), built on reports and information gathered by journalists, was to build a device that would sit on top of one of the many telegraph poles that clutter the streets attracting thousands of birds. The designers created a bird table fitted with a bell. When a woman felt threatened or was subjected to unwanted attention she could use Twitter to 'tweet' the nearest bird table and a bell would ring. The ringing bell would scatter any roosting birds giving a visible sign of a problem in the area. The solution was as poetic as it was practical, highlighting not just the impact of the physical but also the power of journalism as data to help solve a problem.

Open sensors for local data

In 2014, Preston in Lancashire was awarded a £435m, five-year, city deal from central government. The project included plans to spend millions of pounds on a number of new road schemes. Tracking the progress of the deal has, as you would expect, provided a continuous source of content for local news outlets. But researchers at the University of Central Lancashire's DataMakers project[4], where keen to monitor the long-term environmental impact of the deal.

The quality of the local environment is known to have a direct effect on the social and economic wellbeing of a community (OECD, 2015). It generally falls to the government and local councils to prioritise and provide environmental services and measure the impact of projects like the city deal. In recent years, open government legislation has increasingly placed an emphasis on open data as a key part of opening up services to scrutiny and participation. But the quality of environmental data being made open at local level has yet to match the expectations set centrally. Despite a growing assumption that open data encourages participation, the reality is often that decisions are being made on the basis of data that communities cannot see or don't understand, reinforcing the digital divide.

Using data from the local council, the researchers noted that a large number of primary schools where directly next to or near one of the major routes through Preston, a route that had been identified by the council as at risk of congestion during the development of the scheme. The location of the schools made them an ideal base from which to monitor the environmental impact. So the project team asked 30 11-year-olds from local schools to work with games developers to come up with an app that would encourage environmental data collection. The result was Ukko, a sensor-driven mobile phone based *digital-pet* (Dickinson et al, 2015).

The game uses a low-cost environmental sensor connected to a mobile phone. The data gathered by the sensor is used to create the virtual environment for a digital pet that lives on the phone: the better the air quality, the happier the pet. The data and location information is also stored anonymously on a server to help build up a long-term picture of environmental quality with a very local focus.

Like the Wayfinder and Viewpoint projects, the Datamakers team approached the community at large to help gather data. The focus on encouraging ownership and understanding of data at a grassroots level was key, as it meant the community not only had control of the physical process of collecting the data, but also that they *own* the data. It means the community would have raw data they could use to better understand their own environment, or to lobby for better representation in environmental decision-making. Making the data open (for a discussion see www.opendefinition.org) also means that others can take that data and develop their own content and applications, which broadens the impact and value of the data.

Making data open, and benefiting from the network effect that follows has long been an underpinning principle of data journalism (Bell, 2013). But value also lies in its role of making the journalistic process transparent and accountable. As Simon Rogers noted:

> *'News organizations may be campaigners for open information but by withholding that data, become complicit in a system which essentially keeps data private until it's no longer commercially valuable. It's all very well calling for governments to throw open the doors of their data vaults, but if you are not willing to be open too, what is that worth?'* (Rogers, 2012).

The massive expansion in the amount and complexity of open data, particularly coming from governments (open government data), is seen as one of the reasons for the shift of data journalism practitioners to more prominent positions in the newsroom. (Lewis and Usher, 2014). As well as their technical skills – much in demand as the mechanics of getting content online become more challenging – they also bring a different set of cultural practices, more in keeping with open-source communities than the traditional newsroom. As a result, the number of newsrooms making the code for their interactive projects freely available online[5] is on the increase and the focus has shifted from data to the process of managing and presenting that data. However as much as it represents a massive cultural change in the newsroom – undoubtedly encouraging innovation within the industry – it also risks uncoupling openness from transparency, taking the raw data further from the people it is supposed to help and engage.

Stage four: make data real

Despite its successes, sensor journalism is still a developing area and it is not yet clear if it will see any growth beyond the environmental issues that drive many of the examples presented here. Like data journalism, much of the discussion around the field focuses on the new opportunities it presents. These often intersect with equally nascent but seductive ideas such as drone journalism (Waite, 2015). More often than not, they bring the discussion back to the more familiar ground of the challenges of social media, managing communities and engagement – a consistent and fundamental challenge to create a more open journalism6 'which is fully knitted into the web of information that exists in the world today,' (Rusbridger, 2012).

As journalism follows the mechanisms of the institutions we are meant to hold to account into the digital space, it is perhaps a chance to think about how it can move beyond simply building capacity within the industry, providing useful case studies (Gray et al, 2012). It's also a way to ground the increasingly technical process of data journalism, looking beyond the mechanisms of open-source to the underlying ideology of the social benefits of sharing. Perhaps it is a way to for data journalism to help journalism at large re-connect to the minority of those in society who, by choice or by circumstance, are left disconnected.

Thinking about ways to make the data we find and the data journalism we create physical, perhaps through sensors, closes a loop on a process that starts with real people in the real world. Regardless of how rarefied the community data travels through, the results should also end up in their hands. It begins to raise important questions about what journalism's role should be in not just capturing the problems and raising awareness but also creating real, open and accessible solutions. In an industry struggling to re-connect, it maybe also starts to address the issue of solving the problem placing the community back into journalism and making it sustainable. If stage three is to make our own data, perhaps it is time to start thinking about how open strategies and meaningful, hands-on community engagement can get us to stage four of data journalism and make data real.

Notes

[1] Columbia University Graduate School of Architecture, Preservation and Planning Spatial Information Design Lab, available at http://www.spatialinformationdesignlab.org/projects.php?id=97, accessed 23 September 2012

[2] The BBC clearly stated that their sensor had a 20 per cent margin of error http://news.bbc.co.uk/1/hi/in_pictures/7506925.stm

[3] See https://www.newschallenge.org, accessed 19 August 2015

[4] See http://mediainnovationstudio.org, accessed 19 August 2015

[5] For an example see the Knight Foundation's Source project, which offers an interesting jumping off point for exploring open source news development, https://opennews.org/what/community/source, accessed on 5 August 2015

[6] For a good overview of Open Journalism see Melanie Sills 2012 position paper 'The case for open journalism' at http://www.annenberginnovationlab.org/OpenJournalism. However the core concepts are universal and well explored by other attempts to define

the challenge of involving the audience in the journalistic process, such as network journalism and participatory journalism

References

Alba, Davey (2013) 'Sensors: John Keefe and Matt Waite on the current possibilities', Tow Centre for Digital Journalism, 5 June, available at http://towcenter.org/blog/sensors-john-keefe-and-matt-waite-on-the-current-possibilities, accessed 12 August 2013

Allan, Alistain (2013) 'Arduino Uno vs BeagleBone vs Raspberry Pi', available at http://makezine.com/2013/04/15/arduino-uno-vs-beaglebone-vs-raspberry-pi, accessed 2 October 2013

Alvarez, Marcelino (2011) '72 Hours from concept to launch: RDTN.org', Uncorked Words, 21 March, available at http://uncorkedstudios.com/2011/03/21/72- hours-from-concept-to-launch-rdtn-org, accessed 12 August 2013

Associated Press (2008) 'Air Track Project', available at http://hosted.ap.org/specials/interactives/_international/oly_fea_pollution/index.html, accessed 1 October 2013

BBC (2008) 'In pictures: Beijing pollution-watch', BBC News website, 24 August, available at http://news.bbc.co.uk/sport1/hi/front_page/6934955.stm, accessed 12 August 2013

Bell, Emily (2013) 'The NSA files and the network effect', in *the Guardian*, 15 December, available at www.theguardian.com/world/media-blog/2013/dec/15/nsa-files-network-effect-journalism, accessed 19 August, 2015

Blum-Ross, Alicia, Mills, John, Egglestone, Paul and Frohlich, David (2013) 'Community media and design: Insight journalism as a method for innovation', in *Journal of Media Practice*, Vol 14/3, 1 September, pp 171-192

Department of Business Innovation and Skills (2009) *Digital Britain: Final Report*, Stationery Office

Dickinson, Andy, Lochrie, Mark, and Eggelstone, Paul (2015) 'DataPet: designing a participatory sensing data game for children' in *Proceedings of the 2015 British HCI Conference*, British HCI '15. ACM, New York, USA, pp. 263–264

Eggleston, Paul. (2014) 'Bespoke: Unboxed', available at http://mediainnovationstudio.org/bespoke-unboxed/, accessed 18 August 2015

Ellison, Sarah (2011) 'The man who spilled the secrets', *Vanity Fair*, February, available at www.vanityfair.com/politics/features/2011/02/the-guardian-201102, accessed 13 September 2013

Gray, Jonathan, Chambers, Lucy and Bounegru, Liliana (2012) *The Data Journalism Handbook*. Sebastopol, CA: O'Reilly Media. Free version available online at http://datajournalismhandbook.org/

Howard, Alex (2013) 'Sensoring the news', *O'Reilly Radar*, 22 March, available at http://radar.oreilly.com/2013/03/sensor-journalism-data-journalism.html, accessed 12 August 2013

Kalin, Sari (2012) 'Connection central', in MIT news magazine, 21 August, available at www.technologyreview.com/article/428739/connection-central, accessed 22 August 2013

Lewis, Seth C, and Usher, Nikki (2014) 'Code, Collaboration, And The Future Of Journalism' in *Digital Journalism* 0, pp1–11. doi:10.1080/21670811.2014.895504

Livingstone, Sonia and Lunt, Peter (2013) 'Ofcom's plans to promote "participation", but whose and in what?' in LSE Media Policy Project, 27 February, available at http://blogs.lse.ac.uk/mediapolicyproject/2013/02/27/ofcoms-plans-to-promote-participation-but-whose-and-in-what, accessed 23 September 2013

Moradi, Javaun (2011) 'What do open sensor networks mean for journalism?' in *Javaun's Ramblings* blog, 16 December 16, available at http://javaunmoradi.com/blog/2011/12/16/what-do-open-sensor-networks-mean-for-journalism/#sthash.yXXlHoa2.dpuf, accessed 9 August 2013

New York Public Radio (2013) 'Cicada Tracker', available at http://project.wnyc.org/cicadas/, accessed 2 October 2013

OECD (2015) 'OECD Better Life Index' available at www.oecdbetterlifeindex.org/countries/united-kingdom, accessed 19 August 2015

Oliver, Laura (2010) 'UK government's open data plans will benefit local and national journalists' in Journalism.co.uk, 1 June, available at www.journalism.co.uk/news/uk-government-039-s-open-data-plans-will-benefit-local-and-national-journalists/s2/a538929, accessed 12 August 2013

Rogers, Simon (2011) *Facts are Sacred: The Power of Data.* Cambridge, UK: Guardian Books

Rogers, Simon (2012) 'Open Data Journalism' in *the Guardian*, 20 September, available at www.theguardian.com/news/datablog/2012/sep/20/open-data-journalism, accessed 10 August 2015

Rusbridger, Alan (2012) 'Q&A with Alan Rusbridger: the future of open journalism' in *the Guardian*, 25 March, available at www.theguardian.com/commentisfree/2012/mar/25/alan-rusbridger-open-journalism, accessed 22 July 2015

Safecast History (no date) Safecast.com, available at http://blog.safecast.org/history, accessed 25 September 2013

Skoll World Forum (2012) 'Up for debate: why we need solutions for journalism' in Forbes.com, available at www.forbes.com/sites/skollworldforum/2012/11/29/up-for-debate-why-we-need-solutions-journalism, accessed 19 August, 2015

Sopher, Christopher (2013) 'How can we harness data and information for the health of communities?', Knight Foundation, 16 August, available at https://www.newschallenge.org/challenge/healthdata/brief.html, accessed 10 August 2015

Taylor, Nick, Marshall, Justin, Blum-Ross, Alicia, Mills, John, Rogers, Jon, Egglestone, Paul, Frohlich, David M, Wright, Peter and Olivier, Patrick (2012) 'Viewpoint: Empowering Communities with Situated Voting Devices' in Proceedings of the Computer Human Interaction (CHI) conference. New York: Association for Computing Machinery, pp 1,361-1,370

The Guardian (2012) 'Reading the Riots', in *the Guardian*, available at www.theguardian.com/uk/series/reading-the-riots, accessed 2 October 2013

Waite, Matt (2013) 'How sensor journalism can help us create data, improve our storytelling', in Poynter.org, 17 April, available at www.poynter.org/how- tos/digital-strategies/210558/how-sensor-journalism-can-help-us-create-data-improve- our-storytelling, accessed 28 August 2013

Waite, Matt (2015) 'Drone Journalism Lab', available at www.dronejournalismlab.org, accessed 19 August 2015

Hacks, hacking and the NSA: encryption for the working journalist

Gabriel Keeble-Gagnère argues that – following the leaks by Edward Snowden in 2013 – journalists, especially those dealing with sensitive topics, should become familiar with encryption techniques. And he provides an overview of the methods reporters can use to protect themselves from the snoopers

Introduction

The cache of National Security Agency (NSA) documents leaked by Edward Snowden to Glenn Greenwald and Laura Poitras in early 2013, of which only a small percentage of documents have been published as of mid-2015, brought into sharp focus the surveillance efforts of the US government. While it had been assumed for years that the NSA ran surveillance programmes to monitor internet traffic, the leaks have provided documentary proof that these programs are, indeed, operational and in some cases more invasive than previously thought. While the implications for the citizens of the world (since the reach of the NSA is global) are profound, and have been discussed extensively in the media (both on- and off-line), this chapter focuses on the following questions: What are the implications for working journalists, for whom source confidentiality, and the ability to work free of government interference are so integral? And what, ultimately, can be done about it? Journalists, especially those dealing with sensitive subjects, must become familiar with elements of computer security and encryption. In light of this, the aims of this chapter are two-fold: to place the Snowden revelations in the broader context of government intimidation and attacks on journalists, discussing the practical implications; and to give a brief overview of the methods and tools journalists can employ to protect themselves.

What this chapter cannot do is detail how to protect oneself absolutely; instead, it hopes to introduce a number of tools and ideas that can be a starting point for working towards a useful knowledge of encryption and computer security. It must be emphasised that perfect security is impossible, especially on the internet, as this can only be achieved by avoiding it completely. Depending on the situation, this may be a prudent choice.

What we know

The ultimate goal of the NSA/GCHQ (Government Communications Headquarters, the British counterpart to the NSA) surveillance programmes is nothing short of 'map[ping] the entire internet – any device, anywhere, all the time'. As *Der Spiegel* reported, 'every single end device that is connected to the internet somewhere in the world – every smartphone, tablet and computer – is to be made visible' (Müller-Maguhn et al, 2014). Many of the most popular websites and online services – Google, Facebook, Hotmail, Twitter, and Skype among them – actively assist the NSA in accessing their users' data (Greenwald et al, 2013; Ball et al, 2013) even if some, such as Yahoo, initially resisted (Miller 2013). The backbone of the internet – the network of undersea cables which carry the bulk of international phone and internet traffic – is being tapped directly, with all traffic a target for retrieval and storage. Even encrypted data not currently accessible is stored for a future time when it may be: the agency has worked hard to weaken encryption technologies, often in collaboration with the very commercial companies who are supposedly providing these services to clients, even going as far as paying encryption services company RSA $10 million to use an NSA-developed formula, which the NSA knew how to subvert, for random number generation in one of its software packages (Menn, 2013). When the encryption method cannot be broken directly, efforts will be made to gain access to the all-important keys used originally to encrypt the data; the NSA and GCHQ hacked the largest manufacturer of SIM cards in the world, Gemalto, giving it access to potentially billions of mobile communications across 85 countries (Scahill and Begley 2015). If a target proves particularly difficult to compromise, a special offensive hacking unit within the NSA – the Office of Tailored Access Operations (TAO) – can be called on. Among the tools at its disposal are techniques to break into computers not even connected to the internet (Spiegel, 2014a).

What it means

In short, journalists can no longer rely on internet companies, commercial software, or even the rule of law to protect them or their data. Especially at risk are those who work with whistleblowers – as Julian Assange and Glenn Greenwald are perhaps the most aware. It goes without saying that whistleblowers themselves must be especially careful, even more so than the journalists they work with; the experiences of Bradley/Chelsea Manning and Edward Snowden have made this clear. Indeed, following an initial (encrypted) exchange with Snowden (who had not revealed his identity at the time), Laura Poitras was given 'instructions for creating an even more secure system to protect their exchanges'. Snowden had already contacted Greenwald anonymously, with instructions on how to use encryption, but had been ignored

(Mass 2013). In the future, unless journalists have a working knowledge of cryptographic techniques, whistleblowers will, rightly, be unwilling to approach them. Thomas Drake, former NSA executive and whistleblower, recommends journalists familiarise themselves with encryption but also 'good old-fashioned ways of reporting such as meeting in person, paying in cash, taking cryptic notes, and being careful not to do anything that could burden your source' (Pangburn, 2015).

Beginning the journey towards encryption

Journalists, not usually known for their computing skills, may be unsure how to go about familiarising themselves with the various techniques for encrypting their communications and data. This section, therefore, hopes to introduce a number of tools and concepts, together with resources for continued learning; hopefully, it can provide the basis for journalists to begin the journey.

All the tools detailed below, unless stated otherwise, are open-source and freely available for Windows, Mac OS X and Linux operating systems. Given the high chance that Windows and Mac OS X are compromised (see discussion above), it is recommended to use Linux in situations where security is critical. Naturally, as with all software, bugs and security problems are constantly being found (and hopefully fixed); it goes without saying that the latest (stable) version of all the following tools should always be used, and security warnings on the developers' websites checked regularly.

For critical applications, one should already be familiar with the tools in question to avoid potential errors that could compromise security. Most of the tools described below provide comprehensive guides that should be studied carefully.

A note on passwords

Many of the encryption methods detailed below involve the use of a password. The importance of using good passwords cannot be overstated. This is true also for passwords linked to email and other online accounts, though one should take particular care in picking good passwords for encryption as this will determine its reliability. For example, using a strong encryption method but with 'abc' as password is hardly better than using no encryption at all, at least in situations beyond the most trivial. A good password is one that is relatively long (more than 10 characters), involving upper- and lower-case characters, numbers, special characters such as # and *, and not using any words that can be obviously linked to you. As Snowden allegedly told Poitras in their initial exchange, 'assume that your adversary is capable of a trillion guesses a second' (Maas 2013a).

Communicating securely

The most widespread tool for encryption of emails is PGP (Pretty Good Privacy, http://www.openpgp.org), and its open-source implementation GPG (GNU Privacy Guard, http://www.gnupg.org). These tools use the encryption algorithm known as RSA, named after its creators Rivest, Shamir and Adelman. This method relies on two keys: one, the *public key*, is usually shared online (for example, via a personal homepage or through key servers such as http://pgp.mit.edu/) and enables third parties to encrypt messages they wish to send; and the *private key*, without which the encrypted message cannot be decrypted and read. Note that the sender of the encrypted message need not have ever met the recipient; however, they must at least trust that the public key (and associated email address) genuinely belongs to them.

It is important to understand that the strength of RSA relies on a mathematical belief: that very large integers (with hundreds of digits) are difficult to factor (that is, reduce to its prime components). While no known method exists to do this in any reasonable space of time, this does not preclude the possibility that one will be found in the future. Still, the Snowden leaks seem to have confirmed that the NSA has not yet been able to 'crack' the underlying mathematics of RSA (Simonite 2013).

One important factor in the security of RSA is the key size used (measured in bits), which are generally powers of 2 greater than 1024. To be safe, a key size of 4096 bits or more is advised. Another consideration is the implementation of RSA being used. As discussed in the first part of this chapter, proprietary implementations, especially those on embedded devices, are potentially compromised and should be avoided. A Swiss study found that an alarming number of public keys available on the internet shared common factors; the likely reason being sloppy implementations and small key sizes (Lenstra et al. 2012). Given their wide use and history, PGP and GPG can be assumed to be among the most reliable implementations at present.

Another capability of RSA besides encryption is that of digitally *signing* emails and data (this involves using your private key to encrypt – then your public key can be used by anyone to decrypt it and check that the result is the same as the message in question). Such a signature can be used by the recipient of data to confirm that the email has not been tampered with in transit. This is particularly important if an email account is hacked, as it can be used to prove that an account has been compromised.

For real-time communications, an account on the real-time messaging network Jabber (available at http://register.jabber.org), together with an open-source chat client such as Pidgin (http://www.pidgin.im/), allows encryption of messages using the OTR ('off the record') plugin (http://otr.cypherpunks.ca/). Documents indicate that the NSA is unable to decrypt OTR-encrypted chats (Spiegel, 2014b).

With both methods described above, communications are only safe once keys have been exchanged and verified via a *different* communication channel (voice-based is preferable as it is difficult to imitate), where the identity of the intended recipient can be confirmed. This is to avoid so-called *man-in-the-middle* attacks, which may best be explained with an example. Say that Alice and Bob[1] wish to communicate securely, and are presently in physically different locations. If Alice emails Bob requesting his public key (in order to send him an encrypted email), Alice has no way of knowing if Bob's email account has been hacked (by Eve, say) and an alternate public key (for which Eve owns the private key) sent in the reply instead.

If Alice simply uses this key to send an encrypted email with sensitive information, Eve will be able to decrypt it. Hence the importance of verifying keys through another channel – in this case, Alice can simply call Bob and verify the key he emailed is, indeed, his own key. Note that this channel need not be encrypted – in fact, even if Eve is listening in, unless she can change Bob's voice in real-time in a way that convinces Alice, there is no problem (so long as this channel is only used to verify keys). In practice, it is not the key that is verified but its *fingerprint*, a much shorter string of characters that is used to identify the key itself.

Encrypting files

In addition to encrypting communications, journalists will often need to encrypt documents they are working on, such as articles in progress or documents passed to them in confidence. Commonly used compression tools often provide encryption support; though as discussed above, commercial tools are potentially compromised and should not be trusted. A reliable open-source compression tool is 7zip (http://www.7-zip.org/), which supports the AES-256 encryption standard. As noted previously, the strength of the encryption will be compromised by a trivial password. The full set of US diplomatic cables leaked to WikiLeaks was distributed as a 7zip-encrypted file; it was decrypted only after the *Guardian* journalist, David Leigh, published the password in a book by mistake.[2] Another popular tool is Truecrypt (http://www.trucrypt.org; not strictly open-source, though the source code is available), which offers a wider range of cryptographic functions, such as encrypting entire file systems.

It is worth noting that extra care may be needed when working with particularly sensitive information. It follows from the first part of this chapter that any computer connected to the internet is *potentially* at risk of being spied on. In such a situation, the sensitive data can be accessed before it is even encrypted. An extra level of care that can be taken – and one adopted by renowned computer security expert Bruce Schneier while working on parts of the Snowden documents (Schneier 2013a) for *the Guardian* – is to buy a new computer, which is never connected to the internet, and used solely for the purpose of working on, encrypting and decrypting sensitive files (this is known as 'air-gapping'). This way, the plaintext (non-encrypted) data will never be loaded into memory on an online computer.

Accessing the internet anonymously

When connected to the internet, our identity is revealed by a unique IP (internet protocol) address. Each connection we make on the internet (to websites, email servers and so on) may be traced back to us with this address. What this means is that even with prudent use of encryption, the identity of whistleblowers and those they work with can be uncovered (though what they are saying may not be). Because of this, and depending on the situation, anonymous access to the internet may be desired.

One of the simplest ways of achieving this is with the Tor software package (http://torproject.org/), which anonymises connections by sending them through a series of intermediate nodes (computers running the Tor software in 'relay' mode), before finally accessing the website through the final node in the chain, the exit node. One important point to note is that while communications within the Tor network are encrypted, the exit node will transmit data as it was at the beginning – in other words, the user is responsible for encrypting their communications. Failure to do so can compromise anonymity. Care should also be taken when links are followed, since external applications (for example, when opening a linked PDF file) opened will not be running through Tor by default and can unmask you.

While there are a number of potential issues with Tor, and new vulnerabilities are often being found, it is still believed to be a reliable way to achieve anonymity online. Indeed, the NSA's own exploits of Tor have focused on the Firefox web browser supplied with the Tor Browser Bundle (these exploits have since been fixed), not the Tor system itself (Schneier, 2013b). Despite this, the Tor Browser Bundle is still recommended (the website states: 'almost any other web browser configuration is likely to be unsafe to use with Tor') – just make sure to always use the latest version.

Another way of anonymising oneself online is to purchase an account on a VPN (Virtual Private Network) service. In a nutshell, this simply serves as a relay point for your connections; the IP address you appear to be connecting from is that of the VPN server, not your personal computer. Data is encrypted between your computer and the VPN servers (though it should be noted that this is one of the types of encryption that the NSA has worked to compromise). There are a large range of VPN services available, with varying levels of security. One word of caution: many VPN services will log all user activity and hand over this information when pressured by governments and law enforcement (Enigmax and Ernesto, 2013). For true anonymity, a VPN provider that does not log user activity is essential; AirVPN (https://airvpn.org/) and PrivatVPN (https://www.privatvpn.se/en) are two providers that claim not to. More recent revelations have shown that VPN networks are not safe from NSA spying; according to one document, 'from late 2009, the agency was processing 1,000 requests an hour to decrypt VPN connections' (Spiegel, 2014b).

Note that Tor and VPNs can also be used to access websites that have been blocked. In countries which operate particularly aggressive censorship of the internet, such as Iran, China and Saudi Arabia (and let's not pretend that Western governments are exempt – Australia, Italy, France and the UK were placed 'under surveillance' in the annual Reporters Without Borders *Enemies of the Internet* report in 2010 following moves to implement their own filters), access to sites routinely used by journalists such as Twitter may be restricted; a VPN account allows you to bypass such filters regardless of physical location.

The all-in-one solution: TAILS

Tails is a customised version of Debian Linux which has most of the tools discussed above pre-loaded and uses Tor by default to connect to the internet. Importantly, it can be installed on a USB key and used to boot directly into the operating system. Once sensitive tasks have been completed, you can boot back into your usual operating system and no trace of the Tails session will remain. This is the easiest way to get up and running with encryption and anonymity with the least chance of a mistake, but note also that it is not suitable to use as a day-to-day operating system and should only be used to carry out sensitive tasks. It can be assumed to be effective when used properly: The NSA specifically complains about Tails in some of the Snowden documents. Tails can be downloaded from https://tails.boum.org/.

Blowing the whistle securely: SecureDrop

SecureDrop (https://securedrop.org/) is an open-source submission tool that can be installed by media organisations as a way to allow anonymous, secure submission of documents. Among the technologies and techniques it uses are Tor, GnuPG, Tails, and air-gapping, all discussed in this chapter. It was originally created by the late Aaron Swartz and is now managed by the Freedom of the Press Foundation. It is used by many media organisations including the *Intercept*, *the Guardian*, *Pro Publica* and *The Washington Post.*

Learning more

In an ideal world everyone would use encryption; in practice, however, it is beyond the technical skills, and patience, of most people. There have been a number of initiatives recently that seek to educate the broader public on cryptography issues. Started more than a year before the Snowden leaks came to light, the now-global Cryptoparty (https://cryptoparty.org/) emerged practically overnight following an exchange on Twitter initiated from Melbourne, Australia (Butt et al, 2012). It aims to provide a space for those interested in learning about cryptography to learn from users who are already familiar with tools and concepts, through talks and workshops. In New York, an encryption workshop was organised by the 'Hacks/Hackers' group, with the specific aim to educate journalists (Kirchner, 2013). These kinds of initiatives can be expected to become more common in the post-Snowden age. Journalists who are keen to learn should contact local computing groups (such as Linux user groups) or 'hackerspaces' (a comprehensive list can be found at http://hackerspaces.org/wiki/List_of_Hacker_Spaces) and try to organise similar sessions.

The limits

While appropriate and careful use of available technologies can protect journalists from many threats, it has limits. Governments will still try to intimidate and interfere with journalists using the means at their disposal. In particular, laws can be passed criminalising methods detailed above; indeed, it is already a jailable offence to refuse to surrender your password/encyption keys to authorities in the UK, Australia, India, France and South Africa (Price, 2014). While criminalising encryption outright is most likely unworkable in practice, this will not prevent governments from trying.

These actions are part of a worrying broader movement to start treating leakers (and the journalists they work with) as threats to national security, with governments arguing that terror laws are appropriate in this context. In the US, the National Defense Authorization Act for fiscal year 2012 (NDAA) has led to concerns that journalists may be targeted. A lawsuit was filed on 13 January 2013 (Hedges vs. Obama), arguing that Section 1021(b)(2) may authorise indefinite detention of journalists who are suspected of 'providing substantial support' to terrorists. The wording is so vague it has raised concerns that the law can also be applied to journalists who interview or simply write about groups or movements the government is opposed to, such as environmentalists or WikiLeaks (Kuipers, 2012). The case of Barret Brown is another example. Brown, an American writer and journalist, at one point faced 105 years in jail for reporting on hacked private intelligence companies (Goodman et al, 2013). While most charges against him were dropped following a plea deal in March 2014, he was sentenced to 63 months in prison and ordered to pay more than $800,000 in fines in January 2015 (Woolf, 2015).

Given the above, to what extent are journalists really at risk of being snooped on? How much effort should journalists devote to protecting themselves? The answer depends on individual circumstances. The vast majority of journalists will rarely find themselves targeted by governments. However, with large-scale leaks becoming more and more common, and governments' reactions increasingly extreme, few serious journalists can afford not to have at least a basic knowledge of the tools discussed in this chapter. Indeed, it is possible we would still be in the dark if it wasn't for Poitras's positive response to Snowden's initial contact.

Conclusion

Given what we now know, without careful use of encryption, a journalist cannot honestly guarantee the anonymity of a source – in some cases, this might be a matter of life and death. As Snowden has said himself: 'In the wake of this year's disclosure, it should be clear that unencrypted journalist-source communication is unforgivably reckless' (Maas, 2013b). Put another way, Snowden is saying that journalists cannot do their job properly without encryption. Just as the internet revolutionised journalism and the way journalists work (for better or worse), the Snowden leaks highlight the need for another major shift in practices. Journalistic education should reflect this – university courses should provide at least an option to learn about encryption (for example, in collaboration with a computing or maths department).

No matter how good your encryption, it is ultimately no substitute for that most essential ingredient in human relations: trust. Journalists and their sources should probably err on the side of caution. As John Young, founder of notorious leaks site Cryptome (http://www.cryptome.org/), puts it: 'Best be creative, imagine a means to triumph over the advice given here. Don't brag about it' (Cryptome, 2012). The Snowden leaks have revealed that there is, indeed, a war going on – an information war in which cryptography is a key weapon. The true role of journalism is to hold power to account; sadly, as we now know, a power that has evidently overstepped. It's time for journalists to fight back.

Notes

[1] Alice, Bob and Eve are common names used in cryptography books

[2] The password, CollectionOfDiplomaticHistorySince_1966_ToThe_PresentDay#, gives an idea of the care appropriate for sensitive situations

References

Ball, J, Borger, J and Greenwald, G (2013) 'Revealed: How US and UK spy agencies defeat internet privacy and security' in *the Guardian Weekly*, 6 September

Ball, J, Harding, L and Garside, J (2013) 'BT and Vodafone among telecoms companies passing details to GCHQ', in *the Guardian*, 2 August

Enigmax and Ernesto (2013) 'VPN services that take your anonymity seriously, 2013 Edition', *TorrentFreak*, 2 March, available at http://torrentfreak.com/vpn-services-that-take-your-anonymity-seriously-2013-edition-130302/, accessed 30 July 2015

Butt, C and Cook, H (2012) 'Privacy movement finds strength in crypto night' in *The Age*, 23 September

Lenstra, A K, Hughes, JP, Augier, M, Bos, JW, Kleinjung, T and Wachter, C (2012) *IACR Cryptology ePrint Archive 2012*, No. 64

Cryptome (2012) 'How to submit material to Cryptome anonymously', available at http://cryptome.org/cryptome-anon.htm, accessed 30 July 2015

Goodman, A and Gonzalez, J (2013) 'Jailed journalist Barrett Brown faces 105 years for reporting on hacked private intelligence firms' in *Democracy Now*, 11 July, available at http://www.democracynow.org/2013/7/11/jailed_journalist_barrett_brown_faces_105, accessed 30 July 2015

Greenwald, G and MacAskill, E (2013) 'NSA Prism program taps in to user data of Apple, Google and others' in *the Guardian*, 7 June

Greenwald, G (2013) 'The persecution of Barrett Brown – and how to fight it' in *the Guardian*, 21 March, available at http://www.theguardian.com/commentisfree/2013/mar/21/barrett-brown-persecution-anonymous, accessed on 30 July 2015

Kirchner, L (2013) 'Encryption, security basics for journalists' in *Columbia Journalism Review*, available at http://www.cjr.org/behind_the_news/hacks_hackers_security_for_jou.php?page=all, accessed 30 July 2015

Kuipers, D. (2012) 'Activists sue Obama, others over National Defense Authorization Act' in *Los Angeles Times*, 18 April

MacAskill, E, Borger, J, Hopkins, N, Davies, N and Ball, J (2013) 'GCHQ taps fibre-optic cables for secret access to world's communications' in *the Guardian*, 22 June, available at http://www.theguardian.com/uk/2013/jun/21/gchq-cables-secret-world-communications-nsa, accessed 30 July 2015

Maloof, F (2013) 'NSA has total access via Microsoft Windows' available at http://www.wnd.com/2013/06/nsa-has-total-access-via-microsoft-windows, accessed 30 July 2015

Mass, P (2013a) 'How Laura Poitras helped Snowden spill his secrets' in *The New York Times Magazine*, 18 August, available at www.nytimes.com/2013/08/18/magazine/laura-poitras-snowden.html?pagewanted=all&_r=0, accessed 30 July 2015

Mass, P (2013b) 'Q&A: Edward Snowden Speaks to Peter Maass' available at http://www.nytimes.com/2013/08/18/magazine/snowden-maass-transcript.html, accessed 30 July 2015

Menn, J (2013) 'Exclusive: Secret contract tied NSA and security industry pioneer', available at http://www.reuters.com/article/2013/12/21/us-usa-security-rsa-idUSBRE9BJ1C220131221, accessed 30 July 2015

Miller, C (2013) 'Secret court ruling put tech companies in data bind' in *The New York Times*, 14 June, available at www.nytimes.com/2013/06/14/technology/secret-court-ruling-put-tech-companies-in-data-bind.html?pagewanted=all, accessed 30 July 2015

Müller-Maguhn, A, Poitras, L, Rosenbach, M, Sontheimer, M and Grothoff, C (2014) 'Treasure map: The NSA breach of Telekom and other German firms' in *der Spiegel* online, available at http://www.spiegel.de/international/world/snowden-documents-indicate-nsa-has-breached-deutsche-telekom-a-991503.html, accessed July 30 2015

Pangburn, D (2015) 'Advice for whistleblowers and journalists from an NSA spy and Snowden's lawyer' in *Vice News*, available online at http://motherboard.vice.com/read/advice-for-whistleblowers-and-journalists-from-an-nsa-spy-and-snowdens-lawyer, accessed 31 July 2015

Perlroth, N, Larson, J and Shane, S (2013) 'NSA. Able to foil basic safeguards of privacy on web', in *The New York Times*, 6 September

Price, R (2014) 'Can police force you to surrender your password?', in *The Kernel* magazine, 7 December, available at http://kernelmag.dailydot.com/issue-sections/features-issue-sections/11071/police-force-password-cellphone/, accessed 30 July 2015

Rosenbach, M, Poitras, L and Stark, H (2013) 'iSpy: How the NSA accesses smartphone data' in *Der Spiegel*, 9 September

Scahill, J. and Begley, J. (2015) The Great SIM Heist: How spies stole the keys to the encryption castle, 20 February 2015. Available online at https://firstlook.org/theintercept/2015/02/19/great-sim-heist/, accessed on 30 July 2015

Schneier, B. (2013a) NSA surveillance: A guide to staying secure. Available online at http://www.theguardian.com/world/2013/sep/05/nsa-how-to-remain-secure-surveillance, accessed on 30 July 2015

Schneier, B. (2013b) Attacking Tor: How the NSA targets users' online anonymity. Available online at http://www.theguardian.com/world/2013/oct/04/tor-attacks-nsa-users-online-anonymity, accessed on 30 July 2015

Simonite, T. (2013) NSA Leak Leaves Crypto-Math Intact but Highlights Known Workarounds. Available online at http://www.technologyreview.com/news/519171/nsa-leak-leaves-crypto-math-intact-but-highlights-known-workarounds/, accessed on 30 July 2015

Spiegel staff (2014a) Inside TAO: Documents Reveal Top NSA Hacking Unit, December 28. Available online at http://www.spiegel.de/international/world/the-nsa-uses-powerful-toolbox-in-effort-to-spy-on-global-networks-a-940969.html, accessed on 31 July 2015

Spiegel staff (2014b) 'Prying Eyes: Inside the NSA's War on Internet Security', 28 December, available at http://www.spiegel.de/international/germany/inside-the-nsa-s-war-on-internet-security-a-1010361.html, accessed 30 July 2015

Woolf, N. (2015) 'Barret Brown sentenced to 63 months for "merely linking to hacked material",' 22 January, available at www.theguardian.com/technology/2015/jan/22/barrett-brown-trial-warns-dangerous-precedent-hacking-sentencing/, accessed 30 July 2015

D3.js and explanatory approaches to interactive data visualisation

Ændrew Rininsland, newsroom developer on the digital desk at *The Times* and *The Sunday Times*, discusses the development of coding tools and offers tips and advice for would-be developer journalists

Introduction

When searching for the right tool to visualise data, one often encounters two varieties of software. On one hand are *exploratory* tools – for instance, Tableau[1], Google Fusion Tables[2] or DataWrapper[3] – which allow a user to easily create interfaces for sorting or filtering data. Especially at the start of an investigation, these are important tools that often point journalists towards interesting stories. What happens once the journalist finds a story, however?

For quite some time, the next step has often been to write it up and make some version of the exploratory tool available to readers, a practise popularised by *the Guardian*'s Datablog (Aitamurto et al, 2010: 11). This provides transparency and allows readers to personalise the story by letting them look through the data themselves, but it has the potential to sacrifice the story in order to do so – after all, the relationship between data journalist and audience is such that the journalist is there to tell the audience why this data is interesting, and which parts are worth looking at (and, equally, not worth looking at).

On the other hand, some journalists have adopted *explanatory* tools that, instead of merely interfacing with data, allow journalists to pick it apart and show readers only the good bits. D3.js (hereafter just 'D3') popularises this approach by giving competent users a high-level means by which to bind data to web display components. In other words, it lets users map data onto anything they want – whether that be a line, or a rectangle, or most other elements that a web browser can render – and then manipulate those objects using that data. While flexible enough to enable the creation of exploratory tools, D3 really shines when used to create visualisations that highlight the most important pieces of data. D3's speed and utility have made it the de-facto standard for web-based data visualisation for news, with the D3 community leveraging some of the most exciting trends and best practises in web programming. This makes D3 proficiency a valuable skill for aspiring data journalists, newsroom developers, visualisation artists and journo-coders.[4]

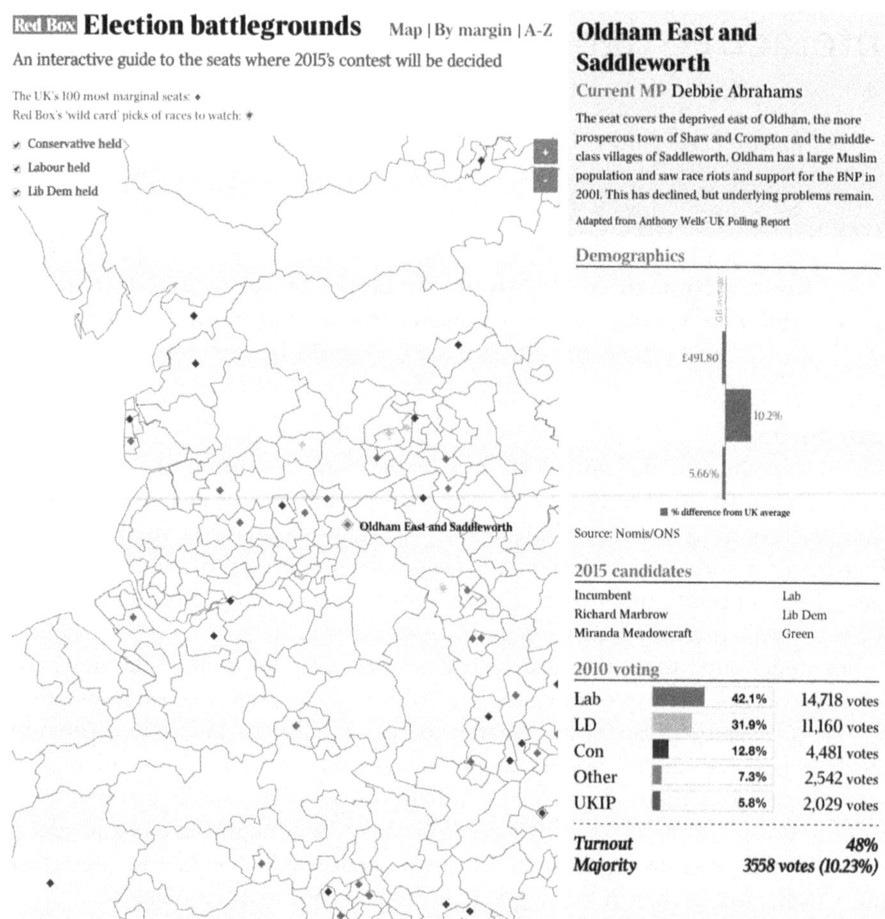

Figure 59: This *exploratory* D3-based interactive allows users to find information about battleground constituencies in the 2015 general election. It follows the classic visual information-seeking mantra of 'Overview first, zoom and filter, then details on demand'. Note that the user isn't directed to a particular end, and is required to use the tool to find relevant data. Source: *Red Box Election Battlegrounds*, Ændrew Rininsland / *The Times* (thetimes.co.uk/redbox/topic/ election-battlegrounds/interactive-explore-the-seats-that-will-decide-2015s-election).

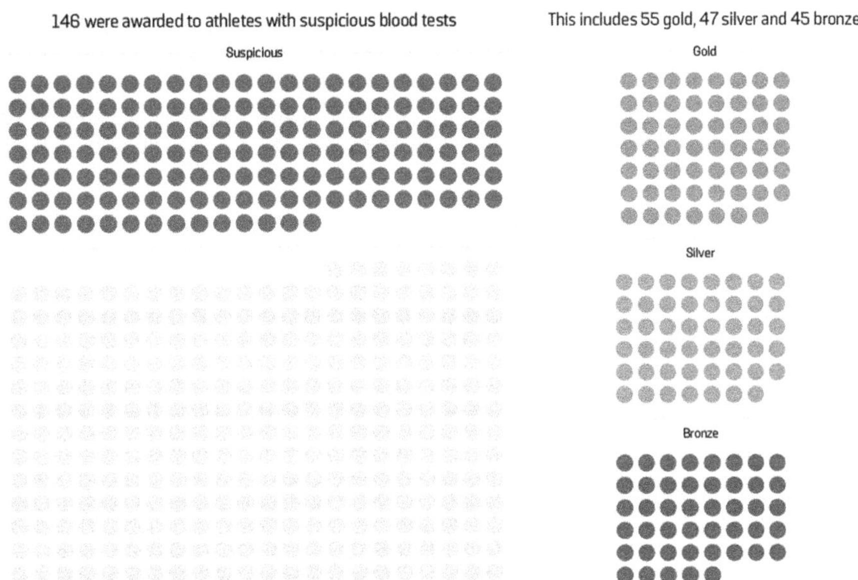

Figures 60 (left) & 61 (right): This *explanatory* D3-based graphic has three states: total medals and suspicious medals (Figure 2), medal breakdown (Figure 3) and country breakdown (not shown here). Users switch between the states using backwards and forwards navigation buttons, which causes the dots to change colour and move to different configurations. The updated groups are then signposted by labelled bounding box and descriptive text. Notice how the user is guided at each step. Source: *The Doping Scandal: Part I – The Medals*, Jeremy Harding and Ændrew Rininsland / *The Sunday Times*. (extras.thetimes.co.uk/web/2015/the-doping-scandal/index.html).

Evolution or revolution?

The internet's development has had several distinct phases. Initially there was the static internet – Web 1.0 – which was constructed mainly using basic HTML pages and this persisted into the mid- to late-nineties. JavaScript, the language of D3, was created by Brendan Eich at Netscape in 1995 to allow the web-browser to be more interactive than before.[5] Throughout the nineties, JavaScript was mostly used to drive many of the uninspiring visual effects that were characteristic of the early web (at a huge cost to computer performance), causing many people for quite some time to turn JavaScript off altogether. It would take many years of development and the emergence of full frameworks like Backbone, Angular and React for people to revisit JavaScript as one of the primary languages of the web. In the meantime, the lack of web-based drawing technologies in early web browsers forced visualisation artists to use static images or graphics technologies like Macromedia Flash (later Adobe Flash).

Following the popularisation of server-side scripting languages (such as PHP, Ruby and others), the Internet is thought to have entered a second iteration commonly referred to as Web 2.0. This new phase was marked by an emphasis on user-driven content and extensible, open source systems for managing it (Graham, 2005). WordPress became wildly popular, and blogs started to appear en masse. The new focus on web-based content creation systems resulted in the emergence of early interactive data visualisation, with IBM's Java-based ManyEyes in 2007 being one of the first examples of Web 2.0 user-driven visualisation tools. Google Spreadsheets enabled basic interactive charts to be added to a news story, then Google Fusion Tables allowed journalists to create complex, interactive maps from spreadsheet data. *The Guardian*'s use of Wikileaks data to map deaths in the Iraq conflict is a prime example of how powerful these tools can be in telling a story (see Rogers, 2010).

Flash and Java, meanwhile, had continued to evolve as web graphics technologies, but were quickly starting to show their age. Not only did Flash not work on Apple's popular iOS platform (Jobs, 2010), but it also added unnecessary resource overheard during an era when most web browsers were starting to be able to draw things natively.[6] Java, on the other hand, reached a tipping point in terms of security and stopped being available as a browser plugin in Mac OS X and eventually became blacklisted by Apple (Kelly, 2013). By dropping its support for these two technologies, Apple drove the visualisation community to re-evaluate how it displayed information online.

As people stopped using the buggy, older versions of Microsoft Internet Explorer, drawing technologies such as SVG (Scalable Vector Graphics) and Canvas became much more viable as a consequence. Not only did these newer technologies use less system resources than Java and Flash, but they were also great in terms of speed and stability. And crucially, SVG and Canvas also worked on mobile devices.

This spawned a whole raft of JavaScript-based graphing tools. Highcharts, Flot and The JavaScript Infoviz Toolkit were among the first, enabling data visualisation artists to easily create interactive, web-native versions of basic graphics like line graphs and pie charts. In the same vein, Google upgraded their visualisation tools to allow interactive visualisations in 2008. Meanwhile, more freeform drawing tools like Raphaël.js and Processing.js emerged for creating interesting visual content, but neither was really created with the intent of supporting sophisticated web-based data visualisation.[7]

Mike Bostock and Jeff Heer at the Stanford Visualisation Group released Protovis in 2009 to create a high-level framework for rendering data with SVG. This JavaScript library allowed data to be bound to various visual objects in the web-browser, and that data is used to manipulate the appearance of those objects. Protovis was fairly successful and a community formed around it. In 2011, Bostock superseded Protovis with the first release of D3.js, which contained numerous improvements to the workflow established by Protovis. Bostock then continued to develop D3 through his tenure as Graphics Editor at *The New York Times*, which he recently left to continue development of D3 full-time.[8]

Data driven documents

D3 provides some convincing answers to quite a few contemporary problems in data visualisation:

Portability

JavaScript, the language D3 is written in, is probably the single most versatile programming language on the internet at the moment. Windows, Linux and Mac OS X all run JavaScript nearly identically.[9] Moving a D3 visualisation from the computer where it's being developed to the production server is as difficult as moving a few files into a web-accessible directory. Further, D3's SVG output can be used in industry-standard tools like Adobe Illustrator, allowing it to be effective middleware in much larger applications and making it very useful when preparing output for print.

Extensibility

D3 can read most popular data formats such as CSV, TSV, XML and JSON. This versatility lets it communicate with most common web services, meaning that visualisations can easily consume live data.

Scalability

D3 visualisations are run on the 'client-side', meaning the viewer's computer is the one that does all the processing work. This avoids laborious server-side data crunching, which can also help prevent many of the scalability issues inherent in high-traffic server-side code. While server-side code can still be used to generate the dataset (as is often the case when using D3 to consume data from web services), in practice precompiled static data sets are often used. In other words, D3 visualisations are less likely to break under high server strain if done correctly.

Hosting

The D3 community commonly hosts its visualisations on GitHub Pages, the free cloud-based file hosting service provided by GitHub.[10] Another GitHub technology, Gists, are used by the community to create examples as a way of explaining how to use D3.[11] Bostock's "bl.ocks.org" tool acts as a convenient viewer for these examples. The upshot of this deployment strategy is that publicly-hosted data doesn't need a complex server setup, can easily be hosted for free, and will scale regardless of traffic requirements.

Mobile accessibility

The vast majority of mobile and desktop web browsers now support SVG. This powerful graphics technology is fast and versatile, but perhaps a bit difficult to use. D3 simplifies the creation of SVG graphics substantially, while doing so from the perspective of exacting, pixel-perfect data visualisation.

Cost

D3 is licensed under the popular open source BSD license, making it free to use, even for commercial purposes. One only needs a web browser to begin creating D3 visualisations — sites like Codepen and Tributary let users experiment with D3 without having to ever configure a code editor.[12]

D3 is useful because it solves many contemporary problems faced by data journalists in the newsroom, which often make it difficult to present their work in a unique or interesting manner. For instance, above I mention the difference between 'server-side' and 'client-side' code, with the former being processed by the big server computers that keep a news organisation's website up, and the latter being run on the news consumer's computer once received from the servers. Scalability is a huge issue for news organisations — a visualisation is often bombarded by huge amounts of traffic for a short time, after which it loses relevance but still must remain online for search engine reasons. If a server overloads and goes down while a piece is newsworthy, the audience impact is diminished considerably. D3's emphasis on cloud hosting through GitHub removes a lot of hardware requirements (especially if combined with a cloud-based script hosting service like Scraperwiki), and allows visualisations to be embedded in news articles via iframes.

This simplicity of use also extends to how easily D3 visualisations can be made to look consistent across multiple platforms. So long as a browser can render SVG and run JavaScript, it will output a D3 visualisation in a similar fashion. Not only that, D3's SVG output can even be pasted into a text file and opened with Adobe Illustrator, enabling it to be useful for creating print graphics.

Brace yourself — some code stuff ahead

It's worth reiterating that D3 is a *JavaScript library*, which means one uses the idioms D3 sets out when one writes JavaScript code, with the effect that many common tasks are simplified. A good example of this is how, in D3, you 'select' specific objects on a page before then executing a sequence of operations on them:

```
var chart = d3.select('body').append('svg').attr('id', 'the-viz');
```

A lot of functionality is packed into the above bit of code:[13]

First, D3's 'select' method (that is, 'd3.select') is told to find 'body' – in a web page, 'body' is the place where content is visible to the web browser.

'select' passes a reference to the page's main visible content area to the next method in that chain, 'append'. The job of 'append' is to add an element to the end of whatever it's been given, and, having been given the 'body' selection, it adds an 'svg' area to the web page.

'append' then changes the focus to the newly-appended 'svg' element, and gives a reference pointing at that to 'attr' (short for 'attribute'), which sets an attribute of an element — in this case, setting its 'id' attribute to 'the-viz'.

After the line of code is processed, a reference to this new SVG area is then stored in a variable named 'chart' so it can be easily accessed later (This is the 'var chart =' part at the very beginning.).

An empty SVG container such as the example described above is a common starting point for many visualisations.

The purpose of this chapter is to discuss the developments leading up to D3 and its general principles, so there won't be further examples of code here. The main point to convey is that D3 isn't so much a graphing library as much as a way of *binding data to display objects*. Once you use another function to open up a dataset while following the workflow above, you often then *select* that SVG container, and *append* a bunch of rectangles to it; then you could bind data (using, unsurprisingly, the 'data' function) to those rectangles, and finally set the height (which is an *attribute*) to whatever value each rectangle had bound to it. Without going into further detail, you now have most of the elements necessary for a basic bar graph.[14] Other elements are often added in a similar manner: first something is *selected*, then items are *appended* to it, then the *attributes* of those items are manipulated in some manner. The 'select, then modify' idiom described above is the most common in D3.

Exploring and explaining

No matter how simple a D3-based visualisation is, it still involves significantly more code compared with simply dropping a spreadsheet into Google Drive and using the Google Visualisation API to render it as a bar graph or line chart. It's worth noting the previous example didn't do anything with scales, margins, axis lines, or have any interactivity whatsoever — all that is taken for granted with an exploratory tool like Datawrapper, but must be explicitly rendered with D3. If you need to draw a basic bar chart (and *especially* if you're uncertain what the data will look like as chart), or if you have tonnes of data and just want to graph it to see whether there are any trends or further subsets of data to interrogate, D3 might not be the best choice – there are a whole host of tools better suited to that which are faster and less frustrating.

However, what if you found one data point that's interesting and you want to highlight it for the reader in an unusual way? What if you want to put all your data into arbitrary categories, and then colour each category? What if you want the chart to grab a related dataset and adjust itself accordingly whenever the reader clicks on an element? Or what if you want to hook everything up to a live dataset, to enable your visualisation to update and always have the latest data?

Scott Murray, author of seminal D3 guide *Interactive Data Visualization for the Web*, describes the difference between exploratory and *explanatory* visualisations as follows:

> *'D3 doesn't generate predefined or "canned" visualizations for you. This is on purpose. D3 is intended primarily for explanatory visualization work, as opposed to exploratory visualizations. Exploratory tools help you discover significant, meaningful patterns in data. These are tools ... which help you quickly generate multiple views on the same data set. That's an essential step, but different from generating an explanatory presentation of the data, a view of the data that highlights what you've already discovered. Explanatory views are more constrained and limited, but also focused, and designed to communicate only the important points.'* (Murray, 2013; emphasis his.)

Typically, if a visualisation needs a lot of dropdown menus or other ways of filtering and constraining data, it's probably more of an *exploratory* visualisation. *Explanatory* visualisations don't typically follow Shneiderman's visual information-seeking mantra of 'overview first, zoom and filter, then details on demand' (1996), instead presenting the user with a rendered snippet of data that separately presents its context in the wider data picture. This extends beyond presentation, however – an *explanatory* visualisation generally doesn't stand on its own because it lacks the context created from a reader's journey through an *exploratory* visualisation. An explanatory visualisation will often be accompanied by a lot of text, or possibly other visualisations intended to cement context.

Are explanatory graphics harder or easier than exploratory? In an interview with Data Stories, Mike Bostock discussed some of the challenges one is faced with when creating an exploratory graphic:

> *'I think it's simply harder to do a good exploratory graphic, and that is because an exploratory graphic sort of implies that you're doing exploration, which means you're doing some amount of work to extract the insight from that graphic. Whereas if you have an explanatory or expository graphic, you're sort of presenting up front "Here's what's the conclusion," or "Here's the interesting insight from that data.*
>
> *[...]*
>
> *'The reason why exploratory is hard is because you have to find that balance where you have some initial insight you want to show in the overview, but there's also that really rich data set that facilitates further insights if you play with it. Not every data set has that level of depth to it. Sometimes, you just want to show those initial insights as quickly as possible and not make people work for it.'* (Bertini and Stefaner, 2013; emphasis mine.)

On some level, Bostock's insights explain why the extra coding effort required to do an explanatory visualisation is worthwhile. But it also implies an obligation to visualise a story in the manner that best suits the data. Using an exploratory approach to communicate a concept that really should just be explained to the reader ultimately does the story a disservice. Additionally, each layer of interactivity requires bug testing, cross-browser testing and cross-device testing, *on top of* the usual journalistic rigour necessary to verify and fact check all the data within the visualisation. If the author is modifying or extending some other JavaScript library, the long-term development effort might be more than that's necessary to build a D3 visualisation from scratch.

Further, D3's learning curve becomes less steep after the first few successful uses, especially if one is already familiar with JavaScript. Learning JavaScript is probably the highest barrier to entry for most users, however it is a valuable skill for data journalists to have due to the language's ubiquity and utility online.

Halfway between explanatory and exploratory: abstractions, and abstracted-abstractions

That's not to discourage users and say D3 is strictly limited to those with the time, effort and money to learn JavaScript. Since the first edition of this book was released, several tools have emerged that leverage D3 in ways that make it much easier to work with, especially for neophyte coders.

On one hand are *abstraction* libraries such as C3, NVD3, D4 and D3Plus. Although these libraries still require a bit of JavaScript skill to use, they can cut down the work required to make a basic chart to roughly a tenth of what it would be otherwise. Each library takes a different approach to how it uses D3 and in what manner it abstracts it: C3 and D3Plus, for instance, have just a few functions that generate a number of different chart styles, while NVD3 and D4 abstract common D3 tasks into reusable models. Therefore NVD3 and D4 are a degree more flexible than C3 and D3Plus, but also potentially more laborious to use.

To be frank, abstractions ultimately are still developer-level tools, but they do streamline the work by creating a linear and structured way to use D3. From the abstraction libraries described above *abstracted abstractions* emerged, which are simple user interfaces enabling data to be fed to D3 in a user-friendly manner. Quartz's Chartbuilder and Axis from *The Times* are two such tools that let users create D4 and C3 charts (respectively), without writing any code and entirely within the browser. Both are open source projects created with the intention of allowing journalists to build charts that are finely tuned to the design styles of their news organisations. Chartbuilder focuses on static charts for print and display, whereas Axis focuses more on interactive charts for the web. Although both tools are fairly usable right out of the box, news organisations still tend to 'fork' either codebase and then modify it to conform to their publication's styling. Unprecedentedly, journalists can now simply supply data to an app which then quickly generates a chart that requires little tweaking before it can be placed in the paper or on the website.

Do these abstractions (and further, abstracted abstractions) change the degree to which D3 can be used in an explanatory capacity? Yes, in the sense that they reduce D3 to a simple chart tool, with the complexity of the abstraction becoming the upper limit to how intricate or nuanced a data visualisation can be. However, these simple charts can also be used as a springboard for building more complex visualisations – for instance, data loading is a key feature that can be used to dynamically update the visualisation, allowing for multi-stage animations. Chartbuilder- and Axis-generated charts can act as components in a much larger data visualisation. Additionally, simpler exploratory tools can be utilised advantageously to produce explanatory visualisations when the exploratory output is enough to showcase the data. For example, a dazzling bespoke visualisation may not be as effective in depicting the data as a clearly labelled series of line charts built by basic chart-making tools. Lastly, of the many trade offs one must consider when visualising data, an important consideration is often novelty versus speed. Does one spend a lot of time developing and testing a bespoke new visualisation concept, or does one fall back on the reliable-but-rudimentary line chart? Whichever is the case, the emergence of high-level abstraction libraries allows D3 to cater to all needs.

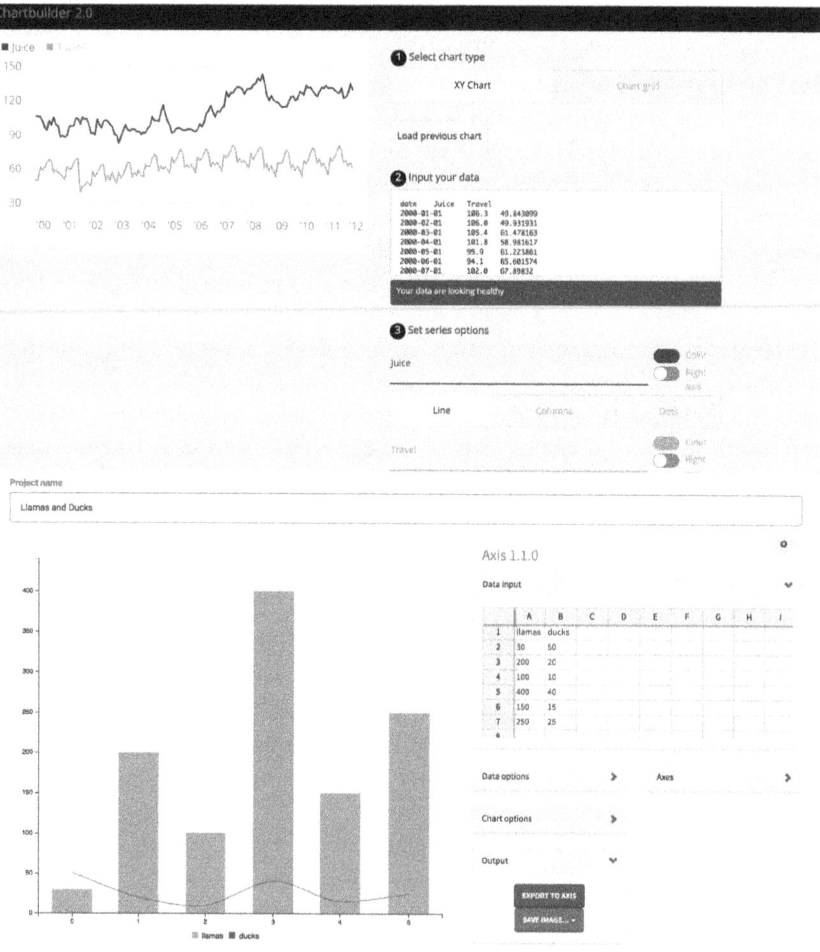

Figures 62 (top) and 63 (bottom): Chartbuilder 2.0 by Quartz (Figure 4; quartz.github.io/Chartbuilder) and Axis by *The Times* (Figure 5; use.axisjs.org) are two open source software projects that leverage D3 to produce simple charts without writing any code.

Conclusion

In this chapter, I have discussed D3; the environment from which it arose; the most relevant use cases for it; some common development idioms; and the differences between explanatory and exploratory data visualisation. D3 certainly has a much higher learning curve than most non-coder visualisation tools, however, this is quickly changing due to the emergence of effective tools that allow high-level use of D3 while writing minimal code. The D3 community is constantly growing, and attracting development talent from many sectors beyond just journalism. The vitality of this community can only be a good thing for data reporters as it means the tools available to journalists will become increasingly nuanced and easier to use over time.

Notes

1. Public version available at tableausoftware.com/public. Free to use.

2. Built into Google Drive, drive.google.com. Free to use.

3. datawrapper.de. Limited free use.

4. Note that this chapter will provide a high-level overview of the technology and won't get too deep into how to actually use D3. For that, please see Murray (2013).

5. For an overview of JavaScript's history, see Severance (2012).

6. Draw, here, refers to the ability of the web-browser itself to display elements like curved lines and circles without having to resort to a third-party piece of code to render such elements.

7. That said, gRaphaël (available for free at g.raphaeljs.com) would eventually be released as an extension to Raphaël.js, making it easier to create simple graphs.

8. See https://twitter.com/mbostock/status/595252571658260481

9. Excepting the aforementioned buggy Internet Explorer.

10. See http://pages.github.com/

11. A really good way to learn D3 is to study and attempt to duplicate some of the examples provided by the D3 community. See: https://github.com/mbostock/d3/wiki/Gallery

12. See codepen.io and tributary.io

13. If you've never written any code, don't worry – this is the sole code example in this chapter.

14. Alternatively, bind the data points to the vertices on a line and you have a line-graph instead. These basic examples understate D3's power, however; the shapes being manipulated can be much more complex, such as is the case with geographic shape data.

References

Aitamurto, Tanja, Sirkkunen, Esa and Lehtonen, Pauliina (2011) *Trends in Data Journalism*, available at http://virtual.vtt.fi/virtual/nextmedia/Deliverables-2011/D3.2.1.2.B_Hyperlocal_Trends_In%20Data_Journalism.pdf, accessed 29 September 2013

Bertini, Enrico and Stefaner, Moritz (2013) 'Data Stories #22: NYT Graphics and D3 with Mike Bostock and Shan Carter', *Data Stories*, available at http://datastori.es/datastories-22-nyt-graphics-and-d3-with-mike-bostock-and-shan-carter/#t=20:52.459, accessed 30 September 2013

Graham, Paul (2005) *Web 2.0*, available at http://www.paulgraham.com/web20.html, accessed 29 September 2013

Jobs, Steve (2010) 'Thoughts on Flash', available online at http://www.apple.com/hotnews/thoughts-on-flash/, accessed 29 September 2013

Kelly, Meghan (2013) 'Oracle issues fix for Java exploits after DHS warns of its holes', *VentureBeat Security*, 13 January, available online at http://venturebeat.com/2013/01/14/java-fix-issued/, accessed 29 September 2013

Murray, Scott (2013) *Interactive Data Visualization for the Web*. Sebastopol, CA: O'Reilly Media, available at http://chimera.labs.oreilly.com/books/1230000000345/index.html, accessed 29 September 2013.

Rogers, Simon (2010) 'Wikileaks Iraq war logs: every death mapped', in the *Guardian*, 23 October, available at http://www.theguardian.com/world/datablog/interactive/2010/oct/23/wikileaks-iraq-deaths-map, accessed 29 September 2013

Severance, Charles (2012) 'JavaScript: Designing a Language in 10 Days', *Computer*, 45/2, pp7-8, available at http://www.computer.org/csdl/mags/co/2012/02/mco2012020007-abs.html, accessed 29 September 2013

Shneiderman, Ben (1996) 'The Eyes Have It: A Task by Data Type Taxonomy for Information Visualizations', *Proceedings of the IEEE Symposium on Visual Languages*, pp. 336-343, available at http://rw4.cs.uni-sb.de/teaching/infovis08/papers/theeyeshaveit.pdf, accessed 29 September 2013

Section 5: Data journalism goes international

Damian Radcliffe

For journalists and academics, it's easy to find great examples of data journalism from the leading English speaking media markets of the USA and the UK. Yet, data journalism is a global phenomenon, and this journalistic reality can all too often be overlooked. In this section we begin to redress this, by hearing from a number of data journalists based outside of these primary markets. What's discernible from their contributions is the universality of several core challenges faced by data journalists. This includes: the data literacy of audiences, cultural change within large new organisations and the format of public data sources, irrespective of where they live and work.

These case studies also highlight how data journalists are driven by the same motivations as traditional journalists. Reporting using data is often underpinned by the rudimentary journalistic principles of seeking to hold authority to account, to tell stories that shine a different light on our world, and to support the creation of an informed citizenry.

A number of these characteristics can be seen in our first contribution, which explores immigration. It's a hot topic in many countries, and one where data journalists can play a pivotal role in discerning the differences between public perception and on-the-ground reality. The Italian designer Matteo Moretti was part of a team who addressed this subject in the North Italian city of Bolzano. Their approach, which is easily replicable, offers a potential model for data journalists around the world who are interested in exploring this topic. The 'People's Republic of Bolzano' project used visualisations, social media and a multi-disciplinary approach to discern if the area really was witnessing a Chinese 'invasion'. Analysis of the data 'painted a very clear picture: Chinese in Bozen-Bolzano were so few and their activities so fragmented across the whole city that an "invasion" was hard to imagine.'

Nonetheless, such perceptions continued to abound, and so the team undertook to 'try to shift the perception of the Chinese among locals in the city' by working with a cultural anthropologist 'to tell the story of the Chinese community in the city via a series of personal narratives, something data alone could not do.'

Following this highly localised approach, Kathryn Hayes takes the temperature of data journalism on a country-wide level, examining how this field is evolving in Ireland. Featuring insights from qualitative interviews with journalism academics and journalist practitioners, she reveals 'that while the landscape of data journalism is improving in Ireland, access to suitably formatted, open and linked data remains a struggle'.

Barriers to progress include 'the unremitting reluctance of some government departments to release information' and the need for appropriate training for data-hesitant journalists. There are, however, reasons for optimism, ranging from a newly strengthened Freedom of Information (FOI) Act through to a national track record of 'a number of political and social controversies [which] have been have been unearthed through original and investigative journalism.' These foundations often lay the cornerstone for data journalism to flourish, so it will be interesting to see if data journalism in the Emerald Isle is able to build on these fundamentals.

Eva Constantaras, who advises the NGO Internews on data journalism, offers a different perspective, building on her extensive experience of launching data journalism initiatives in developing countries such as Kenya, Afghanistan, China, Myanmar, El Salvador and Mexico.

Although clearly an advocate for this emerging practice, she notes that data journalism – globally – has yet to fulfil its potential. The reasons for this are multiple, and in developing markets they include apathy, social media buzz being mistaken for real change and impact, as well as 'the assumption' often by funders and Western media 'of the role of the media itself as a public service watchdog'. Journalistic realities in these markets are often very different, she writes:

> *'Actually getting to the bottom of things and identifying a chain of responsibility can be much riskier than exposing corruption in general terms in countries where corruption, graft, mismanagement, incompetence are all expected and scratching too deep can be dangerous. Therefore, the motivation to exercise the kind of analytical thinking skills required for the kind of data journalism that helps solves problems is often missing.'*

Proponents of data journalism in developing countries therefore need to take account of these realities and consider this when funding and supporting new initiatives. To help them do this, Eva outlines how to overcome the 'fatal design flaws' that she identifies with the current boot camp model and the 'huge potential' afforded by global data investigations. 'It's no surprise that so many initiatives fail,' she says, 'but it is all the more important that we identify elements that work, build a new model for data journalism in developing countries and support rising stars.' After reading her contribution, you'll be inclined to agree with her.

One developing country with a growing myriad of data initiatives is India. Sanjit Oberai, data editor of Quintillion Media, walks us through a number of these enterprises, highlighting the importance of mobile in this market and aspirations of the county's wider 'Digital India' initiative. John Samuel Raja, of How India Lives, tells us that:

> *'..data journalism that involves working with raw data and converting that data into interesting analysis hasn't picked up. That's because newsrooms don't have the resources or the required training skills to execute this kind of journalism.'*

However, he believes that there is 'immense scope' in this arena. 'We believe the way forward is to build communities and use them to gather data,' he says.

This optimism – although not necessarily the approach – is shared by many of his contemporaries in India's data journalism space. For this potential to be unlocked, barriers to use such as data cleaning and finding 'valid and up-to-date data' need to be overcome. The importance of this in India, as elsewhere, is increasingly important. As Factly's Rakesh Dubbudu explains:

> *'Misinformation and rumour also frequently trend on social media, but little of it is substantiated. Wrong data/information or a morphed picture that might be sensational has a greater chance of being shared by many people on social media than genuine information. This was the motivation behind Factly, to make public data more meaningful to the public and encourage them to look for facts or genuine data.'*

It's an approach that data journalists the world over will empathise with.

Reporting the 'invasion': perception and reality of Chinese migrants in Bolzano, Italy

Matteo Moretti recounts how he and colleagues used data journalism to tackle Chinese migrant xenophobia in the Italian city of Bolzano

Introduction

The 'People's Republic of Bolzano' is a visual journalism project that tried to debunk the cliché of a Chinese invasion in Bolzano, a south Tyrolean city in Italy, populated 25 per cent by German speakers and 75 per cent by Italian speakers. Due to historical and political reasons rooted as far back as 1918, when south Tyrol was annexed by Italy, the history of Bolzano and how the Italian and German communities live together, is a very long and not easy to tell story. In my personal experience as a lecturer and then a researcher at the Free University of Bozen-Bolzano since 2010, I found the local culture very sensitive to the concept of 'invasion' because of historical occupation by Italian troops. It is only in the last 20 years that the two communities learned to co-exist together, and migrants played a crucial role in this integration process. This change in dynamics raised new questions to answer.

This premise helps to explain why, despite the fact that a Chinatown doesn't exist in Bozen-Bolzano, and Chinese make up just 0.6 per cent of the population - 633 of 105,713 citizens - (Astat, 2014) – some locals expressed fears of an 'invasion' of Chinese people in the city. A number of factors also contributed the feeling of an invasion. First of all, Chinese people work in public spaces – in restaurants, bars, shops and hairdressers; they are more visible in the city than other migrant communities that usually work away from public view in construction sites or in the apple fields that surround the city - South Tyrol is a well-known apple-producing region, producing 950,000 tonnes each season, equivalent to 50 per cent of the entire Italian apple harvest annually, and much of this work is done by migrants (Chamber of Commerce of Bolzano/Bozen). Second, the most read newspaper by Italian people in Bozen-Bolzano, the *Alto Adige*, stirred up migrant worries, running articles with headlines warning of the creation of a 'Chinatown' ghetto (Conti, 2011); of a 'Chinese advance' (*Alto Agide*, 2012), and 'Chinese megastores' (Valletti, 2012) depicting a context very different from the reality, most frequently in years of 'big' Chinese business openings between 2007 and 2011. In 2010 the city saw 19 Chinese businesses open. For a small city such as Bozen-Bolzano this is significant, as much from a social perception perspective as economic.

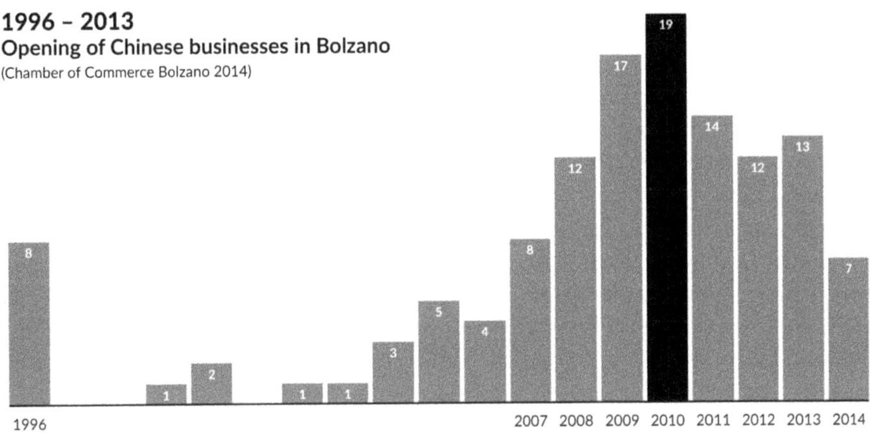

Figure 64: Chart demonstrates the opening of Chinese run businesses in the city between 1996 and 2014

Reporting reality versus perception

All the factors above contributed the cliché of the 'invasion'. While there were issues in other Italian cities with migrants, the reality in Bozen-Bolzano would have been best described as integration instead (Chinese in Italy number 1.8 per cent of the population, while in Bozen-Bolzano the population was 0.6 per cent, as described above (Astat, 2014)).

With journalist Fabio Gobbato, we decided to investigate. We began experimenting with new ways to tell stories with data in order to open a window into the Chinese community of Bozen-Bolzano; to show who the Chinese living in the city were; what they thought of Italy; and moreover that the story of 'invasion' was far from reality. We started looking at the data: we asked Atstat – the South Tyrolean statistics agency – for details of the Chinese population of Bozen-Bolzano. The Chinese government doesn't allow dual citizenship, meaning Chinese migrants have to choose between their mother or destination country citizenship. Often, as is the case in Bozen-Bolzano, a majority keep their Chinese citizenship in order to spend their retirement in China.

The 633 Chinese we considered includes only citizens with a Chinese passport and not second generation Chinese-Italians, or Chinese that have taken Italian citizenship (though these are few in number). We didn't include them in our data analysis because from a legal point of view, they are Italian. As previously stated Chinese residents number just 633 out of 105,713 - 0.6 per cent of the city's population. If we look at the population growth trend we notice an increase in 2007-2008 but the increase in the Chinese population in the city is very small; even newborns are few in number - just 16 in 2013. It was clear based on the statistics that fears of an 'invasion' were unfounded.

Economic 'invasion'

We then analysed economic statistics provided by the local Chamber of Commerce to examine if an economic 'invasion' had happened in the city. We searched for businesses opened by Chinese citizens for the previous 20 years. We found that out of the 9,543 companies in Bozen-Bolzano, only 126 (1.3 per cent) were Chinese-run. The data from 1996 to 2013 showed us that the businesses were located all over the city and not in any particular spot; and that the type of Chinese-owned businesses had changed during the period (from bars and restaurants to a huge variety of activities such as shops and hairdressers). The data again refuted the idea of a Chinese invasion or a 'Chinatown ghetto'. We discovered some interesting statistics: out of 441 bars, 51 (11.5 per cent) were managed by people with Chinese nationality; of 261 restaurants, 32 (11.8 per cent) were Chinese, the 11.8 per cent of the total. Evidence certainly that Chinese nationals who have settled in the city are entrepreneurial in the service industry, but hardly evidence of much else.

We visualised the economic data on an interactive map, using a stop motion animation that displays the evolution of economic activity since 1996. We also split each timeline year unit into smaller coloured bars in order to visualise the proportion of different business activities opened in each year: in earlier years businesses concentrated around bars and restaurants, however since 2009 there has been a diverse range of businesses opened. Through the data map, we were also able to demonstrate that a Chinatown district didn't exist – as the map clearly showed businesses owned by Chinese nationals were spread throughout the city – despite reports by local newspapers.

Figure 65: Map demonstrating spread of Chinese-run businesses in the city

Shifts in perception

The data painted a very clear picture: Chinese in Bozen-Bolzano were so few and their activities so fragmented across the whole city that an 'invasion' was hard to imagine. But for us it was very important not only to demonstrate this but also try to shift the perception of the Chinese among locals in the city. Too many clichés has been allowed to develop, and misinformation had contributed to the creation of a distorted perception.

To accomplish that, we decided to combine qualitative and quantitative investigative methods and took an integrated approach to the story. We met, and then included, Sara Trevisiol in our team, a cultural anthropologist with a strong knowledge of Chinese culture and deeply connected to the Chinese community of Bozen-Bolzano. With her, we shot eight qualitative interviews. This human-interest approach allowed us to tell the story of the Chinese community in the city via a series of personal narratives, something data alone could not do. The series also demonstrated how the Chinese community of Bolzano is composed of a huge variation of members, contrasting the perception that Chinese only own restaurants. Thanks to her work, we were able to represent how multi-faceted the Chinese community members of Bozen-Bolzano are. Through their voices, we were able to break through a number of misconceptions of Chinese people living in the city.

For example, one of our interviewees, YiYi Chen, discussed the concept of *Guanxi*, a traditional personal network of influence that allow Chinese people to save large amounts of cash in order to fund their businesses, rather than relying on banks for finance (Gold et al, 2002). This interview also allowed us to debunk the myth (very common in Italy) that Chinese businesses were supported by the Chinese mafia. Another interviewee, Yingjun, discussed the Italian education system, which she described as easier than the Chinese system. She arrived in Italy when she was 14 and managed to learn fluent Italian as well as graduate high school with honours alongside other Italian students her age within five years. These are just two of the eight stories that we collected in our efforts to tell the story of the Chinese people of Bozen-Bolzano. We believe these demonstrated that far from an invasion, rather we were witnessing Chinese migrants integrating. Thanks to the anthropologist's work and approach, we accessed qualitative data that may have been difficult to collect otherwise.

Telling the story from different sides

The interdisciplinary team, composed of two designers, a journalist, a cultural anthropologist and a computer scientist, told the story from their respective points of view, revealing different sides of the same phenomenon. I found inspiration in the work of Otto Neurath, an Austrian philosopher, sociologist and political economist, who invented ISOTYPE - a universal language to educate people after the World War I. Neurath, was also foremost in the shift of thinking about data visualisation as purely a form of analytics toward thinking of visualisations as both educational and informative, through the work of interdisciplinary teams combining experts, graphic designers and a 'transformer' - a role that he defined as 'responsible for organising the information in visual terms so that it could be understood easily' (Twyman, 1975: 7-18), a sort of visual and cultural mediator. This interdisciplinary approach was useful in our long-form investigation using data, where the journalist told the story; the designers visualised it in order to make it more appealing; the computer scientist created the interactions to engage the users in the navigation; and the qualitative interviews enriched the narrative.

The project took six months of work. We worked in a different way from the traditional (linear) approach where usually the experts provide the data, then the journalists write the story and finally the designer packages it. We constantly shared all information among the group in order to ensure everyone was up to date, and we worked simultaneously on the project, from each respective point of view. We could define this approach as 'organic', where a change in a single variable provoked the re-design of the whole story. We had a number of back and forth processes; we re-thought and re-designed part of the story according to the changes or as new data was found. It was a time consuming approach, most probably time that a newsroom couldn't afford, but it was worth it. Most of the six months spent on the project were spent thinking and re-thinking the story in order to develop the narrative, based on a complex and serious social issue.

Figures 66 and 67: Screengrabs from qualitative video interviews with Chinese residents

The project, which can be seen at www.peoplesrepublicofbolzano.com, was presented on 26 September 2014 at the 'Long Night of Research 2014' at the Free University of Bozen-Bolzano (2014), and was also published as a double page spread in the local edition of the national newspaper Corriere Della Sera. In order to change attitudes of the local community toward Chinese integration, we also opened our work up to public debate - especially among readers of the Alto Adige (the most read Italian newspaper in Bozen-Bolzano), in order to show them the difference between their perceptions of the issue and the reality.

After our work was published it gained a lot of traction on social media via our Facebook page, though little local coverage. However four months later the story was picked up by Der Spiegel. The Italian correspondent of the German news group spotted the story on Facebook and wrote an article for the magazine, which also appeared online. Due to the minority German-speaking population of the Bozen-Bolzano, and the fact that local media are very responsive to what happens in Germany and in the German media - in particular when the story concerns the city - our story began to get local traction. The week after publication in Der Spiegel we were interviewed by local television and a local newspaper, and even the Alto Adige newspaper published our work in print, on their website and - very important for measuring the debate - on their Facebook page.

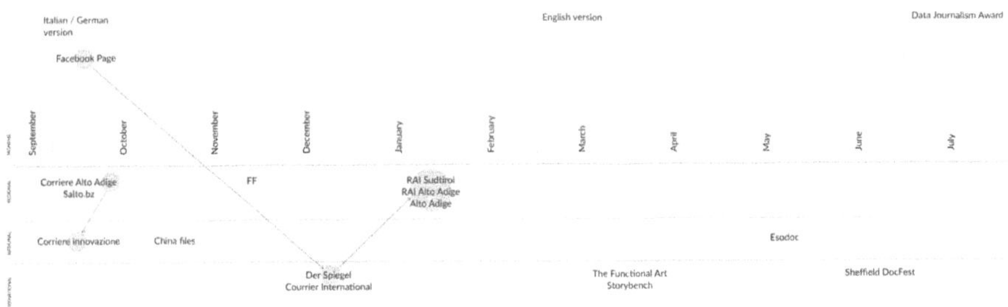

Figure 68: A timeline of the website interactions by the local, national and international media

We had observed that when the Alto Adige Facebook followers debated migrant issues in the past they usually they split in two, with a majority expressing anti-emigrant sentiment. In our case we compared two Alto Adige Facebook posts on the Chinese topic, the first post was about the article 'too much permission given to Chinese retailers, according to Italian traders' (*Alto Agide*, 2011) while the second was the one about our project, with the title 'There's no invasion: The Chinese are just 0.6 per cent' (*Alto Agide*, 2015).

We analysed sentiments expressed in the comments of both posts, in order to map and then compare the opinions. The results were interesting: in the first case, followers were split evenly in their views, with both negative and positive sentiment expressed toward Chinese; while in the second case (the one relevant to our project) we noted that most comments were positive.

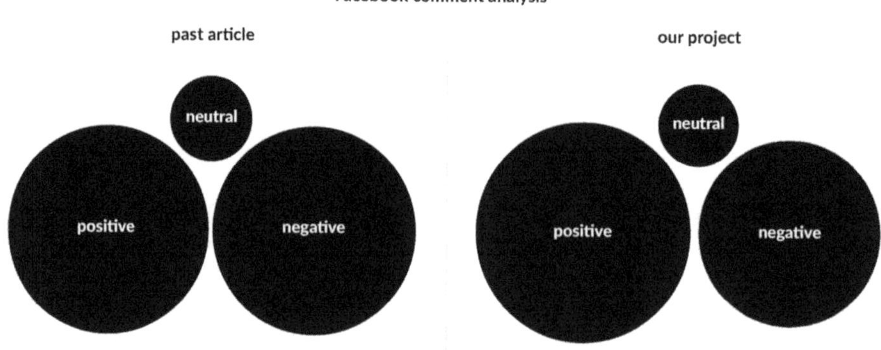

Figure 69: Comparison of the sentiment analysis of the post comments on Facebook

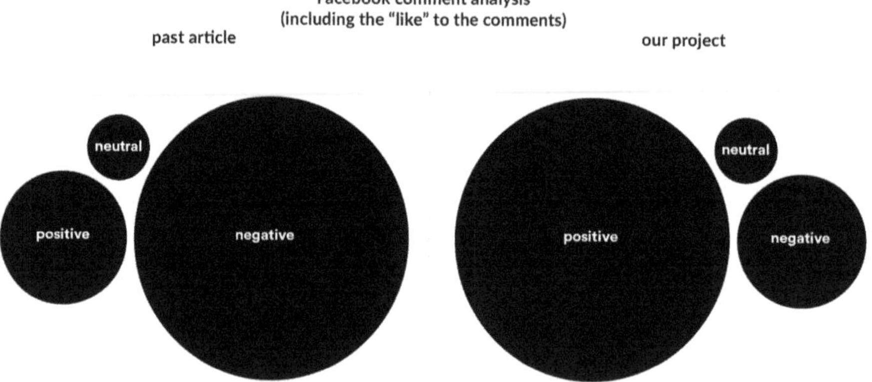

Figure 70: Comparison of the sentiment analysis of the post comments including 'like' on social media

Of course there are many caveats. Some time had passed between the two posts – the first in 2011, while the second was in 2014. Society had changed and grown, even if nationalist ideologies against migrants still persisted. Despite this, the positive comments expressed about Chinese integration was significant and cannot be ignored. We are happy to have contributed to this change in attitude toward Chinese migrants in the local community of Bolzano.

References

Alto Adige (2011) 'Protestano i negozianti di Bolzano: troppi permessi ai cinesi' via Facebook post, 14 June, available at https://www.facebook.com/AltoAdigequotidiano/posts/209142142455113, accessed 28 August 2015

Alto Adige (2015) 'Macché invasione, in città i cinesi sono solo lo 0,6% della popolazione' via Facebook post, 8 January, available at https://www.facebook.com/AltoAdigequotidiano/posts/10155024420955542, accessed 28 August 2015

Alto Adige newspaper, available at http://altoadige.gelocal.it/, accessed 28 August 2015

Conti, Alan (2011) 'Bar cinesi verso quota 150 La Chinatown bolzanina è in via Claudia Augusta', in *Alto Adige*, 13 March, available at http://altoadige.gelocal.it/bolzano/cronaca/2011/03/13/news/bar-cinesi-verso-quota-150-la-chinatown-bolzanina-e-in-via-claudia-augusta-1.4214772, accessed 28 August 2015

Gold, Thomas, Douglas Guthrie, and David Wank (2002) *Social Connections in China: Institutions, Culture and the Changing Nature of Guanxi*. Cambridge: Cambridge University Press

Instutito Privinciale di Satistica (Astat) (2014) available at http://www.provincia.bz.it/astat/it, accessed 28 August 2015

Südtirol (ND) 'Eden's apple orchard' available at www.southtyroleanapple.com/en/our-territory/cultivation-area.html, accessed 28 August 2015

Twyman, Michael (1975) 'The significance of Isotype in Graphic communication through ISOTYPE' Reading, UK: Department of typographic and graphic communication University of Reading

University of Bozen Bolzano (2014) 'Long night for research' (translation) available at http://langenachtderforschung.it/it/lunga-notte-della-ricerca-2?set_language=it, accessed 28 August 2015

Unnamed author (2012) 'Lega Nord: freniamo l'avanzata cinese' in *Alto Adige*, 28 February, available at http://altoadige.gelocal.it/bolzano/cronaca/2012/02/28/news/lega-nord-freniamo-l-avanzata-cinese-1.4352991, accessed 28 August 2015

Valletti, Ricardo (2011) 'Il primo megastore cinese sfida i negozi di via Torino' in *Alto Agide*, 12 June, available at http://altoadige.gelocal.it/bolzano/cronaca/2011/06/12/news/il-primo-megastore-cinese-sfida-i-negozi-di-via-torino-1.4250007, accessed 28 August 2015

Closed shop? Irish data pioneers battle to access information in 'open' regime

Despite efforts by a few notable data pioneers, data journalism is still in its infancy in Ireland, where access to digital records remains difficult despite official commitments to open data, writes Kathryn Hayes

Introduction

While journalists in Ireland have been using data as part of their work for decades, Irish media organisations have been slower to engage with large data driven projects compared to their UK and American counterparts, where journalists have used open data to contextualise everything from the socioeconomic background of the London rioters to aiding the evacuation efforts of New York residents in advance of hurricane Sandy (Byrne, 2015). While the size of the country and economies of scale cannot be ignored, a lack of access to structured data is considered one of the main reasons for the delayed Irish data take off. An 'innate conservatism' in Irish media is also cited as partly to blame as is the deliberate obfuscation of many of the institutions, which hold the most valuable data sets in Ireland (Linehan, 2015). In recent years there has been a lot of rhetoric in Ireland around open government, however the culture of secrecy that has dominated the civil service since the foundation of the State has delayed any determined drive towards an 'open data' movement. The manner in which data held by some Irish government departments is still often released in PDF format or even sent by post has also hindered any large-scale data driven journalism.

Through a series of qualitative interviews with journalism academics, and journalists working in the national media in Ireland, this chapter explores the state of data journalism in Ireland; a country where despite a history of prolonged struggle with opaqueness in government, a significant number of political and social controversies have been have been unearthed through original and investigative journalism. Responses from those interviewed suggest that while the landscape of data journalism is improving in Ireland, access to suitably formatted, open and linked data remains a struggle. The unremitting reluctance of some government departments to release information is also problematic. Appropriate training is also seen as necessary for some journalists who wish to overcome their fear of figures or increase their technical knowledge of how to extract and analyse information from large datasets.

Reviewing the Irish data landscape

The turbulent conditions surrounding the birth of the Irish Free State in 1923 – following the Irish War of Independence against the English Crown and a consequent Civil War – meant openness and transparency in government were not high on the agenda of Ireland's new legislators, who were instead intent on defending against subversive elements in order to ensure survival. Democracy was born at a time of considerable violence and the new Irish civil service was heavily influenced by the Westminster model of government, where citizens had no right of access to information and their relationship with government was deliberately kept at a distance. Chubb (1992: 4) suggests that Irish political culture was heavily influenced by Britain as a result of geography, political, social and economic domination, and culture. From its foundation the fledgling Irish Free State was regarded as centralised and secretive and far from a 'model of openness and transparency' (Felle and Adhsead, 2009).

As an example of the State's efforts at control, the 1923 Censorship of Films Act was one of the first acts on the statue book of the new government. It gave power to an officially appointed censor to keep from the public films, which it believed to be 'indecent, obscene of blasphemous' (Censorship of Films Act 1923, Section 7(2)). Early Free State governments brought in the notion of Cabinet collective responsibility, and confidentiality in Cabinet decision-making. Cabinet handbooks stated that all memoranda for government were to be enclosed in special envelopes and marked for Minister's personal attention and sealed with wax. Documents not likely to be used again were personally burned by the minister's private secretary.

The Emergency Powers Act introduced in 1939 – on the eve of World War II – gave the government wide ranging powers to censor all broadcasts and newspapers in the Free State. In 1963 the Irish government amended the Official Secrets Act, making it a criminal offence for any civil servant to reveal anything, no matter how trivial, without express permission of the minister responsible. That early pattern of control and secrecy continued during the outbreak of the Troubles in Northern Ireland in the 1970s and the invocation of Section 31 of the 1960 Broadcasting Act, which prohibited Raidió Teilifís Éireann (RTE), the national public service broadcaster, from broadcasting anything that could be interpreted as supporting the aims or activities of organisations that 'engage in, promote, encourage or advocate the attaining of any political objective by violent means'. In essence the censorship was used to prevent RTE from using interviews with spokespersons for Sinn Féin and the IRA. The Section 31 ban as it was commonly known was not lifted until 1994 by the then Arts Minister and current president of Ireland Michael D Higgins. Likewise, the Emergency Powers Act was also not lifted until the same year.

While Ireland did begin to open up, the pace was glacial. Modernisation of government as well as a number of other factors such as Ireland's membership of the EEC; the introduction of accountability laws around audits and Ombudsman legislation; and demands from civil society, all led to the opening up of Irish government and bureaucracy. Ireland introduced freedom of information legislation in 1997, and it was widely seen as a watershed moment in the relationship between citizens and the State in terms of openness, transparency and accountability. The former Labour Minister who introduced the legislation Eithne Fitzgerald said at the time she wanted to turn the culture of the Official Secrets Act on its head and in its place create a changed culture in the civil service (Fitzgerald, 2015). Finance documents were made available to journalists for the first time along with emails sent by civil servants. Citizens for the first time could access their medical and social welfare records. Ireland, many believed, was finally opening up.

But the FOI Act was, perhaps, too successful. Notwithstanding how these initiatives reflected a move towards challenging the 'cult of secrecy' in Irish administration (Doyle, 1996-7: 64-67), the culture of secrecy which dominated the State's first 50 years of existence had undoubtedly left an enduring legacy, which continues to haunt the open data movement. After a while civil servants stopped putting sensitive or controversial information in emails and started using the phone instead (Hennessy, 2008). A number of embarrassing exposés of incompetence by ministers and other rows and mishaps, as revealed by journalists following FOI requests, led in 2003 to the introduction by the then Fianna Fáil led government of the Freedom of Information Amendment Act. That Act introduced fees for making requests; extended the time when access to the records of government was available to 10 years rather than five; gave full protection to communications between ministers concerning matters before government; and introduced blanket bans on information that could be withheld. It was regarded as a 'severe setback' to openness in Ireland (Foley, 2015) and was described by the then Information Commissioner Emily O'Reilly as a 'step back from the commitment to openness, transparency and accountability' that had underpinned the spirit of the original Act (Office of the Information Commissioner: 2008, 13). A year after the amendments were enacted the use of the Act by journalist fell by 50 per cent (*The Irish Times*, May 17, 2004).

In 2014, a subsequent Fine Gael Labour coalition government reintroduced a strengthened FOI Act, reversing most of the amendments and abolishing fees. The legislation was also extended to cover the police and state financial bodies such as the Central Bank – important in the Irish context following the 2007 collapse of the Irish economy and near collapse of the banking system, in part blamed on weak banking regulation and poor oversight by financial watchdogs. That same government committed to an open data regime (see below).

While the history of Irish democracy and the story of FOI are not in and of themselves reasons for a lack of development of a strong data journalism community in Ireland, they do go someway toward explaining why media organisations have struggled to access data. The impact of the 2007 economic crash on media organisations and newspapers; shrinking newsrooms; lack of investment in innovation by media and lack of appropriate data training for journalists and in journalism schools has also contributed to the delayed Irish engagement with data driven projects.

Open government and open data

Large national datasets are held, or at least in most cases controlled, by official bodies. While the Irish government has been historically slow to respond to calls for more openness, there have been moves toward data transparency and the government has committed to the principles of the Open Government Partnership – the worldwide movement toward open and transparent administration. Launching Ireland's Open Data Portal in 2014, the Irish cabinet secretary responsible, Brendan Howlin, said open data formed a core element of the country's first Open Government Partnership (OGP) national action plan.

The initial minimum target of Ireland's strategy was for open data to be published at a minimum 3-star format (non-proprietary machine-readable format). The ultimate aim was to strive towards the implementation of a 'five star open data deployment standard' where all future data would be released in an interactive HTML format or as linked data (Department of Public Enterprise and Reform, 2014). However, the lack of specified time frame to achieve this goal has already been highlighted as a cause for concern (Byrne, 2015) along with the fact that the foundation document for the development of Ireland's Public Service Open Data Strategy was itself released as a PDF – the most unusable format possible.

Notwithstanding the moves towards opening up government data, Ireland is still ranked 36th in the 2014 Global Data Index. The UK tops the list followed by Denmark, France and Finland. Germany is also ranked in the top ten after Australia, New Zealand and the US (Global Open Data Index, 2015).

Data successes

Despite Ireland's continued legacy of secrecy and control, much of the data obtained for some of the biggest examples of public service journalism in Ireland during recent years was sourced through freedom of information requests as highlighted in a survey carried out by RTE's Ken Foxe and published in *the Guardian* (Greenslade, 2013). For example:

- In 2011, Independent TD (Member of Parliament) Michael Healy-Rae agreed to pay €2,500 to the taxpayer following revelations in the *Irish Daily Mail* about hundreds of premium rate phone calls to a reality TV show in which he appeared.

- The *Irish Mail on Sunday* revealed that the then education minister Ruairi Quinn was paid expenses for driving to and from his holiday home.
- Spending of around €105,000 a year on secretarial assistance and mobile phones for former prime ministers ended following a series of stories in *The Sunday Times.*
- The number of staff employed by the office of the Speaker of the Irish Parliament was reduced, thus saving €300,000 annually, following revelations by the *Sunday Tribune.*
- Ministerial travel in 2007 to coincide with St Patrick's Day festivities exceeded €500,000. In 2012, the figure was just €53,142. It followed a series of articles by the *Sunday Tribune* and other newspapers.

In the following sections, this chapter hears from the front lines where interviews with Irish data journalists explore the extent to which newsrooms are using data to tell stories; the problems they face accessing datasets; and what training if any is available to Irish journalists working with data.

The data pioneers

As previously noted, apart from the work of some individual trailblazers, data journalism has been slow in establishing itself in Ireland. The founding of dedicated data initiatives such as *The Irish Times* Data Project follows years of journalistic work that has often born the hallmarks of data journalism but not carried the label. The *Irish Examiner* has done a number of major data-based projects on health; the *Irish Independent* on policing; the *Irish Mail on Sunday* on clamping; and RTE's newly established Investigations Unit has done a number of programmes underpinned by the use of data journalism. In 2012 an RTE investigation into prostitution used data from escort websites to prove that prostitution was not about individual escorts working for themselves, but rather highly organised networks with links to people trafficking. However, the efforts of individuals were perhaps best described as rudimentary. 'Being very honest newsrooms just weren't adapted for it,' admits *The Irish Times* editor Kevin O'Sullivan, 'even though we would have done stuff over the years, I was very conscious that this is a very important digital front and that *The Irish Times* should be involved in it' (O'Sullivan, 2015). O'Sullivan's comments were echoed in other newsrooms.

The Freelance

Investigative journalist Gavin Sheridan is a doyen of Irish digital journalism and was considered a trailblazer when it comes to data driven reporting in Ireland. After becoming aware of www.theyworkforyou.com, a web site dedicated to transparency in the British Parliament, Sheridan established KildareStreet.com, a service that tracks activity in the Irish Oireachtas (parliament) and which is designed to allow citizens keep tabs on their TDs (members of parliament) and

Senators. Sheridan describes the site as the 'go to' place for citizens who want to know who their local representative is, how often they speak in parliament, what their expense claims are and what donations they have received. Sheridan is also co-founder of TheStory.ie, which is a chronicle of his FOI requests to diverse branches of the Irish government and a growing public database of government records. According to its mission statement TheStory.ie is dedicated to 'sharing documents, combing and combining data and promoting transparency in public life' (www.thestory.ie). One of the first posts on TheStory.ie involved the conversion of word docs and PDFs to spreadsheets, analysing all published donations to TDs (members of parliament) from 1997-2008.

The broadsheet newspaper

The Irish Times Data Project was launched in February 2015 and is regarded as an important digital front by the newspaper, which is determined to give its readers more 'immersive journalism' (O'Sullivan, 2015). One of its opening data projects 'What's the most reliable car in Ireland?' (O'Brien and Scott, 2015) involved distilling complex sets of figures to work out what cars are most likely to pass the Irish MOT test. Another 'Is your name going out of fashion?' (Duncan, 2015) used tens of thousands of data points to work out which baby names are going in and out of fashion. The baby name story attracted more 170,000 readers in the first week and was hugely popular on social media according to O'Sullivan. In March 2015 an investigation by the newspaper into donations to the Sinn Fein political party in America saw the team digitise 20 years of filings made by Friends of Sinn Féin (FoSF), the party's US fundraising arm, allowing for analysis of cumulative donations made by donors (Duncan and Carswell, 2015). The filings are publicly available on the US Department of Justice website in PDF format, however as with most information held in PDF form, the data had to be uploaded into a format which would allow the data team to calculate totals for individual donors and the total amount raised in particular US states. The project also required that each and every row and column, 14,879 entries (or almost 60,000 individual cells), were manually checked. (Duncan 2015) According to the editor of the *Irish Times* Kevin O'Sullivan, the Sinn Féin expenses story required a huge amount of 'graft'; combined with old fashioned and modern journalism techniques, to ensure the figures were accessible and clearly understood.

> *'It is demanding, and it does require special resources. But if it is fulfilling our needs in terms of being more digital and also generating journalism that is more immersive or journalism that has more of a news edge then we can justify doing it, and I will certainly think we are going to do more of it,'* (O'Sullivan, 2015).

The broadcast newsroom

Ireland's national broadcaster RTE established a multimedia Investigations Unit in 2012 after one of its flagship programmes *Prime Time Investigates* was axed following an investigation into the station's reportage of allegations against a Catholic priest. The station paid a six figure sum to the priest after unfounded allegations in the 'Mission to Prey' programme that wrongly alleged he had raped a minor and fathered a child by her while working in Kenya in the 1980s. After the Investigations Unit was established, part of its ambition was that it would focus not only on long-form TV projects, as it had done in the past, but expand its brief to include online and data driven projects (Foxe, 2015).

Since joining the Unit in 2013, reporter Ken Foxe has been involved in a number of investigative projects driven by the use of data including a story on political expenses (Foxe, 2015) which he admits was one of the most labour intensive projects he has been involved in to date. 'I probably would not have been able to do that project in any other environment other than RTÉ because of the time involved as the nature of the existing records is quite haphazard and an awful lot of it had to be done manually,' he explained.

Nonetheless, Foxe believes the idea that all data journalism projects are incredibly labour intensive is often more of a fear than a reality. One of the biggest problems in Irish journalism is inertia, he argues, and a fear of doing something because it might not work out, take too long, or end up causing embarrassment. Media companies are all fully aware that their future lies in the better use of technology – whether they are able to adapt to the change is more often the question, rather than their willingness to try.

> *'I think perhaps we need to make a distinction between data-based journalism, which I think has been relatively common in Ireland – and what has become known as 'data journalism', which is probably the attempt to display this information in a fuller, more visual, or interactive way, rather than it just being an article or TV programme based on datasets or statistics. This modern interpretation of 'data journalism' obviously lends itself to an online experience for visual and interactivity reasons. And certainly Ireland has been behind the UK and the USA in online innovation right across the media, not just in this area,'* (Foxe, 2015).

The mid-market tabloid

The Independent News and Media (INM) group, which owns a number of national newspaper titles in Ireland including the *Irish Independent*, has put significant resources into its 'digital first' strategy and 'understands that the future of news for their readers is data led' (Caffrey, 2015). In February 2015 the *Independent* ran a six-part series 'Future Proof: Planning where we live' that examined the housing need in each county in Ireland, and explored the challenge of providing key services including water, transport, schools, childcare, and health services in communities of the future. The articles about the future of residential planning were based on data from Ordnance Survey Ireland, according to the paper's Environment Editor Paul Melia.

> *'People are willing to engage in big worthy projects if they are presented right and if they are easy to understand and if the information is all in the one place. That's going to be*

the trick for publishers. People want to see the trend but they want to be able to drill down to their own area,' (Melia, 2015).

Another recent example of data-driven project undertaken by the *Irish Independent* highlighted the correlation between penalty points and accidents and examined where motorists were most likely to get penalty points in Ireland. Melia believes everyone is on a learning curve when it comes to embracing data journalism and lack of good data, time and skill shortages are also reasons for the delayed engagement (2015).

Getting to the data

There have been some positive developments from individual public bodies. Located in north County Dublin, Fingal Council is the third largest local authority area in Ireland by population. Fingal Open Data launched in November 2010 was the first Open Data website in Ireland. Other public bodies in Ireland have since started publishing Open Data including Dublinked – the Dublin Region Innovation and Open Data Initiative; data.localgov.ie – the Irish Local Government Open Data Portal; and data.gov.ie, the Irish Government Open Data Portal. But the pace of publication has been painstakingly slow, according to RTE's Ken Foxe:

'The government's open data programme is a positive step but obviously I would have concerns that it would turn into a bit of a cosmetic exercise to appear as forward thinking. You go to the data.gov.ie website currently and it just seems like a bit of a data dump at the moment. There is very little there to assist people in finding what they are looking for or to help them understand what exactly it is they are looking at,' (Foxe, 2015).

While there is a certain amount of data available in Ireland from government departments and agencies such as the Central Statistics Office (CSO); the Health Service Executive (HSE); the Road Safety Authority (RSA); and the Environmental Protection Agency (EPA), there are significant amounts of data that is not readily available. Moreover there have been a number of high profile cases in Ireland where transparency only occurred after scandals were exposed. In 2005 an RTE *Prime Time Investigates* programme 'Home Truths' on the state of nursing home care at the Leas Cross facility in Dublin, prompted a national debate on how the elderly were being looked after in Irish nursing homes and mounted pressure on the HSE to publish inspection reports on private nursing home care. (Holland, 2006) Following the Leas Cross controversy, the Information Commissioner Emily O'Reilly said it was vital that such reports were made public (O'Reilly, 2006).

The widespread abuse of the penalty points system within the republic of Ireland's national police force, An Garda Síochána, was only exposed after it was highlighted in 2012 by whistleblowers Sergeant Maurice McCabe and former Garda John Wilson. The allegations led to the subsequent publication of the Guerin Report in 2014, which found that serious crimes were improperly investigated by police. The report was also critical of the treatment of the whistleblowers (Guerin, 2014). Recent changes to FOI legislation in Ireland has seen the law extended to cover more public bodies including the police, however only administrative files can be requested. Data that is deemed sensitive or related to intelligence matters is not covered by the act (Freedom of Information Act, 2014). There is a lot of inconsistency in how data is released, and what data is available.

The release of high value linked datasets has the potential to reveal answers to important societal issues that could otherwise go unanswered; allowing journalists and academics opportunities to explore previously undiscovered trends while affording citizens opportunities to make more informed decisions about their lives. For example if someone wanted to know more about the area in which they were purchasing a house they should be able to access information about crime statistics for the locality and information on schools and local health services. 'If you want to buy a house and you want to get crime stats, the best way of finding out if your house is in a dodgy area is to ring up the local Garda (police) station and the local Garda will generally tell you. That's pretty much how it's being done,' said Paul Melia, Environment Editor, the *Irish Independent.*

While the Irish government's new data initiative has positive goals, including the mandatory incorporation of all public bodies under one uniform data release programme where reports will be released in the same format and at similar frequency, the portal where all this data is to be accessed, (www.data.gov.ie), has as yet been slow to reveal any of the promised linked data.

Culture and training

But it's not just a lack of available data that has hindered the development of data journalism in Ireland. News organisations have been slow to embrace change, and many journalists have little training in data techniques. Fully embracing data requires a change in mind set from news organisations, which must start working towards embracing collaborative and team-based working models. Journalists don't do enough of that according to *The Irish Times* chief reporter and a member of their data team, Carl O'Brien:

> *'We tend to be sole operators. When you look at other disciplines like maybe science it's very much a team based healthy model where you can bounce ideas off each other and cross pollenate ideas. It's a very effective way of working – that's a good learning curve for everybody,'* (O'Brien, 2015).

Most Irish journalists have also traditionally have had little or no numeracy or data training. With the exception of libel law training, historically journalism has never been associated with up-skilling and continuous professional development, which is often far more common in other disciplines. If Irish media organisations are to fully embrace data driven journalism, there is a need for appropriate training rather than simply relying on self-taught tech savvy reporters and developers or individuals willing to educate themselves. Those interviewed identified a role for journalism schools to introduce data training as part of their journalism education programmes.

Conclusion

The establishment of dedicated data initiatives is a positive step towards making data journalism an everyday practice in Irish newsrooms. The influence of the work that is being done abroad and by individual data pioneers in Ireland has also demonstrated the benefits of exploiting the full potential of this approach to storytelling. However, with the circulation of Irish newspapers in decline, it's difficult to determine where the resources will come from for large-scale data driven projects. According to figures from the National Newspapers of Ireland (comparing January-June 2009 and January-June 2014) Ireland's biggest selling daily the *Irish Independent*, had 26 per cent wiped off its circulation while *The Irish Times* lost almost 30 per cent. The population size and economies of scale cannot be ignored when comparing Irish media outlets with big hitters in the US and UK who have embraced data-driven journalism. With a population of 4.6 million Ireland has a limited audience of potential readers (for advertisers to target) thereby limiting the budgets available to newsrooms for investment in data projects.

However in a modern digital society, where information is increasingly stored in data it is imperative that journalism in its duty to inform fully explores the potential of data. Journalists must find ways to access, analyse and explain this information, especially if the 'truth lies in the data' (Linehan, 2015). Equally, the government's commitment to the principles of the Open Government Partnership must be honoured with the provision of good data.

The role of data journalism in the future of journalism is undoubtedly significant and while for some journalists it might remain a specialism, for others it will be used as an important tool in their armoury. The basic tenets of journalism – cultivating sources and finding stores – remain as relevant and valuable as ever.

References

Byrne, Robbie (2015) Howlin: 'New data strategy 'a major milestone'. So what's it about' in the *Irish Examiner* 19 June, available at www.irishexaminer.com/viewpoints/analysis/howlin-new-data-strategy-a-major-milestone-so-whats-it-about-337973.html, accessed 9 September 2015

Chubb, Basil (1992) *The Government and Politics of Ireland*, (3rd edn) London: Longman

Caffrey, Elaine (2015) 'Independent.ie – A digital first strategy' available at http://digitalmarketingstrategy.ucd.ie/independent-ie-digital-first-strategy, accessed 9 September 2015

Department of Public Expenditure and Reform (2014) 'Ireland and the Open Government Partnership', available at www.per.gov.ie/en/open-government-partnership-ogp, accessed 8 September, 2015

Duncan, Pamela (2015) 'Is your name going out of fashion?' in *The Irish Times* Data Blog, 3 February, available at www.irishtimes.com/news/ireland/irish-news/is-your-name-going-out-of-fashion-1.2089357, accessed 8 September 2015

Duncan, Pamela and Carswell, Simon (2015) 'Sinn Fein's money' in *The Irish Times* Data Blog, 5 March, available at http://www.irishtimes.com/news/ireland/sinn-feins-money, accessed 8 September 2015

Felle, Tom and Adshead (2009) Democracy and the Right to Know: 10 years of the *Freedom of Information Act* in Ireland'. Limerick: University of Limerick Papers in Politics and Public Administration, 2009/4

FitzGerald, Eithne (2015) 'Ending the culture of secrecy: What we wanted to achieve when we introduced the original FOI legislation' in Adshead, Maura and Felle, Tom (eds) *FOI@15: Ireland and the Freedom of Information Act.* Manchester: Manchester University Press

Foley, Michael, (2015) 'Keeping the State's secrets: Ireland's road from 'official' secrets to freedom of information' in Felle, Tom and Mair, John (eds) *FOI 10 years on: freedom fighting or lazy journalism*? Bury St Edmunds: Abramis

Department of Public Expenditure and Reform (ND) 'Foundation Document for the development of the Public Service Open Data Strategy', available at www.per.gov.ie/en/open-data, accessed 10 September 2015

Foxe, Ken (2012) 'Ruairi Quinn's mystery mystery €1,400 mileage claim: Minister says he drove 5,100kms but his diary shows only 1,000kms' in The Irish Mail on Sunday, 19 February, available at www.dailymail.co.uk/news/article-2103184/Ruairi-Quinns-mystery-mystery-1-400-mileage-claim-Minister-says-drove-5-100kms-diary-shows-1-000kms.html#ixzz3lG09dOVZ, accessed 9 September 2015

Global Open Data Index, available at http://index.okfn.org, accessed 10 September 2015

Government of Ireland (1963) *Official Secrets Act.* Dublin: Government Publications Office

Government of Ireland (1997) *Freedom of Information Act 1997.* Dublin: Government Publications Office

Government of Ireland (2003) *Freedom of Information (Amendment) Act.* Dublin: Government Publications Office

Government of Ireland (2014) *Freedom of Information Act 2014.* Dublin: Government Publications Office

Greenslade, Roy (2013) 'Irish journalists alarmed at Freedom of Information pricing proposal' in *the Guardian* online blog, available at www.theguardian.com/media/2013/nov/13/irish-journalists-alarmed-at-freedom-of-information-pricing-proposal, accessed 8 September, 2015

Hennessy, Mark (2008) *The Irish Times* journalist in comments to expert focus group on freedom of information 'Democracy and the Right to Know' seminar at University of Limerick, Ireland, 29 February, 2008.

Holland, Kitty (2006) 'Harney to consult AG over Leas Cross report' in *The Irish Times*, 3 October, available at www.irishtimes.com/news/harney-to-consult-ag-over-leas-cross-report-1.1010360, accessed 8 September 2015

Guerin, Sean SC (2014) 'Review of the Action Taken by An Garda Síochána Pertaining to Certain Allegations Made by Sergeant Maurice McCabe' (Guerin Report), available at www.merrionstreet.ie/en/wp-content/uploads/2014/05/Final-Redacted-Guerin-Report.pdf, accessed 8 September 2015

Information Commissioner (2008) *Annual Report of the Freedom of Information Commissioner 2007*. Dublin: Government Publications Office

Irish Government Data Portal www.data.gov.ie

Linehan, Hugh (2015) 'Data Journalism: Reinventing news for 21st century digital society.' in *The Irish Times* 27 February available at www.irishtimes.com/opinion/data-journalism-reinventing-news-for-21st-century-digital-society-1.2119160, accessed 9 September 2015

News Brands Ireland (2015) 'Circulation' available at http://newsbrandsireland.ie/data-centre/circulation, accessed 8 September, 2015

O'Brien, Carl and Scott, Paul (2015) 'What's the most reliable car in Ireland?' in *The Irish Times* Data Blog, 5 March, available at www.irishtimes.com/news/environment/what-s-the-most-reliable-car-in-ireland-1.2073954, accessed 8 September 2015

O'Reilly (2006) 'O'Reilly "disappointed" Garda not subject to FOI' in *The Irish Times*, 11 May, available at www.irishtimes.com/news/o-reilly-disappointed-garda-not-subject-to-foi-1.782425, accessed 9 September 2015

Saorstát Éireann (1923) *Censorship of Films Act*. Dublin: Government Publications Office

TheStory.ie (ND) 'Our Goals' available at www.thestory.ie/our-goals, accessed 8 September, 2015

Interviews

Duncan, Pamela, Data Journalist, *The Irish Times*

Foley, Michael, Lecturer in Journalism, Dublin Institute of Technology

Foxe, Ken, Investigative Journalist, RTE Investigations Unit

Melia, Paul, Environment Editor, *Irish Independent*

Kerrigan Mick, Principal Data Scientist, *Irish Independent*

O'Brien, Carl, Chief Reporter, *The Irish Times*

O'Sullivan, Kevin, Editor *The Irish Times*

Global models for starting data journalism in developing countries

There is a pressing need for data journalism training in developing countries but the appeal of the boot camp model is starting to fade, writes Eva Constantaras

Introduction

In a recent data journalism workshop hosted by the Media Initiatives Center in Yerevan, Armenia, a young journalist discovered that after years of leading the European Union in the rate of incarceration, with a steady uptick over 5 years, the rate had suddenly stalled. Not only that, it had dropped. How did she account for that? Had a bunch of prisoners been freed? Was there a drastic decrease in criminality in Armenia? Had the criminal justice system in Armenia changed policy or practice in a significant way? Instead of being excited about this possible scoop, the journalist looked at me and shrugged. She said that everyone knows that the government is corrupt and cyclically arrests and pardons enemies and allies and the media house wouldn't be interested in funding her to find out who had been released or why. Sure, she could learn to graph the trend, but, why bother? This is a question not only for the global data journalism community but also for the open data community in general. From the perspective of the open data community, Jonathan Gray recently questioned the certainty of the data revolution:

> *'We might consider moderating some of the mythologies of spontaneously self-organising actors that will optimise society, if only we can create the right conditions for them to flourish.* Who, *specifically, do we anticipate will use public information? And how, specifically, do we anticipate that they might use this information to bring about the kinds of social and political objectives that we desire? … If we do not scrutinise these questions we risk being left with, for example, data without users or analysis without action' (2015).*

Data journalists have a potentially tremendous role to play in acting out its role as a public-service watchdog by transforming the flood of publically available data into insight that facilitates citizen engagement in the democratic process. From Nigeria to Rwanda, Chile to El Salvador, Pakistan to Cambodia, Twitter is exploding with anecdotes of successful data journalism conferences, boot camps, hackathons and fellowships propelling forthwith propaganda-ridden, analog, ambulance-chasing yellow journalism into the world of news apps, investigations and citizen engagement.

But even in the United States, that's not an accurate description of the journalism revolution. But what appears on Twitter is not a reflection of the day-to-day reality of the practice of journalism either in Western or developing countries. Despite the potential of digital and data tools, in most newsrooms, they simply aren't there. According to *The Goat Must Be Fed* authors, 'Our biggest finding is that data journalism is out of whack with the hype – and we need to acknowledge that we've been part of the problem,' (Adair, Kamalakanthan, and Stencel, 2014).

Why digital tools are missing

In donors' excitement to embrace the open government and open data movement, they have pumped lots of money into the quickest, cheapest and flashiest path to data journalism: boot camps, hackathons and conferences. Yet these approaches boil down the barrier to data journalism into one simple problem: technology. These boot camps are designed to provide technology solutions, with the tacit assumption that the rest will follow, but they have misdiagnosed the essential root problem. *Goats* and a vast array of experience in failed data journalism initiatives tell us, it's not the tools, at least not primarily.

The primary challenge is rooted in the assumption of the role of the media itself as a public service watchdog. It speaks to the apathy I saw demonstrated in Yerevan. Flipping through a few Kenyan newspapers, the number of headlines with direct quotes is overwhelming. The role of media in many places is not to report the truth, but rather, to quote powerful people espousing their version of the truth. Once the quotation marks are removed and replaced by data, the journalist assumes some responsibility for content verification and in a place where governments and their data are distrusted, this is not something many journalists want to stake their reputation on. Actually getting to the bottom of things and identifying a chain of responsibility can be much riskier than exposing corruption in general terms in countries where corruption, graft, mismanagement, incompetence are all expected and scratching too deep can be dangerous. Therefore, the motivation to exercise the kind of analytical thinking skills required for the kind of data journalism that helps solves problems is often missing. And, as my Armenian colleague pointed out, with high levels of public apathy, it might not be worth the effort. Those journalists who are interested in that kind of work are usually busy, really busy, and not likely to sign up for flashy data journalism events.

A critical barrier to data journalism in countries where it has the greatest potential for good (the most corrupt, unequal and impoverished) the biggest challenge is simple data literacy both among the media and among citizens. A recent study examines why journalism students at the University of Georgia don't study computer science, a key ingredient for data journalism, finds:

- They don't know they should
- They think they will fail
- They don't think they'll enjoy CS classes (Cook, 2015)

Data literacy for mid-career journalists in developing countries, which is also tech-intensive, can seem equally irrelevant, intimidating and unrewarding.

Thirdly, the absence of a media industry crisis, no matter how imminent, offers a paradoxical barrier to innovation and exploration of digital content, including data journalism. Publishers, editors and journalists see no need to engage in a difficult, expensive, risky endeavour when for now, their traditional business model is stable. People are still buying newspapers, listening to radio and tuning into the nightly news. Additionally, nobody has produced a compelling business model based on data that can win over publishers. Those plug-and-play tools that seem like an easy way to get newsrooms started in data are often not supported by the CMS. Web traffic is so low that editors don't want to bother adapting.

Models for growing data journalism

In many cases, these challenges are glossed over and with no real metrics for impact of data journalism interventions, years later, the same activities are still being rolled out and failing despite the social media buzz they generate. To understand these challenges, I will evaluate three common models for seeding data journalism in developing countries– fellowship, boot camp and cross border–and recommend ways to improve them.

The fellowship revolution

Fellowships are a popular strategy for trying to blend journalistic and data science skills in the newsroom. Either a developer is embedded in a newsroom or aspiring data journalists are removed from the newsroom and participate in intensive training and project creation for the fellowship period. With the challenge to basic data literacy and widespread analytical capacity as high as it is, it is unrealistic to expect most journalists to take on the programming that is often used in developing interactive data products. The logical course is to try to lure developers and programmers into journalism (Susman-Peña, 2015).

Data literacy, journalist engagement and online platforms' limitations are often not factored into the developer fellow model, borrowed from Code for America. As this fellow is generally neither a journalist nor a teacher, often he or she faces a yawning data and digital literacy gap and unable to revolutionise the newsroom alone, builds an isolated news app or dashboard that may or may not ever be migrated to the host news organization because of limitations to the CMS.

One of the few official studies of these embedded fellowship programs evaluated Code4Kenya, a project of the Africa Media Initiative Code4Africa Program and the World Bank in 2012. Code4Kenya aimed to develop applications that would create demand for government data and in the process, catalyse institutional change as well as how citizens engage with the government through fellowships with the mainstream media. According to the study, Code4Kenya sites received an average of only approximately 3,000 daily page views (with a 78 per cent bounce rate – i.e. visits to the home page without further interaction on the site).

Most of the websites are still in beta mode, incubated in the main Code4Kenya site as opposed to live sites maintained by host organisations. It seems that the media houses and civil society organisations did not have a sense of ownership of these applications and were therefore still relying on the Code4Kenya pilot program to maintain and develop further the applications (Mahihu and Mutuku, 2014).

Journalists of host outlets, some of whom had attended data journalism boot camps, did not write stories around the data. The Star Health Dodgy Doctors App, developed over a year after the fellowship ended, has been touted as the future for data-driven business models, enabling citizens to pay a fee to research their doctor's credentials (Looney, 2015). Yet the link to the app on the Star Health site leads instead to a citizen reporting app and has only been downloaded from Google Play between 10-50 times and is only one of two apps available from Code4Kenya. There is not even a link on the Star homepage that leads to the Star Health page, which features the database.

More successful developer embed programs have taken place in media houses with an established data journalism team, such as the Knight International Journalism Fellowship program. This program has embedded a fellow for several years in La Nación of Argentina, South America's leading data journalism outlet and sponsored a fellow at InfoAmazonia, a data-driven environmental reporting platform in Brazil that is supported by several international donors.

Learning from the Code4Kenya experience, Internews in Kenya piloted a data journalism fellowship modelled after the Stanford Knight Fellowship. This paid fellowship removes media professionals from the newsrooms for an extended period of time to focus on skills building in and out of formal classroom settings, and develop ambitious journalism projects with technical and editorial assistance. The Internews in Kenya office, which had a 10-year history and relationships with all the major media owners, offered a competitive five-month fellowship to three journalists, a graphic designer and developer in 2013. These were young professionals from mainstream newsrooms who participated in an intensive training, mentoring and editorial support program with the five-person

Internews in Kenya data team. Editors and publishers committed to continued employment for the fellows as well as to publication of their completed stories.

The fellowship overcame data literacy barriers and produced high-impact investigations, though mostly through low-tech data visualisations distributed through print and TV. The 'Change for Health' series published by the *Standard* in Kenya prompted several county administrations to contact the journalist for further data and advice on developing a health budget for the following fiscal year (Wafula, 2013). 'When the sun sets in Turkana; Hunger stakes and stripes in the North' the lead news story on NTV (Juma, 2014) revealed that that diverting funds from emergency food aid to food security programs could end famine and let to the implementation of a drought relief strategy. A front-page investigation led by the *Standard* fellow into corruption in the donor-funded system of cash payments for poor Kenyans (Wafula, 2014) led to an audit and overhaul of the system (Wafula, 2015) Policy changed, but only after five months of sweat and tears and continued follow-up.

Fine-tuning the fellowship

The challenge of fellowships, deciding between mass media and elite media, again mirrors the division in the United States.

> *'There's no question that some news organisations are doing wonderful, innovative data work that has created extraordinary journalism. They have mined large data sets, invented tools and used new reporting techniques to expose corruption and explain complex issues in ways that weren't possible before the digital age. They've been aided by millions of dollars from foundations that have funded innovation through grants, pilot projects, training and journalism education. And yet, hundreds of news organisations are still stuck in the analogue past, doing meat-and-potatoes reporting that doesn't take advantage of the new tools'* (Adair, Kamalakanthan, and Stencel, 2014).

Working with the latter groups is challenging but has a potentially greater public impact by democratising access to data-driven content. Bringing together journalists with other members of the technology community through group fellowships result in high-profile projects in mainstream media that engage citizens in a public debate and encourage a reaction from policy makers. These fellowships grow data literacy and public service journalism while also teaching the interactive multimedia content production skills that media houses seek. Civic hackers come to regard journalists as a valuable partner in disseminating data findings that shape public policy. However, these fellowships are only appropriate in strong media markets where media houses can afford to release a fulltime staff member for an extended fellowship. They are also resource intensive for the training institution, which requires a fulltime staff of locally-based data professionals. A less intensive approach may be a part-time year-long fellowship where media professionals commit to a certain number of days and stories per month.

Embedded fellows for niche data-driven media houses are often easier and more resource efficient. There are a growing number of niche digital data-driven media outlets across the world that could benefit from the embedded developer fellowship model. Many digital outlets have the data literacy to leverage embedded data experts to scale up production. The debate is whether the audiences for these media are too elite and whether there can be true public engagement through these platforms.

The data journalism boot camp buzz

For many in the data journalism community, data journalism boot camps and hackathons invoke an uncomfortable déjà vu of years spent explaining to donors that transforming a media ecosystem – converting a propaganda-heavy media cycle to a bastion of independent media – requires more than a 40-hour workshop, no matter how well designed. Data journalism boot camps and hackathons, which began as a place to generate buzz around the open data movement, have now become a cheap substitute for actual sustainable investment in data journalism capacity. The media development literature is overloaded with lessons cautioning that short-term, parachute training engagements have limited to no impact, especially in low data and digital literacy and high development priority environments such as South Sudan where two-day workshops are popular yet 'many journalists lack the most basic writing skills' (Fojo. 2012). In many countries, journalists are poorly paid, a promise of a daily stipend is motivation enough to attend a workshop for a few days. Some form of long-term educational engagement designed specifically for adult learners will be necessary for data journalism (Susman-Peña, 2015).

Despite a flurry of Twitter traffic, guest appearances by famous Western stars of data journalism and flashy prototypes produced by invited developers, the glowing appeal of the boot camp model is starting to fade. Besides the immediate challenge of a crash course in data science, learning data journalism skills requires an uncomfortable attitude shift for many journalists to a more scientific and collaborative work style. As Paul Bradshaw, a veteran data journalism professor explains, 'It is an open approach to reporting that borrows more from the culture of programming than journalism's own culture of guarding information jealously' (Bradshaw, 2015). Even if a run-through of a tool in a boot camp goes smoothly, once a journalist gets back to the newsroom, that tool is not going to work perfectly and the journalism may give up.

The popular boot camp model is crippled by a few fatal design flaws:

- Huge, 50-plus person events without a pedagogical strategy for teaching the necessary theoretical and technological skills for basic data literacy;
- Failure to recruit promising journalists with the analytical skills who are most likely to thrive in data journalism but would not prioritise attending a massive boot camp;

- Wasted resources to bring in high-profile speakers with little understanding of the local data or media environment;
- Focus on developing prototypes for news apps and recycling cutting edge-digital product ideas from previous boot camps that are far removed from the goal of enriching the quality of traditional media reporting with data and analysis;
- Lack of buy-in from editors and publishers to publish stories produced by budding data journalist and at worst, an after care system where a Western data journalist provides remote support to trainees and effectively produced a data story for him or her.

Rescuing the bootcamp

Many media development organisations are experimenting with composition, intensity and post-event support needed to ensure data journalism workshops have the desired impact: getting data-driven stories out through mass media. There is a huge potential for intensive training to overcome key barriers to data journalism, namely:

- Sustained training in data literacy basics that lays the groundwork for more balanced, purposeful and objective reporting in countries with a weak history of independent journalism;
- Identifying and supporting journalists who want to pursue public service journalism and linking them with other members of the open data community who can work together to lower the barrier to data journalism production; and
- Actively persuading publishers and editors that data journalism can be a valuable asset in the face of digital convergence and discussion the transition for breaking news to in-depth reporting.

One approach piloted in Cambodia was a 14-day workshop funded by the German government and implemented by DW Akademie that trained 12 local participants including journalists, communication officers, and a journalism professor in data journalism skills. All trainees posted a final project including story and visualisation published on the training blog (DW Akademie, 2014). The project went a step further and conducted community meetings to ensure that the content made its way to an offline audience as well (James, 2014). IREX has implemented a similar approach in China where a combination of in-house workshops, grants, competitions and events has created a distinct space for data journalism in a country in the middle of a digital transition (2014).

In countries without the opportunity to implement a fellowship training program, such as in Afghanistan, Internews has designed a series of data journalism interventions around specific themes including elections, public health and economics, with mentoring and small production grants, to support journalists to continue growing their skills between training periods. Stories produced by these trainees touch on governance issues such as arms trafficking, opium production, corruption perception and violence against journalists. Another model developed by Internews for pilot testing is the Data News Lab, where participants spend six weeks working intensively in a data-driven daily newsroom environment run by a team of trainers, combining capacity building and production for home outlets. More research into the goals of capacity-building activities, the impact of different training models and closer tracking of workshop outputs would help shift a model based on open data hype to one of journalistic content.

Cross-border global data investigations

The burgeoning field of cross-border reporting has catapulted the media of several countries into the world of data thanks in part to efforts such as the Organized Crime and Corruption Reporting Project (OCCRP) and the International Consortium of Investigative Journalists (ICIJ). Both of these organisations harness national and international databases to uncover financial abuses in a globalised world. OCCRP provides a unique example of locally-driven investigations with a goal of changing regional governance with members spanning Eastern Europe through to Central Asia. Members come from media houses across the region to share data and produce collaborative stories such as 'The Russian Laundromat', which investigated the regional reach of Russian money laundering by organised crime networks from Russia to Europe (OCCRP, 2014).

Alexandre Léchenet's new research into cross-country data journalism collaborations found, many success stories come from media that prioritises working together for richer content. According to Léchenet, 'an open-source and collaborative culture lends itself well to projects that seek to untangle a story hidden in a large dataset. Finding information as well as writing complete stories afterwards can be complicated for one person alone' (2015).

The underlying logic of cross-border collaborations: discrete, non-competing audiences in different media markets and localised content for each member's audience and political context underpin a lot of the success of data-driven investigative projects. It applies even more to smaller media rather than international behemoths competing for the same online audience, which Léchenet cites as a possible future deterrent to collaborative reporting (ibid). Yet cross-border data journalism faces the same capacity issues that many data journalism initiatives do in developing countries. ICIJ, for example, isolated and distributed data relevant to journalists, country-by-country for 'Offshore Leaks'. OCCRP works primarily with already trained data journalists who are members of their network.

'Offshore Leaks' and 'Migrants Files' proved that strong project management, by people understanding the data well, is crucial in carrying out a big investigation of this kind. The data-journalist can assume this role by being the main contact with other journalists who are not so good with the data (2015). A recent collaboration between ICIJ and African journalists illustrates the limitation. The African journalists involved in the 'Fatal Extraction' investigation of Australian mining companies in Africa were, at the most, junior partners, publishing independently in their own outlets and not as authors of any of the principle ICIJ products (2015). The Africa Network of Investigative Journalists played a supporting role. Contributions by African members provided local fact-checking of the situation, logistical, data and editorial support but little in-depth data analysis, further evidence that data skills do not simply 'rub off' on journalists through exposure to other data journalists but require sustained investment of resources. The muscle behind the database analysis was ICIJ's data team. Arguably, the local governments have the largest role in future regulation of extractive industries and thus exploration of local data had potentially greater policy impact. But, as with other cross-border projects, such as 'Migrant Files', the focus is primarily on Western media and a Western audience for a policy response.

In his criticism of another ICIJ project that examines displacement of populations by World Bank projects, Nicholas Benequista pointed out, to fix an international development issue, the most effective strategy is to go after the people who have a vested interested in their local reputation and better yet, go after them through local media (2015). This begs the question about the objective of cross-border data journalism. Is the goal to expose the wrongdoing in order to give the right public the information they need to solve the problem or is it about scandal? As Jonathan Stray suggests '…it is always about scandal - what has been called "*the journalism of outrage*". This has sometimes made investigative journalism powerless in the face of huge systemic issues without a clear locus of wrongdoing' (2015).

Globalizing audience for cross-border data journalism

With a dearth of quality international news coverage during a persistent media industry crisis, cross-border reporting may be the future for in-depth global coverage and journalists in developing countries should be taking a more and more active role. Projects such as 'Influence Mapping', a new initiative supported by Open Society Foundations seeks to document relationships between people, organisations, and political processes. Perhaps even more importantly, it seeks to facilitate collaboration on investigating these relationships. It will enable databases from different countries to talk to each other and hopefully spur their journalists to do the same as well. This should enable investigations that range from the global to the hyper-local through media most likely to prompt change.

Conclusion: making the jump from tools to change

Western media pundits are wringing their hands about the role of journalism, with terms like explanatory journalism, context journalism, and solution journalism being discussed as potentially both lucrative and competitive in a digital media environment. This goal is a given for donors seeking to fund data journalism in developing countries with the express goal of fostering transparency and accountability. According to Stray, who is also one of the leaders of 'Influence Mappers', 'in a recent study comparing the same story with and without a proposed solution, readers who read the solution reported being more likely to share the article on social media, and read other articles on the same site or on the same issue.' Or, if the aim is to educate citizens to be more informed and active in the democratic and government process, that also requires a more sustained approach. 'If we're serious about the notion of an independent check on government, we need to get systematic about it' (2015).

In countries desensitised to corruption, efforts to grow data journalism need to get serious. Transforming the legacy media's messengers of breaking news into change agents for government accountability requires an array of skills, a shift in the media industry's attitude and the coalescence of an open data community around this common goal. It also requires overcoming public desensitisation to the daily scandal, front-page corruption stories and permanent dysfunction. With this in mind, overcoming apathy will require not just a couple of data driven stories, but a structured journalism approach to covering governance consistently over time. It's no surprise that so many initiatives fail, but it is all the more important that we identify elements that work, build a new model for data journalism in developing countries and support rising stars, such as Ani Hovhannisyan, another participant in the Armenia workshop, who after hitting a wall in getting hospital data, personally went to Yerevan's hospitals to document hygiene conditions and X-ray machines, both of which she suspected are widespread health hazards in the country (2014a, 2014b). She persuaded the Yerevan municipality to hand over budgets for renovations and inspection reports that document significant public health risks. Though conditions in the clinics have not yet changed as a result of her reporting, the recent public demonstrations against an energy price by the Russian-owned distributor gives her hope that change is possible and she is pursuing a Fulbright Fellowship to study data journalism in the United States in the hope of returning and continuing her campaign to reform the country through data journalism.

References

Adair, Bill, Kamalakanthan, Prashanth and Stencel, Mark (2014) *The Goats Must Be Fed: Why digital tools are missing in most newsrooms*. Atlanta, Georgia: Duke Reporters' Lab at the DeWitt Wallace Center for Media & Democracy in the Sanford School of Public Policy, available at http://www.goatmustbefed.com, accessed 26 August 2015

Benequista, Nicholas (2015) 'Journalists Covering International Development Don't Get this One Thing'. Medium, 17 April, available at https://medium.com/@benequista/journalists-covering-international-development-don-t-get-this-one-thing-7b94d697d761, accessed 26 August 2015

Bradshaw, Paul (2015) 'Data journalism isn't just a technical skill – it's a cultural one too', *Online Journalism Blog*, 24 June, available at http://onlinejournalismblog.com/2015/06/24/data-journalism-isnt-just-a-technical-skill-its-a-cultural-one-too, accessed 26 August 2015

Cook, Lindsey (2015) 'Why Journalism Students Don't Learn CS', *Source Open News*, 7 May, available at https://source.opennews.org/en-US/learning/journalism-students-and-cs, accessed 26 August 2015

DW Akademie (2014) *DW Akademie Blog*, 31 January, available at http://ddjtraining.org/blog, accessed 26 August 2015

Fojo Media Institute (2012) 'Moving away from "parachute" journalism training in South Sudan' 4 September, available at http://lnu.se/1.73416/moving-away-from-parachute-journalism-training-in-south-sudan, accessed 25 August 2015

Gray, Jonathan (2015) 'Democratising The Data Revolution: A Discussion Paper'. Cambridge, United Kingdom: Open Knowledge Foundation, available at https://assets.okfn.org/files/reports/DemocratisingDataRevolution.pdf, accessed 26 August 2015

Hovhannisyan, Ani (2014) 'Expired X-ray Machines: Dangers of Radiation a Shut Topic in Armenia.' *Hetq Online*, available at http://hetq.am/eng/news/59954/expired-x-ray-machines-dangers-of-radiation-a-shut-topic-in-armenia.html, accessed 26 August 2015

Hovhannisyan, Ani (2014) 'Yerevan's Polyclinics: Take Advantage of the Free Health Care but Stay Away from the Toilets.' *Hetq Online*, available at: http://hetq.am/eng/news/58378/yerevans-polyclinics-take-advantage-of-the-free-healthcare-but-stay-away-from-the-toilets.html, accessed 26 August 2015

International Center for International Journalists (2015) 'Fatal Extraction', 10 July, available at http://www.icij.org/project/fatal-extraction, accessed 26 August 2015

IREX (2014) 'Chinese Journalists and Programmers Crunch Numbers' in IREX, 13 May, available at https://www.irex.org/news/chinese-journalists-and-programmers-crunch-numbers, accessed 26 August 2015

Juma, Mercy (2014) 'When the Sun Sets in Turkana: Hunger Stakes and Stripes in Turkana' in *NTV*, 21 January, available at https://www.youtube.com/watch?v=Ga8CEYVALo4, accessed 26 August 2015

James, Kyle (2014) 'Getting online data to offline communities', OnMedia Deutche Welle Akademie, 19 August, available at http://onmedia.dw-akademie.de/english/?p=20775, accessed 26 August 2015

Léchenet, Alexandre (2015) *Global Database Investigations: The role of the computer-assisted reporter.* Oxford, United Kingdom: Reuters Institute Fellowship Paper, University of Oxford, available at http://reutersinstitute.politics.ox.ac.uk/publication/global-database-investigations, accessed 26 August 2015

Looney, Margaret (2014) 'Africa's newsrooms experiment with charging for data', *IJNet*, 12 March, available at https://ijnet.org/en/blog/africa%E2%80%99s-newsrooms-experiment-charging-data, accessed 26 August 2015

Mahihu, Christine M and Mutuku, Leonida (2014) *Open Data in Developing Countries: Understanding the Impacts of Kenya Open Data Applications and Services.* Nairobi, Kenya: iHub Research, available at http://www.opendataresearch.org/sites/default/files/publications/ODDC%20Report%20iHub.pdf, accessed 26 August 2015

Organized Crime and Corruption Reporting Project (2014) 'The Russian Laundromat', 14 August, available at https://www.reportingproject.net/therussianlaundromat, accessed 26 August 2015

Stray, Jonathan (2015) 'The Editorial Product' in *Tinius Trust*, 27 May, available at https://tinius.com/blog/the-editorial-product, accessed 26 August 2015

Susman-Peña, Tara (2015) *Understanding Data: Can News Media Rise to the Challenge?* Washington, DC: Center for International Media Assistance, National Endowment for Democracy, available at http://www.cima.ned.org/publication/understanding-data-can-news-media-rise-to-the-challenge, accessed 26 August 2015

Wafula, Paul (2013) 'Change for Health' in *The Standard*, 12 November, available at http://www.standardmedia.co.ke/health/changeforhealth, accessed 26 August 2015

Wafula, Paul (2014) 'Poverty Fund: Sh600m paid to "ghosts"' in *The Standard*, 17 January, available at http://www.standardmedia.co.ke/?articleID=2000102507&story_title=poverty-fund-sh600m-paid-to-ghosts, accessed 26 August 2015

Wafula, Paul (2015) 'Treasury, CRA on collision path over new formula to allocate Sh6b equalisation cash' in *The Standard*, 12 May, available at http://www.standardmedia.co.ke/business/article/2000161913/treasury-cra-on-collision-path-over-new-formula-to-allocate-sh6b-equalisation-cash, accessed 26 August 2015

Baby steps: a slow start but data journalism in India is gathering pace

Sanjit Oberai, data editor of Quintillion Media and one of the early pioneers of data journalism in India, talks to leading Indian data enthusiasts about their efforts to found various start-up data journalism initiatives. They have had mixed results but all are positive for the future

Introduction

Data journalism is at a nascent stage in India. There are currently very few websites that are operating in this area, and news organisations still have a long way to go to reach the global benchmark. The good news is that it has picked up and caught the attention of the Indian government, news organisations, analytics companies, and data visualisation companies. Data can be used to bring about accountability and transparency among people and that awareness is catching people's attention. It is also fast becoming an important part of the armoury of newsrooms in India and plays an important role in multimedia and digital reporting.

The concept of 'open data' is a relatively new phenomenon, and is gathering momentum as many governments voluntarily decided to release data to the public. While India may have been one of the first few countries to join the open data movement after the US and the UK, the idea of open data evolved over a period via the National Data Sharing and Accessibility Policy (NDSAP), since March 2012. This initiative gathered pace when the National Informatics Centre (NIC), in collaboration with the US government, created an Open Government Data Platform, data.gov.in, as an open source portal to provide single point access to all the datasets published by different government departments in open format. The NIC is part of the Indian Ministry of Communications and Information Technology. It assists in implementing information technology projects, in collaboration with central and state governments.

Further, the 'Digital India' initiative under Prime Minister Narendra Modi is expected to help transform India into a digitally empowered society and knowledge economy. Digital India is an initiative of the Government of India to integrate government departments and the people of India. It aims to ensure that government services are made available to citizens electronically by reducing paperwork, and to connect rural areas with high-speed internet networks.

Following these moves at the federal level, a number of start-ups and other media organisations have begun to explore data storytelling and visualising data, with varying successes. In the following chapter, I discuss with leading Indian digital pioneers their experiences to date in being a part of these initiatives.

How India Lives - *John Samuel Raja*

There are two types of data journalism: the first looks at data as a unit of information, processes the data and get interesting analysis out of raw data; and the second uses published data reports like national crime statistics or government survey reports to write stories around them. The second type of data journalism has picked up in India quite rapidly, with many media houses - both traditional and new ones - doing such stories on a regular basis. This is welcome because it will bring insights into reports and surveys that were not previously reported extensively. However, data journalism that involves working with raw data and converting that data into interesting analysis hasn't picked up. That's because newsrooms don't have the resources or the required training skills to execute this kind of journalism. One would need a person with programming skills who can help scrape data and arrange in a database, and then write code to visualise the data. A newsroom where a programmer works alongside journalists, and who understands the data, is needed to execute such work. With government moves to increasingly make data available, there is immense scope to do such type of data journalism. Such moves increase transparency, as we will be making it available to public so that anyone can make sense of it.

How India Lives started

How India Lives is a Delhi-based start-up. The internet-based application aims to organise a massive amount of public data on India, and make it available in a searchable, comparable and visual format. The idea is to offer something of value to everyone who uses public data, be it for decision-making – like the company executive, the government official, the researcher – or for information-seeking. It was founded by a team of journalists with more than 60 years collective experience and has a technology team that has executed large data projects for Mint, Shine.com, The Caravan magazine and others.

What 'How India Lives' does

How India Lives' efforts are two-fold. The first is to make data easy to search, compare and visualise. We feel there is a huge gap between people who know how to access data, and those who don't. We would like to bridge this gap. We do this in a number of ways, namely:

- bringing data from different sources into a single database and making different datasets compatible so they can be cross-referenced
- enabling tag-based search for user friendliness
- visualising data for easy understanding

By making data available from different sources in an easily searchable manner, we believe more journalists will start using data. By making public data datasets available through data interactives, greater numbers of ordinary citizens can also access stories they are interested in, and be informed. For example, we used vehicle theft data for Delhi and visualised it like a dashboard (How India Lives, 2015). We believe the way forward is to build communities and use them to gather data.

Challenges we face

The biggest is data cleaning. Data is in difficult formats - often in scanned PDFs, so it takes the majority of our time just to clean the data. Second, a significant majority of people in India only have access to the internet via mobile devices, and most smartphones have limited storage capacity. This means there is no space to download more apps. So the importance of a mobile-friendly website is vital. And on top of that, presenting data interactives and visualisation in mobile-friendly formats is difficult.

Health Analytics - *Syed Nazakat*

Health Analytics India is a data journalism initiative dedicated to providing the most illuminating reporting on healthcare. We're not going to blindly accept the data, but we're not going to be blind to it either. We crunch the numbers, investigate the issues behind the numbers and turn them into facts and figures based stories that matter to people. Our aim is to make Health Analytics India a single-point source of healthcare data and information in India.

Our initial challenge was to set-up the infrastructure and to build the team. Designing and curating website for data visualisation and analytics was also quite a challenge. Health, as a subject, was chosen because it touches us all. And there is so much scope to improve the health reporting in India. Millions of people are dying in this country from the diseases, which are totally preventable. Lack of health facilities is such a shameful story. Yet the stories hardly make news. Our challenge remains to build engagement with audiences and to present data to them in a way that will help them to understand complex stories. We're conscious of data overload so our daily challenge is to handle and interpret large data.

One of the biggest challenges is to find valid and up-to-date data. We collect data on the healthcare system by searching for the different studies or reports of the union health ministry, or from 29 state health ministries, or from other international organisations such as WHO and research institutes. Sometimes we're surprised by how much you are able to find. But then there are vast data gaps, which leave you with an impression that nobody really knows anything concrete about healthcare data in India.

Recently while doing a story about death of rabies, we were told that the union health ministry does not collect data on its own. The data comes from 29 states and seven union territories. But in many states there were no cohort studies; community-based studies; and until 2014 one of India's biggest states Punjab hadn't even a department to collect rabies data. Elsewhere, in many states, there are proper rules and guidelines about data collection – but there is no data.

Data journalism is one way in which the media can help the cause of information, transparency, watchdog reporting and quite legitimately hold the government to account. However the lack of data and loopholes in data collection are problematic.

Factly - *Rakesh Dubbudu*

Factly is a platform that brings various aspects of life that directly or indirectly affects the common man but with one major difference: each news story on Factly is backed by factual evidence/data that is either available in the public domain or that is collated/gathered/collected using tools such as the Right to Information (RTI) Act.

Motivation behind launching Factly

In the last 10 years of my experience in this space, I came across a lot of government (public) data. A lot of that data is extremely important to the public. But because this data was not easily accessible and even in cases where it was, it was not easily understood. Hence public data was anything but 'public'. Misinformation and rumour also frequently trend on social media, but little of it is substantiated. Wrong data/information or a morphed picture that might be sensational has a greater chance of being shared by many people on social media than genuine information. This was the motivation behind Factly, to make public data more meaningful to the public and encourage them to look for facts or genuine data.

All our data comes from government sources such as government websites, answers to questions asked in parliament, government reports and for some, we use RTI. We zero in on a topic and then find relevant data. We also did not want to stop at making data alone meaningful; we wanted to make government information in general more meaningful to the public. We plan to explain policies/laws that are relevant to people in simple language that can be understood by everyone. We are already doing that to a certain extent.

How is it going to be helpful to people?

We have three aims when producing stories based on official data. The first is to make people more knowledgeable about issues with relevant data and information. That is what Factly is doing right now by packaging data in easily understandable stories, well designed infographics and easy to understand visualisations. The second is to mobilise people using this knowledge; and the third is to engage with them. We are currently at the first stage and are working towards introducing tools and other features that can take us to the second and third stages. There are many cases where our data stories have been very useful to people. By mobilise, we essentially wish to inspire people to take action or engage with the system based on the data or information. It could be a local issue to do with how their funds were spent or a state or national issue. We do not want to lead movements ourselves, but be a force that can inspire the activism and subsequent engagement with the system.

For example, we explained how petrol and LPG are priced, which was a big mystery to many. We also explained surrounding planning and land purchases so that the public could easily understand them. Examples of these stories can be found at https://factly.in/petrol-price-breakup-in-india-infographic and https://factly.in/9-point-check-list-for-buying-agricultural-land-in-telangana-ap.

Future plans?

We are working on building some data tools and information products. We hope to be ready with the first ones by the end of this year. With all these, we want to expand our base, encourage more people to engage and mobilise for causes based on this data. We are also looking at options to take this offline for those who do not have access to the internet by partnering with a few non-profits that work on the ground. For example we would like to make templates available for stories such as the performance of MPs (see this link https://factly.in/sachin-tendulkar-mp-progress-report-infographic); or local spending on village budgets so that anyone can select their MP or village and download copies of the same. These can be printed and be used for offline work. We wish to do similar work in other areas such as governments and schools and tie up with NGOs that work in those local areas.

IndiaSpend - *Govindraj Ethiraj*

IndiaSpend is the country's first data journalism initiative whose vision is to improve the quality of public discourse by using data to write stories in areas of public interest. In March 2014, the same team also launched www.factchecker.in, a dedicated fact checking initiative that examines statements and assertions made by individuals and organisations in public life for both accuracy and context. Both initiatives have a strong social media presence. IndiaSpend's articles are now distributed to India's leading newspapers, magazines, television stations, online dailies and wire services and area usually cited in at least a dozen major media platforms daily. IndiaSpend/FactChecker are registered as non-profit organisations. They analyse government policy on issues such as the economy, education, health, agriculture and security. The team have reported on a number of important stories, such examples include:

- Why child rapes have soared 151 per cent in five years: This article looks at the sharp increase in registered child rapes in India and the states that have had the highest cases. In some nine of ten cases, victims knew their attackers. The article is available here: http://www.indiaspend.com/cover-story/why-child-rapes-have-soared-151-in-5-years-25891
- How 46 million Indians are being slowly poisoned: This article explores why millions of Indians are exposed to contaminated water, which could lead to serious health issues such as crippling skeletal damage, kidney degeneration, cirrhosis of the liver and cardiac arrest. The article is available here: http://www.indiaspend.com/cover-story/how-46-million-indians-are-being-slowly-poisoned-40865

DataMeet India - *Nisha Thompson*

DataMeet is a community that started in 2011 on a Google group, and now has more than 1,000 people throughout India coming together to discuss data issues and civic-minded topics. DataMeet has 6 chapters - Bangalore, New Delhi, Mumbai, Ahmedabad, Pune, and Hyderabad - who meet monthly offline to discuss, learn, share experiences and skills and also organise events.

DataMeet hosted the first Bangalore Open Data Camp in India in 2012, and since then the yearly Open Data Camp has been a great way to bring together people in the data civic space. Since then Hyderabad and New Delhi have had Open Data Camps to organise communities in their cities. These camps are great venues to discuss large ideas and problems encountered in different sectors. At the 2014 Bangalore camps that focused on elections, the community came together and shared Assembly and Parliamentary boundary shape files. The 2015 camp focused on education, and it brought civil society and government together to try to work out issues around education data in India.

DataMeet also has worked with the government on how to open more data in India. After the passage of the National Data Sharing and Accessibility Policy in 2012, we gave them feedback on standards and also implementation issues. When Data.Gov.In - India's official open data portal – launched, we worked with the officials to make sure they were aware of what high priority datasets were. For example we had requested that the Census be available and currently it is available on the portal.

Part of the open data movement is to raise data literacy. DataMeet has hosted and supported data training events for journalists, with partners like Oorvani Foundation and The Hoot. We also got involved in data expeditions on urban data along with Hyderabad Urban Labs, and other events with Field of View and

IIIT Bangalore. These events help introduce data concepts and skills to people who want to learn more and use data more often.

Conclusion?

Clearly 'better late than never' is an apt description for India with respect to data journalism. Many of the initiatives that have started are making their presence felt in their various areas of expertise. However, this is just the start and as people start recognising the importance of data, it will soon be the sought after area for decades to come.

References

Data Meet Bangalore, available at http://datameet.org/chapters/bangalore/, accessed 16 August 2015

Factly India, available at https://factly.in/team/, accessed 16 August 2015

Government of India (2012) 'National data sharing and accessibility policy – 2012 approved', available at http://pib.nic.in/newsite/erelease.aspx?relid=80197, accessed 16 August 2015

Health Analytics India, available at http://healthanalyticsindia.com/, accessed 16 August 2015

How India Lives, available at http://howindialives.com/, accessed 16 August 2015

How India Lives (2015) 'Which are the most stolen cars, bikes and scootrs in Delhi?', available at http://howindialives.com/testchart/dlicrthft/, accessed 16 August 2015

India Spend, available at http://www.indiaspend.com/, accessed 16 August 2015

National Informatics Centre Data Portal India, available at http://www.nic.in/projects/data-portal-india, accessed 16 August 2015

Parihar, Isha (2015), 'On the road to Open Data: glimpses of the discourse in India' *World Bank Blog*, 17 February, available at http://blogs.worldbank.org/ic4d/road-open-data-glimpses-discourse-india, accessed 16 August 2015

Singh, Shreya (2013) 'The beginnings of India's open data movement', available at http://www.igovernment.in/opinion/20131/the-beginnings-of-indias-open-data-movement#sthash.eUJxO8NM.dpuf, accessed 16 August 2015

Section 6: The future

Damian Radcliffe

Journalists have long used public data, such as health records or crime statistics, to inform their work. However the explosion of public and private data, coupled with a growing range of both easy to use - and highly sophisticated - visualisation tools have all contributed to the rapid growth of data journalism in recent years. For new graduates, an ability to produce data driven journalism (DDJ) is fast becoming an essential part of their journalistic toolkit, alongside wider skills in the digital and social realms.

Their prospective employers also are also increasingly aware of the opportunities and importance of data driven journalism, particularly in the digital arena. Infographics, online visualisation tools, gifs, great - and illustrative - pictures and video are all part of the new era of online storytelling. Data can often underpin much of this work, as Nicole Smith Dahmen notes:

> *'Digital technologies allow audiences to experience information in a way that is not possible in print; in a digital environment, audiences can engage and interact and thereby immerse themselves in the information experience.'*

She goes on to demonstrate how publishers such as *the Guardian*, *The New York Times*, and the *Washington Post* have created memorable and impactful 'data visualisations that *enhance* the storytelling function by allowing audiences to truly *engage* with the story.' There is a plethora of different ways to do this, from pie charts to interactive maps and other data visualisation methods, and so 'media producers must be meticulous in selecting the correct type of data visualisation for the intellectual task of the communication.' This means that although DDJ is an increasingly valuable instrument for journalists and publishers, enabling stories to go 'beyond the basic who, what, when, and where...to give content perspective, especially regarding the reporting of how and why…' traditional journalistic abilities - such as a strong story sense – are still fundamental to doing your job; and doing it well. Blend these different elements, she suggests and 'data visualisation may indeed be a sustaining value of journalism, and thus, a critical pillar of the future of journalism'.

In order to do this, Jacqui Taylor argues, we will need to understand and deploy more rigorous scientific approaches to visualisation efforts. This will be especially important if publishers are to capture the attention of younger – and global - audiences. Journalism has long benefited from such cross-disciplinary approaches; with computer assisted reporting (CAR) and the rise of computational journalism (offered by Cardiff University, Stanford and others) being just two examples. Visualisation, she suggests, is another area which could enjoy similar benefits.

Without this, echoing many earlier contributors, albeit from a different standpoint, she argues that 'the value created by matching topflight journalism skills and evidencing the resulting stories has not yet been fully realised.'

Alexander Howard wraps up our book with an extract from his acclaimed 2014 Tow Centre report 'The Art and Science of Data-Driven Journalism'. Howard contends that 'the world needs journalists with new skills more than ever,' and 'in the near future,' he says, 'expect basic data-science skills to become baked into how investigative journalists gather sources, find evidence, and present their findings - from building databases, to creating visualisation, to applying powerful analytical software.'

Although many large legacy media organisations are struggling to successfully pivot their business model towards digital, 'there is a tremendous upside for adoption and use of current tools and vast green fields for digitally native media organisations to experiment, create, and find audiences, as billions of people come online for the first time globally.'

Data lies at the heart of much of this digital future; as a source for stories and to gain richer insights into audience behaviours. Better tools and apps will sit side-by-side with more robo-journalism and journalists steeped in the social sciences and statistics. '…but know that human relationships and storytelling still matter,' he says, with collaboration and more diverse newsrooms all helping to produce better data journalism.

No one can accurately predict the future, although Howard does identify 14 trends we're likely to see in this space. Alongside the input of our other expert contributors, these insights suggest that data journalism has only begun to scratch the surface of what it can do. He writes:

> *'Complemented by human wisdom and intuition, data journalism still won't save the world or news, but it will help us all understand it better.'*

As such it's a trend that no journalist can ignore, and a tool for enriching our understanding the world that all of us should want to embrace.

Data visualisation and the future of journalism

Visualisations enrich the story telling experience for journalists but also the interactivity for readers and viewers, argues Nicole Smith Dahmen

Introduction

Journalism is an industry of storytelling. Data visualisations can help us craft more effective stories. Data visualisations, or infographics, are not new to journalism; what is new, however, are the emerging technologies that allow static infographics to become dynamic infographics, for a new realm of information visualisation. In 2010 Anthony Calabrese, a leading technology blogger, predicted that data visualisation is the future of online journalism. Defining data visualisation as 'the visual representation of information served up with a healthy dose of innovation and creativity,' Calabrese (2010) refers to it as a 'new form of visual communication for the 21st Century'.

Digital technologies allow audiences to experience information in a way that is not possible in print; in a digital environment, audiences can *engage* and *interact* and thereby immerse themselves in the information experience. Consider, for example, *the Guardian*'s interactive data map illustrating women's global political rights (http://www.theguardian.com/world/datablog/interactive/2013/mar/08/international-womens-day-political-rights). Rich in data, the visualisation allows – and in fact encourages – audiences to create their own interactive information experience. Rather than being a cumbersome and laborious mountain of text, audiences can take great delight in seeking out and engaging with the data for a truly unique learning experience.

Based on the capabilities afforded by digital technologies regarding engagement and interaction – and with Calabrese's prediction in mind – this chapter argues that data visualisation may indeed be a sustaining value of journalism, and thus, a critical pillar of the future of journalism.

Journalism in the digital news and social media age

In an age of digital news and social media, the traditional elements of a news story – the who, what, when, and where – emerge quickly. And they emerge from a multitude of sources, both from traditional media sources and newly available information sources, such as news aggregators and citizen journalists. Journalism must learn to re-invent itself for the age of digital news and social media. One way this re-invention can happen is through data visualisations that *enhance* the storytelling function by allowing audiences to truly *engage* with the story.

But there are necessary conditions for the journalism profession and for journalism educators to ensure that data visualisations enhance storytelling for *real* understanding to thus become a sustaining value of journalism. Before the discussion of these conditions, this chapter begins with an overview of the benefits of data visualisations as storytellers.

Visualisations as storytellers

We must begin talking about *how* data visualisations help us craft more effective stories. In other words, what are the critical characteristics of data visualisations that make them powerful communication tools? The following section discusses a number of these:

Visual reporting

Data visualisations could be considered to fall under the canopy of visual reporting, with the understanding that visuals are more than just aesthetic or decoration. Visuals – photographs, graphics, videos, data visualisations – are information and thereby communication. As a popular form of data visualisation, weather maps, for example, quickly give audiences great amounts of information, such as color-coded temperature and participation scales. As another example, data visualisations can provide information through comparison, either in a before or after sense or by presenting relative comparisons. To illustrate, one might know that the Burj Khalifa in Dubai is the tallest building in the world. But audiences can get a real sense of just how tall the building is when it is visually compared to other recognised skyscrapers: a simple bar-type pictograph of the world's tallest skyscrapers quickly illustrates to audiences that the Burj Khalifa in more than two times as tall as the Empire State Building in New York City.

Audience attention

Data visualisations quickly catch audience attention. Pages of text can be easily ignored. Visuals attract audiences. Eye tracking research done by Poynter has shown that news stories with visuals more quickly catch audiences' attention (Adam, Quinn and Edmonds, 2007). As such, stories with visuals, such as data visualisations, can more effectively tell stories because they can more quickly catch audience attention, which is critical in a mass media market oversaturated with content.

Universal language

Data visualisations can be considered a universal language. Because data visualisations are a *visual* information source, audiences do not face a language barrier in interpreting the news, as with written or spoken news. Certainly there can be cultural differences in understanding and interpreting visuals – and most data visualisations do contain a significant amount of text – but you do not necessarily need to be able to read or speak a different language to understand the basic premise of a pie chart, for example.

Visual processing

Data visualisations can be processed more quickly than written news. Recent research has shown that the human brain can process images at a rate 60 times faster than the rate at which words are processed (Weinroth, 2014). As such, audiences can more quickly process stories that contain or feature imagery, such as data visualisations. This is especially true for stories that emphasise technical data or big data.

Easier to recall

Data visualisations can be remembered. Academic research has shown that pictures are easier to recall than words (see, e.g., Paivio, Rogers and Smythe, 1968). The ability of the human brain to recall imagery, in turn, contributes to the formation of easily recognised and understood visual icons. Imagery has the ability to become part of our shared collective consciousness. Consider, for example, the almost universally recognised symbols for 'male' and 'female' or 'play' and 'stop'.

Audience interaction

Data visualisations can create experience. In a digital news environment, visualisations can create experience by allowing audiences to interact with the content. Digital technologies allow audiences to experience information in a way that is not possible in print. In a digital environment, audiences can engage and interact and thereby immerse themselves in the information experience. As an example, audiences intellectually know that the universe is vast. But it can still be hard to fully understand the limitlessness bounds of space. 'If the Moon Were Only One Pixel,' a brilliant interactive experience, allows audiences to immerse themselves in the content, which leads to real understanding of the vastness of our solar system (http://joshworth.com/dev/pixelspace/pixelspace_solarsystem.html).

Data visualisations and the future of journalism

With this understanding of the critical characteristics of data visualisations that make for effective storytelling, we can return to the discussion of their value as a sustaining pillar in the future of journalism. Again, data visualisations, or infographics, are not new to the journalism industry; some research suggests that data visualisations date back to the mid 1500s (Friendly, 2008).

The new elements, as already noted, are the emerging technologies that allow for an immersive and self-guided information experience, and thus, a new realm of information visualisation (Calabrese, 2010). Digital technologies allow audiences to experience information in a way that is not possible in print; in a digital environment, audiences can engage and interact and thereby immerse themselves in the learning experience. Audiences can also make purposeful decisions to self-direct their own information experience. As Calabrese (2010) predicted, data visualisations can be one critical path to ensure the continued value of journalism in the age of digital news and social media.

But there are necessary conditions for the journalism industry and for journalism educators. Firstly, the truth must always prevail. Bearing in mind the social responsibility theory of the press, journalism is a business of facts, and facts must always remain supreme in order for journalism to fulfill its function in a healthy democracy (Siebert, Peterson and Schramm, 1963; SPJ, 1996). Words can mislead, misrepresent, and lie. So can visuals, whether they are photographs, videos, or data visualisations. And audiences can be easily misled, as they are potentially less visually literate regarding data visualisations (Geidner and Cameron, 2014). As data visualisation guru Edward Tufte argues, 'there are right ways and wrong ways to show data; there are displays that reveal the truth and displays that do not,' (1997: 45).

To ensure that data visualisations present the truth, media producers must have a thorough understanding of the content and message to be presented, as well as the available forms and technologies of data visualisation. A good journalist should understand content beyond the basic who, what, when, and where. Data visualisations can help to give content perspective, especially regarding the reporting of how and why. As an example, a data visualisation could present data on climate change or gun violence, but if there is no connection to relative information or to cause and effect, the information could potentially be out of context or misrepresented and, thus, misunderstood. Tufte (1997) argues that data visualisation producers must always understand the 'intellectual task'. In other words, *what* is it that you are trying to convey?

With a thorough understanding of the facts, media producers must then decide which type of data visualisation is most effective for the data and the intended intellectual task. All data visualisation types are not created equal and they are not all interchangeable. A pie chart, for example, is ideal for showing the values of parts in relation to the whole, whereas as a line (or fever chart) shows quantity over time. And within the realm of digital technologies the options for types of data visualisations become even greater. Media producers must be meticulous in selecting the correct type of data visualisation for the intellectual task of the communication. And they must use good moral judgment in ensuring that the visual presentation of the data sheds light on the facts of the story and not a version of the story with a certain agenda.

Consider, as an example, this interactive data map from *The New York Times* that presents the story of the spread of drought across the United States (http://www.nytimes.com/interactive/2014/upshot/mapping-the-spread-of-drought-across-the-us.html?abt=0002&abg=1). The data map effectively conveys the intellectual task of mapping the rise of drought across time and geographic location. Through updated data, longitudinal findings, locator information, and effective use of data labelling and colour classification, the data maps clearly show audiences that drought conditions in the United States are becoming increasingly more severe and more widespread. This data visualisation is rooted in facts and ethically and accurately crafts the story of drought.

A second key criterion for successful work is the inclusion and transference of emotion (Tufte, 1983). As visual journalists and scholars, we tend to overlook infographics and focus on photographs as the leading visual source for emotion. Certainly, photographs can be emotionally moving (see Ephron, 1978; Goldberg, 1991; Goodwin, 1983; Perlmutter, 1999; Zelizer, 2010). But truly engaging data visualisation can also bring audiences to their knees. As an example, Tufte argues that Charles Minard's infographic documenting Napoleon's fateful 1812 march to Moscow is powerful because it 'tells a rich, coherent story' (1983: 40). With multiple variables connected to a locator map, Minard turned a static graphic into a visual story of data that makes us mourn for the decimation of 400,000 troops (ibid).

As a more recent example, *The Washington Post* created a haunting data visualisation project that brings real understating to the presumed fate of the disappeared Malaysia Airlines Flight 370 from March 2014 (http://apps.washingtonpost.com/g/page/world/the-depth-of-the-problem/931). The data visualisation is successful for multiple reasons, but its greatest success is in its audience involvement. The graphic allows audiences to engage with the information and literally bring them to the presumed resting place of the airplane in the depths of the Indian Ocean and the reality of the problems of locating the plane at such a depth. As the audience scrolls down the graphic, the tension mounts and the horror intensifies. This graphic could be printed; it would provide information and understanding in print. But, in print, it is limited. The audience cannot engage. It is that digital act of scrolling deeper and deeper that draws in the audience and makes us yearn for it to end. It forces us to concede the fate of those 239 people on board. It forces us to face human mortality. And it forces us to care.

Thirdly, journalists, editors, and publishers must fully embrace the capabilities of digital technologies in presenting information to audiences. A static bar chart online is going to be just as dull as a static bar chart in print. As Calabrese (2010) notes, data visualisation must be innovative and creative. A prime example is the previously mentioned, stunning data visualisation project on the vastness of space, 'If the Moon Were Only One Pixel'. But successful data visualisations can take time and resources. In a journalism industry that is strained for both time and money, digital journalism too often continues to be print-based material shuffled to the web. Media organisations must be willing to devote resources to developing innovative and creative data visualisation projects. However, there are two critical caveats. First, media producers must be cautious to not fall prey to the lure of interactivity just for the sake of interactivity. There are times when a static bar chart may actually be the most effective way to present the content in question. Visualisations that utilise technology and interactivity must do so *only* when that digital experience will enhance the information value. Second, it is important to note that successful data visualisation projects do not necessarily have to be expensive or complicated to be successful. The *Washington Post* data visualisation on the fate of Malaysia Airlines Flight 370 is not complicated; it is simply brilliant.

Finally, as journalism educators, we must find new ways to train and challenge our students. We must force them to think critically and to think creatively. They must learn new ways of considering, understanding, and presenting information. To do this, we must encourage them to take an array of courses, from philosophy to ethics to history to computer science to art. We must encourage them to embrace diversity and to challenge norms. We must encourage them to care. While writing, design, and critical thinking will always be foundational, we must also train students to think across platforms. Indeed, today's journalism graduates must be capable of telling stories across multiple platforms. And they must understand the content and the technologies to make informed decisions about the most effective way to craft a story given the topic, audience, and medium.

Conclusion

This chapter argues that in an age of digital news and social media, data visualisation can be a sustaining value of journalism. Data visualisations that are rooted in facts, effectively presented through the correct data tools and technologies, and make a connection with the audience can be a means to crafting better stories. But we must be willing to devote time and resources, both within the journalism industry and within our journalism classrooms. Data visualisations that enhance the storytelling function by allowing audiences to truly engage with the information are a critical pillar of the future of journalism.

References

Adam, Pegie S, Quinn, Sara and Edmonds, Rick (2007) *Eyetracking the News: A Study of Print and Online Reading*, St Petersburg, FL: Poynter Institute

Calabrese, Anthony (2010) 'Six stunning projects that show the power of data visualisation,' 5 October, available at www.pbs.org/mediashift/2010/10/six-stunning-projects-that-show-the-power-of-data-visualisation278, accessed 2 June 2015

Ephron, Nora (1978) *Scribble Scribble Notes on the Media*, New York: Alfred Knopf

Friendly, Michael (2008) 'A brief history of data visualisation' in Chen, Chun-houh, Härdle, Wolfgang Karl and Unwin, Antony (eds) *Handbook of Data Visualisation*, Berlin, Heidelberg: Springer pp 15-56

Geidner, Nicholas and Cameron, Jaclyn (2014) 'Graphic Deception: Individuals' Reaction to Deceptive Information Graphics', Visual Communication Division,

National Conference of the Association for Education in Journalism and Mass Communication, Montreal, Quebec, Canada, 9 August 2014

Goldberg, Vicki (1991) The Power of Photography: How Photographs Changed Our Lives. New York: Abbeville

Goodwin, H Eugene (1983) *Groping for Ethics in Journalism.* Ames: Iowa State University

Paivio, Allan, Rogers, TB and Smythe, Padric C (1968) 'Why are pictures easier to recall than words?' *Psychonomic Science*, Vol. 11, pp 137-138

Perlmutter, David D (1999) Visions of War: Picturing Warfare from the Stone Age to the Cyber Age. New York: St. Martin's Press

Siebert, Fredrick S., Peterson, Theodore and Schramm, Wilbur (1963) *Four Theories of the Press.* Chicago: University of Illinois Press

SPJ (1996) 'Code of the Society of Professional Journalists', available at www.spj.org/ethicscode.asp. Accessed 5 June 2015

Weinroth, Adam (2014) 'Infographic: The science of storytelling', 22 May, available at www.onespot.com/blog/infographic-the-science-of-storytelling, accessed 19 April 2015

Zelizer, Barbie (2010) *About to Die: How News Images Move the Public.* New York: Oxford University Press

Data visualisation: now for the science

As more and more of the world's population access news digitally, evidencing journalism is becoming a key way of further enforcing the message of storytelling, and the science behind visualisation is becoming ever more important, writes Jacqui Taylor

Introduction

Not a day goes by without me seeing another data visualisation (or infographic if you prefer, I treat the two definitions as interchangeable) telling a story based on data. I'm aware that the sceptics exist, that their view is 'this is just another pretty picture', and I assume if you hold that view you are already irritated by the title of this chapter. Data journalism came into my world by accident: I'm a web scientist and had no previous experience of dealing with the heady world of journalism. Sometimes the happy accidents of life bring great rewards. At a data conference I was fortunate to meet Simon Rogers, who was at the time Editor of the 'newish' *Guardian* Datablog, and as all good data folks do we talked about possibilities. I offered to help out pro bono the next time he had a challenging dataset he needed to visualise and thus began the journey.

Four years on, we have created many key data visualisations initially in collaboration with *the Guardian* and latterly independently published on our Public Cloud platform. Arguably the most important data visualisation was the first, not least because it is credited as the launch of our industry due to the impact it had. We visualised the 'Human cost of 10 years of war in Afghanistan' by mapping every death using data provided by Wikileaks. Even at the time we were all aware we were at the beginning of a new journey for data. I remember we discussed whether anyone would understand what we had presented and whether the essential story in the data would be communicated. The response we received stunned us all, millions of people around the world interacted with the visualisation and it proved to be very sticky, with people spending on average between eight and 10 minutes with the data. This is a screenshot of the visualisation.

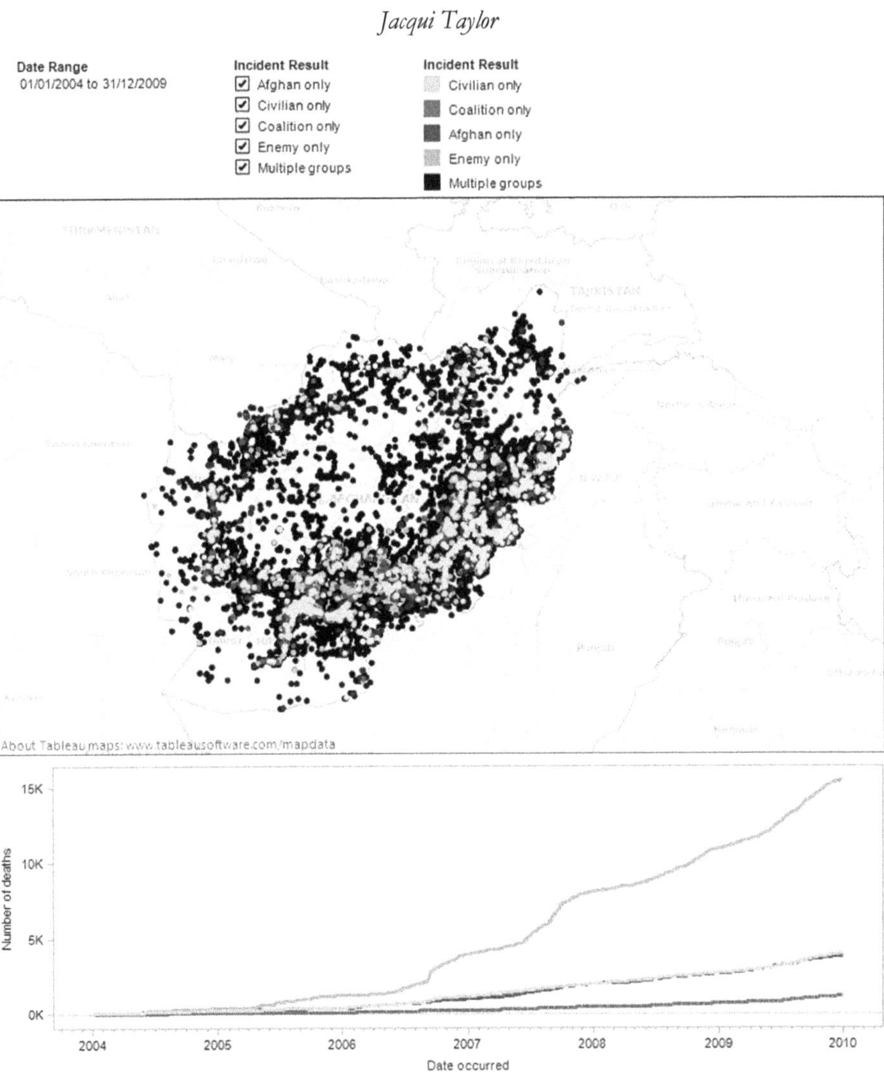

Figure 71: 10 years of war in Afghanistan - the human cost

The grey scale image is a poor reflection of the interactive visualisation that captured people's imagination. The interactive live visualisation is available online at http://public.tableausoftware.com/views/AfghanistanDeaths02/DeathsinAfghanistan

Even in this grey scale version, the deaths in the south of the country and the impact of the landmines on the 'road to Basra' can be clearly seen, a major factor in the death toll.

Looking to the future of data journalism

Today I don't have to persuade any student of journalism that they should have some basic data skills and ensure that they include a data specialist as a key contact to bounce ideas off. These are now essential supplementary skills in the journalistic world. Indeed I expect that specialist teams like those who create *the Guardian* Datablog will be a fixture of any media organisation as we move towards more evidence based journalism. The value created by matching topflight journalism skills and evidencing the resulting stories has not yet been fully realised. At the time of writing we have 43 per cent of the world's population online (Internetlivestats.com, 2015): this is set to rise to over 80 per cent in the next few years. The result of this huge rise in potential audience and the engagement possible from utilising interactive visualisations is a largely untapped market.

What most people are unaware of is that the engagement possible from using visualisations is dramatically different if some of the basic science related to our human interaction with visuals is incorporated during the design of the visualisation. This science is the foundation of the way we at FlyingBinary build our data visualisations. From the beginning, and on an ongoing basis where we embed our visualisations on the web, we have put our cloud platforms to work analysing how we can refine the science to ensure the interactivity is the most compelling for our audience. Evidencing journalism is becoming a key way of further enforcing the message we are articulating and increasingly static representations of data are being superseded by interactive visualisation as the demographics of the workforce change.

Impact of the Generations

Currently Generation X (the baby boomers) are in a dominant position of leadership in our media organisations, however this will change over the next three years as Generation Y become predominant in our workforce. Generation Y (or as they are sometimes known, the Millennials) are a highly visual generation and are increasingly comfortable with the use of visual presentations to present facts or data. As a result of this the science behind visualisation becomes ever more important.

From a future viewpoint it is important to consider the increasing Generation Z audience. They also have key visual abilities but these are combined with kinaesthetic (movement, touch) capabilities. This audience shift will require us all to make increasing use of interactive visualisation capabilities in order that we serve this generation in a way that harnesses their biological capabilities. There are those of us who already know of the need to move from static visualisations to interactive visualisations to meet the needs (or more likely demands) of this new audience. We made this change at FlyingBinary two years ago, and have found that the science we apply to visualisations had to be updated to reflect the needs of this new audience.

We teach the Science of Data Visualisation as a one-day workshop as part of a series of training modules to develop the capabilities needed to ensure that the work produced is compelling for the newer audiences. I have chosen to outline in this chapter the science behind the work we do to reflect the needs of the Generation Z. A Generation Z audience has the combination of visual and kinesthetic skills and this has required us to revamp the essential training we give in these workshops. The links to the interactive visualisations are examples of the combination of visual and kinesthetic visualisations designed to engage with Generation Z.

At the moment many visualisations are serving up static capability and if you measure your audience engagement you will be able to track the data as it begins to decline. However I recommend that you move to interactive visualisations now and capture the increasing new audience as well.

Introducing web science

The first science we apply is web science. It is unlikely that most readers will be familiar with this new discipline, which was created just over six years ago by the original web scientist, Sir Tim Berners-Lee. Web science is an emerging, new and exciting discipline. It draws on existing areas of study, but requires new scientific methods and techniques to be developed. The web's diverse nature means that it has to be able to be considered from a broad range of perspectives both independently and in unison, for this reason web science is an interdisciplinary subject that draws on many different academic areas.

Nothing like the web has ever happened in all of human history. The scale of its impact and the rate of its adoption are unparalleled. This is a great opportunity as well as an obligation. All of the data visualisations we develop are designed to be web enabled whether or not they are eventually deployed on the web. When Sir Tim Berners-Lee appeared in the opening ceremony of the 2012 Olympics Games held in London, our web science message was signalled around the Olympic Stadium, 'it's for everyone'. This is another reason why the move to interactive visualisations is key, web science aims to be inclusive. The most flexible way of ensuring that this ideal is met is by using some key design principles to support the development of our data visualisations.

Understanding cultural differences

We use our social intelligence 'big data' platform to understand audiences beyond our current reach. It is this work that has highlighted differences in the engagement of audiences with our visualisations in particular geographies. Whilst this does not relate to the specific science we use to visualise data, it does underline important cultural differences we have found across the world, which require us to design visualisations that translate across the cultures. However there is a key cultural difference that needs to be decided upon at the outline design stage. It is important to decide whether your main audience is likely to be in a western or eastern geography. In the West we read from left to right in contrast to the East where right to left is the norm. Essentially the design needs to consider which audience this is targeted at. In the detailed science I will explain why it is important to organise the data story to be on one page. With a single visualisation this is easy, however multiple visualisations need to be positioned with panes on the screen using a left, right and top, down sequence. This allows a western user to follow the story you are relating intuitively.

Visualisation design principles

We often get questions on our data visualisation courses about how to decide how much data to present. Ultimately you are looking to produce an intuitive design for a user who has no prior domain knowledge of the subject. We will aim to produce an uncluttered visualisation, minus any bling, with a 'less is more' philosophy. However it is important to recognise that some users will need additional support to assimilate the data story.

When you use interactive visualisations you can optimise the user experience by the adoption of a progressive reveal technique. This allows you to showcase the data story in stages rather like the traditional journalism techniques applied to data: headline, byline, body text etc. Additionally what this also does is make the engagement with the interactive visualisation very sticky, on average eight to 10 minutes for our web facing visualisations. The 'stickiness' of these visualisations is a direct result of giving the user the ability to explore the data in this way. A number of companies are pioneering this feature to drive traffic and therefore revenue through their websites. It is expected that as we move to an ever more open and social engagement model this will move beyond the early adopters and become the pervasive method of user engagement.

Impact of the human visual system

In the meantime there are a number of techniques you can use when designing your interactive visualisations that utilise the basics of our human biology to make your visualisations more intuitive and therefore more compelling. Our vision is by far our most powerful sense, approximately 70 per cent of the receptors in our body are related to our vision system. Given that Generation Y and Z both demonstrate highly visual abilities we can maximise the impact of visualisations by designing and displaying data in the most impactful way for these users.

The human visual system is able to discern patterns in a most powerful way. We use the combination of the power of our eyes to perceive those patterns and interpret them via the brain. This uses a key set of rules that ensures that we can unlock the power of data presented via a massively parallel process. This is a complex subject, however an understanding of the basics of visual perception can transform the impact of a visualisation. If we do not engage our audience using the power of visual perception we run the risk of our message not being communicated. This is best illustrated:

3 2 4 5 0 7 6 8 9 4 3 0 1 2 3 4 5 9 8 7 6 4 5 6 7 0 9 2 3 4 5 6 7 8 7 2 4 3 6 3
7 8 2 0 2 4 4 5 0 0 2 2 4 6 5 8 9 4 3 0 1 2 3 4 5 4 8 7 6 4 9 8 7 6 4 5 6 7 3 2
3 0 1 2 3 4 5 4 8 7 6 4 9 5 6 7 0 2 3 4 5 6 7 8 1 2 4 3 6 7 8 5 0 8 4 4 5 0 0 2
2 4 6 5 8 1 3 2 4 5 0 7 6 3 2 4 5 0 7 6 8 3 4 3 0 1 2 3 4 5 2 8 7 6 4 5 6 7 0 5
2 3 4 5 6 7 8 9 2 4 4 3 0 1 2 3 4 5 3 8 7 6 4 5 6 7 0 9 1 6 7 0 2 3 9 5 6 7 8 1
2 4 3 6 7 8 5 0 8 4 4 5 0 0 2 2 4 6 5 8 3 2 4 5 0 7 6 8 3 9 3 0 1 2 3 4 5 2 8 7

Figure 72: Greyscale illustration

As quickly as possible count the number of 9s that appear in the table of numbers above. I expect this took quite some time as attentive processing is slow because we carry out the task sequentially. How many 9s did you count? By contrast if I asked you to count the number of 9s in the table below you will likely get the correct answer very quickly.

Figure 73: Greyscale illustration with use of highlighted colour

How did you do? I expect you found this quite quick to do and by contrast with the first list of numbers you got the right answer. In both lists there are ten 9s. This second list was much easier because you used the visual perception functions of your visual system. Numbers to our visual system are just a series of squiggles whereas if we colour a particular number (in this case all the 9s) our brain can process the black 9s separately from all the other numbers coloured grey. This is called pre-attentive cognition.

Maximising preattentive cognition

In the field of visual science there are 17 pre-attentive cognition attributes but we can group these into categories: colour, position, form and motion. It would require an all-day workshop to understand how best to use all these categories in your visualisation design (and more particularly why), however there are some key attributes that we use regularly in our work and I will focus on these. We are all familiar with the use of size and position to encode data, for example the use of line and bar charts to represent data visually. So I intend to cover how to encode data correctly with area, colour and shape to maximise the impact of your visualisations. I will explain this in the context of quantitative, ordinal and nominal data to ensure that the different treatment of each data type is explained in detail.

I am limited to grey scale only images for this book. The reader should assume colour encoding for all examples unless explicitly stated. Firstly we will look at data we are most familiar with when we are looking to visualise data, quantitative data, a set of numbers, for example: 1, 2, 3, 4, 5 or 3.2, 5.1, 6.0, 7.1, 9.9.

Encoding quantitative data using area: I have used 8 circles to represent a large set of values. We are typically interested in general comparisons rather than exact distinctions, so a large range of sizes is acceptable, with no practical limit.

Encoding quantitative data using a colour ramp: I have used a continuously varying shade of a single colour to represent the full range of values being visualised. We are typically interested in general comparisons rather than exact distinctions.

We can use both area and colour encodings to engage our pre-attentive cognition capabilities in our visual system to make sure the story in the data is visible to our audience. However the use of shapes instead would not be appropriate for quantitative data. Individual shapes cannot convey the intrinsic order within a range of numbers. When the data which needs to be visualised is ordinal, this is when data has an intrinsic order, is non numeric and is usually but not always text. An example of ordinal data is the months of the year, January, February, March, etc. Again we can use both area and colour encodings although for ordinal data it is important to be able to distinguish clearly the different values of the encoded data. So for these reasons we use a smaller range of sizes for comparison purposes.

Encoding ordinal data using area: I have used four circles here but we have a practical limit of 5 circles to compare the area of the circles easily.

Encoding ordinal data using colour: I have used a palette of four shades of one colour to compare ordinal data for the same comparison reasons we use with area.

Finally we will look at how we can best represent nominal data to ensure we are using the power of the human visual system. This last type of data is non-numeric data with no intrinsic order, for example: apple, orange, blackberry and raspberry. For nominal data it is inappropriate to encode data using area because the size of the area would imply an order where none exists. We can however use colour as a method of choice to encode this data, but now we use the actual colour rather than the shade.

Encoding nominal data using colour: I have used a palette of eight colours that has a practical limit of ten colours.

Nominal data is an example of where shapes can be utilised for our visual perception to be utilised, as simple shapes can be pre attentively perceived in a way that complex shapes (eg numbers) cannot.

Encoding ordinal data using shape: I have used eight different shapes and whilst there is no practical limit to the number of shapes you can use, it is important to ensure that the shapes are sufficiently distinct to enable visual differences to be discerned.

We have now covered the encodings to use with different data types. You will find it useful for your data visualisation work to have a list of the top three encodings for each of the types of data we have already considered. This gives a basic guide on the best choices to make to ensure you are maximising the capabilities of human visual perception when designing your visualisation.

Quantitative data: Top three encoding choices

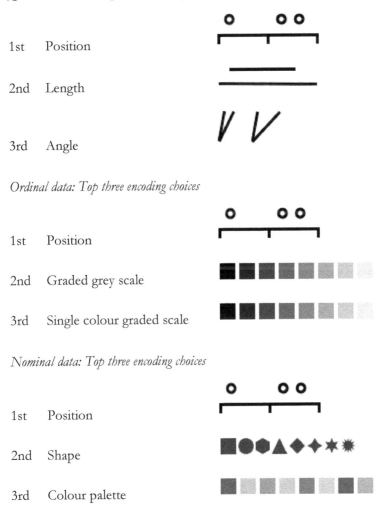

1st Position

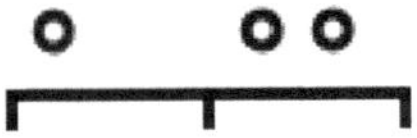

2nd Length

3rd Angle

Ordinal data: Top three encoding choices

1st Position

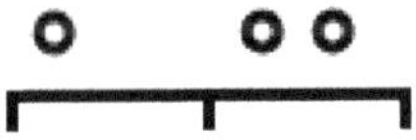

2nd Graded grey scale

3rd Single colour graded scale

Nominal data: Top three encoding choices

1st Position

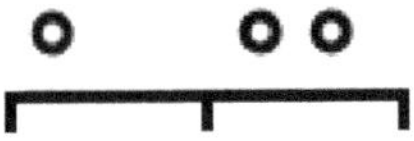

2nd Shape

3rd Colour palette

As you can see in all three cases position is our number one choice for encoding data to harness the power of our visual perception. We should make different choices in our design if we have to use a second and/or third encoding, dependant on which type of data we are visualising.

Understanding Short-term memory

I have dealt in some depth with visual perception, which is linked to the iconic memory of our brain where the processing of what we see occurs. However we also use both short-term and long-term memory when processing visual information. There are some key issues with our short-term memory that we should take into account when designing interactive visualisations, namely:

It is limited in the information it can store,

Only a portion is dedicated to visual memory,

It is temporary storage.

We can only store about three chunks of information in our short-term memory at any one time. Individual numbers in a table may constitute a chunk of memory, whereas a pattern of numbers represented graphically (eg by a bar on chart) can convey many numbers in one chunk. Whilst the good design principles we have already discussed are key to ensure an intuitive visualisation, an understanding of the limits of short-term memory can be equally important when designing great interactive visualisations. It is important to present related data as a set of data visualisations on a single page/screen, commonly called a dashboard. The dashboard allows the user to understand the related data stories, with no need to rely on their short-term memory to process the data.

Where possible group the detailed data into particular segments of the dashboard, this will allow the user to interact with the detailed components of the data story in an exploratory manner in a sequence that is most important to them. When you arrange data on a dashboard within a user's vision. that data can be processed and understood extremely quickly.

An example of a complex story that is designed to allow a citizen wide audience to participate in transformation of health services is the Social Intelligence story we curated for NHS Citizen on behalf of NHS England. FlyingBinary are core technology suppliers in this new approach to citizen participation at the heart of the NHS. Our Social Intelligence platform moves the NHS on from a surveillance approach to the social platforms such as Facebook and Twitter to a new citizen participation model. This visualisation helps NHS England understand how it is delighting and alternatively disappointing citizens and patients within the limits of our short-term memory.

As before the greyscale limits the visual impact of the interactive visualisation we built. You can get the best appreciation with the online version http://flyingbinary.com/nhs-citizen-social-intelligence.

NHS Citizen - A Social Intelligence story

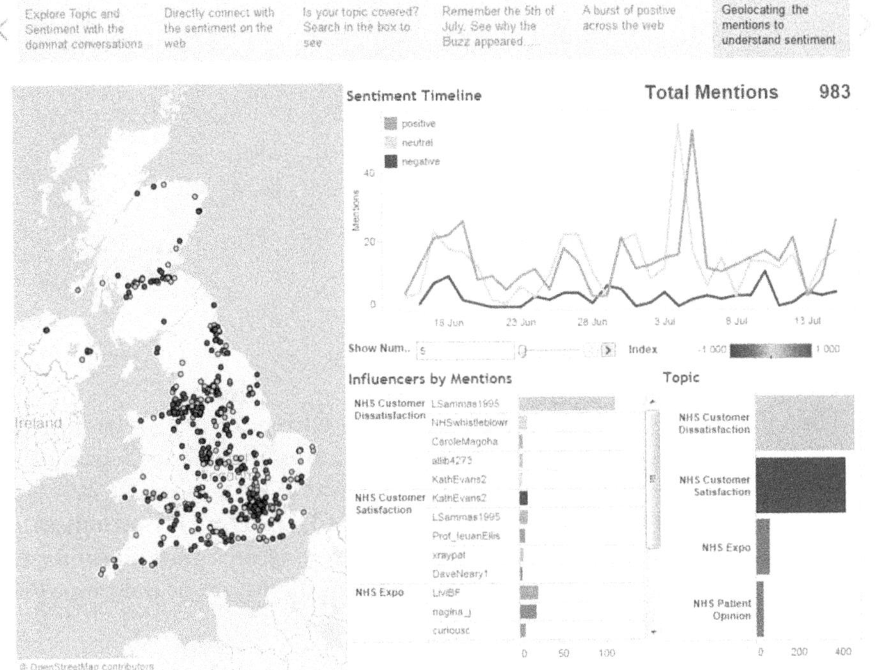

Figure 74: NHS Citizen – A social intelligence story

This visualisation was part of a data halo strategy we designed for NHS Citizen where non-NHS data could be curated and shared as an evidence base for the transformation of NHS Services. Additionally the data evidenced an advocacy network of influencers who represent patients who are not digitally connected or harder to reach. This has allowed the NHS to better understand how to develop a curated space which is inclusive to all those who wish to be part of NHS Citizen. NHS Citizen is a world leading initiative in the transformation of health services with citizen participation at the heart. This initiative uses data stories to communicate this new evidence base, which is powered by the science of data visualisation.

Conclusion

The use of data as evidence for journalists to amplify their work has created a new communication medium. Data is a language that only a few will learn but we can use the data visualisation to communicate this language of data to a global audience. However we can augment all that we do with data visualisation by understanding the science of the human visual system. This will ensure that our designs are intuitive and compelling. I encourage you all to go viz!

On to the future

When journalists combine new technology with narrative skills they can deliver context, clarity and a better understanding of the world around us, wrote technology editor Alexander B Howard in an acclaimed 2014 Tow Centre report entitled The Art and Science of Data-Driven Journalism. In an extract from that larger report, he offers 14 recommendations and predictions for the future of data reporting

Introduction

Journalists have always needed to be able to write, interview, and fact-check their work. Today, photography, social media, video editing, and mobile devices have already become integral elements of the toolkits of many journalists. Whether news developers are rendering data in real time (McClure, 2012), validating data in the real world (Boiko-Weyrauch, 2012), or improving news coverage with data (Cruz, 2012), good data journalism still must tell a story, solve a problem, or speak truth to power. Smartphones, notebooks, cameras, social media, and data sets can extend investigations in important ways. The world needs journalists with new skills more than ever. The same trends changing journalism and society (Howard, 2012) have the potential to create significant social change throughout the world, as nation states move from conditions of information scarcity to abundance, causing vast disruptions to governance and governments.

In the near future, expect basic data-science skills to become baked into how investigative journalists gather sources, find evidence, and present their findings—from building databases, to creating visualisation, to applying powerful analytical software. Along with those skills, journalists will still need to apply critical thinking and show how they reached conclusions.

While the need is acute and journalism schools are responding, significant cultural, fiscal, and technical barriers to the adoption of data journalism and digital skills remain. In May of 2014, a new report by the Duke Reporters' Lab at the DeWitt Wallace Center for Media and Democracy in the Sanford School of Public Policy surveyed 20 newsrooms to find which digital tools are still missing. The top-line conclusions from Mark Stencel, Bill Adair, and Prashanth Kamalakanthan (2014) painted a sobering picture of an industry in flux. The report found that many US newsrooms aren't taking advantage of new, low-cost digital tools for reporting and presenting journalism, instead continuing to use familiar methods and practices. Its authors suggest that journalism awards and popular media conferences have created the perception that the adoption of digital tools and data journalism is more prevalent than it is.

While local newsroom leaders told the researchers that budget, time, and people were their primary constraints, deeper infrastructure and cultural issues are hindering adoption. The report describes an industry with a gap between 'have and have-nots,' with national organisations experimenting with data journalism and new digital tools while local newsrooms are not. *'The local newsrooms that have made smart use of digital tools have leaders who are willing to make difficult trade-offs in their coverage,' write the authors. They prioritise stories that reveal the meaning and implications of the news over an overwhelming focus on chasing incremental developments. They also think of the work they can do with digital tools as ways to tell untold stories—not 'bells and whistles*', wrote the authors.

Writing at Poynter.com, Howard Finberg (2014) noted that the Duke report's conclusions support findings of Poynter's recent 'Core Skills for the Future of Journalism' report, which was based on a broader sample of the industry—that is, more than 2,900 responses from media organisation professionals, independent or freelance journalists, educators, and students. 'Professional journalists in legacy media rated new digital skills as much less important than traditional skills,' he wrote. 'Educators, students, and independent journalists rated digital skills as much more important than the professionals.'

Finberg's discussion of the report's finding and data journalism is a reality check on the challenges that remain for its adoption, revealing a schism between educators and professionals:

> *'The ability to find and make sense of information is almost the definition of newsgathering, so it seems safe to call this an essential skill for the beginning journalist. We asked professionals and educators to rate the importance of two key aspects of newsgathering that require this ability. Both the ability to analyse and synthesise large amounts of data and the ability to interpret statistical data were rated as more important by educators than by professionals.*
>
> *'When it comes to the ability to analyse and synthesise large amounts of data, a little more than half (55 per cent) of the professionals responded that this was important to very important. Almost three-fourths (73 per cent) of the educators rated this skill as important to very important. The response to the question about the ability to 'interpret statistical data and graphics' was similar: 59 per cent of professionals and 80 per cent of educators called this skill important to very important.*

> *'Given the large amounts of data available on the Internet and the growing importance of presenting information in a pleasing and informative visual manner, the gap between educators and professionals is disturbing. The ability to make sense of our complex world by distilling meaningful information from the vast river of data is one of the great values professional journalists can offer their audience'* (ibid).

The third report, on innovation at *The New York Times*, was prepared by a team inside the newspaper for an internal audience, not public consumption. After the document leaked online in May of 2014 to Buzzfeed and Mashable (2014), however, it was hailed by Joshua Benton, the director of Harvard's Nieman Journalism Lab, as 'one of the key documents of this media age' (Benton, 2014a).

There's a tremendous amount of insight and introspection in the 97-page report, which surveyed the media landscape of today in depth, drawing on interviews with dozens of staff at *The New York Times* and dozens more with outside observers, including this author. I spoke with a researcher from the *Times*' team last year about the paper's approach to digital journalism, editorial analytics, social media and data, along with my own reading, sharing, and commenting habits.

The report paints a picture of an extraordinary organisation housed within an institution and business grappling with the same fundamental shifts that broader society is enduring in the 21st Century, struggling at times to escape a 20th Century legacy of tools, infrastructure, and culture. Even though the digital audience of *The New York Times* is larger than its print readership (31 million unique visitors a month to nytimes.com versus 1.6 million total daily circulation), the daily editorial workflow described remains focused on the paper, not the pixel.

The report described the routine of a newsroom focused upon Page One and an incentive structure in which reporters are measured against their A1 stories. Instead of going 'digital first' over the last decade, the publisher and leadership have continued to focus on the print edition. As the report notes, the paper currently derives three quarters of its revenues from print. That focus, however, cites a failure to convert the 14.7 million articles in the *Times*' archive into structured data. Not doing so has meant that the newspaper is not capitalising on one of its primary assets by making it more discoverable through search, sharing through social media, and data mining.

There are many reasons to think that 'The Gray Lady' could become much more than she used to be in the years ahead. The first redesign of nytimes.com in eight years went live in January of 2014, optimised for mobile devices and integrating native advertising. The parent company was profitable in the first quarter of 2014. In March of 2014, the *Times* expanded its digital offerings to include NYT Now, a lower-priced mobile app sold to iPhone users that summarises the day's top stories, and Premier, which offers expanded access to behind-the-scenes stories, e-books, videos, and crosswords. The *Times* may also explore events, a lucrative concern for other media companies. As noted earlier, The Upshot launched in April of 2014, to general acclaim (Somaiya, 2014).

The Upshot's team includes the graduate student in statistics who helped to build the news quiz on dialect while he was an intern (*The New York Times*, 20 December 2013). This interactive went on to be most read and shared content in the history of nytimes.com. In May of 2014, the *Times* launched a lovely closed beta of a new cooking Web application with more than 16,000 recipes (Benton, 2014b). If the outlet can build a personalised recipe recommendation engine on top of its decades of dining and cooking archives, the platform could have tremendous potential. The new executive editor of *The New York Times*, Dean Baquet, endorsed the report and the digital-first strategy contained in it, both internally and publicly, once it leaked online. Whether he and his colleagues can execute against its recommendations remains to be seen.

The conclusions of these three reports, however, should still be sobering. The *Times* may be fine, but other papers will not be. Newsrooms face tight budgets, deep set cultural challenges, liabilities and debt, and historic lows in public trust. On the positive side, there is a tremendous upside for adoption and use of current tools and vast green fields for digitally native media organisations to experiment, create, and find audiences, as billions of people come online for the first time globally.

So what should we watch for next, and where? The following list of recommendations and predictions sketch out what to expect in the next decade and where publishers will need to adjust.

1) Data will become even more of a strategic resource for media

If text is the next frontier in data journalism (Bouza 2012), it should be used in the service of telling stories more effectively, enabling digital journalism and digital humanities to merge in the service of a more informed society (Cohen, 2012). Modern media organisations should become sources for trusted data (Lorenz et al, 2011). Increasing amounts of data will be hosted by media organisations and leveraged as an asset. In some cases, media companies may be able to sell access to their archives and APIs. Given the sensitivity of some datasets and the responsibility news organisations hold to confidential sources and whistleblowers, the media will need to improve its security practices. Recent widespread hacking incidents at major newspapers around the United States highlight the need for improvement (Perlroth, 2013).

2) Better tools will emerge that democratise data skills.

Even though the resources to learn data journalism are improving daily, there's still a high barrier to entry for people with no experience practicing it. That's changing as more powerful resources come online. Many of these tools for creating or presenting data-driven journalism will come from start-ups or non-profits, like CartoDB, DocumentCloud, Timeline.js, Mapbox, Frontline SMS, Zeega, Kimono, Enigma.io, Amara, Plot.ly, DataWrapper, and Graf.ly. Other tools will be provided by technology giants, like Google, Amazon, and Esri, as free Web services and open source code, or with enterprise licensing and API fees. Uncertainty about sustainability will drive foundations to fund tools and platforms, including pilot projects, entrepreneurial ventures, or components of open source civic infrastructure. The rest of the tools will be built by independent news hackers, university students, and data journalists as passion projects aimed at scratching someone's itch; these may well end up helping many other people solve similar problems as well. Just as publishing text and editing photography or videos became accessible to hundreds of millions of people, analysing and presenting data in maps, apps, and visualisations will become easier to do as well.

3) News apps will explode as a primary way for people to consume data journalism

There have been hundreds of millions of iPhones, iPads, and Android devices sold in recent years, with billions of lower cost devices to follow as more of humanity goes online on mobile broadband networks. According to the Pew Internet and Life Project, 42 per cent of American adults over 18-years-old owned a tablet in January 2014 (Zickuhr and Rainie, 2014). Designing narrative stories, videos, and news applications for the growing number of readers using smartphones, phablets (a new class of mobile phones designed to straddle the functionality of phone and tablet), tablets, and laptops will only become more important to media organisations. That puts a premium on data journalists who can create apps, lightweight data visualisations, and story presentations that are optimised for mobile devices. Increasing demand for apps, quizzes, and interactive games will make news application developers a highly sought-after specialty at media companies.

Despite the growth in news apps, the narrative story format will endure as a complement to the news app, the summary for a blog, and access to the underlying data and model.

4) Being digital first means being data-centric and mobile-friendly

As more and more people access the Internet and consume media on mobile devices, adopting a data-centric approach to collecting and publishing journalism will only grow in importance. The need to flexibly deliver content to multiple platforms and formats means that applications' programming interfaces (APIs) that can supply data to any platform will continue to be a smart investment for organisations, particularly if they seek to be digital first. The *Washington Post*, NPR, and the *New York Times* have already moved in this direction. Others will follow, or lead.

Media companies will be competing for attention, and advertising and subscription dollars, with technology giants like Google, Yahoo, Facebook, and start-ups that publish or curate user-generated content, along with vast amounts of data underpinning information services like mapping, shopping, or search. Facebook's Paper app, Google Play, Yahoo's News Digest, Narrative Science,

Flipboard, and the automated information services yet to be created will be strong competition for media companies in the future.

5) Expect more robo-journalism, but know that human relationships and storytelling still matter

We will see wunderkinds apply computational journalism to finding secrets and creating knowledge at a vast scale, just as data scientists do in Silicon Valley, quants do on Wall Street, or spooks do at the National Security Agency. 'Robo-journalism' for commodity news from services like Narrative Science is already in the wild and will grow in use, particularly for areas that might have been previously uncovered by a beat reporter or for which a full-time journalist is no longer economically viable. Wearable computers, drones, sensors, and algorithms are going to play a bigger role in the gathering of data and consumption of media.

Despite changes in technology, humans will still matter in building relationships and making data into stories relatable to people. While the platforms and toolkits for journalism are evolving and the sources of data are expanding rapidly, many things haven't changed. The ethics that have long guided the choices of the profession remain central to the journalists working today, as National Public Radio's (NPR) new ethics guide makes clear (NPR, undated). 'Governments and others are going to learn how to hide their actions from open data,' said Stray. 'Personal relationships and scepticism will continue to be extremely important.'

6) More journalists will need to study the social sciences and statistics.

'Philosophically, I think data journalism shares something with social science and also there's a real connection with the digital humanities,' said Jonathan Stray, who teaches the subject at Columbia. 'The emphasis is not just algorithms, but what do these algorithms tell us? How should we interpret all this fancy output?' These questions have been integral to how sociologists, anthropologists, and ethnographers have conducted research for decades, particularly with respect to data collection and statistics. This means that if members of the media seek to practice data journalism, they'll need to be numerate, ethical, and thoughtful about the biases embedded in the data they're interrogating.

This is not a new idea, given how deeply Philip Meyer's 'precision journalism' is grounded in applying social science to investigative reporting, but everyone who wishes to practice and publish sound data journalism is going to need to understand it. Social scientists and biologists alike know that the sources for data and conditions under which it is collected will shape and bias any subsequent research conclusions made from it. To serve broad audiences, data journalists have to go beyond acquiring and cleaning data to understanding its provenance and source. Then, they'll need to make sure that its presentation doesn't tell a different story than the data itself allows.

None of that is easy for people trained as scientists, much less journalists. Some projects and analyses may exceed technical competence or subject matter expertise of select members of the media. Collaborating with academia and technologists will be preferable to flawed journalism, analyses, maps or visualisations that mislead readers, given the impact that inaccurate conclusions would have upon trust in the authors or publications.

7) There will be higher standards for accuracy and corrections.

Getting a fact wrong or screwing up a quote can sink a news story, leading to a correction or even retraction. Making a mistake in an algorithm or interpretation of data can similarly undermine the entire premise of an act of data journalism. The mistakes and errors made in a post at FiveThirtyEight.com that sought to map kidnappings in Nigeria offer an instructive case study (Chalabi, 2014). The post relied upon data sourced from the Global Database of Events, Language and Tone (GDELT). As the correction to the story acknowledged, the journalism that was published was fundamentally flawed because the journalist failed to see that the data represented the rate of media stories as a proxy for the rate of kidnappings, did not account for duplicated reports, and used a default location if none was given. Decontextualising the GDELT data led to a flawed post (Solomon, 2014).

Data journalism will attract numerate readers who are not only interested in the data behind stories and the analysis used to arrive at conclusions, but with the interest to try to reproduce them. For instance, a FiveThirtyEight story on the Bechdel test in movies earned in-depth scrutiny from Brendan Keegan, who was able to replicate the findings. What that means in practice is that any media company that publishes such work should have a corrections policy in place for data journalism (Keegan, 2014).

Andrew Whitby, an economist at Nesta, upon encountering examples of bad data journalism, (Whitby, 2014) proposed four principles of his own to improve upon the form:

1. **Choose the right stories**: In cases like this, a well-written review of the scholarly literature is likely to better inform public debate. Otherwise, stick to (a) lightweight but fun topics or (b) fast-moving topics yet to attract academic attention.

2. **Embrace complexity**: No interesting causal relationship involves only two variables.

3. **Use statistics intelligently**: A scatterplot of two variables with a least-squares regression line is not 'doing statistics'. Bad statistics is worse than no statistics.

4. **Finally, be modest**: If you have so many caveats as to completely undermine any conclusion, then don't offer a conclusion.

8) Competency in security and data protection will become more important.

In the United States, email hosted on private sector servers outside of a media company's control does not have the same legal protections as email within an office. Until the Electronic Communications Privacy Act is reformed, journalists should be cautious about hosting sensitive email or data on other platforms. People practicing data journalism or civic hacking need to know about the Computer Fraud and Abuse Act (CFAA) (O'Donovan, 2014), along with proposals for its reform (Zeng, 2014). Journalists or members of the public who are unsure of the legality of data access or use, and don't have the legal resources of major media organisations behind them, should think twice or thrice before clicking.

In general, journalists must consider when it's appropriate to scrape data, access data, store it – or not. Does the story require storing personal information? If so, such sensitive data will need to be protected with the same vigour that journalists have protected confidential sources. Unfortunately, the information security practices of many media companies are not as robust as they will need to be to prevent determined intrusions by organised crime or nation states.1

9) Audiences will demand more transparency on reader data collection and use

Automated, personalised advertising or native advertising will be part of some living stories and news apps. The creators of these platforms it will have to carefully consider the context for matching ads with content. Editorial and business departments are going to run up against difficult conversations about data access and sharing, with respect to audience analytics. Non-profit organisations may not rely on advertising, instead taking underwriting or sponsorships, but they too will face pressure from funders and foundations to quantify their audiences and the impact of their journalism with data. As editors, reporters, and publishers learn more about who is reading, sharing, and commenting on journalism through gathering data, they'll have to decide how transparent they'll be with readers about data collection and usage.

10) Conflicts over public records, data scraping, and ethics will surely arise

For good or ill, we're likely to see more controversial online maps and interactive apps that show donations, votes, contributions, permits, convictions, and other public records. Along with voluntary disclosures, the data will be scraped, FOIA'ed or otherwise sourced from government publications, agencies, and websites.

Over time, much more of this data will end up in private hands, along with media, non-profits, foundations, snarky online media outlets, and hacker collectives like Anonymous. Some of the resulting maps and charts will no doubt be found to be incorrect, made so by incompetence or malicious intent, resulting in misidentified people who will be subject to harassment or worse. In turn, governments will try to deny access to data, heavily redacted documents, demand takedowns, and criminalise scraping or API calls. They will apply filtering, or extra-legal censorship through pressure on payment processors, seize servers or even direct denial of service attacks. Companies may deny access to their platforms for apps or services that use controversial data, similar to when Apple rejected an app showing drones strikes (Wingfield, 2014), or even accuse reporters of being hackers if they find data breaches or unprotected data online (Gallagher, 2013).

Around the world, the conflict in societies with more closed governments and constricted information flows is likely to be explosive. Open data is not enough (Kaplan, 2013): investigative journalism will remain essential. In the United States we'll run into more difficult First and Fourth Amendment issues as a result of all of this. It's going to be extremely messy. The chilling effects of mass surveillance on digital journalism will continue to be an issue for years to come. Just as sources may not trust the idea of a private conversation with a reporter, the provenance of data may be difficult to mask.

As a public comment to the Review Group on Intelligence and Communication Technologies convened by President Barack Obama from Columbia Journalism School and the MIT Center for Civic Media highlighted, mass surveillance makes investigative journalism much harder:

> *'Put plainly, what the NSA is doing is incompatible with the existing law and policy protecting the confidentiality of journalist-source communications. This is not merely an incompatibility in spirit, but a series of specific and serious discrepancies between the activities of the intelligence community and existing law, policy, and practice in the rest of the government. Further, the climate of secrecy around mass surveillance activities is itself actively harmful to journalism, as sources cannot know when they might be monitored, or how intercepted information might be used against them,'* (Bell et al, 2013).

11) Collaborate with libraries and universities as archives, hosts, and educators

The government shutdown in the United States in the fall of 2013 demonstrated the need for media organisations and civil society to back up government data. At the time, many non-profits, foundations, and individuals acted to preserve and mirror what they could. Around the rest of the globe, data sources may be even more tenuous. In the years to come, journalists, universities, tech companies, businesses, and local governments will share a messy ecosystem of APIs, public, and private databases. There's already an emerging geocommons around OpenStreetMap, supported by rapidly improving open source tools and an emerging 'geo-journalism' speciality.

One strategy that may be fruitful is for city, county, and state governments to engage local media, universities, and libraries in public or civic data hosting and preservation (Burke et al, 2013). Librarians and academics have always been stewards of knowledge, in the forms of books and periodicals. As such, they and their institutions are well placed to host data for the public good, although legislators and executives will have to think through the economics of them doing so.

12) Expect data-driven personalisation and predictive news in wearable interfaces.

In 2013, the most popular online content at the BBC was an economic class calculator. User-centric apps and services will enable people to understand how a given story or policy applies to them, their children, or their business. These kinds of news apps and data-driven platforms like Homicide Watch hint at what lies ahead. The current state of the art only scratches the surface of the ways that data will be personalised for individual readers as the use of analytics grows in media companies, helping editors get smarter.

As people express their interests through searches, clicks, saves, and shares, algorithms will use the data generated to suggest related editorial content and match advertising algorithms for relevant businesses or services with it. Recommendation engines will improve, across media companies, and be followed by predictive news that using social network analysis to suggest stories to users.

Over the next decade, a new wave of mobile computing will provide new platforms for nimble media companies to publish stories, from iWatches, to Google Glass, to smart appliances and wearable interfaces connected to an Internet of Things. Some of these wearables won't just display data, they'll collect it. Such will include health data, geo-location, and air quality, which can then be used in citizen science and monitoring projects. They'll be part of a rich fabric of connected devices that, when combined with people, mobile phones, and civic media, will enable citizens to monitor infrastructure or water quality in China, extending into networked civil society (Zuckerman, 2014). The data generated from them will be rich source material for journalists to investigate and share.

Drones and sensors are both part of this picture and represent rich topics for more experimentation and inquiry, as explored by my colleague Fergus Pitt in his own research and workshops at the Tow Center (Pitt, 2014).

13) More diverse newsrooms will produce better data journalism.

Diversity has been a challenge in the media for decades. Although far more minorities and women work in professional journalism than a century ago, a 2013 survey of American Society of News Editors (ASNE) found that of the 38,000 journalists currently working at 1,400 US newspapers, 4,700 are minorities (2013a). Another 2013 ASNE survey of 68 online news organisations found that 63 per cent of them had no minorities at all (2013b). The hiring choices at Vox Media, FiveThirtyEight, First Look Media, and other news start-ups garnered criticism in the spring of 2014 (Prince, 2014) including an open letter from the National Association of Black Journalists expressing concern regarding the lack of diversity (2014).

Diversity concerns are particularly relevant in the data journalism space, given the broader issues with women in technology that have become evident in recent years. Online and off, misogyny and discrimination endure in the industry, along with subtler sexism and racism. The challenge that editors face in hiring a diverse team of data journalists is structural, reflecting broader societal issues. As of 2010, 18 per cent of undergraduates receiving degrees in computer science were women, according to the National Center for Women and Information Technology (Ashcraft and Breitzman, 2012). In 2013, just 0.4 per cent of all female college freshmen said they intended to major in computer science (Rampell, 2013). Given that context, perhaps it shouldn't have come as a surprise when Nate Silver said that 85 per cent of the applicants to FiveThirtyEight were men.

There are reasons, however, to be cautiously optimistic about diversity in data journalism. Interviews with women and minorities in the United States suggest that the communities that have grown up around computer-assisted reporting over the decades may be more accepting of different faces than others in the technology world, perhaps because of the culture focused on peer-to-peer learning that celebrates mentorship. 'NICAR is a pretty healthy place to be a non-white, non-male person working in journalism,' said Tasneem Raja. 'I can't speak to issues of class, ability, gender identity, and other types of difference, other than to say we're almost definitely less good at them, and that needs to change.' She went on:

> *'I don't have experience with the way folks in this community handle issues of inclusion issues when they come up, but I have seen evidence of folks working pre-emptively to create environments that are less exclusionary than the norm in Web development, quantitative analysis, the visual arts, or journalism. Maybe it's because there haven't been that many of us webby data journos till recently. Data journalists are pragmatic by nature, and maybe it just didn't make sense to alienate potential swaths of new recruits. That's not to say everything is rainbows and sunshine, but I'm gonna take a rare moment of optimism here and say that I'm proud to represent this community, because in my experience, it's genuinely committed to inclusion,'* (Howard, 2014).

No matter the country in which a media company operates, making an effort to include more women; minorities; gay, lesbian, bisexual, and transgender individuals; and people from multiple socioeconomic backgrounds will improve the work product and work environment. A diverse staff diminishes stereotypes and produces second-order reflection on unconscious biases, which in turn can lead to improved, more equitable evaluation of work, performance, promotion, and compensation. The absence of women, minorities, or GLBT persons in start-ups, media organisations, development teams, and in editorial or product leadership positions can signal to others that they aren't welcome.

Recruiting and hiring differently pays off: Media organisations that have diverse staffs are likely to produce better journalism, from story choice to source selection. Research suggests that teams with both men and women on them are more profitable and innovative. According to the National Center for Women and Information Technology, mixed gender teams produced information technology patents that are cited 26 per cent to 35 per cent more often than the norm.

As the demographics of the United States shifts, stories and data that focus upon minorities, women, and the GLBT community will also gain more audience share, which in turn will create a business opportunity for media companies. That's true around the globe as well. Given the opportunity, women and minorities have produced world-class data journalism. The world needs more of them, along with anyone else who wants to treat data as a source.

14) Be mindful of data-ism and bad data. Embrace scepticism

Journalism will survive the death or diminishment of its institutions, as the Tow Center's report on post-industrial journalism explored (Andersen, Bell and Shirky, 2012). In the decades ahead, media that integrate technology, data, and narrative skills into their work will play critical roles in societies around the world, from holding the powerful accountable to connecting people with information.

As people struggle to make sense of what matters or is true in a tsunami of new media, data journalism will be held up as a way to provide trustworthy insights to debunk pseudoscience, propaganda, misinformation, and online rumour. Just as yellow journalism, penny papers, and tabloids created a market opportunity that led to the creation of a more rigorous, ostensibly objective brand of journalism at *The New York Times* 160 years ago, today's fast-moving, chaotic media environment creates opportunities to publish data journalism as a corrective to punditry.

There are rocks and stormy waters ahead here, however, created by bad data journalism. The early 21st Century has seen the growth of 'data-ism,' (Brookes, 2013) where knowledge can be derived through analysis of huge amounts of data now generated by various sources (Cukier and Mayer-Schoenberger, 2013a). This belief has antecedents in variants of positivism, the philosophy of science that holds information derived from logical (algorithmic) and mathematical analysis of data and sensory experience is the source of authoritative knowledge; and scientism, the belief that that the scientific method can be applied universally. All have a critical weakness – bad data, biased data, and flawed experiments can and will be used ignorantly or cynically to twist the truth, mislead, or misinform, even by journalists who wish to do the opposite. Even good data and solid research may be misrepresented or mistaken, a risk that will grow if journalists are pushed to create data visualisations or analyses without training in information design, statistics, and social science.

Data has led many numbers-driven executives astray, in business, government, media, or academia (Cukier and Mayer-Schoenberger, 2013b). The antidote to this malady is for journalists to interrogate data just as they would human sources, checking facts and assumptions, comparing results, and documenting the process and results of their investigations as a social scientist or biologist would. Complemented by human wisdom and intuition, data journalism still won't save the world or news, but it will help us all understand it better.

- *This is an extract from* The Art and Science of Data-Driven Journalism. *New York: Columbia Journalism School / Tow Center for Digital Journalism, funded by the Tow Foundation and the John S and James L Knight Foundation. The full report is available here: http://towcenter.org/wp-content/uploads/2014/05/Tow-Center-Data-Driven-Journalism.pdf*

Note

[1] For more on data security, ethics, privacy, and journalism, consult the Tow Center's white paper, McGregor, Susan E (2015) *Understanding Journalists' Information Security Choices.* New York: Tow Centre/Columbia University, available at http://towcenter.org/understanding-journalists-information-security-choice, accessed 26 August 2015

References

American Society of News Editors (2013a) '2013 minority percentages at participating online news organisations' in ASNE Newsroom Census, available at http://asne.org/files/Minority%20percentages%20at%20participating%20ONLINE%20organizations%20copy%282%29.pdf, accessed 27 May 2014

American Society of News Editors (2013b) 'Table B - minority employment by race and job category' in ASNE Newsroom Census, available at http://asne.org/content.asp?pl=140&sl=416&contentid=416, accessed 27 May 2014

Andersen, Chris, Bell, Emily and Shirky, Clay (2012) 'Post industrial journalism: adapting to the present' in Tow Center for Digital Journalism, 27 November, available at http://towcenter.org/research/post-industrial-journalism, accessed 21 May 2014

Ashcraft, Catherine and Breitzman, Anthony (2012) 'Who invents IT? An analysis of women's participation in information technology patenting' at National Center for Women in Information Technology (NCWIT) online, available at http://www.ncwit.org/sites/default/files/legacy/pdf/PatentExecSumm.pdf, accessed 27 May 2014

Bell, Emily et al. (2013) 'Letter to review group on the effects of mass surveillance on journalism', 10 October, available at http://towcenter.org/blog/the-effects-of-mass-surveillance-on-journalism, accessed 23 May 2014

Benton, Joshua (2014a) 'The leaked *New York Times* innovation report is one of the key documents of this media age' in Nieman Journalism Lab, 15 May, available at www.niemanlab.org/2014/05/the-leaked-new-york-times-innovation-report-is-one-of-the-key-documents-of-this-media-age, accessed 25 May 2014

Benton, Joshua (2014b) 'The *New York Times* has a (lovely) new cooking site' in Nieman Journalism Lab, 14 May, available at www.niemanlab.org/2014/05/the-new-york-times-has-a-lovely-new-cooking-site, accessed 25 May 2014

Boiko-Weyrauch, Anna (2012) 'From where? Validating data in the real world' in IRE, 25 February, available at http://ire.org/blog/2012-car-conference-blog/2012/02/25/where-validating-data-real-world, accessed 25 May 2014

Bouza, Teresa (2012) 'Text is a "new frontier" in data journalism, says Head of the IRE' in Computational Reporting, 2 February, available at www.computationalreporting.com/2012/02/27/text-is-a-new-frontier-in-data-journalism-says-head-of-the-ire, accessed 25 May 2014

Brooks, David (2013) 'The philosophy of data' in *The New York Times*, 5 February, available at www.nytimes.com/2013/02/05/opinion/brooks-the-philosophy-of-data.html, accessed 25 May 2014

Burke, Brian et al (2013) 'Enabling Open Government For All: A Planning Framework for Public Libraries' at the Center for Technology in Government, University of Albany, available at https://www.ctg.albany.edu/publications/reports/enabling_open_gov_for_all/enabling_open_gov_for_all.pdf, accessed 25 May 2014

Chalabi, Mona (2014) 'Mapping kidnappings in Nigeria (Updated)' in FiveThirtyEight DataLab, 13 May, available at http://fivethirtyeight.com/datalab/mapping-kidnappings-in-nigeria, accessed 25 May 2014

Cohen, Dan (2012) 'Digital journalism and digital humanities' in Dan Cohen blog, 8 February, available at www.dancohen.org/2012/02/08/digital-journalism-and-digital-humanities, accessed 25 May 2014

Cruz, Mayra (2012) 'Improving news coverage with data' in IRE, 25 February, available at http://ire.org/blog/2012-car-conference-blog/2012/02/25/improving-news-coverage-data, accessed 25 May 2014

Cukier, Kenneth and Mayer-Schoenberger, Viktor (2013) 'Robert McNamara and the dangers of big data at Ford and in the Vietnam War' in *MIT Technology Review*, 31 May, available at www.technologyreview.com/news/514591/the-dictatorship-of-data, accessed 25 May 2014

Cukier, Kenneth and Mayer-Schoenberger, Viktor (2013) 'The rise of big data' in *Foreign Affairs*, available at www.foreignaffairs.com/articles/139104/kenneth-neil-cukier-and-viktor-mayer-schoenberger/the-rise-of-big-data (accessed 25 May 2014).

Finberg, Howard (2014) 'Journalism needs the right skills to survive' in Poynter, 13 April, available at http://www.poynter.org/how-tos/journalism-education/246563/journalism-needs-the-right-skills-to-survive, accessed 25 May 2014

Gallagher, Sean (2013) 'Reporters use Google, find breach, get branded as "hackers"', in Ars Technica, 21 May, available at http://arstechnica.com/security/2013/05/reporters-use-google-find-breach-get-branded-as-hackers, accessed 25 May 2014

Howard, Alex (2012) 'Four Key Trends Changing Digital Journalism and Society' in *Radar*, O'Reilly Media, 28 September, available at http://radar.oreilly.com/2012/09/open-journalism-open-data-news.html, accessed 25 May 2014

Howard, Alex (2014) 'Tasneem Raja urges newsrooms to adopt pair programming for better data journalism' in Tow Center for Digital Journalism blog, 2 May, available at http://towcenter.org/tasneem-raja-urges-newsrooms-to-adopt-pair-programming-for-better-data-journalism, accessed 25 August 2015

Kaplan, David (2013) 'Why Open Data Isn't Enough' in Global Investigative Journalism Network, 2 April, available at http://gijn.org/2013/04/02/why-open-data-isnt-enough, accessed 23 May 2014

Keegan, Brian (2014) 'The need for openness in data journalism,' in briankeegan.com blog, 7 April, available at www.brianckeegan.com/2014/04/the-need-for-openness-in-data-journalism, accessed 23 May 2014

Lorenz, Mirko, Kayser-Bril, Nicholas and McGhee, Geoff (2011) 'News organizations must become hubs of trusted data in a market seeking (and valuing) trust,' in Nieman Journalism Lab, March, available at www.niemanlab.org/2011/03/voices-news-organizations-must-become-hubs-of-trusted-data-in-an-market-seeking-and-valuing-trust, accessed 25 May 2014

McClure, Jon (2012) 'Rendering real-time' in IRE, 25 February, available at http://ire.org/blog/2012-car-conference-blog/2012/02/25/rendering-real-time, accessed 25 May 2014

National Association of Black Journalists (2014) 'An open letter to news media start-ups' 14 March, available at www.nabj.org/news/164828/NABJ-An-Open-Letter-to-News-Media-Startups.htm, accessed 27 May 2014

National Public Radio (ND) *NPR Ethics Handbook*, available at http://ethics.npr.org, accessed 25 May 2014

O'Donovan, Caroline (2014) 'Hacking in the newsroom? What journalists should know about the Computer Fraud and Abuse Act' in Nieman Journalism Lab, March, available at www.niemanlab.org/2014/03/hacking-in-the-newsroom-what-journalists-should-know-about-the-computer-fraud-and-abuse-act, accessed 25 May 2014

Perlroth, Nicole (2013) 'Hackers in China attacked *The Times* for last 4 months' in *The New York Times*, 31 January, available at www.nytimes.com/2013/01/31/technology/chinese-hackers-infiltrate-new-york-times-computers.html, accessed 25 May 2014

Pitt, Fergus (2014) *Sensors and Journalism*. Tow Center for Digital Journalism. New York: Columbia Journalism School, available at http://towcenter.org/wp-content/uploads/2014/05/Tow-Center-Sensors-and-Journalism.pdf, accessed 25 August 2015

Prince, Richard (2014) 'Diversity protests get startups' attention' in Maynard Institute for Journalism Education, 14 March, available at http://mije.org/richardprince/diversity-protests-get-startups-attention, accessed 27 May 2014

Rampell, Catherine (2013) 'I am woman, watch me hack' in *The New York Times*, 27 October, available at www.nytimes.com/2013/10/27/magazine/i-am-woman-watch-me-hack.html, accessed 27 May 2014

Solomon, Daniel (2014) 'GDELT and the problem of decontextualized data' in Source: OpenNews, 14 May, available at https://source.opennews.org/en-US/articles/gdelt-decontextualized-data, accessed 25 May 2014

Somaiya, Ravi (2014) 'With app and premium plan, the *Times* expands online offerings' in *The New York Times*, 27 March, available at www.nytimes.com/2014/03/27/business/media/the-times-is-expanding-its-digital-subscriptions-offerings.html, accessed 25 May 2014

Stencel, Mark, Adair, Bill and Kamalakanthan, Prashanth (2014) 'The goat must be fed', Duke Reporters' Lab at the DeWitt Wallace Center for Media and Democracy in the Sanford School of Public Policy, May 2014, available at www.goatmustbefed.com, accessed 25 May 2014

Unnamed author (2013) 'How y'all, youse and you guys talk' in *The New York Times*, 20 Dec ember, available at www.nytimes.com/interactive/2013/12/20/sunday-review/dialect-quiz-map.html, accessed 25 May 2014

Unnamed author (2014) 'The full *New York Times* innovation report' in Mashable, 16 May, available at http://mashable.com/2014/05/16/full-new-york-times-innovation-report, accessed 25 May 2014

Whitby, Andrew (2014) 'Bad data journalism' in andrewwhitby.com blog, May, available at http://andrewwhitby.com/bad-data-journalism, accessed 25 May 2014

Wingfield, Nick (2012) 'Apple rejects app tracking drone strikes' in *The New York Times* Bits Blog, 30 August, available at http://bits.blogs.nytimes.com/2012/08/30/apple-rejects-app-tracking-drone-strikes, accessed 25 May 2014

Zeng, Allen (2014) 'Hack or Hacker? Know when it is appropriate to access data and when it is not' in Knight Lab, Northwestern University, 5 March, available at http://knightlab.northwestern.edu/2014/03/05/hacks-or-hackers-when-it-is-appropriate-access-data-and-when-it-is-not, accessed 25 May 2014

Zickuhr, Kathryn and Rainie, Lee (2014) 'E-reading rises as device ownership jumps' in Pew Research Center, 16 January, available at http://www.pewinternet.org/2014/01/16/e-reading-rises-as-device-ownership-jumps, accessed 25 May 2014

Zuckerman, Ethan (2014) 'What comes after election monitoring? Citizen monitoring of infrastructure' in My Heart's in Accra blog, 26 April, available at http://www.ethanzuckerman.com/blog/2013/04/26/what-comes-after-election-monitoring-citizen-monitoring-of-infrastructure, accessed 25 May 2014

Lightning Source UK Ltd.
Milton Keynes UK
UKHW021255300421
382904UK00005B/1002

9 781845 496630